THE NEW COMPLETE *English Springer Spaniel*

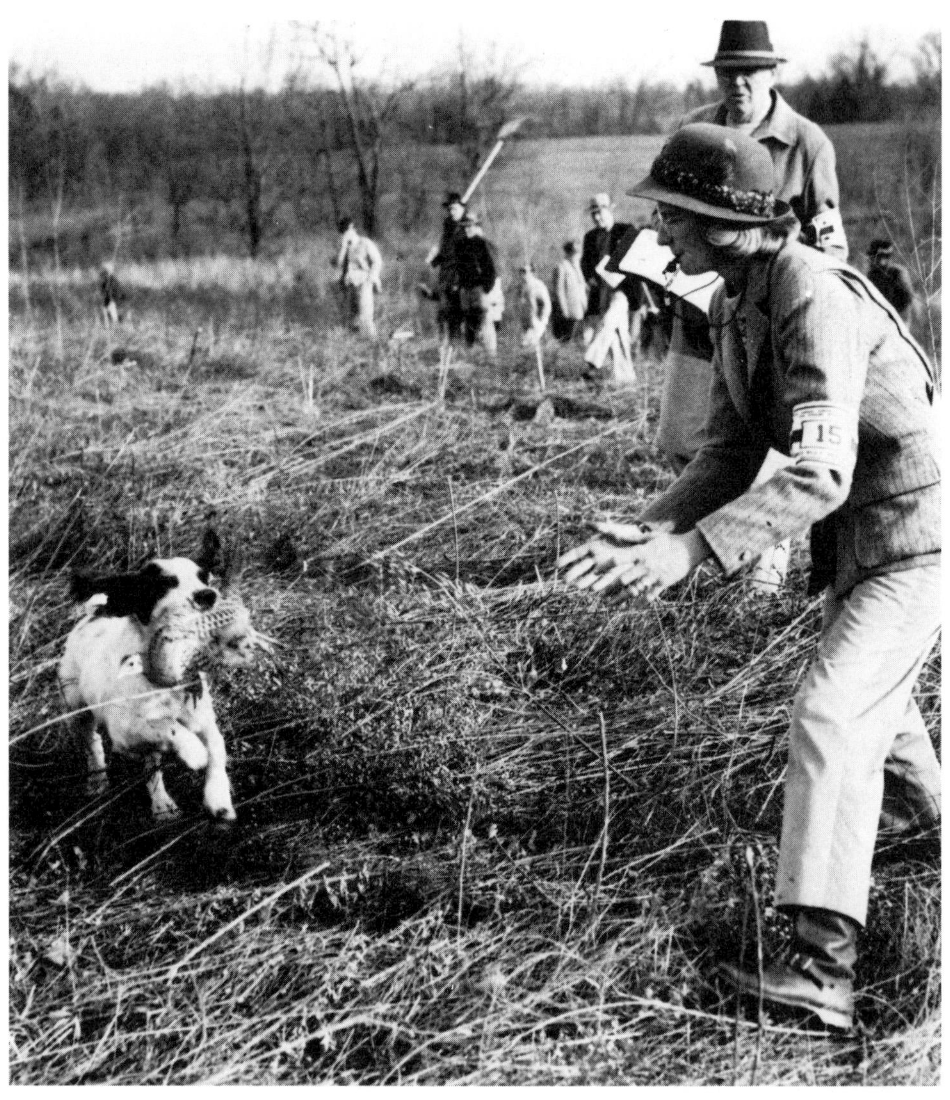

Mrs. P. D. (Julia) Armour accepts delivery of a pheasant from National Champion Carswell Contessa as the late Robert McLean, co-judge, looks on. Mrs. Armour's 1960 National win was the first for a woman in the U. S., Great Britain and Canada. It was twenty years before her great achievement was duplicated by Mrs. C. A. (Janet) Christensen, D.V.M. *Shafer*

THE NEW COMPLETE *English Springer Spaniel*

Julia Gasow

(with Kellie Fitzgerald)

and

Edward K. Roggenkamp III

New York

Maxwell Macmillan Canada
Toronto

Maxwell Macmillan International
New York Oxford Singapore Sydney

Howell Book House
Macmillan Publishing Company
866 Third Avenue
New York, NY 10022

Maxwell Macmillan Canada, Inc.
1200 Eglinton Avenue East
Suite 200
Don Mills, Ontario M3C 3N1

Macmillan Publishing Company is part of the Maxwell Communication Group of Companies.

Library of Congress Cataloging-in-Publication Data
Gasow, Julia.
The new complete English springer spaniel / by Julia Gasow and Edward K. Roggenkamp III.
p. cm.
Rev. ed. of: The new complete English springer spaniel / by Charles S. Goodall and Julia Gasow. 3rd ed. 1984.
ISBN 0-87605-119-0
1. English springer spaniels. I. Roggenkamp, Edward K. II. Goodall, Charles S. New complete English springer spaniel. III. Title.
SF429.E7G36 1994 93-24441
636.7′52—dc20 CIP

Macmillan books are available at special discounts for bulk purchases for sales promotions, premiums, fund-raising, or educational use. For details, contact:

Special Sales Director
Macmillan Publishing Company
866 Third Avenue
New York, NY 10022

10 9 8 7 6 5 4 3 2 1

Printed in the United States of America

Contents

SECTION II: The English Springer Spaniel in the Show Ring and Obedience Competition, and as a Family Companion

by Julia Gasow (with Kellie Fitzgerald)

FTC Busy Bruning of Ashaba, owned, trained and handled by A. P. Moecher. Busy was the second Springer to earn the title in the West.

Ch. Chinoe's Eminent Judge, CDX.

Foreword

THIS BOOK is the newest edition of a much-heralded classic and a legacy for modern enthusiasts of the English Springer Spaniel, however they choose to enjoy him.

The first edition appeared in 1958 and was authored entirely by the legendary shooting man Charles S. Goodall. In that edition, Goodall gave the reader a view of the Springer that was steeped both in field dog lore and solid breed knowledge. That loving tribute to the Springer was the prototype all subsequent editions would be based on. During the book's long, distinguished history, there would be many significant changes in format and content—all responding to the changing needs of the English Springer Spaniel and those who have made a place in their lives for the breed.

When the second edition was published in 1974, it became two books in one. Goodall wrote the section on Gun and Field Springers and Julia Gasow, the Mistress of Salilyn, furnished the section on Show and Obedience Springers, and that is how it has remained. The third edition succeeded the second in 1984 and again the formidable team of Goodall and Gasow presented the English Springer with ten years' more history to relate. As in the earlier collaboration, *The New Complete English Springer Spaniel* was a success story.

This success was predictable—both Goodall and Gasow were icons to fanciers of the breed. These revered authorities held the Springer up for the admiration of all. Whether the dog was presented as a hard-charging gun dog crashing through heavy cover in a Nebraska wheat field to flush his bird, or putting on an inspired performance at the Nationals, or pouring his heart out under the unforgiving floodlights of Madison Square Garden, readers could savor the real essence of the English Springer Spaniel. That was what the last three editions were about. That's what this edition is about.

Today, Charles Goodall, the man, is no longer among us, but his influence will abide forever. Julia Gasow continues to breed superlative show dogs and after a lifetime of devotion to the breed has achieved what all dog show people dream of but few ever achieve. She has earned her rewards.

In this edition, Section I has been retitled and is written by another accomplished shooting man, Edward K. Roggenkamp III. Whether your interests embrace the field or not, read the section. The English Springer Spaniel is, after all, a Sporting dog.

We hope you enjoy this new, fourth edition. As with you, the English Springer is very important to Howell Book House, and we are proud to bring yet another edition of this great classic to the breed's many friends.

THE PUBLISHER

I

The English Springer Spaniel in the Field— Dog of Many Talents

---

by Edward K. Roggenkamp III

Bird Dogs, side-by-side shotguns, field trials and hunting trips are my *hobbies, not my wife's. However, she indulges my interests even when it intrudes upon her life. Writing this book was yet another way in which I prevailed upon her good nature. This time, she served as an informal editor, using her considerable literary skills to wrestle with, revise and puzzle out my sometimes convoluted thoughts and sentences. For these reasons, I dedicate the Field Section of this book to my wife,*
Rheva.

Edward K. Roggenkamp III, author of the Field Section, is a longtime spaniel fan, sportsman and prolific writer on Springers and hunting.

The Author

EDWARD K. ROGGENKAMP III is a veteran outdoorsman with an in-depth knowledge of field-bred English Springer Spaniels and the happy ability to write effectively about them.

With over twenty years of active participation in Springers, Edd Roggenkamp has hunted pheasant, grouse and other upland birds as well as ducks and geese in numerous parts of the United States and Canada. He has had extensive hunting and field trial experience through most of his tenure in the sport.

He began to campaign Springers extensively at American Kennel Club field trials in 1982, and his dogs have competed in thirteen States and Canada. Registered with the prefix REWARDS, Roggenkamp's Springers are run in at least ten trials each year and have distinguished themselves on numerous occasions. There have been five championships and several interclub trophies brought home, and most of these achievements were made by way of the training and handling of the author—an amateur and proud of it!

Edd Roggenkamp is also a popular field trial judge and, as this book goes to press, has officiated in twelve trials in eight states. He judges only once a year, but is still actively sought out by trial organizers.

A member of the English Springer Spaniel Field Trial Association since 1982, Roggenkamp has served on the Board of Governors and is co-chairman of the committee to redefine "The Rules of Conduct of Field Trials." He was also invited to work with the AKC on spaniel activities, including a stint on the original committee to develop the first draft of the rules for conducting and judging AKC hunting tests for spaniels.

He also conducts a careful breeding program that has resulted in a number of field trial champions during the past ten years. These Springers have brought pride and pleasure to Roggenkamp and to many who have acquired dogs from him.

In keeping with Edd Roggenkamp's awareness of the needs of others, he has written numerous articles on hunting with spaniels; these have appeared in such popular, influential periodicals as *Gun Dog*, *Spaniels in the Field*, *The New York Conservationist*, *The Drummer* (Ruffed Grouse Society magazine) and others.

We at Howell Book House are proud and honored to have this popular, well-respected sportsman follow in the tradition of Chuck Goodall in writing the Field Section of this book. We are sure you will enjoy it as much as you will learn from it.

Happy reading.

Acknowledgments

IN 1958 the first edition of this book was authored and published by Charles S. Goodall and Julia Gasow. Goodall focused on the field side, which he knew so well; Gasow focused on the show side, where she is a legend. Over the years, the book went through several revisions and numerous reprints but it always remained true to its roots and purpose to "be a guide to the English Springer Spaniel enthusiasts."

I never knew Charles Goodall personally, but since the day I acquired my first Springer, I have used his book extensively as a reference manual, a guide and a second opinion on all training matters. Mr. Goodall is revered in the field-bred English Springer Spaniel community and highly respected for his many contributions.

By the time I had actively entered the field trial arena on the East Coast, Mr. Goodall had retired to his Arkansas retreat and was no longer active in the sport. In the mid-1980s he passed away. Fortunately, his vast knowledge is collected and immortalized in his several books and numerous articles.

Because Mr. Goodall's original book is considered by many spaniel trainers to be the bible of the sport, I have endeavored throughout this section to maintain the essence of Mr. Goodall's ideas—in some places simply quoting passages he penned so many years ago. But time marches on. In other areas, where the breed, the sport or the times have changed, this edition includes several new chapters and many major revisions that reflect current training practices and updates on the status of this wonderful breed of working gun dogs.

—Edd Roggenkamp

Reproduction after etching by Ben Marshall (1767–1835), a noted British artist. Spaniels such as these were the early ancestors of present-day Springers, and were known at the time as Norfolk Spaniels, Springing Spaniels and by other names appropriate to the locality or use.

Preface

IT IS HARD TO BELIEVE that nearly forty years have passed since Charles Goodall penned the first edition of this book. By conservative count, that is at least ten generations of Springers. In ten generations some significant changes have occurred due to selective breeding practices and today's preferences for type in the dogs themselves, style and performance.

In *type*, the field dog looks much as it did forty years ago with the possible exceptions that it is a little higher on leg, has a bit less coat, generally shows more white in its coloring and may tend toward somewhat lighter bone.

However, in *temperament*, the dogs are much softer, less able to take harsh discipline and are trained with a more subtle approach. Sheer numbers indicate that dogs in competition today are either better trained or are more trainable. Veteran trialers tell stories of twenty-five–dog trials in the 1950s when half of the field would break (chase a bird) or fail due to an obedience problem. Today, it is not uncommon to see a forty-dog stake where only two or three dogs are eliminated from competition due to breaks or discipline problems. It is my opinion that most of these developments are due to trainability and emotional stability in the dog's genetic makeup. That puts a burden on the trainer to teach the dog slowly and in a manner that in no way breaks the spirit, dulls the enthusiasm or turns off the desire to please.

The English Springer Spaniel has, for all practical purposes, evolved into two distinct strains; a field strain and a show strain. Although they are registered as one breed by the American Kennel Club and can be legally interbred, this is seldom done by knowledgeable breeders. This same separation between show varieties and field varieties is true in virtually every major hunting breed. But recognize that this separation happened in an evolutionary way. No one ever set out to develop two strains; the separation simply occurred as people focused on their primary interest—show or field. So many inherited traits are required in a fine gun dog—nose, retrieving instinct, athletic ability, biddability, trainability—that it is easy to see why field breeders overlook what they see as minor conformation flaws. On the other hand, show breeders must focus on so many key physical and mental attributes to adhere to the Standard and so excel in the show ring (size, coat, head, ears, gait, attitude) that it is easy to see how nose and range became low priorities, especially if never tested in the field.

I make no excuses for my totally biased love of and belief in the field-bred Springer. I want any hunter who selects a Springer for the field to be pleased with the dog, and I think the odds are much higher if a puppy of proven field stock is selected. However, if your interests are show or obedience, by all means select a puppy of appropriate breeding.

These two strains happily coexist under the aegis of the English Springer Spaniel Field Trial Association (ESSFTA), parent club for the breed in the United States. The ESSFTA along with the American Kennel Club sets the breed Standard and the rules for all forms of competition. Although the two sides throw some good-natured barbs at each other, we (show and field) work together for the betterment of the breed.

Both Julia Gasow and I fully agree that any purchaser of an English Springer Spaniel puppy should carefully consider his or her long-term interests and select a puppy of appropriate background.

During my business and dog-related career, my family and I have lived in Iowa, New Jersey, California and Michigan. Hence, my Springer experience and friends stretch from coast to coast. It would have been impossible to complete this book without the enthusiastic help of many people all across the United States and Canada. Some supplied information, some photos, some dug through their archives to find old catalogs, entry lists and data. In every case it was obvious that the people truly love this wonderful breed and sport and want to see both carefully documented. I therefore gratefully acknowledge the contributions of the following:

Janet Christensen, DVM
Don Cande
John Isaacs
Dr. David McCurdy
John Eadie
David Lorenz
Dan and Marie Langhans
Gary Wilson
Joe and Frances Ruff
Art Rodger and *Spaniels in the Field* magazine
English Springer Spaniel Field Trial Association
All the professional trainers documented in Chapter 13
Jim Lightfoot
Jim and LuAnn Devoll
Kevin Martineau
Ed Whitaker
Ruth Greening
Roy French
The Lou Craig Estate
George Wilson
John Blanock
Ben Martin
B. J. Hopkins

American Kennel Club (AKC)
United Kennel Club (UKC)
The English Springer Spaniel in North America by Beatrice P. Smith

Keith Erlandson (Wales)
Dick and Sylvia Lane
David Hopkins
Jack Williams
Dan McIntosh

Special appreciation goes to Lori Brewster for her wonderful word processing skills, to John Friend for access to his extensive photo archives, and to Steve Ellis for his diagrams.

This English print by P. Reinagle, engraved by I. Scott, was published in London by Richard Bentley in 1846. Although the title is "Field Spaniels" it is obvious that the dogs in the print are markedly like today's field-bred English Springer Spaniels and are flushing fowl before the hunter's flintlock. This print was made long before the English Springer was officially recognized in the United Kingdom as a unique breed.

1

Origin, History and Development of the English Springer Spaniel

THE ENGLISH SPRINGER SPANIEL has been called by several of today's major gun dog writers the leading contender for the title of best all-around gun dog. But it is an ancient and respected breed whose ancestors can be traced back into the dim and distant reaches of time when dogs were first used to help man gather food. Thus, a sportsman who is thoroughly equipped to train and use these fine dogs in the field should have a basic knowledge of the breed's origin and early history as a means to utilize completely its many and great hunting talents.

There are several theories as to where the ancient parent stock of spaniel-type dogs originated. Some say they originated in Great Britain. The majority opinion, however, holds that they first came from Spain, as the breed name implies. This position is sustained by eminent authorities, the first of them being the French nobleman Gaston de Foix (often called Gaston Pheobus). He wrote *Livre de Chasse* in 1387, most of which was reproduced in *The Master of Game*, written between 1406 and 1413 by Edward, second Duke of York. The Duke wrote that spaniels were good hounds for the hawk and that even though they came from Spain, there were many in other countries. Further evidence of their distribution throughout Europe may be found in the statement of the late Freeman Lloyd, a twentieth-century sportsman-writer of note, who wrote in 1934 of seeing an Italian tapestry from about the first century A.D. depicting a spaniel-type dog fawning at its master's feet. Most reliable twentieth-century authorities on spaniels attribute the breed's origin to Spain.

Another noted authority who held with the theory of Spanish origin was the sixteenth-century British scholar Dr. John Caius, whose *Of Englishe Dogges*, a short treatise written in Latin and published in 1576, states: "Of gentile dogges serving the hauke, and first of the spaniell called in Latine Hispaniolus." Caius described two kinds of spaniels: "one which spryngeth the birde and betrayth flight by pursuite." This dog was "the first kinde of such serve the Hauke" (because this was before fowling guns, the flushing type spaniel was used to force birds to fly for the hawks). Caius went on to describe a second type that located game by pointing it, and the game could then be captured by throwing a net over it. As Caius explained, "The common sort of people call them by one generall word, namely spaniells, as though these kinde of Dogges came originally and first of all out of Spaine." The late nineteenth-century British writer J. R. Walsh, who used the nom de plume "Stonehenge," wrote that the Romans, who began their occupation of the Isles in 43 A.D., learned the sport of hawking from Britons and improved upon it by introducing the Land Spaniel to the country.

Numerous ancient authorities considered spaniels as belonging to two distinct types. The larger group comprised the *Land Spaniels* (some flushed and some pointed their game). The flushers beat out, flushed and chased game for the hawks or hounds. The setting kind crouched to enable the hunter to cast or drop his net over the game, and occasionally the dog, too. The second type were the *Water Spaniels*, which retrieved waterfowl. These facts are well documented in early literature and art objects as the principal methods of hunting in the fourteenth, fifteenth and sixteenth centuries.

Mental Evolution of the Spaniel

The invention in France around 1630 of the flintlock changed hunting forever. By reducing the time lag between the trigger pull and the discharge of the projectiles from the muzzle, "flying shooting" (wing shooting) became possible. By the late 1600s this piece was introduced into Britain and precipitated the beginning of the art of gun dog training. Trying to shoot over one or a brace of wild, uncontrolled spaniels with any kind of gun was as useless then as it is now. As a consequence, over the next 300 years spaniels were transformed from untrained wild beaters, flushing birds for soaring hawks, into smoothly polished gun dogs that must hunt within gun range and retrieve with a tender mouth in order to save the game for the table.

The invention of the flintlock was the driving force that determined the mental instincts and biddability needs of spaniels. Spaniels, which were more tractable and which quickly learned to hunt to the gun (and not for themselves), were the most useful for the new method of wing shooting. These more trainable dogs were most frequently selected for breeding and thus passed on their temperament—an essential fact about spaniels and one reason why modern field strains

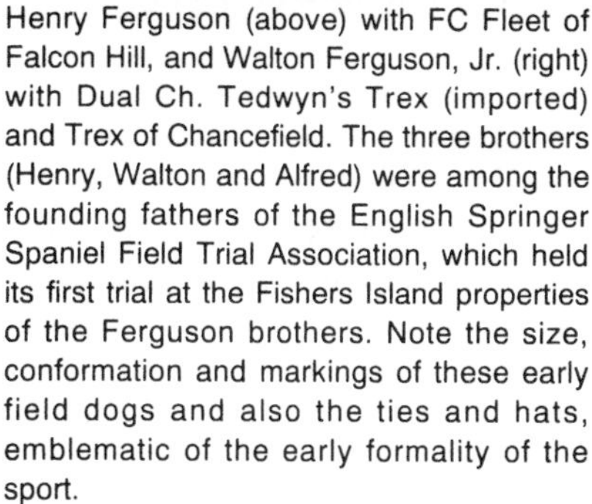

Henry Ferguson (above) with FC Fleet of Falcon Hill, and Walton Ferguson, Jr. (right) with Dual Ch. Tedwyn's Trex (imported) and Trex of Chancefield. The three brothers (Henry, Walton and Alfred) were among the founding fathers of the English Springer Spaniel Field Trial Association, which held its first trial at the Fishers Island properties of the Ferguson brothers. Note the size, conformation and markings of these early field dogs and also the ties and hats, emblematic of the early formality of the sport.

Probably no one contributed more to the early start of the English Springer Spaniel in America than the three Ferguson brothers. They owned large tracts of land on Fishers Island where the trials were held for the first twenty-five years of the sport. Walton Ferguson, Jr., was especially influential as an early president of the ESSFTA, a host to trials at his Fishers Island estate and home, an importer of many fine foundation dogs to America and as a benefactor who paid the expenses of English judges who came to this country to help properly institute the sport.

William Humphrey, of England, was instrumental in working with the founders of the ESSFTA to develop the rigorous but practical field trial format that is, to a great extent, still used today. Humphrey, a famous spaniel man and owner of Horsford Kennel in Shropshire, was brought to America by the founders of the ESSFTA as an adviser. Shown with him are FC Anghrim Flashing, the first U. S. field champion, and Horsford Hale. For several years—well into the 1930s—the Fishers Island founders group continued to bring over veteran spaniel people from England (and pay all expenses) to judge the annual field trials.

have such deep-seated instincts of biddability. The hunting strains through the ages have been selected and bred not only for hunting desire, but also for their ability to accept training kindly.

Physical Evolution of the Spaniel

The spaniel's change from a variety of local physical types into today's consistent spaniel breeds was an evolutionary one. By the seventeenth century, one writer described land spaniels of thirteen different kinds in a variety of colors, sizes, shapes and manner of handling game. Thomas Bewicke (1752–1828) was actually the first writer to use the words "Springer" and "Cocker" in referring to specific types of spaniels. His beautiful woodcuts of the twenty-five "breeds" of hunting dogs of his day illustrate Springers and Cockers in great detail. Even in the nineteenth century it was not unusual to find two or even three types in the same litter. Small ones (under twenty-five pounds) came to be called *cocking spaniels* (cocker comes from the quarry—woodcock), whereas the larger ones were called *springing spaniels* or *setting spaniels*. The setting spaniels undoubtedly were the ancestors of present-day setters. The first real attempt to standardize the physical and mental characteristics of the Springer was made by the Boughey family, whose stud book dates back to 1812.

Some beautiful art exists depicting the many varieties of spaniels over the last century and a half. The recently published book *Dog Painting—1840–1940*, by William Secord and published by the Antique Collectors Club Press, shows numerous examples of spaniel art. Four paintings stand out for their beauty and relevance: George Garrard's oil painting of a spaniel depicts Springer breed type; William E. Turner's 1868 oil painting shows a spaniel flushing a grouse; Arthur Wardle's 1906 oil painting features *Field Spaniels of the Twentieth Century* with a beautiful rendering of Ch. Velox Powder, one of the foundation sires of the English Springer Spaniel breed; and George Earl's 1870 oil painting *Champion Dogs of England* also depicts a beautiful Springer. You might want to check your local library or art museum to peruse the book.

The Springer Becomes a Popular Breed

Organized competitive sport for spaniels began with the founding of The Spaniel Club in England in the 1880s. The club drew up standards for bench (physical conformation) competition and shows were held. Another club, The Sporting Spaniel Society, was organized to test spaniels for their hunting ability. Soon both clubs were holding field trials (the first one in January 1899). At the third or fourth event a Springer dog named Tring beat all other spaniels and was thus the first Springer to become a trial winner by beating out the Cocker and Clumber competition.

In 1902 the English Kennel Club recognized the English Springer Spaniel officially as a breed. Some twelve years later the first Springer field champion in the world was C. A. Phillips's Rivington Sam, whose influence still stands behind many outstanding present-day Springers.

EFC Rivington Sam, a key foundation sire of the breed, was owned by C. A. Phillips and trained by James Thompson, both of Scotland.

George E. Watson, Sr., with Horsford Handcraft, winner of a 1930 trial at Fishers Island. Mr. Watson was an avid spaniel competitor and the grandfather of Forsyth Kineon and Betsy Watson (Brackenbriar Kennel). Mr. Watson was also involved in early activities of the ESSFTA.

During the first quarter of the twentieth century six great fountainhead strains of Springer bloodlines were established in England, according to the late eminent Scottish authority C. Mackay Sanderson:

1. Ch. Velox Powder, whelped in 1903.
2. Rivington Sam, whelped in 1911.
3. Denne Duke, whelped in 1908.
4. Dash of Hagley, whelped in 1905.
5. Caistor Rex, whelped in 1908.
6. Cornwallis Cavalier, whelped in 1914.

Most of the top field dogs in Britain and America today have one or more of these great stud dogs far back in their pedigree.

By the early 1900s the English Springer Spaniel (field type) had developed from a wild, unruly dog, one allowed to flush birds into the air for falcons and hawks, into a biddable, close-working gun dog that flushed game for the gun. Selective breeding intensified the traits necessary for our modern style of hunting while the basic size, style and physical traits of the Springer remain very similar to those of the early twentieth century.

Springers in England

Although virtually all of the famous English breeders of the first half of the twentieth century have passed on and their famous kennel names are no longer alive, the English breeders since 1950 have produced many premier dogs that have either won major championships in American competition or produced offspring that have capably competed on the American scene.

By the third quarter of the twentieth century, with World War II over, British dog enthusiasts were back to enjoying their pursuits and continued the development of the breed. Probably no British breeder has contributed more to the American scene than John Talbot Radcliffe, the record-breaking breeder of Saighton Springers that would win American field trials. In the 1960s he predicted he would "produce a strain of Springer blood with great native ability to scent, drive and run. . . . dogs that would be trainable and would handle." His predictions were remarkably accurate. The United States win record for Saighton-bred Springers includes 10 National wins, 9 Seconds, 7 Thirds and 6 Fourths. In addition, many other Saighton-bred Springers have won field championships in England and the United States.

British sportsmen have long used professional trainers to help train and develop their Springers with great drive, speed and enthusiasm for hunting, with nose to match the speed and temperament to handle kindly. There have always been many fine professionals in England, such as the legendary Joe Greatorex, who trained almost twenty field champions. Andrew Wylie and his brother, J. S. Wylie, produced their share of field champions. John MacQueen and his son, John, Jr., were cousins of Larry MacQueen, who came to the United States and became a top professional trainer here. Jack and Keith Chudley, another

Eudore Chevrier of Manitoba was a key figure in establishing the English Springer Spaniel throughout North America. Chevrier, a colorful personality, imported over 850 Springers to Canada from the United Kingdom and then resold them far and wide. These early dogs, in the hands of enthusiastic hunters, did much to laud the talents of the Springer for American-style hunting. Freeman Lloyd, dog editor of *Field & Stream* magazine, was a close friend of Chevrier, and Lloyd published many articles recommending the English Springer Spaniel as an ideal dog for American hunting pursuits.

At this 1956 Canadian Trial at Port Colborne, Ontario, the ribbons went to several renowned owners and handlers (left to right): Andrew Dunn of Port Credit, Ontario. Mr. Dunn imported many dogs from England in the early years. Herb and Edna Routley of Peterborough, Ontario, owners of the Trent Valley Kennels. The Routleys competed widely and even won some early trials at Fishers Island. They imported many dogs from England and contributed much to the popularity of the breed. The Routleys were the original importers of the Rivington and Breckenhill lines to the Americas. John and Jessie Blanock of Detroit, Michigan, active trialers and Springer fanciers then and today. John "Colonel" Blanock is president of the Southern Michigan Spaniel Training Club, and the Blanocks still host a weekly training session at their estate in Oxford, Michigan. *Nicholson*

team of brothers, developed winning ways at their Harpersbrook Kennels and delighted many owners with their smooth, polished results. In North Wales, Keith Erlandson built a strong reputation very quickly and in just a dozen years handled five Springers to their field titles. He also bred many great dogs, including a double U.S. National Field Champion and a double U.S. Amateur National Field Champion (Gwibernant Ganol and Gwibernant Gefni). Erlandson also bred the famous Hales Smut, a dog that is one of the most prominent sires in the history of the breed.

Readers desiring information on Springer activity in other countries are referred to the well-written book *The Popular Springer Spaniel* by Dorothy Morland Hooper, published by Popular Dogs Publishing Company, London.

Spaniels in America

Spaniels arrived in America at an early date, according to G. Mourt's *Journal of the Beginning of the English Plantation at Plymouth* circa 1622. He said one of the Pilgrims had a "spaniell" that chased deer. *The Sportsman's Companion*, published in New York circa 1780, describes spaniels as one of several varieties of fine shooting dogs when carefully trained. In the last half of the nineteenth century the sporting literature lists the names of more than fifty sportsmen who owned and used spaniel gun dogs.

It was not, however, until 1910 that the first Springer was registered by the American Kennel Club—a bitch named Denne Lucy. In 1914 the Canadian Kennel Club registered a dog named Longbranch Teal. But the real popularity of the breed in the United States did not occur until Eudore Chevrier of Winnipeg shot over that fine Springer gun dog Longbranch Teal in 1920. Chevrier was so impressed with Teal's hunting ability that he began to import English-bred Springers in great quantity for resale to American sportsmen.

Chevrier, along with G. T. Wolfe, Hayes L. Lloyd, E. T. Marsh, W. H. Gardner and other Canadians, founded the English Springer Spaniel Club of Canada in July 1922; the first North American trial for the breed was held just two months later near Winnipeg. One of the winners was Alderbury Drake, son of the great British field champion Dalshangan Dandy Boy (a grandson of the first British field champion, Rivington Sam).

The first Springer club in the United States, the English Springer Spaniel Field Trial Association (ESSFTA), was also organized in 1922 in the New York area by Samuel G. Allen, William Hutchenson and the three Ferguson brothers (Walton, Jr., Henry and Alfred) of Fishers Island, New York. These five sportsmen had on-hand advice and counsel from William Humphries, owner of the famous Horsford Kennels in England, who spent much time here in America. The first trial was held at Fishers Island in October 1924, and was won by Aughrim Flashing, owned by Humphries and later sold to Mrs. M. Walton. That dog became the first United States Field Champion. In 1927 the American Kennel Club recognized this club as the "parent club" of the breed and shortly thereafter "Standards and Regulations" for field trials and bench shows were established, modeled carefully after their English counterparts.

In 1962, Talbot Radcliffe (right) made one of his many visits to the United States and is shown here with Lem Scales, handler/trainer of NFC Kansan, 1962 National Open Champion. Radcliffe, of Anglesey, Wales, is the founder/breeder of the famous Saighton Springers. Over the years, Saightons have won many field championships and National Field Championships in the United States. *French*

This historic photo shows eight well-known spaniel men posed for the victory photo at the 1963 National Open Championship. They are (top row, left to right): Harold Jones (California), vice president of the Championship; Arthur "Ruffy" Aiken (Pennsylvania), Judge; Howard Zingler (California), Judge; Richard Migel (New York), President of the Championship. (bottom row left to right): John Blanock (Michigan) with Meadowcourt Daniel, awarded "Best dog owned and handled by an amatuer." (In those days only 1st, 2nd and 3rd placements were awarded); Clarence Wingate (Pro of Michigan) with NFC Waveaway's Wilderness Maeve, 1st place and National Champion, owned by William E. Lane of Michigan; Cliff Wallace (Pro of Illinois) with Shineradee, 2nd place owned by John Olin of Winchester Arms fame. (Shineradee was imported from England by Mr. Olin.); Dave Lorenz (Pro of Illinois) with 3rd place Brackenbriar Snapshot owned by Brackenbriar Kennels (Forsythe Kineon and Betsy Watson). Snapshot went on to become National Champion in 1967 and later sired many successful dogs. *Craig*

During this Ohio Valley Club trial held in the early 1970s, several well-known trialers competed for the Open All-Age victory. The competitors and the dogs were destined to make a lasting impact on the sport and the breed. They are (left to right): Dave Lorenz, holding on his right a dog that was to become 1972 National Champion, NFC Dot of Charel owned by Charles and Eleanor Curdy; Warren Wunderlich, M.D., with two-time National Amateur Champion (1973, 74) NAFC Sunray of Chrishall (sired by the legendary Hales Smut); John Riepenhoff, M.D., well-known Ohio handler who has owned and handled several National Champions; Fred St. Clair of Jeffersonville, Ohio.

Clubs carefully consider the experience and knowledge of those they invite to judge their trials. At this trial, two very experienced judges worked together to select the winner. Both John Buoy of Illinois (left), owner/handler of several National Champions, and the late Larry McQueen of New Jersey, professional trainer/handler of many field champions and several National Champions, were major factors in the sport in this half of the twentieth century. John Buoy is still very active in trialing and served as a longtime member of the ESSFTA Board of Governors.

NFC Tillan Ticket, trained and handled by the late Elmore Chick (shown), and owned by Charles A. Mee, won the 1972 National Open Championship. Mr. Chick handled several other National Champions including NFC Brackenbank Tangle in 1959, owned by E. W. Wunderlich, and NFC Staindrop Breckonhill Chip in 1957/58, owned by Ruxroy Kennels. *Lightfoot*

The team of Wally Retzlaff of Wisconsin and NFC/NAFC/NCFC Solo Sam is legendary. Sam was the only survivor in his litter, so Wally gave him very personal treatment. Sam repaid Wally's kindness and careful training with three National Championships in the mid 1970s—all coming when Mr. Retzlaff was well along in years. Sam, a rather small dog, was bred quite extensively, thereby perpetuating a line of small but high-performance Springers. *Lightfoot*

These two National Champions, FC, NAFC Misty Muffet (left) and NFC, AFC, CFC Dewfield Bricksclose Flint (right), are shown with Jim Lock of Essex, England. Mr. Lock exported both dogs to the Christensens of Oregon. Then Misty was handled by Janet Christensen, DVM, to the 1970 National Amateur Championship, and Flint was handled by Dr. C. A. (Chris) Christensen to the 1973 and 1975 National Open Championships.

These three men made a major impact on and contribution to the sport in the 1960s, 1970s and 1980s. They are: Dr. C. A. "Chris" Christensen of Oregon, shown with two-time National Open Champion NFC, AFC, CFC Dewfield Bricksclose Flint. Dr. Christensen was noted for his highly competitive dogs, many of which were British imports. His wife, Janet Christensen, DVM, is also a very successful field trialer and breeder. In the late 1970s, Dr. Christensen retired from active competition and now mainly hunts, fishes and guns field trials for recreation.

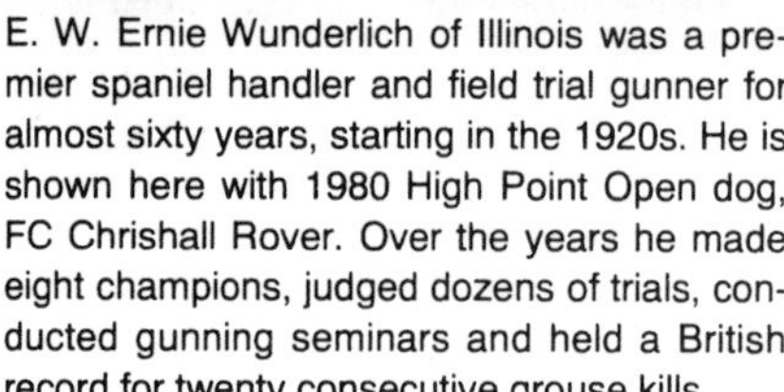

E. W. Ernie Wunderlich of Illinois was a premier spaniel handler and field trial gunner for almost sixty years, starting in the 1920s. He is shown here with 1980 High Point Open dog, FC Chrishall Rover. Over the years he made eight champions, judged dozens of trials, conducted gunning seminars and held a British record for twenty consecutive grouse kills.

Ed Whitaker served for many years as president of the ESSFTA and is a devoted trialer who has campaigned many successful dogs, made many Champions and introduced many newcomers to the sport of spaniel field trials. He is shown here with AFC Whyte Winter Drift.

The breed was touted and recommended extensively in the 1930s and 1940s by such famous outdoor writers as Freeman Lloyd, Bob Becker, Will Judy, Maxwell Riddle, Gordon McQuary and others. Their recognition of the breed's hunting talents did much to popularize it with United States hunters. Later on, such fine writers as William Brown, editor of *The American Field*, Henry Davis, Jack Baird, Joe Stetson, Mrs. Evelyn Monte, David Michael Duffy and Arthur Swanson kept the sporting public well informed of the merits of the Springer, until it was found in American hunting fields and duck blinds by the thousands.

During the second quarter of the twentieth century, the United States pheasant population grew by leaps and bounds as a timely replacement of the ever-dwindling supply of native game birds. It was then that Springers found a real "home" on these shores. By 1950 more than thirty field trial clubs were holding competition and the breed was established as a true American institution.

Since 1950 the English Springer Spaniel has continued its preeminent position as a sophisticated gun dog. The field and show strains continued to separate until there was little or no breeding interaction between the two. Although recognized as a single breed by the AKC, only people with minimal knowledge of the breed would fail to recognize the differences between the two.

Certainly having a classy field-bred English Springer Spaniel in the White House as the "First Dog" during George Bush's presidency enhanced the popularity and public relations of the breed. "Millie," and later her son "Ranger," lived in the White House with great aplomb. Millie came from Will Farish's Lanes End Farm in Kentucky. Mr. Farish, a friend of President Bush and a noted horse breeder, imported Millie's forebears from the United Kingdom, which is why she looks like a traditional Springer of English estate breeding.

Today, more than seventy clubs across the United States and Canada hold field trials and competitive events. The field trial format for Springers is closely guarded to insure that it approximates a normal day's shooting afield. This has encouraged development of a Springer that is valued as a hunting companion. Thus, the field trial Springer remains an excellent choice for the average hunter. Meanwhile, some pointing dog and retriever trial formats became so artificial that they encouraged breeding of dogs that had no relevance to a typical hunter's day afield. Springer Spaniel field trial enthusiasts focused on breeding dogs that could win trials but were still valued gun dogs and companions.

Whether you choose to use your dog for all-out field trial competition, an occasional day hunting pheasants, hunting dog tests to earn an AKC suffix or simply want to train an awesome gun dog to impress your friends, the English Springer Spaniel can admirably meet all your expectations.

A well-trained English Springer Spaniel will always flush game within gun range. The Springer's inherited instinct to work close is enhanced by proper training. Here a dog flushes a pheasant then "hups" at the flight. If the gunner drops the bird, the spaniel should await the command to retrieve. Note that this bird was flushed well within gun range. *Friend*

The spaniel is a versatile dog that retrieves on land and water as needed. Here a Springer retrieves a cock pheasant that fell in an adjacent pond, a common occurrence in upland hunting. *Friend*

2

The English Springer Spaniel: Where Does It Fit in as a Gun Dog?

ONE OF THE MOST EXCITING experiences for a sportsman anywhere is to see a fine gun dog of any breed, well trained, well conditioned and experienced, expertly performing in the field. But since there are many hunting breeds often performing quite differently, the question frequently arises—how are the several types of gun dogs supposed to accomplish their work? This chapter answers that question.

In the United States, purebred hunting dogs are registered with one of three organizations: the American Kennel Club (AKC), the Field Dog Stud Book (FDSB), an arm of the American Field Publishing Company, or the United Kennel Club (UKC). The AKC, which is by far the largest of the three with 135 recognized breeds, has divided all these breeds into a variety of groups with the *bird dogs* (retrievers, spaniels and pointing dogs) forming the Sporting Group.

Today, all English Springer Spaniels are registered with the American Kennel Club. Years ago, many Springers were dual registered with the AKC and the Field Dog Stud Book, but that practice faded away and today the AKC is the only common registry organization.

The Canadian Kennel Club (CKC) recognizes the English Springer Spaniel in the same way as does the AKC, and through a simple but somewhat tedious process, dogs can be registered back and forth. Springers registered in the United Kingdom can also be AKC registered when imported to the United States.

Spaniels such as English Springers and Cockers are called land or flushing spaniels. They search for game by nose and flush it (make it run or fly) when they come upon it. They are probably the second-oldest hunting-breed type (behind hounds).

The pointing dogs are of two main types: the older and more popular English Pointers and the three Setters, and then all the other "continental breeds" such as the Brittany, German Shorthaired Pointer and the Vizsla. Pointing dogs seek game by scent and indicate it by freezing or "pointing" it when in close proximity.

Retriever breeds are typified by the Labrador Retriever, the Golden Retriever and the Chesapeake Bay Retriever. Retrievers were developed to walk at heel or sit in a blind instead of searching in front of the gun. They then retrieve anything downed by the hunter.

Each breed is a specialist, and years ago many wealthy sportsmen kept several of each type in their kennels. Today, few people's lifestyles would allow for such a luxury.

Noted authorities such as the noted dog writer David Michael Duffy, the hunting dog editor of *Outdoor Life*, Larry Mueller, and others generally concede that of all types of gun dogs, the English Springer Spaniel is a leading contender for the title of all-around gun dog for the one-dog-sportsman who wants to hunt upland game and waterfowl. Having hunted and shot over many dogs of the several breeds and types over the years, I agree completely. English Springer Spaniels are great all-around dogs. They can do almost anything—some things better than others—but almost anything.

As Charles Goodall explained it back in the 1950s:

> The properly bred, well-trained and experienced Springer Spaniel is a joy to gun over. He should walk obediently at heel without leash, and when ordered to hunt will fairly explode, and always in the direction in which he is sent (right or left of the gunner).
>
> When he reaches the desired distance to either side of the hunter, he will reverse direction and speed back in front of the hunter with great dash and hunting desire (almost as mechanically as the windshield wiper on an automobile). The spaniel is a beater who covers all his ground to either side and in front of the handler, never leaving any game but always in gun range. When he strikes game (foot scent) he will drop his head and put his nose to the ground like a hound. He will persistently puzzle out the line (foot scent) increasing his speed as he approaches the bird or rabbit with his tail beating furiously and his animation quite visible. When his nose tells him that game is close, he will raise his head, take the body scent and drive in with a great rush that is guaranteed to drive it out from its hiding place.
>
> If the game is shot, the spaniel will mark the fall and retrieve it on command; if it is missed, he will resume hunting on command. If the game was only crippled, he will put his nose to the ground at the fall and trail it out with eagerness and dispatch—10, 50, or 200 yards—seize it in his mouth with a gentle grip and return it to his owner's hand. An experienced, trained, and suitably bred dog of this type will not only fill the game bag but will provide many thrills and excitement for the hunting party. A real sportsman who thinks the hunt is equally as important as the

The bright eyes and eager expression of NFC Misty Muffet—National Amateur Champion—owned by Janet Christensen, DVM, of Oregon demonstrates why the field enthusiasts of the English Springer Spaniel breed feel that beauty is in the eye of the beholder. No hunter or outdoor person could fail to appreciate the beauty, enthusiasm and talents of such a dog.

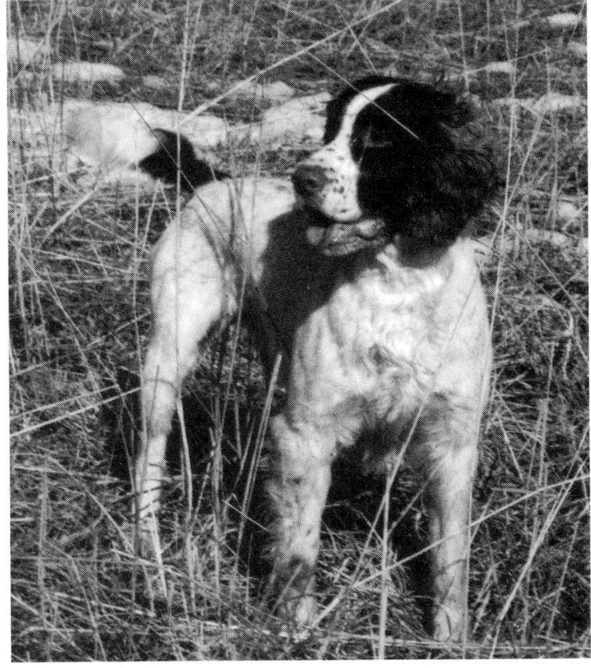

When fully grown, a field-bred English Springer Spaniel will often have the markings, size and athletic build similar to FC/AFC South Chase Brady (shown here). Brady is owned and handled by Dr. Pat Fischer of Green Bay, Wisconsin

quantity of game brought home will never hunt without a trained gun dog. The Springer is the pheasant dog par excellence.

But consider this: Spaniels, by their nature, hunt with the hunter. That means you will be in the cover with the dog. In today's world of exercise, jogging, hiking, workouts and health concerns, the spaniel is an active dog for active people. When it comes to gunning, spaniels are for sporting shooters. Springers will give you plenty of warning by their body language and tail action, but you won't often have time to plant your feet, shoulder the gun and get set. This is snap shooting at its best; tremendous fun for true sports and a game of fast, exciting action.

Many dogs are imported to the United States and Canada from the United Kingdom. ENFC Cortman Garry was imported to Canada by Alex Stewart of Manitoba. Garry is shown here with a woodcock and a traditional British side-by-side shotgun.

3

Selection of a Springer Gun Dog Puppy

TO THE PERSON setting out to acquire a Springer for field work, this is the most important chapter in the book. Selecting a puppy worthy of and able to benefit from your effort is the first step in training an English Springer Spaniel to work to the gun. This is a most difficult situation to control, because most people acquire their first dog for reasons of sentiment rather than on cold, hard logic. The best advice that can be given to anyone interested in acquiring a high-class Springer gun dog puppy is to go to the spaniel *field trial* club or a professional trainer in your vicinity and ask for the names of individuals who breed field-type Springer Spaniels. Or, you could call *Spaniels in the Field* magazine (513-489-2727) to get a breeders list and an issue of the magazine, which always features many ads for field-bred puppies.

Because many of the numerous championship titles and performance certificates that can be acquired by an English Springer Spaniel have no bearing on the dog's ability to find game, retrieve or accept training of the type necessary to produce a good field dog, you should be aware of the meanings of the various titles.

At this point I quote Charles Goodall directly from the third edition of this book:

> At the risk of incurring the undying enmity of Springer breeders who specialize in producing show type dogs, the author in all sincerity is compelled to say that Springer dogs primarily of show bloodlines are usually poor risks if one wants to have a really high class gun dog. Also, the Obedience titles C.D. or C.D.X. or

U.D. mean only that the dogs have been trained to perform certain routine acts such as walking at heel, remaining in one spot on command, or carrying a wooden dumbbell in its mouth while jumping over a hurdle, etc. There is nothing wrong with Obedience trials where dogs are tested on their ability to perform the above acts, and are graded according to their ability to do so. But there is no guarantee, however, or even suggestion, that a dog with these abilities (or its offspring) can scent a bird ten yards away, or exhibit an eagerness to crash into a duck pond on a chilly November day to retrieve a fat mallard drake that has fallen to the gun. The same facts hold true for puppies whelped from a mating of one or more show champions. The title of champion (Ch.) means only that the dog has near perfect body conformation and that its legs are straight, its coat the proper color and quality, its body formed in the manner prescribed by the breed Standard, and its ears the proper length, etc. It is basic logic to assume that Springers or their offspring which have been selected for these characteristics alone (this is true of most show strains) are not as well fitted to exhibit an overwhelming desire to hunt on a bitter cold day, or with the sun beating down in 90° temperatures as occasionally happens during the dove shooting season, the partridge season, or in a good duck marsh. And of equal importance is the fact that show strain bloodlines have not been selected for the ability to accept training and to respond kindly, as have the Springers which have descended from hunting strains that are pure and proven for many generations.

Goodall goes on to say:

> Again, it must be repeated and stressed that there is nothing wrong with the sport of showing dogs, or the dogs that are shown, or the people that show them on the bench or in Obedience trials. Both sports provide a valuable form of recreation which is greatly needed in our most complex and high pressure society. It is wrong, however, to expect the son or daughter of a show champion (Ch.) or Obedience winner (C.D., C.D.X. or U.D.) to develop into a high class shooting dog—just as it is wrong to expect the offspring of the best field dogs to do well or win at bench shows. The two types are as far apart as if they were two different breeds.

Obviously, Mr. Goodall felt very strongly about the subject and his viewpoints are just as predominant among knowledgeable field Springer enthusiasts today.

The more I'm involved in the breeding of dogs, the more I believe in inherited traits. If you start with a puppy of parentage that has not in any way proven its worth in a hunting or field situation for several generations, you have no way of knowing what traits for hunting, if any, the dog possesses. You are severely testing the odds and may be setting yourself up for a great deal of hard work and disappointment.

Field Champions

For some breeds, specifically pointers and setters, where the trials are conducted from horseback, or retrievers, where trials are based mainly on rigid obedience tests, the title "Field Champion" may not be applicable to an average day of hunting on foot. However, rest assured that the Springer field trial format

For the first three weeks, the puppies need mainly warmth and mother's nourishment. These puppies snuggle up to nurse and are warmed by a Scott electric whelping pan. *DeVoll*

Soon the puppies will be very active, and by five weeks they will be ready to explore and play. Springer puppies crave affection and children make wonderful socializers. Of the five puppies in this litter, two became field champions and all became successful hunting dogs. *Roggenkamp*

Socializing a puppy is very important; being in the house is especially good for the development of a Springer's personality. If you can manage it, try some in-house time every day. Here Dr. Dave Kettleson's puppy rests on a bed the owner prepared under the family room coffee table. This level of family closeness builds a solid bond with the owner and strong self-confidence in the dog. *DeVoll*

rigidly adheres to the premise given in the American Kennel Club's *Registration and Field Trial Rules and Standard Procedures for Spaniels* that in a field trial "the performance should not differ from that in any ordinary day's shooting except that in the trials, a dog should do his work in a more nearly perfect way." Therefore you can select a Springer of field trial parentage and expect a dog with natural ability to perform in the field in a way that will please the average foot hunter.

If you want a hunting dog, select a puppy from known and proven hunting or field trial stock. Study the five-generation pedigree, which most reputable breeders gladly supply. High-class gun dogs do not always result, even from the proper breeding, but the percentage of success is a great deal higher when you start with proven stock. You should, on all accounts, beware of breeders who promise dual skills in any dog. Also, beware of people who make vague claims of hunting prowess. Ask for details, demonstrated abilities and references.

Field-bred Springers are much less uniform in size, color and markings than the show types; and a few differences are noteworthy. Field dogs tend to have much more white and abundant ticking in their coats. Many breeders actually strive to achieve a substantial amount of white in the coat for field visibility. Field strains generally have notably shorter ears, less feathering on the legs and underbody and much longer tails (usually docked to be six to twelve inches long at maturity). Field dogs tend to be lighter boned and leaner, with ribs often showing.

You should also research pedigrees, looking for titles with an "F" signifying Field; FC—Field Champion; AFC—Amateur Field Champion; CFC—Canadian Field Champion; or the very exclusive NFC, NAFC or NCFC—National Field Champion. Springer Field Championships are very demanding and difficult to earn. For example, in 1991, in the entire United States, only 21 Field Champions (FC) and 13 Amateur Field Champions (AFC) were titled. In that same year, 217 Springers earned show championships (Ch.) and 128 Springers completed their CD Obedience titles.

The AKC hunting test suffixes are of value as well and, although still very new and less prevalent, do have meaning. They are JH—Junior Hunter; SH—Senior Hunter; or MH—Master Hunter. Obviously, the higher the level the better; and at this point I would consider only MH of any real value for breeding reference. The Hunting Tests are still relatively new; therefore, JH, SH and MH suffixes are still relatively rare.

Picking a Puppy

Never forget that the gift puppy from the accidental breeding of some neighbor's Springer bitch, or the bargain puppy bought on impulse from a spur-of-the-moment decision, may be a most expensive addition to the household. The initial cost of the puppy is a very minor part of the long-term expense, so it truly pays to buy the best. It costs just as much to properly feed and care for a puppy of minimal potential as it does a good one; and it may cost a great deal

Bloodlines *do count.* Here Dr. David McCurdy's (Nova Scotia) Champion FC/AFC/CFC Saighton's Sharp (center) is surrounded by six of McCurdy's Glenrock field champions. The consistency of type is unmistakable. *McCurdy*

Kara Roggenkamp thinks this puppy is the sweetest and nicest one in this litter . . . "Can't we keep it, Dad?" *Roggenkamp*

Some of the best Springer hunting dogs and trial dogs are house dogs. Here Dr. Kettleson's puppy awakes from a snooze in his new owner's favorite chair, which seems to please the puppy and the owner. Surely anyone could love a field-bred Springer this cute! *DeVoll*

more to train a poor one because it has not inherited the desirable qualities to enable it to fully utilize your training efforts.

Most puppy purchasers focus on two factors almost exclusively—sex and markings. Frankly, neither will have any bearing on the long-term success of the dog as a hunter, companion or competitor. Almost every successful field trialer has run and trained a few of each sex. Markings, though interesting at first, soon fall on the scale of importance. The real traits of importance are evident to a trained eye even in very young puppies and include boldness or inquisitiveness, aggressiveness or playfulness, dominance or docility. Although it is difficult, try to look beyond markings and sex when picking your Springer partner.

Bringing the Puppy Home

Most breeders ship puppies at seven weeks of age, and today it is easy to fly puppies cross-country with no traumatic effect. The most heralded breeders generally have a waiting list for puppies and require a deposit. Once the new puppy arrives, immediately have your veterinarian inoculate it for diseases as recommended and religiously repeat this practice every two weeks for as long as the veterinarian suggests until the dog has received its permanent shots.

The puppy, once it is home, should be settled into the place you have previously prepared for its living quarters. If it is an outside kennel, with a concrete or other hard surface run, be sure it is equipped with a tight, draft-free dog house. Remember, a puppy can stand cold weather and a certain amount of wet weather, but it cannot withstand both cold and wet weather at the same time. Puppies do not have the sense of older dogs and will frequently play in the rain until thoroughly wet and then spend the night sleeping wet. This is almost sure to result in dire consequences.

If the puppy is to be a house dog, prepare a bed in a draft-free, out-of-the-way spot in the house. Most hunters today use an airline crate for travel, but it can also serve as a combination bed, home and housebreaking device. Even the smallest puppies seldom soil a confined space like a crate if taken out for relief regularly. Small children in the household, as well as adults, should be reminded that little puppies require lots of sleep to maintain good health and cannot be played with all the time.

4

Before You Begin to Train

MOST PEOPLE reading the field section of this book are doing so because they have embarked upon the task of training their Springer for hunting. Now, with a Springer puppy under their left arm and this book in their right hand they are ready to embark on that training program.

Let me start by assuring you that most of the things you must do during the first year involve your natural parenting instincts. Humanization and basic training for dogs are as natural as the nurturing and bonding process we develop with our children. Because today's *field-bred* Springer Spaniel has a very soft temperament, the first few months with you and your family builds and instills a level of self-confidence in the animal that is necessary if it is to become the bold and assertive hunting dog you want. Four times I have tried to formally train a dog that was virtually ignored or left alone in a kennel for the first six months of its life. In all four cases I failed. These dogs all lacked the self-confidence and human bonding necessary to develop into a bold, confident hunting dog.

I firmly believe that humanization and exposure to the world during the first six months are critical. Naturally, quality food and competent regular veterinary care are also essential, but most of all your young dog needs love, exposure to the world and slowly—very slowly—instilled consistent basic training.

However, there is a negative side to too much attention. Often the new puppy is the light of the hunter's eye and the owner can't wait to get started on the advanced training described in Chapter 7. This over-eager trainer is soon out in the field with a twelve-week-old puppy trying to teach very complex skills that should only be expected at the age of two years. Avoid this pitfall! Relax, take your time. If you are too anxious or compulsive, go fishing or play golf while you give your dog time to mature. You want to achieve a happy balance, which lies somewhere between over-training the puppy to the point of utter boredom versus ignoring it to the point that the puppy is an untrained, unresponsive, undisciplined wild animal with no respect for you or the human world in which it lives.

With that bit of advice, let's get into the basic skills and training. As you begin with your young dog, teach the skills in this order: Obedience, Range, Fetch, Find and Flush, or ORFFF:

O—***Obedience*** to commands
R—***Range*** within gunning distance
F—***Fetch*** birds
F—***Find*** birds
F—***Flush*** birds

This order may seem a little strange, but it is the proper one for training. The most rudimentary gun dog should have some level of these basic skills and control. The difference between a novice started gun dog and a very accomplished Master Hunter (MH) is the level of quality, polish, control and consistency exhibited. If, in the future, you should decide to compete in field trials, you and your dog must perform these same five functions but within the rigid structure of the field trial format and with the ultimate level of style, speed and consistency.

The table at right details the qualities you should strive for in a good Springer gun dog.

Yard Training versus Field Training

I have always found it helpful to separate yard training from field training in the earliest stages by thinking of yard as rules and field as fun.

Yard training is a place for disciplined learning. This is classroom where "Come!", "Fetch!" and "Hup!" should be taught with strict and consistent expectation of quick and responsive obedience. Don't equivocate. Expect compliance *every time* once the puppy knows what is expected.

Field training, on the other hand (most especially during the first six months), is a playground, a fun place to run and play; build enthusiasm; learn the wind and gain self confidence—but no birds in the first few months.

Later, when you are sure that both yard obedience and field enthusiasm are firmly instilled in the puppy's mind, it is time to begin transferring and merging the yard discipline into the field setting. Soon your youngster will be charging around in the field with that same level of enthusiasm but with an ear attuned to your whistle and a brain ready to respond to your commands.

The term "puppy" in Spaniel language means a dog under age two years that is eligible for all AKC competitive events designated for puppies. This is a

Obedience	This begins at seven weeks, the day you get your puppy and is most intense for the first twelve months of the dog's life. After that, most obedience will not be training but merely reinforcement of previously learned commands. This can and should be taught at home and is commonly referred to as "yard training."
Range	Starts at seven weeks and should be firmly entrenched in the dog's psyche by age nine months. However, it will need to be reinforced frequently. This can be taught in parks, school yards or fields. This is a basic understanding in the dog's mind that it should *never* range more than forty yards from you.
Fetch	Can start as early as seven to nine weeks with most puppies and should be fairly well refined by age nine months. All the basics can and should be taught in your yard.
Find	Starts at about four or five months and intensifies from nine months to a year. This is part inherent talent, part learned ability and part skill. It gets better as the dog ages and learns from experience. Can be started in the yard but requires a field with suitable cover for most efforts.
Flush; desire to find birds	Boldness, eagerness, birdiness, hunting desire, ability to follow a moving bird until it is forced into flight are learned skills that are usually started at six or seven months. These skills progress rapidly with experience. This is field training.

wise choice of terms and timing. A two-year-old is about the human equivalent of a late adolescent, and until age two most dogs (regardless of the level of polish in their performance in the field) are still somewhat immature and in the learning phase of their life. In this book I refer to any dog under age two as a "puppy," and although your pupil will reach full growth by about nine months, mentally it should be treated like an impressionable youngster and handled accordingly.

Training to Encourage What Comes Naturally

Several noted dog behaviorists have written extensively about the obviously inherited (instinctive) behavioral patterns of different breeds of dogs. Whereas most humans make decisions and learn on a primarily conscious level, animals for the most part are driven by their natural inclinations (instincts).

Training a spaniel is different from training any other type of gun dog. Your goal is to enhance the positive instincts and control the negative ones. An example is teaching a spaniel to heel. Keith Erlandson, the well-known Welsh breeder and dog trainer, explains in his book *Gun Dog Training* that teaching a retriever to heel is relatively easy and should be done early in the dog's life. On the other hand, he notes, most spaniels don't like to heel—an action that is in direct conflict with their natural instinct to quest and hunt whenever walking with their master. Erlandson states that "rigorous heel keeping early on could inhibit hunting which is to be avoided at all costs, as hunting is the primary function of a spaniel."

Another example of overcoming a dog's natural instinct is training the dog to be steady to wing and shot. It is a spaniel's nature to boldly run in on a game bird and then chase it to the horizon when it flies. Teaching the dog to stop and hup when game flies is totally counter-instinctive. If you are ever going to have any hope of training your dog to be steady to wing and shot, you must lay a very solid foundation of discipline and control, sufficient to overcome the dog's natural instinct to chase game.

As you begin training, try to think through each new training command to decide whether you are reinforcing a natural instinct (such as retrieving) or overcoming a natural instinct (such as chasing a flying bird). This will help you make training decisions.

Patience in Training

The greatest fault displayed by most trainers is that in their enthusiasm they rush the training beyond the dog's capacity to absorb it. A puppy six months old has a very short span of attention. He may not remember things very long and cannot concentrate on any one thing for more than a few minutes. He gets bored easily and cannot stand much nagging or hacking. So the lessons must be brief and to the point and must *always* be discontinued while the dog is still enthusiastic about the work. It is easy to break a puppy's spirit or to make him hate the training sessions. If the trainer is in doubt, the lesson should be stopped at once.

Levels of Training

Perhaps this will be your first real effort to formally train a Springer gun dog. That is not to say that you haven't had experience with other breeds or experience with hunting dogs, but you have never attempted to reach for a training level that tapped the fullest potential of your training talent or your dog's ability. I find it easiest to visualize the training effort in levels—basic, intermediate and advanced. It is rare, if not impossible, to get to the advanced level without going through the basic and intermediate steps. In the end, the final level of performance the dog achieves corresponds to the level of training it has received, the trainer's talent and the dog's basic capacity to learn.

The new AKC hunting tests have defined levels of performance that in many ways correspond to the three levels of training. For example: **Basic training** should yield a solidly started gun dog—one that is reasonably obedient, comes when called in the field, hunts within gun range, finds game with its nose, flushes the game boldly and, when game is shot, retrieves it tenderly to the hunter. That description roughly echoes the AKC hunt test definition of a Junior Hunter. A gun dog of this level can be great fun in the field and a valuable hunting asset. I have spent many marvelous days afield with young dogs with no more training

English Springer Spaniels crave attention and affection not just as puppies but throughout their lives. Here John Isaacs (Pro) of Ohio, who is well over six feet tall, gets down on the puppy's level and provides some hands-on bonding and petting time. *Friend*

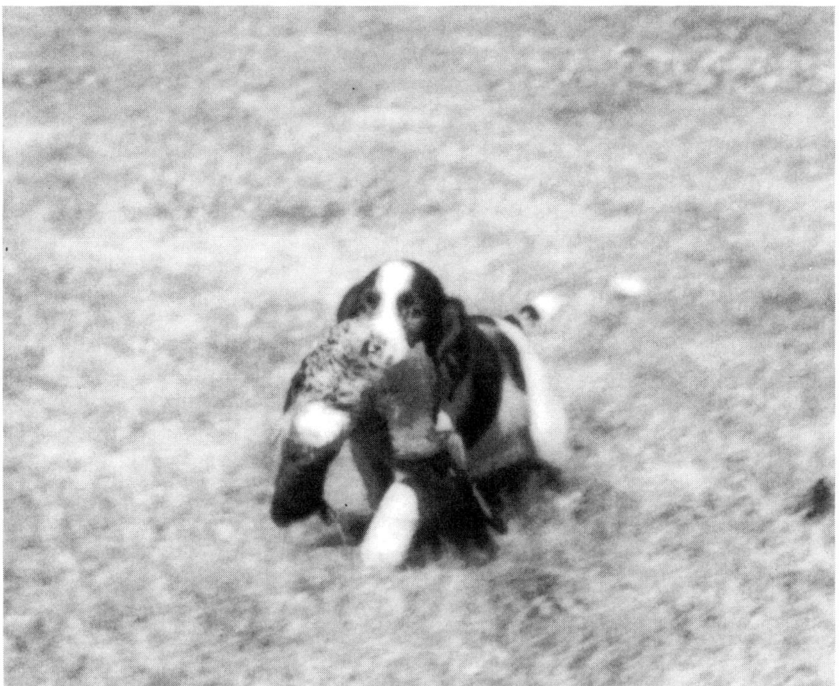

Even the smallest puppies often show a natural inclination to retrieve. This puppy raced out and picked up a dead pigeon that was being used with an older dog. Notice the natural high head carriage and the instinctive turn to the handler as the retrieved object is picked up. *Roggenkamp*

than this basic level and had wonderful and productive hunts. I estimate that 90 percent of all dogs are never trained beyond this level.

Intermediate training takes more of your time, more ability, more patience and requires more dog talent. In addition to all the attributes of a basic gun dog, the intermediate gun dog must have a high level of obedience in the field, i.e., quarter at your direction, limit its chasing after missed birds, boldly attack cover in its search for game, "hunt dead" (to find downed but unseen falls at your direction), and handle basic water retrieving. In general, this dog reflects the qualifications of an AKC Senior Hunter. A dog of this level is a valuable hunting companion, able to handle almost any situation and willing to work with you and for you—a true hunting partner. Hunting with a dog of this caliber is a distinct pleasure. I estimate that roughly 7 percent of all Springer gun dogs are trained to this level of competence.

Advanced training imparts a final added level of excellence to a very solid gun dog and turns it into a polished and complete hunter, a dog fully steady to wing and shot, able to handle blind retrieves on land and water. He is able to track wounded birds and always hunts in control, handles easily, works with the hunter. The AKC requirements for a Master Hunter carefully define such traits and the requirements to earn such a title. Such a dog inspires fireside conversations, legends and memories. Only about 2 percent of the dogs will ever achieve this level of excellence.

Finally, the very advanced level of **Field Trial training** builds upon the aforementioned training and adds a dimension of competition, style, speed and obedience that goes beyond that required of a gun dog. These dogs should be the crème de la crème. Fortunately for the Springer as a breed, the field trial format so closely simulates hunting that some dogs are hunted on the way home from trials or, more important, trialed on the way home from hunting trips. This is the ultimate level of performance. Dogs that achieve a championship at the field trial level of performance have proven their talent, and most breeders consider this the true test that qualifies dogs for breeding programs, in the belief that they will pass on their talents through their genes.

Choosing a Target Level

The level you achieve will depend upon your ability as a trainer, the innate abilities of your dog and the amount of time and effort you invest in the process.

I bring up levels of training at this point for a reason. In all likelihood, you are not yet certain what level of training you will want to achieve in your puppy. Many people are very optimistic and already have grand plans to win a National Championship with their first dog. That is possible—in fact, it has been done! However, if you do want to achieve success in the highest levels of competition, you must be very careful not to attempt risky shortcuts in the early stages of training. Shortcuts often ingrain subtle faults that can prove to be very negative during the judging of major events. More about this subject appears in the chapters on advanced training.

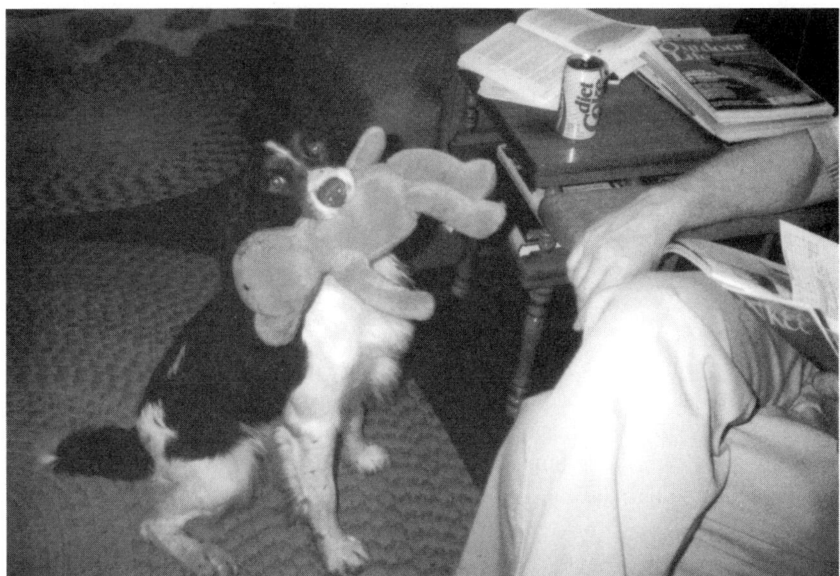

Not all retrieving must be in the yard! To most spaniels, retrieving is fun and they do it with great enthusiasm. Here a Springer retrieves his very own teddy bear that the owner keeps in the house as a toy for the dog. *DeVoll*

FC/AFC/CFC Ru-Char's Rise & Shine bounds back with a retrieve. This photo was taken when Shine was just a puppy, but he continued his enthusiasm for retrieving throughout his many All-Age victories. *Gary Wilson*

Other Spaniel Breeds as Gun Dogs

There are several other flushing spaniel breeds. All Spaniel breeds (except Irish Water) accomplish field work in basically the same manner. However, the speed, dash, boldness and natural abilities vary from breed to breed according to the breed's physical capabilities and the amount of field work talent in the individual's breeding. Most are smaller than Springers except for the Clumber, which is a large, heavy-boned dog. Several, such as the Field Spaniel or Sussex Spaniel, are very rare. Although Cocker Spaniels are a very popular breed, relatively few were found in the field ten years ago. Today, there is a resurgence of interest in using Cockers for field work, especially the English Cockers. With luck, the spaniel puppy of your choice has some parentage with field/working genes, which will greatly enhance your probability of success.

In any event, the training methods explained in this book are applicable to any flushing spaniel and can be used as described.

No Single Best Method

Finally, as you begin to train, please understand that there is no single best way to train a Springer gun dog. This book explains some of the more usual and proven methods, but each puppy is different and variations tailored to the individual are often appropriate. That is one reason why so many of us choose to train with some experienced partners, because they often have insights and ideas that don't occur to us on how to break through some training difficulty.

A COMMAND CHECKLIST

Don't overlook this simple but important obedience training checklist. It will make your life easier and your hunting trips more enjoyable. And a bit of advice—don't name your dog anything that sounds like these commands. It becomes very confusing to your dog when you yell, "Moe, No!"

Command	*It Means*	*Age to Begin Training*
"No!"	Stop that right now	7 weeks
"Kennel!"	Get into your kennel, run or travel box . . . now [makes travel much easier]	7 weeks
"Come!"	Come here right now	7 weeks
"Fetch!"	Go get it . . . then bring it back . . . don't tarry	3 to 5 months
"Git!"	Go over in the corner of your kennel or in your dog house while I clean your run [makes your job easier]	4 months

''Hup!''	Sit down right there . . . don't move [This is Spaniel jargon for ''Sit!'']	4 to 6 months
''Stay!''	Don't move an inch until I tell you to	8 months
''Heel!''	Walk closely by my side [spaniels are not known for their easy heeling nature]	12 months (maybe never)
Advanced Commands		
''Over!''	Take my hand signals . . . go where I point	18 months
''Go back!''	Go fetch where I point . . . further away	18 months
''Hunt dead!''	There is a bird shot down near where I'm standing . . . find it . . . try hard	18 months

This is one simple, yet effective way to discipline a puppy. John Isaacs (Pro) of Ohio shows how to lift a puppy, make eye contact and say *No! No! No!* Most dogs are most uncomfortable with all four feet off the ground, and it makes a lasting impression. A strong "No!" command is important in the training of a Springer. Some people are very hesitant to discipline a puppy in a forceful enough manner to ingrain a strong impression; such people are doing both themselves and the dog a disservice. A quick response to a "No!" command can save a dog's life. *Friend*

Frank O'Grady, professional trainer from Ontario, walks a very enthusiastic CFC Springville's Crispy Crunch at heel as they go to the line at a 1993 Southwestern Ontario Spaniel Club field trial. *Roggenkamp*

By three months of age many puppies are enthusiastic and reliable retrievers. In early training, a fence encourages the puppy to return with the retrieving object. *Roggenkamp*

5

Basic Training for a Springer Gun Dog

WHEN AND HOW to start training a puppy is widely debated even among experienced trainers. Each trainer uses a slightly different method, sequence or routine, but certain elements are basic. Care must be taken to match the training to the aptitude and mental development of the puppy being trained. Each puppy is slightly different in its timing, and the trainer's ability to assess this readiness is a valuable skill.

This chapter, in keeping with its title, will deal with the most rudimentary training. However, professional Springer trainer Ben Martin emphasizes that "you must build a proper foundation for the most advanced training and it always starts with the basics." This chapter explains how to:

- Teach basic obedience commands
- Stimulate natural retrieving instincts
- Encourage natural hunting instincts
- Introduce live birds
- Teach "Hup!" and "Stay!"
- Introduce the pup to gunfire.

I suggest that you read through this chapter at least once before you start training. The chapter outlines a natural training sequence, but as your training goes along you will find that you need to intertwine the various strands to achieve the whole.

What Is Basic Training?

A young dog that achieves the defined level of Basic Training is a passable gun dog. It should follow basic commands, hunt reasonably close to you and find and fetch birds, but will probably chase missed birds to the horizon, a practice that can be both frustrating and dangerous.

The basic training of a gun dog takes, at a minimum, ten months. If you go faster, you do so at serious risk. Dogs learn in stages and each successive stage builds on the previous one. Just as people must first learn basic arithmetic before they can master algebra, geometry and calculus, dogs must also learn the basics before the more advanced concepts can be introduced.

Before training is begun, it is essential that the puppy is well acquainted with the trainer and that there is a feeling of mutual respect, trust and regard between trainer and trainee. This may be accelerated by the trainer's doing most of the required feeding and grooming. Further progress can be made by taking the dog for frequent ''relief'' sessions or walks (around the block), and by devoting a few minutes each day to playing and romping with the young student. Even though I live in the suburbs, I rarely put a leash on even the youngest of puppies in my yard. It is my intent from day one to teach the puppy to stay near me without the constraint of a leash. I believe this reinforces the natural bond between us. (How you handle this can be a bit dicey if you live in an area with heavy traffic. A fenced yard is ideal.) Ten days should suffice for this phase. If a mutual attachment for each other has not been formed by the end of ten days, perhaps you have the wrong dog or your get-acquainted methods are faulty.

Basic Yard Commands: Obedience

Basic yard training is the lifelong foundation for control. It also helps build a bond and a rapport with your puppy. However, since you are starting with a puppy, you must have a realistic expectation of the learning process timetable. For example, I begin to teach the ''kennel'' command at seven weeks by repeating the command every time I put the puppy in a run or crate. However, it is not until about age three months that, suddenly, the puppy obeys the command. In fact, in my experience, most of the puppy's early learning is so gradual as to go almost unrecognized until one day you give a command that elicits exacting compliance. At that point all your efforts are rewarded.

In Chapter 4 I suggested keeping yard training (obedience) and field training (enthusiasm) separate in the puppy's mind for the first several months. Early yard training—in the first three or four months—should firmly instill three commands: No!, Kennel! and Come! Before progressing further, the dog *must* obey each with prompt exactness.

No! is taught by being firm and roughly lifting the puppy off the ground by the scruff of the neck, turning his eyes to you and saying firmly, No! No! No! He will very soon back off and desist whatever he is doing when you shout No! No! This is a very important command because it could save your puppy's life. For instance, if he is running toward the street and a car is speeding down the street, and you yell No! No!, will he obey? If you are working in the garage and notice he is chewing on an electrical extension cord, and you yell No! No!, will he stop? Your answer can be yes only if the command is ingrained early and with enough *trauma* or *intensity* that it will always break through the background clutter of noise, enthusiasm and external stimuli to reach the puppy's conscious brain.

Some people teach *No*! by lifting the dog by the scruff of the neck, others stand over the dog and shout and wave their arms; others roll the dog on its back and teach it in a dominance mode. Whichever way you choose, it must be done early, consistently and with impact.

Kennel! is taught by simply giving the command in a firm manner whenever you push the puppy into his crate. Be firm. Be consistent. Repeat it frequently and soon the puppy will jump in on his own whenever you command "Kennel." This is the only instance where I believe a food reward can work effectively.

Later, when you want to teach your dog to merrily jump into a crate in your car or truck, the procedure is the same. Again, a food reward helps. Be advised that dogs are very leery of jumping into a place they can't see into, so when teaching *Kennel*! be sure the dog can see into the crate. This is especially true when trying to teach the dog to jump into a crate in a car or truck.

Come! is the second most important command. It is a strong command that must break through whatever the puppy is doing and draw him to you, as if on rails or on a rope. When the puppy is very young, get on your knees, slap your legs, say Come! Come! Come! When he does, heap lavish praise upon him and pat him generously on the head. Repeat this act frequently. Soon he will be scampering to you at your command to get his daily quota of hugs. It is also easier to teach this command when you can run out and catch the puppy if it disregards your command.

In the early stages of training, *Come*! is taught as an enthusiasm command. The puppy will race to you to play. He loves you and wants your affection. Unfortunately, at some point he will enter his "teen-age" phase and decide he can get along quite nicely without your love pats. At this point you must reteach *Come*! as an obedience command. For this I use a rope and a choke chain to emphasize my ability to force compliance to the *Come*! command. For several days in a row do not give the *Come*! command without a sharp jerk on the rope: Reel the dog in hand-over-hand and make sure he knows you can enforce your will. That is usually all it takes, although you may have to go through this phase three or four times in the dog's lifetime.

Again, *Come*!—especially in combination with *No*!—is the basis of control and can save your dog's life. In a panic situation, a shouted No! No! Come! has taken many a good Springer out of harm's way.

Walking on a Lead

Having the dog walk on a lead—or leash—is an accomplishment of varying importance to different people. It has never been a major training effort with me. It happens almost naturally over time. Some puppies learn to comply with the pressure of a lead very easily, whereas others fight it aggressively. In the main, it is simply a matter of using a relatively short lead and a choke-chain collar and firmly, but carefully, applying pressure to force the puppy to follow where you walk. Many Springer puppies, due to their mouthy nature, will want to bite the lead as you walk. That is okay, so long as they still follow your direction. A five minute on-lead walk every other day for three weeks usually imparts the basic understanding. Frequent normal usage for walks, visits to the vet and trips to the park ingrains the lesson. By five months the puppy should be fully leash-compliant. During these sessions if you frequently and firmly say "Heel!", the dog will soon associate the word with walking on your left side.

Preliminary Retrieving: ***"Fetch"***

Even though most Springers have a natural desire to retrieve, it is important to fix the habit of retrieving firmly before the dog learns to hunt.

The first lesson in retrieving may be started with a puppy as young as two or three months of age. Understand that the puppy is acting mostly on instinct at this point. Here is how: Use a new, clean, paint roller or a handkerchief knotted several times to serve as the object to be retrieved. A tennis ball also excites your puppy's interest in retrieving because it bounces and moves as if alive. Just you and the puppy (no one else) should go to a sheltered spot in the kennel or yard, or even the basement or garage. Allow the puppy to sniff around until all the strange new scents have been investigated, then call him to you and tease him with the object until his interest is aroused thoroughly. While the puppy is still interested in the object, hold it just out of reach and toss it slowly, but only three or four feet away. Eight puppies out of ten (Springer puppies, that is) will run immediately to the object, grab it, and with a little coaxing return immediately to you. The puppy should then be rewarded with plenty of petting and friendly words. Make it a fun game. Soon the puppy will retrieve it from habit.

Your chances of success are much greater if the puppy is trained in a closed area such as a hall or between two fences where the only path of escape is back to you. And never let the puppy have the retrieving object as a toy. This object is strictly for retrieving.

In the beginning, be careful not to throw the object more than four or five feet and always with a slow motion, as very young puppies cannot see very well and quick motions may be just a blur to their eyes. Repeat this no more than six times and always stop while the dog is still enjoying the game. Always reward the puppy with petting each time he performs properly. Six to twelve throws each day for a week will work wonders. Always try to stop on a positive performance and pet the puppy lavishly.

After a few days, begin to give the command *Fetch*! in a firm but subdued tone of voice each time the object is thrown. This will form an association in the dog's mind between the act of retrieving and the command Fetch! Never fool the puppy by failing to throw the object, and never indulge in a tug of war to

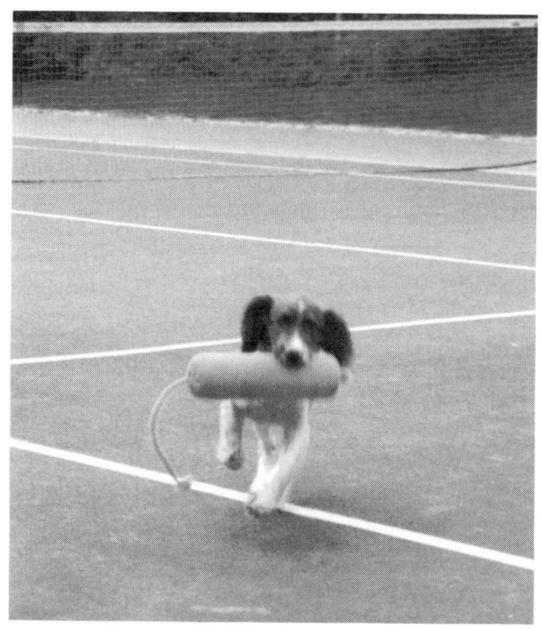

Retrieving can be taught almost anywhere if the distractions are minimal. Here, a very bold little puppy races back from retrieving a big buck across a tennis court. *Roggenkamp*

John Friend of Ohio accepts a perfect delivery from his dog, "Duke." All the elements of a proper delivery are shown in this photo. The dog has hupped, facing the handler, head up, then releases the bird when the handler says *Give!* Note the gun safety; the breach is open so the gun will not fire and the barrels are pointed at the ground. This is what you are working to achieve in a delivery. But be patient. Few dogs will perform such a delivery until about one year of age. In the interim, try to avoid bad habits such as dropping the bird, which will make later training for a proper delivery more difficult.

get the object from his mouth. If his grip on the object is too firm, which is most likely, a little gentle pressure exerted by squeezing the lower lip against the teeth (on the side of the jaw) will usually induce the dog to release his grip. The command *Give!* should be repeated if this is done, in order to teach the dog to release the object. Don't forget to make a fuss over the dog and pet him generously.

After a week or so, the trainer should clap his hands together to produce a single sharp report each time the object is thrown. This is preparation for introduction to the gun and is most important. Within a few days, the puppy will come to expect the noise each time the object is thrown.

To test your progress, clap your hands together sharply without throwing the object. If the groundwork has been laid properly, the puppy will whirl immediately and look for something to retrieve when the sound is heard. Again, do not fool the young dog. Always be sure there is something to retrieve each time a throwing motion, or the noise of the hand clap, or the command *Fetch*! is given. A child's cap pistol should be substituted for the hand clap after a week or two, when in the trainer's opinion the young prospect will not be alarmed by the noise.

The little guy will probably retrieve beautifully for a few days or even a few weeks and then suddenly refuse to bring the object to hand. This is normal behavior, and it is also normal when he attempts to bury the retrieving object in the ground or under some leaves in the hedge. Sometimes the trainer can nip this undesirable behavior in the bud by making an exaggerated show of appearing to run away from the puppy, thus causing him to run after the trainer with the object still in his mouth. If this subterfuge does not work, try attaching a ten-foot fishing line to the puppy's collar and bring him gently to you with very light pressure on the fishing line after he has picked up the retrieving object. If you pull too hard, the puppy will probably drop the retrieve. These lessons should be continued for several weeks until they have been well learned and have become a habit.

Older dogs can be started on their retrieving in the same manner if desired, although the retrieving may prove a little more difficult. Teasing and coaxing and holding the object just out of the dog's reach may have to be repeated a number of times with a dog as old as one year so as to arouse his interest. His reactions will be similar to those of the puppy except that he will be less playful.

The trainer must always remember to show his pleasure when the dog performs properly. Petting, many kind and approving words and a friendly attitude are recommended. A reward of food or some tidbit is a poor practice for a field dog. Often the dog will drop the retrieve and race to you for the treat. A good gun dog performs because he loves it and wants to work for his master.

Later, when the dog has become well conditioned to retrieving, a suitable retrieving buck should be substituted for the paint roller, handkerchief or tennis ball. Retrieving bucks of varying sizes, textures and firmness are available from pet stores and gun dog supply catalogs (see Chapter 15). I've found that most Springers dislike the hard knobby rubber retrieving bucks used for retriever breed training, so I normally use the canvas-over-cork type.

Retrieving enthusiasm never ends for a Springer. By six months the puppy should be racing boldly to the fall and racing proudly back with the retrieve. But even my twelve-year-old veterans get excited when I get out the retrieving bucks and eagerly await their turn to "make the retrieve."

A word of warning: One of the prime prerequisites of a good gun dog is that it retrieve with a soft and tender mouth. Starting young puppies to retrieve on a dead or shackled bird may sometimes result in the condition known as "hard mouth." This is a serious and objectionable fault and case-hardened offenders may ruin much of the game they retrieve. For now, always use the retrieving buck with a young dog.

Delivery to Hand

Once, while visiting with some people to whom I had sold a puppy, they explained what they considered a problem. "When she retrieves anything, she follows me around until I take it out of her mouth." The owner wanted the dog to drop the retrieves at his feet; but he was totally wrong. Your properly trained Springer delivers the game it retrieves *into your hand*. In executing a perfect delivery, the dog returns promptly with the retrieve, hups directly in front of you and gently yields the bird to you when you reach down, grasp the bird and say, "Give!"

Of course, very few dogs do this naturally and most require some training. You can do the finish-delivery training at ten to twelve months—but don't ingrain bad habits earlier like letting the dog drop the retrieve at your feet. If you are having a problem, try letting the pup jump up and stand with its paws on your stomach when bringing back retrieves. With young puppies, take the object from the puppy as soon as he returns with it.

Hand Signals

Whenever a young puppy fails to mark the fall of the buck, the trainer should use the occasion to teach the dog to take hand signals by indicating the location of the buck with a wave of the hand. A few such experiences are usually enough to teach the dog that if he hunts in the direction indicated by the trainer's hand signal, he will find the bird or buck promptly. Later, when the dog is working live game, another effective way of teaching a dog to respond to hand signals is to plant a few birds to the right or left of the imaginary line on which the trainer walks as he works the dog. Now the trainer gives hand signals to the dog where to find a half dozen or more live birds. This will speed up the learning process greatly.

Mental Readiness for the Next Phase of Training

One of the most important aspects of dog training is the evaluation of the pupil's readiness for further training. The professional trainers call this "reading the dog" or "the right time" or "when the lights come on," or will say "he is

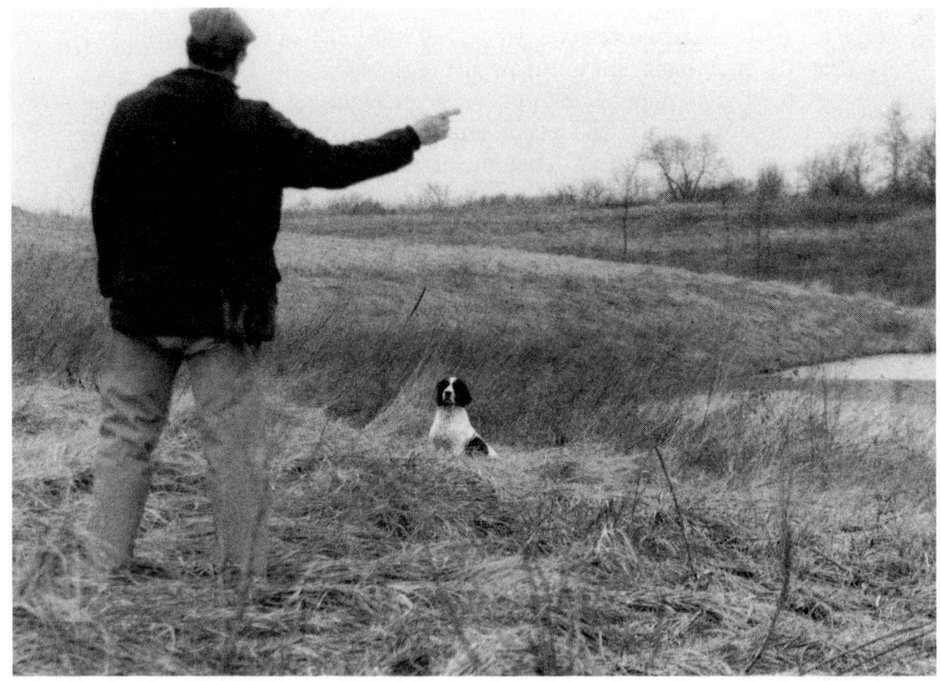

Teaching the young dog to take hand signals is a part of the gradual training process. Hand signals direct the dog when quartering, hunting or when searching for a difficult retrieve. Here Paul Rupert of Ohio signals his dog, AFC Lora's Patches, to a retrieve. *Roggenkamp*

When the dog is completely enthusiastic about retrieving and racing off madly after the tossed buck, fire the cap pistol in the air when the puppy is some distance away. John Isaacs demonstrates how. *Friend*

ready for . . .''; all these catch phrases are a way of saying that in their opinion, through careful observation and experienced judgment, the puppy is ready for the next step in training. All trainers must be alert for signs of boredom (which may mean it's time to expand learning), eagerness (which often means the puppy is open to new ideas), or confusion (which can mean, ''I'm overwhelmed, slow down''). My wife, who has done an outstanding job of raising our children while I travel on business, helps me in the early phases of puppy care. She builds the social bond with the puppy, an effort so vital to future learning. But she also reads their readiness for learning and often tells me, ''Your puppy is ready for more training; he is bored and needs a challenge.''

Noise Acclimation

From the very first day that you get your puppy, noise must be a part of its life. Because your adult dog will be forced to deal with many noisy situations, it is best to acclimate the dog early through a simple process of using household noises. With two teenagers and numerous household appliances, daily life at my house is a rather noisy affair anyway. We have developed a procedure for housing the puppy in an airline crate in the laundry room for the first few months. The sounds of the washer and dryer, traffic through the mud room, doors banging, rock music, the television blaring in the next room all accomplish the noise acclimation. When the time for the blank pistol comes, it's just another noise in an already noisy world.

Introduction to the Blank Pistol

After the dog has become well acclimated to the sound of the cap pistol and has associated the sound with the act of retrieving, it is time to substitute a .22 blank pistol for the cap gun. The little *22 crimps* should be used. It is most important to first use the blank pistol during the act of retrieving. If the cap pistol has been used religiously, there will be no adverse reaction on the part of the dog the first time the .22 blank is substituted. There is really no need to hurry this; when the puppy is four or five months old is soon enough.

Take the dog to your normal training area or another familiar spot and work him on his favorite buck. Fire the .22 blank the first time when the dog is still some distance away (forty feet or so) on his journey to pick up the buck. Fire the gun behind your back and pointed away from the dog. If the noise appears to startle the dog, throw the buck even farther the next time and be sure that the dog is at the furthest point away when the pistol is fired. Two or three shots are enough the first time the transition is made from the cap gun to the .22 blank. If the dog appears to fear the noise, stop the shooting and go back to the cap gun for several weeks. The reason for this extreme caution is to avoid gun-shyness, which is explained later in this chapter.

Note: It is suggested that the trainer wear hearing protection from this point on whenever a gun or blank pistol is fired. Most of us who have trained dogs for some time have some moderate hearing loss from our carelessness years ago before today's inexpensive, comfortable and effective hearing protection was available.

If the noise appears not to bother the dog, the .22 may be used each time the dog retrieves until the sound has been heard at least twenty-five times. If no adverse reaction is observed, the trainer may gradually reduce the time interval between throwing the buck and firing the .22 until the shot is being fired while the dog is at heel. *Never* discharge the pistol at, over or in front of the dog. The gun should be held behind the trainer's back to eliminate muzzle blast in the dog's ears. Granted that a .22 does not make much noise; but the puppy does not know this, and his sensitive ears may find the sound objectionable if the blank is discharged in front of his face. This gradual procedure of acclimation greatly reduces the chance of gun-shyness.

Do not, at this point, get over-confident or careless and shoot a shotgun near or over the dog. The dog's first gunfire must be carefully planned, as explained later in this chapter.

Building Field Enthusiasm

When the puppy has been retrieving reliably for several weeks and is acclimated to the sound of the .22, he is ready for romps in the field. One of the great advantages of owning a Springer is that he can be trained in a small area. The dog's first introduction to game can be in a small field with some tiny clumps of cover. Such property is usually available even near our largest cities. Most puppies love to chase rabbits, squirrels, chipmunks or small birds; they should be allowed and encouraged to do so when safe from vehicular traffic.

Once the process is started, trips to the field should be scheduled as frequently as possible and certainly weekends should be utilized fully. The early field sessions should not exceed fifteen or twenty minutes, but can be lengthened gradually as the dog's muscles develop and his wind and desire to run increase. After he has chased a few rabbits and squirrels, the puppy should be introduced to live birds—usually pigeons.

Soon the puppy will be full of enthusiasm and will dash away as soon as he is released at the edge of the cover. He will be eager to use his nose as well as his eyes to hunt for game. The position of the dog's head while hunting is a clue to the development of his hunting instincts. If his head is up and above the level of his body, the puppy is probably sight hunting. But if his head is level with his body or lower, he is probably hunting by scent.

It should be remembered, however, that the puppy must *always* be worked in the field with the wind blowing into the face of the trainer. There are two reasons for this: 1.) It enables the puppy to scent game much better than when worked downwind. 2.) It will help, in most cases, to keep the puppy closer to the handler while the dog is working.

Retrieving lessons should be continued at home, and although retrieving can be tried in the field, it may result in the dog's ignoring the buck. Once the puppy learns to hunt, he may not be too interested in retrieving, except at home. This is normal, and the retrieving lessons should be given for five minutes at home before the trips afield.

Finding and Retrieving Live Game

Most trainers who use traditional English method do not let a puppy come in contact with live or dead birds until they reach eight or nine months of age. However, many Americans—myself included—may give a precocious puppy one or two dead or closely shackled (taped) pigeons at the age of three or four months. Don't overdo it! Three or four contacts per week are ample and don't be surprised at *any* puppy reaction. At first, some bark, some grab the pigeon's tail and run in circles carrying the bird, some lay down and mouth it. But soon, with coaxing, your puppy will proudly bring this exciting new object back so you can toss it for more retrieves. I have always believed that a few live birds excite a young puppy and keep him from becoming bored with the retrieving buck and routine practices.

Years ago in this country and still today in England, young dogs were introduced to game on wild rabbits, pheasants and other game birds. However, today feral pigeons will serve as a substitute. Pigeons may be secured from farms or from poultry markets. Always place the pigeons (with flight feathers taped) in cover and let the young dog find them. Repeat this many times. This will arouse the dog's interest, teach him to use his nose and create much excitement on his part. He will catch the taped-wing bird and, if the early retrieving work was done properly, will deliver it to you. After several field sessions with taped-wing birds, the trainer can "plant" a few full-winged flyers for the puppy to flush and chase.

If the first flying bird that gets up startles him so much that he does not chase, you should encourage him to do so. You should make a show of running after the bird for a few yards and exhibit great excitement. Most field-bred puppies will be off like a flash and chase the flying bird for at least a few yards—perhaps even as far as a few hundred yards.

Develop a firm understanding in the puppy that he will find game when he "hunts" in the field. At first, plant birds so they can be easily and quickly found. As time goes on, you can spread the planted birds farther apart and make finding them more challenging. The dog should eagerly race around to find the four or five planted birds on every trip to the field.

How to Plant Game

Charles Goodall explained his method for putting a pigeon in cover to be found by the dog as follows:

> Planting a pigeon is an easily learned skill. The method employed by many trainers is to grip the bird firmly over its wings with the right hand encircling the bird's

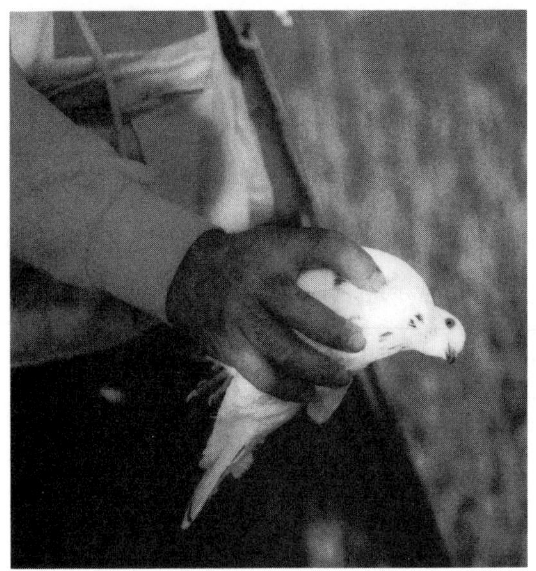

Planting feral pigeons or pen-raised pheasants is a key job for the spaniel trainer. Pigeons are whirled until dizzy and then dropped into light cover. Planting a dizzied pigeon is quite simple using Chuck Goodall's method, as described in this chapter. To dizzy a pigeon, grip it around the body then spin the wrist quickly. Usually about twenty turns does the trick. Watch the bird's head and eyes to see if it is dizzy. When it is quite dizzy toss it into light cover.

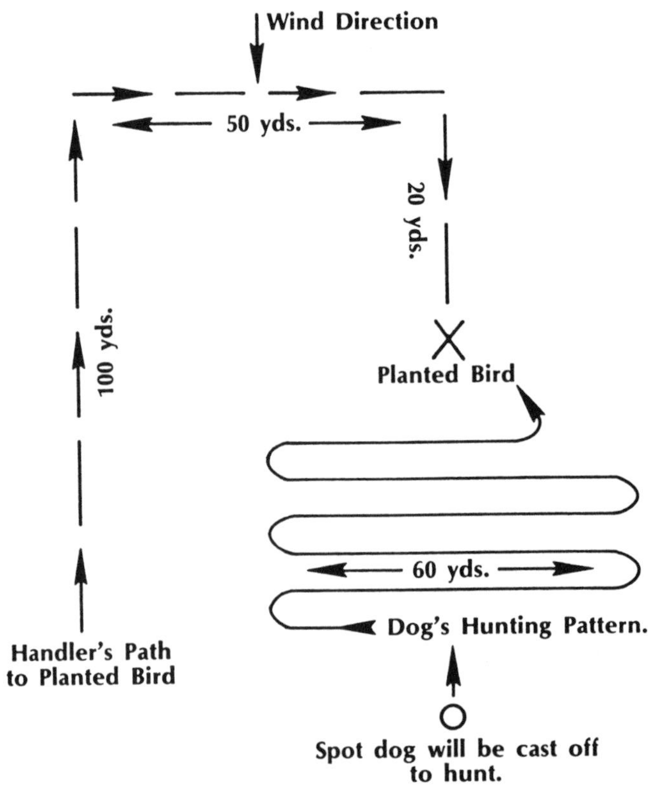

You don't want your young dog to learn how to track out your footprints to find the planted birds, so walk to the training area via a circuitous route as outlined in this diagram.

body. Using lots of wrist action, the pigeon is whirled rapidly for fifteen or twenty turns. The bird is then planted (tossed or dropped) in the cover and will remain where it is placed. Best results are obtained by mashing down the cover into a nest approximately the size of the trainer's foot. This will permit the bird to flush without becoming entangled when the dog rushes in.

Some care must be taken in planting birds so the young dog will not learn to trail back to the bird by following the "bird planter's" footsteps. This may be prevented by walking in from the side of the area which the dog will work. One can also carry pigeons in the pocket of a game coat and "dizzy" them (as explained above) while the dog is hunting. The bird can then be thrown with considerable force into a spot of cover on the right while the dog is working to the left. Never let the dog see the bird planted. A little practice will develop considerable skill in planting by both methods and little or no difficulty should be experienced. Pheasants can be planted using the simple method of tucking their head under their wing and laying them gently in heavy cover.

Teaching the Dog to *Hup!*

To teach the dog to "hup," or sit, walk him on a short leash to a quiet place in the garage, basement or yard with no onlookers or distracting influences. As you walk the dog at heel, give the command *Hup*! in a firm but quiet voice and instantly press down firmly but gently on the dog's rump or hindquarters. Force him to sit with your hand on his rump, maintaining the pressure for five or six seconds. Then remove the pressure and continue to walk him around on the short leash. Again give the command *Hup!* Immediately press down on the dog's rump, again forcing him to assume the sitting position. Again maintain the pressure for five or six seconds, then walk the dog around for ten or fifteen seconds. Repeat this performance, but not more than ten or fifteen times at the first lesson. Begin to mix in the whistle and your hand signals. *Hup!*-peep-hand up, etc., until whenever you give this command, the dog sees and hears all three signals. Every training session should include ten or fifteen "hups" for a period of two or three weeks until the dog immediately sits on command when on the lead without the need for hand pressure.

Within a week or ten days he should respond perfectly. The dog should also be ordered to hup every time he is fed and should not be given the food until he responds properly. At other suitable occasions, the command should be given and the dog required to obey instantly. This command, followed by an immediate response by the dog, is extremely important and must be learned well without exception.

Teaching the Dog to *Stay!*

The next step in early yard work is to teach the dog to stay. This is slightly more difficult and some young Springers do not learn it as fast as others. It is relatively simple, however, if one is persistent and patient. The handler may start this training by taking the dog to a secluded training area in the yard or the basement and giving the command *Hup!* At the same time, the trainer should raise and extend the right arm upward with the palm outward and command in a stern voice *"Hup! . . . Stay! . . . Hup! . . . Stay! . . . Hup! . . . Stay!"* then take a step or two slowly backward while repeating the command. If he moves, carry him back to this spot and put him down and repeat the procedure. In many cases, when he is commanded to hup the dog will remain in position without being commanded to stay. The trainer should then walk back to the dog while repeating the command *Stay! The trainer goes back to the dog* and pets the dog where he sits. At this point, do not call the dog to you from a hup position; rather, reward him with petting where he has obeyed. This procedure should be repeated ten or more times during the first lesson, with the trainer taking two or three slow steps backward from the dog.

In many cases, the puppy will learn what is required in a few lessons. But if he does not understand at first or if he attempts to follow the handler or move from the spot, the puppy must be picked up bodily and returned to the original spot where the hup command was given. Once the puppy is obeying the stay command, the distances may be lengthened gradually over a two-week period until the trainer can walk up to twenty feet without having the puppy move. When the puppy is responding properly, the lessons may be continued in the yard and then in the field each time before the puppy is cast off to hunt.

If it is deemed necessary, the learning process may be speeded up with a very mild form of punishment such as a chuck under the chin or a mild shake to indicate disapproval. Try to be patient and not lose your temper. Always try to maintain an attitude of patience and firmness when teaching this command. If you begin to lose your temper, cease the session at once and do not resume it for the rest of the day.

If the puppy does not appear able to grasp what is desired, another method may be employed in teaching the stay command. In this method a light cord or a length of nylon rope is attached to the puppy's collar. The line is then passed through a hook in the garage wall, around a tree limb or around a fence post. Upon giving the commands *Hup!* and *Stay!*, the trainer can soon convince the dog that it is essential to remain in the sitting position. The choke collar will help with the learning process. This sounds easier than it is, since a puppy tangled up in the rope is almost always the result. If you use this method, continue to work the dog with a slack line for a few weeks after he begins to respond. When the dog responds properly, reward him by petting and proceed with the lessons with the line attached, but dragging on the floor. After the dog remains at the stay several times, remove the line and proceed with the lessons with the dog free of all restraint.

If you remember to give the command three ways—voice, whistle and hand—every time, within two or three weeks it will be possible to make the dog hup and stay by merely raising your hand or tooting the whistle. This command will prove useful in the field throughout the dog's life.

The Circle Walk

At the end of two weeks, enough progress should have been made to enable the trainer to hup the puppy, give the command *Stay!* and then walk in a complete circle around the puppy at a distance of fifteen yards or more. I place great importance on the accomplishment of being able to walk a full circle around a hupped dog and continue to use it as a reinforcement technique even with three- or four-year-old dogs. To sit quietly while the master walks a circle requires solid obedience and discipline from the dog. A puppy eight months old or more should demonstrate enough progress to make this possible after two or three weeks of training, provided the trainer has followed a routine of working with the dog almost daily.

After the hup and stay commands are fully learned, begin to vary the routine. Sometimes hup the dog and walk the circle. Other times hup the dog and then walk to the dog to pet it. Still other times, hup the dog and demand *Come!* Rarely, however, should you simply hup the dog and then release it to run around. Remember, the command *Hup!* is the foundation for steadying to wing and shot.

Compliance with Commands

When I first started training dogs, the very wise and experienced Ruth Greening of the renowned Ru-Char Kennels told me never to give a dog a command that I wasn't ready, willing and able to enforce immediately. Consistency is a key factor in dog training, since dogs learn, to a great extent, by repetition and rote compliance.

Let me give you an example. You and your spouse are about to go out to a fancy party and both have on your best evening clothes. You will be gone several hours and know the eight-month-old puppy needs to go out to relieve itself if it is going to make it until you return home. So you let the pup out to run around in the backyard while you stand on the patio trying to avoid the puddles and the muddy flower beds, wet and dripping from an afternoon rain shower. This is not the time to use *any* commands. If you say *Hup!* and he doesn't comply, what will you do? Will you run out into the wet grass to enforce the command? No way! Try to avoid even saying *Come!* At the right time, simply get the dog's attention, then tease or lure him back in to the kennel, lock the door and go to the party. Timing is important.

Training with Common Sense

Again, a word of caution to the over-conscientious trainer: *guard against overtraining the dog*. Too frequent use of the commands may destroy the puppy's initiative and might cause him to stop learning. It is necessary to mix a little common sense with the training routine; if the young dog appears to be bored or intimidated, back off a little and go a few days with almost no commands. The wise trainer will observe the action of the dog's tail—much can be learned by observing its action and position. If the puppy enjoys the work, and he certainly should, the tail will be up and in motion most of the time. If the tail is always tucked between the legs and the puppy goes about his work with a fearful look in his eyes, you may be overdoing it. Most Springers drop their tails during intense training sessions, but if the tail is down all the time, go gently.

Basics of Teaching the Turn Whistle

As a part of basic training, whenever walking the dog the handler should take a serpentine path, frequently changing direction. This will encourage an observant puppy to keep an eye on you even while it looks for butterflies and investigates new and fascinating smells. Over time, as the dog grows, he will expect you to roam around and he will gradually learn to cast around you at reasonable range. This is a way to build the natural tendency to stay in touch.

While the pup is investigating some new and interesting items, you should walk away from him. When he's some distance away, get the pup's attention with a "Hey you" or the pup's name. Usually when he notices that you are getting farther away, he will scamper in your direction. As he begins to come in your direction, keep walking and blow the whistle twice (peep, peep). Keep doing this a few times every day and soon the puppy will associate two peeps with your change in direction or moving away and his need to change course to stay with you. The next chapter addresses how to strongly reinforce this command and demand absolute compliance.

Shooting over the Dog

Up to this point, I have avoided a discussion of gun-shyness. There is a special reason for this. Many novice trainers do one of two things: (1) they either worry too much about introducing the young dog to the gun, or (2) they don't worry enough. It seems that there is no happy medium. I hope that by this point you will have the matter in proper perspective and will have laid a noise acclimation foundation to make shooting over the dog a simple process.

Anyone who has had any association with bird dogs and hunting has seen or heard of many cases of a bad reaction to gunshot. A cringing, slinking, fearful dog of any breed is a sad thing, for it was *made* gun-shy by some unthinking or uninformed individual. The condition is almost certainly produced by man, for very few, if any, dogs are ever born gun-shy. Usually, if one takes the trouble to investigate each case of gun-shyness, it is due to ignorance, lack of patience or stupidity.

One of the worst cases I ever observed was a fine Springer bitch who would practically go into convulsions, not only at the sound of a gun, but also at the sight of a broom or any other object that bore even a faint resemblance to a gun. Several of her littermates were great gun dogs. She too loved to run and hunt so long as no gun was in hand. Unfortunately, she had been taken to a gun club at the tender age of three months and her inexperienced owner ignored her obvious fear. After two hours of guns being fired, the dog was terrified of the noise. That terror remained with her.

A second common cause of gun-shyness is the Fourth-of-July firecracker. The burning fuse usually attracts the puppy's attention and, if he attempts to seize the firecracker or to paw it, the results are sure and positive. The noise and the flash burn will condition the puppy adversely and gun-shyness is too often the result. Many puppies are born in the early spring and the Fourth of July comes at a time when they are very vulnerable to noises. Always keep all your dogs (young and old) inside and protected on this holiday.

Young dogs may also become gun-shy by being shot over without the proper preparation. Gun-shyness is very hard to cure and, if it can be cured at all, it is a long, slow process. Months of reeducation may be required to overcome the phobia, but it is very easy to avoid this condition by proper early conditioning. How to deal with the fault of gun-shyness is discussed further in Chapter 7.

You will recall the suggestion that a sharp hand clap be associated with the early retrieving lessons. It was also suggested that a cap pistol, and later a .22 blank pistol, be introduced gradually as part of the retrieving routine. Hence, it should come as no surprise to learn that any dog that was conditioned by this method has learned to associate gun sounds with fun and is probably well on its way to being ready to be shot over. However, the next step in the procedure should be carefully monitored to be sure that the puppy is handling the gunfire easily.

When you go to the field to shoot over the puppy for the first time, be absolutely sure that you and your gunner understand the importance of the day. Some people are just naturally trigger-happy and regardless of your instructions may get excited and shoot too near the dog.

Actually, the first five or six birds should *not* be shot. The gun should be fired at least sixty or seventy yards from the dog and in a direction away from the dog and the bird. Let the dog chase. If the dog pays no attention to the first five or six shots, good. If he shows any fear, go back to the blank pistol. Regardless of the dog's reaction, that's all for the first day—go home.

On the next trip to the field, the guns should be far out from the dog and can shoot the bird, but only if it is high in the air and the muzzle is not pointed over the dog (see diagram on page 64).

Other Hints: Use light loads. Some loads are quieter than others. Experiment at a gun club before you shoot over the dog. Long-barreled guns are quieter than short-barreled models. Some people suggest starting with a 20-gauge or even a 410, but I think a long-barreled 12-bore with light loads is no louder than the smaller gauges.

Gradually, if the dog shows great enthusiasm and intensity and no adverse reaction to gunfire, the guns can move in closer. However, the dog should never be subjected to muzzle blast during the first few months of shooting over the dog (see diagram on page 64). Trigger-happy guns have ruined many a promising

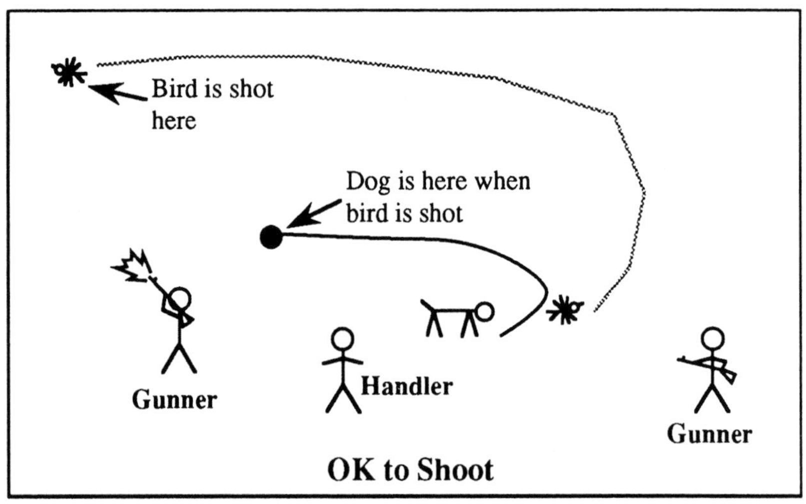

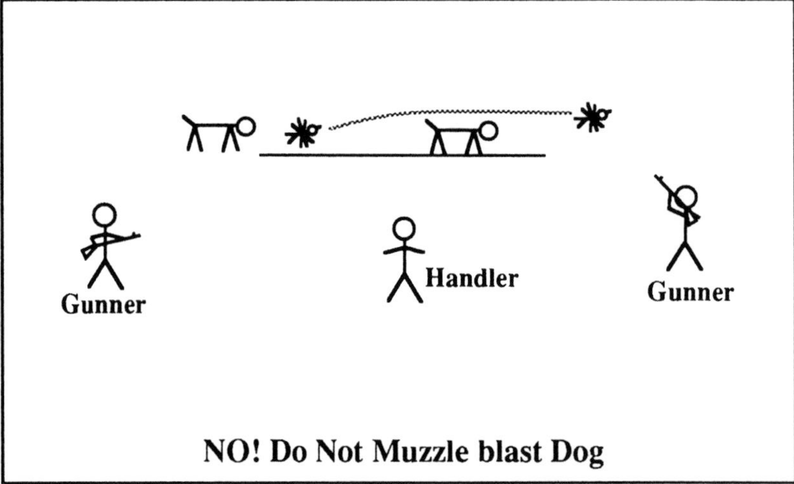

Never muzzle blast a young dog. Experienced and cautious guns will shoot only when the bird is high in the air and well clear of the dog. It is always better to let a bird fly away than to chance needlessly endangering a young dog or causing gun-shyness.

Ellis

Communicating with Your Dog in the Field

Desired Action	*Voice*	*Whistle*	*Hand*	*Pictorial*
Sit down	"Hup!"	One strong blast	Hand and arm raised, palm open toward dog	
Come to me	"Come!" or, "Heel!"	Peep-peep-peep or continuous trill	Drop hand to knees	
Turn toward me, quarter back toward me	None	Peep-peep	Point in direction dog is to take	
To direct a dog to a retrieve	"Over!" or, "Go Back!"	None	Give direction	

young dog. As more and more birds are shot for the dog, he will begin to associate fun and gunfire and it will become a stimulus that excites the dog.

Shooting Game

If you have followed the steps carefully, you will at this point be able to rapidly progress to shooting birds over the dog. Now, at each training session, mix taped-wing birds, dead birds and fliers. The taped-wing birds keep the dog flushing boldly. When the fliers get up, the dog will chase wildly so shoot carefully. If the retrieving training was done well, the dog will quickly pick up the downed bird and race back to you. The dog has just demonstrated its ability to Find, Flush and Fetch. The dog should have at least a dozen sessions on shot birds before you try to progress to the next level of training.

Your Solidly Started Gun Dog

If the schedule of lessons recommended in this chapter has been completed and the dog has learned each task, you should have a very competent started gun dog. His abilities will correspond closely to the requirements for an AKC Junior Hunter. The dog will demonstrate his competence in the critical areas of Obedience, Range, Fetch, Find, and Flush (ORFFF).

At this point, your dog of ten or twelve months of age is a very pleasing hunting companion. He will hup, stay and come on voice, whistle or hand command. He will hunt aggressively to find and retrieve shot game. He is acclimated to gunfire and shows no adverse reaction. He knows that the turn whistle (peep, peep) means you are changing direction and he responds by turning as well. You can proudly see the results of your work and you and your fine, young started dog are ready for more advanced training.

6

Intermediate Gun Dog Training

THE PROCEDURES explained in this chapter are designed to take your basic gun dog to the intermediate level, which corresponds generally to the Senior Hunter level of the AKC Hunting Tests. The training outlined in this chapter will help you:

- Refine and instill the dog's hunting pattern;
- Elicit prompt and consistent response to the turn whistle;
- Stimulate your dog's natural instincts to hunt in heavy cover;
- Help your dog learn how to track moving game;
- Learn the importance of and one method for teaching your dog to limit its chasing of missed birds.

In the main, this chapter is devoted to controlling, polishing and developing natural talents. It also includes a section on faults. If a major fault such as gun-shyness or hardmouth has surfaced, you must deal with it before you give the dog further training or make the painful decision that the fault cannot be corrected.

Quartering the Ground

Not only must gun dogs of all breeds learn to hunt aggressively, but they must also learn to hunt in the places where game is most likely to be found. The big, wide-ranging, bird-wise pointers or setters used on southern quail plantations will reach out to hunt the birdy places such as fence rows, where their experience tells them that quail are likely to be found.

Your Springer Spaniel will learn to work birdy places, too, but because he is a "flushing dog," he must be trained and encouraged always to stay within gun range. It is easy to see that a fast, eager Springer, if allowed to line out like a pointer, would soon be out of gun range. Therefore, spaniels are taught to quarter back and forth in front of the handler. In the early work, your training should strive to make the young Springer quarter the ground in front of the gun in an almost mechanical manner. Later on, as the dog gains experience, he will break this rigid pattern to work birdy patches, but he must be well grounded in the fundamentals of quartering when young in order to produce consistent ground work when mature.

Earlier I suggested that a young Springer should always be worked into the wind. Working into the wind makes it easier to lay the foundation for teaching the dog to quarter. In fact, many young Springers of field breeding appear to have inherited a characteristic to quarter naturally. When this is the case, the trainer's job is relatively simple. All you need to do is widen the dog's hunting pattern (encourage him to cast out farther to either side of the trainer to the distance you desire) and then work the dog enough to make consistent quartering a habit.

However, if the dog has not started to quarter naturally, he will need some guidance. Work on quartering this way: Sit the puppy down in front of you and then send him out to the right side with a wave of the hand and your release command. (Your release command can be the traditional spaniel word "Hi-on"; or, like me, you can just use "O.K." and a wave of the hand. Some people say "Let's go.") Walk directly into the wind and usually the young dog will cast about rather than just run and hunt straight ahead. Give him a wave to the right and start to walk that way, an action to which he will most likely respond by running farther to the right. Now you swerve to the left as he reaches the edge of range and you give two toots of the whistle. The dog should respond by running back past you. The trainer repeats this several times and continues to walk in a zig-zag into the wind (see diagram).

It also helps to have gunning partners stationed about thirty feet to either side of you. These gunners can also encourage the dog to reach out and run toward them by waving their hat or calling the dog's name until the "toot-toot" of the handler's whistle turns the dog back to him. Three or four lessons should get the idea over to the pup that he is to hunt out to either *side* of the trainer rather than straight out in front. *Always* walk into the wind in early field work. The wind alone is almost enough to cause the dog to hunt the pattern that all spaniel trainers desire, but if it is not, the trainer must encourage the dog to quarter.

The very basic hand signals, which you used in the early retrieving lessons, are very useful at this point. The purpose of hand signals is, of course, to direct the dog to likely spots or parts of the field he has missed. It is amazing how, as the rapport between dog and hunter grows, very subtle hand gestures can be used to "put" the dog almost anywhere.

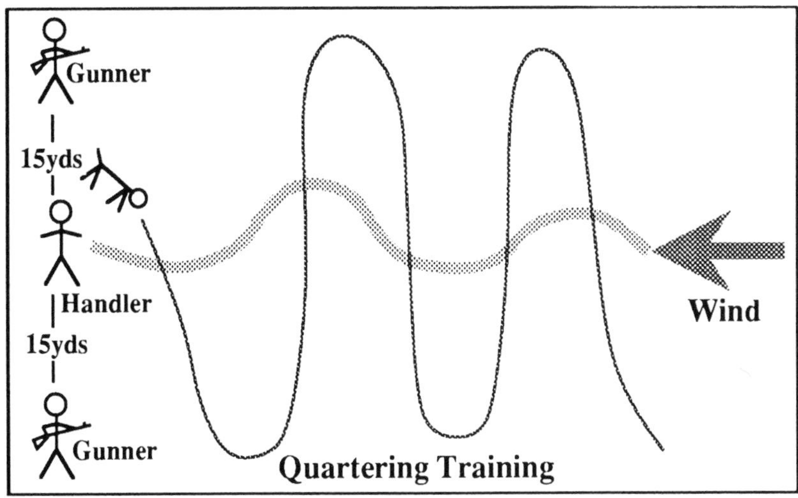

Use this diagram to properly align the gunners into the wind. Then the handler should walk a slightly serpentine path. The dog will follow your lead, hand signals and whistle commands, and will soon learn to quarter from gun to gun. In the early stages the gunners should encourage the young dog to run to them, then feign indifference to the dog when the handler "toot-toots" the turn whistle. *Ellis*

Your goal is a dog that will quarter at a brisk pace but within gun range and with a minimum of whistle and hand signals. After the dog and handler (hunter) have gained an understanding, the dog will usually follow the handler's very slight and subtle directions. It is this kind of teamwork that results in success when hunting. *Lightfoot*

Reinforcing the Response to the Turn Whistle

While the dog is learning to quarter be sure you use the whistle to signal turns, as indicated previously. At first the dog will glance at the handler and probably follow directions as indicated by a wave of the hand. Even if the dog is already turning, give two toots to ingrain an association between turning and the turn whistle. Eventually he will merely change his direction whenever the two whistle toots are given, sometimes without even looking for direction. If the dog does not respond to the whistle, you should shout at him very gruffly, indicating that you mean business. If that fails to produce the prompt response you expect, you should run out and give the dog a brisk shake of the collar and sound two blasts of the whistle. A few such actions from you will make it clear that the dog must respond to your whistle signal every time. Never let the dog ignore your turn whistle.

There are other methods, such as attaching a check cord to the dog's collar and forcing him to change directions when the whistle signal is given. Like some trainers, you can even blow the hup whistle whenever the dog ignores the turn whistle, which should cause the dog to stop (if the early training has been thorough); then, when the dog's attention is directed wholly to you, indicate the direction in which you want the dog to hunt. One or a combination of these techniques will produce the desired results.

In a few tough cases, you will have to be very firm, forceful and consistent to elicit an exacting turn response. *Do not* compromise. Exacting response to the turn whistle is the key to field control. Usually, by repetition, a dog's reflexes become thoroughly conditioned to perform or respond to a certain stimulus or command in a certain way. Once that happens he becomes a most dependable animal.

Learning to Track Live Game

On this subject, the training of a gun dog and a field trial dog often take divergent paths. Most field trial trainers take the dog fully through the steadying process on pigeons (and in general, pigeons do not move or walk about in the field). Hence a field trial dog gets very little moving game until it is introduced to pheasants, usually at about fifteen to eighteen months of age. This allows the field trial trainer to focus on the finer points of steadying and control early in the dog's life.

The trainer of a gun dog, on the other hand, can expose the puppy to moving game *prior* to the steadying process. There are several ways to do this; one of the easiest is to let the pup run rabbit trails. However, the most common is to use pheasants—preferably hens—properly tagged to comply with your state game laws. A lightly planted pheasant will run rather than fly. Roll the bird lightly into medium cover about five minutes ahead of the dog and be sure to mark the spot so you can quarter the dog back to it later.

Next, work the dog into the wind to the drop area, then let nature take its

Pheasants are planted by placing the head under the wing and laying the bird very gently in the cover, where it will sleep for a few minutes before becoming alert. For tracking practice, the bird must run ahead of the dog, so these birds should be planted very lightly and allowed to wake up quickly. Another method is to lightly roll the bird into heavy cover where it will hunker down for protection. *Craig*

At this stage of training, the dog must instantly "Hup" to your command. The hand signal for "Hup!" is simple but important. The dog should immediately respond to voice, whistle or hand signal—individually or in combination. Use all three signals during training sessions. Here George Wilson gives the "Hup!" signal to CFC Rewards of Barney. *Roggenkamp*

When you begin to hunt the dog alone (without training gunners), the dog will learn to stay within single gunner range. Here Dean Brunn (Pro) of Indiana trains FC Denalisunflo's Frosty without gunners, and quarters the dog with hand signals. *Roggenkamp*

course. Even though young dogs can track much more easily into the wind, this learning process can take a while. Young dogs will make many miscues, backtracks, retracks and become generally befuddled. But eventually (sometimes after a dozen birds), they get the hang of it and improve rapidly with each new experience. From here on, improved tracking ability simply involves getting more experience for the dog so he can learn how to use his nose and for you to learn how to read the dog's body language.

Wild birds present the ultimate tracking challenge and one good trip to the Dakotas can teach a dog more in a week than a year of training sessions.

One key to spaniel control is being able to stop a dog—to hup him down while he is in pursuit of a running pheasant. This isn't easy unless you have thoroughly ingrained the hup! command to the point that it will break through to the dog even if it is hot on the trail of a big rooster.

The reason you want this control is to give you a chance to catch up. Suppose your dog is hot on the trail of a fast-running bird and gets out to the edge of gun range. If you can hup the dog, you can quickly catch up, then turn the dog loose to regain the trail. Usually after two or three stops and restarts, the wary rooster will duck in and hunker down allowing the dog (and you) to catch up and have a shot within gun range. It is this talent, the ability to track moving pheasants and force them to fly and the ability to track out and retrieve wounded birds, that makes a Springer the pheasant dog extraordinaire. You can't really teach a dog to track, but you can help him learn by providing the right experiences.

Teaching a Dog to Hunt Heavy Cover

Some Springers are born addicts of heavy cover who seem from the age of a few months always to want to thrash around in the densest, roughest, most tangled web of weeds, sticks and briars. Others need some time and exposure to learn that heavy cover often holds the most birds. The dog's enthusiasm for birds increases drastically as he gets older—his enthusiasm coupled with learning where to hunt often makes for a perfect combination. Very few Springers are cover-shy, but exposing the dog properly is well-advised.

First, train your young puppies in light cover no more than knee high and thin enough to run through easily. This encourages a brisk and aggressive hunting style. Don't plant birds in such heavy cover that the dog can't race in boldly.

Late in the dog's first year, when the dog begins to track, put the birds in heavier cover. The dog's intensity on a hot trail often means the heavier cover will go virtually unnoticed.

A dog that is totally intent upon finding birds will crash through the thickest tangles in pursuit of game. I find woodcock hunting to be a strong learning experience for young dogs. The American woodcock is noted for its love of the most difficult tangles. After a youngster has crashed through the woodcock tangles for half a day and filled the bag limit, it will have learned the value of hunting in heavy cover.

Introduction to New Species

Don't be surprised, when hunting a new species of game bird, if the young dog seems confused. Almost any dog must find, flush and fetch at least one or two birds of a new variety before it understands that this is now the quarry. The introduction is fairly easy for pheasant, chukar and quail, since you can start the dog on pen-raised birds; ducks, woodcock and grouse are seldom raised in captivity. Hence, I always take the first bird shot over a young dog and use it to give the dog several retrieves. That is normally all it takes to add a new species to the dog's hunting list. If you are hunting both an experienced dog and a puppy, you can use the game shot over the veteran to teach the puppy the smell of the quarry.

The Controlled Chasing of Fly-away Birds

At this point you have a decision to make. For if you plan to fully steady your dog to wing and shot, there is no need to train for a controlled chase. In fact it is not a building block for steadiness. On the other hand, a controlled chase is much faster to teach and is much preferred to the actions of a totally unsteady, freely chasing dog. The controlled chase can mean that the dog runs after flyers and retrieves those that are shot. However, when a bird is missed, the dog breaks off and returns to the handler after only a twenty- or thirty-yard chase. It is preferred that the dog hold steady to wing and shot but be allowed to break to retrieve if the bird falls to the gun. Other times, the dog lopes slowly after the bird but turns back if the bird is missed. A controlled chase can be taught faster and more firmly than field trial steadying since you are not as concerned about the hard flush. You can see why this is of value and a controlled chase is a requirement in the Senior Hunter title of the AKC hunting test format.

There must be twenty different methods for teaching a controlled chase, but this is one of the more prevalent. Controlled chase training is completed in three parts that are then merged into the final desired response. The dog needs to 1) understand the futility of chasing birds that are missed; 2) be solidly and reflexively steady to shot and 3) be basically controllable and willing to hup down on thrown taped-wing birds without chasing. If the dog fully understands that it has no chance of catching a flying bird, if it instantly drops to any shot as a reflexive response and if it willingly hups to your command, even when a live bird is in the air you are probably going to be able to control the chase of the dog. This should allow you to keep the dog out of harm's way if it flushes a bird near a busy road or to pull the dog off a chased bird to keep it from disturbing game farther down the hunt site.

Controlled chase dogs often take several steps forward while the bird is in the air or may slowly lope after the bird until the dog knows if the bird is hit. So long as it does not fully chase to the horizon, you have accomplished your goal. However, do understand that, while of great benefit to the hunter, a loping follow-through on the flush will knock you out of field trial competition in about three seconds.

Learning the Futility of Wild Chasing

Making the dog understand the futility of chasing depends on the dog. Some dogs learn this quite easily. Other dogs never seem to get the message and would chase a flyer through a barbed-wire fence. It is not unusual for dogs in the eleven- to thirteen-month range to learn to break off a futile chase on their own. At this point, several noted trainers give a dog that shows signs of controlling its own chase as many as a dozen strong flyers in a row without shooting at any. Carefully consider the logic here. Six or eight strong flyers in succession will tire a young, chasing dog to a frazzle. If no shots are fired, the dog soon learns there is little or no chance of the bird coming down to be retrieved (just like a hen pheasant in most states—no shots, no retrieve). *Do not*, for this exercise, shoot at all and recognize that long, flutter-down retrieves of 150 yards send a message to the dog that if he chases far enough he can catch the bird and retrieve it. Plant no fluttering taped-wings in this phase either. Again, taped-winged birds only serve to remind the dog that if he just runs farther and faster, he can catch the bird. There is about a 50/50 chance that a dozen really strong fly-away birds will teach your dog that chasing is pointless. However, if the dog is a mindless, overly aggressive chaser, giving the dog more flyers will only increase the problem. So don't do this step under such circumstances.

Steady to Shot

Steadiness to shot can be ingrained reflexively in the dog through aggressive yard training, but only after the dog is fully acclimated to gunfire. If you attempt this step earlier, you may make the dog gun-nervy or uncomfortable with the sound of gunfire. Keep it up and you invite gun-shyness.

Start by walking the dog on a lead on your left with a blank pistol in your right hand. Suddenly without warning, fire the blank pistol and instantly, loudly and aggressively jerk the lead, yell "Hup!" and force him to drop to the sitting position. Over a period of a month, repeat this forty or fifty times. If you have been aggressive and consistent, he will soon develop a reflex to hup at the sound of gunfire.

Now take it a step further; force the dog to hup at a distance on the sound of gunfire. Continue this frequently for a while. Throughout the dog's life, an occasional refresher will be needed to maintain the reflexive "Hup!" reaction.

The next step in the training program is to make sure that "stopping to shot" is a firmly ingrained habit even when the dog is quartering in the field. Often, when hunting, game is shot out of the dog's sight. If the dog drops to shot instantly, it will then look to you for direction to the fall of game—a very valuable asset. Recall that during the retrieving training you fired the pistol when the buck or birds were thrown. Some bright Springer pups are able to grasp the idea quickly from this early work, and they begin to stop and look for direction to a retrieve after just a few training sessions. Devote some additional time to focused training to make the dog faultless in this requirement. One of the best

A well-trained Springer will respond and adapt to a changing situation. FC, AFC King George of Westphal is a good example. "George" is a legendary Springer who was owned first by Rick O'Brien and later by Russ Smith. Over the years, both owners, as well as John Isaacs (with whom he is shown), handled the dog to wins and placements. John Isaacs handled the dog to five Open All-Age wins, the first in 1983; the last in 1991 when George was ten years of age. Such longevity is highly valued in a hunting dog.

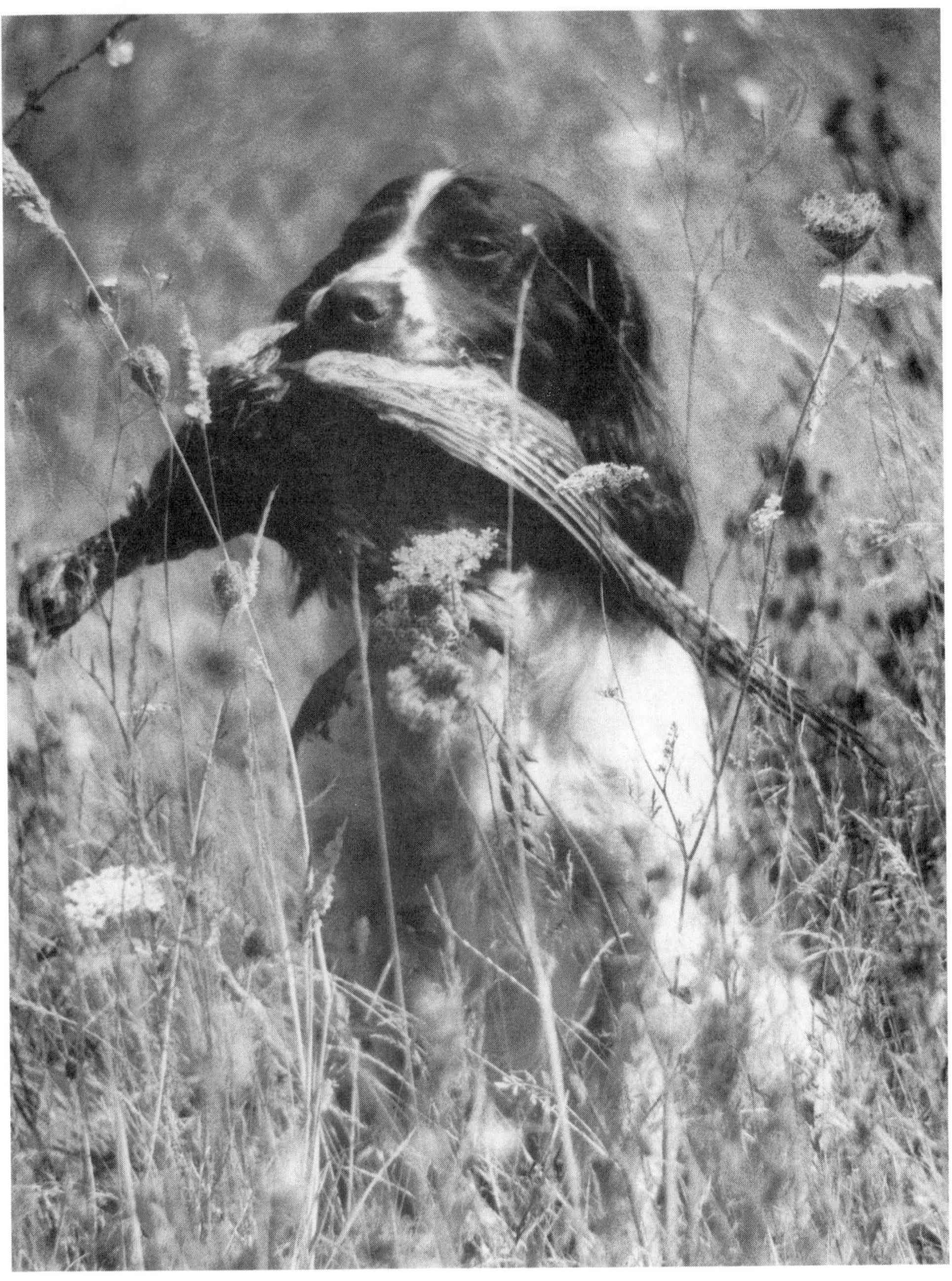

A perfect delivery! NFC/NAFC/NCFC Saighton's Scud retrieves a hen pheasant and makes a perfect delivery to Janet Christensen. Hen pheasants are often used for field trials and are as viable as roosters for dog training. Note here that Scud demonstrates a good mouth by bringing back a *live* bird that was wounded by the gun.

ways to give this training for steadiness to shot is in the field using a blank pistol or a shotgun. Quarter the dog with no planted birds and no wild birds. While the dog is quartering and responding to the whistle and hand signals, fire the shot. If the dog hups, great. The only thing the trainer must do is to repeat the act four or five times and follow through with the same procedure for the next five or six trips to the field. If the dog does not stop and sit at the crack of the shot or jumps around looking for the reason for the shot, you must immediately give the verbal or whistle command to "hup" and run to the dog and enforce it.

If you use a blank pistol, hold it high over your head when firing and give the "Hup!" command by voice and whistle at the same time. This will soon condition the dog to stop as he sees the trainer raise his arm overhead to discharge the pistol. This training procedure should be repeated at frequent intervals until the dog becomes thoroughly conditioned to hupping both to shot and to the trainer's upraised arm. Always demand compliance. If the dog fails to respond, you must rush out fast and scold the dog in a stern voice and shake his collar. Soon the spaniel's reflexes will become thoroughly conditioned. He will hup down instantly by reflex when the gun goes off.

If you have properly taught steadiness to shot, the dog will have such a strong reflex to sit when he hears gunfire that it will break through the intensity of chasing a flying bird for an instant and give you a chance to gain control before he races off madly to the horizon. When you train, at least once during every session, fire a shot in the air while the dog is quartering and demand an instant hup.

Basic Steadying to the Thrown Buck or Bird

Read carefully the training instructions for basic steadying in Chapter 7 and train for the level of control you deem appropriate to limit your dog's chasing. Certainly you will want to go through at least the yard-steady portion to be sure that you have control of the dog in a duck blind.

Finally, to control the chasing, merge the three subjects—chase futility, basic yard steadying and steady to shot—in a series of consistent field training sessions. Here you must roll in the birds very close to you and, using well-controlled gunners, shoot only every other bird. Make a major no-nonsense-allowed effort to control the dog on the fly-away birds. The result should be a dog that will momentarily stop when the gun goes off, will probably look at you and, if you have seriously ingrained the control commands, will limit his chase to a few dozen yards. *That* is success!

If you have completed all the training in Chapters 5 and 6 and the dog has learned well, you now have a well-trained gun dog that should give you great pride.

With just a few more instructions from Chapter 7 (specifically as to water retrieves and use of wind), you will have a very polished gun dog. You might even seriously consider participating in an AKC hunting test in your area to add several months of recreation to your hunting season.

FAULTS

There are a number of significant faults that Springer gun dogs may display. The most common ones are discussed here. Please keep in mind that it is much simpler to train a dog properly in the first place than to attempt to correct a fault. Attempt is the right word; for once a fault becomes habitual, it is hard to overcome. A Cornell University study proved that you *can* teach an old dog new tricks, but it required ten times as much effort to reeducate the dog as was expended in learning the improper act or fault in the first place.

The most common faults of Springer gun dogs fall into two broad categories: 1) inherited faults or characteristics, and 2) learned or acquired faults or characteristics. The two most serious inherited faults are a lack of desire to hunt and a tendency toward hard mouth. The three most common acquired faults are blinking or bird-shyness, gun-shyness and hunting out of control.

It is possible for a dog to acquire other bad habits that render him unsuitable as a reliable gun dog. But limits of space preclude a discussion of other than the most common faults.

Inherited Faults

Lack of Desire

The worst possible fault that a prospective gun dog can have is the lack of desire to hunt. This condition is to be found in all breeds and all strains within the breeds, but fortunately is extremely rare in field-bred Springers. The owner of a new puppy should not expect him to start hunting immediately. Although the desire to hunt is an instinct, it develops slowly in some bloodlines, faster in others. It must be given a chance to manifest itself in the dog. As a rule, no puppy will hunt the first time he is taken into the field, but will learn to hunt if given full opportunity to develop his instincts over time.

If a young dog between the ages of six months and a year is put on suitable game (birds or rabbits) fifteen or twenty times, he will generally get very excited when turned loose in the field and start to search for more game to find and chase. If he does not, the owner should consult a professional or good amateur trainer and ask for advice. If an older dog (over two years) exhibits no interest in hunting after repeated exposure to game birds or planted pigeons, you would do best to consult an experienced gun-dog trainer for advice.

Hard Mouth

One of the most controversial subjects among spaniel trainers is the fault of hard mouth. Obviously, a spaniel has a hard mouth if he picks up a dead bird and mangles the carcass to the point that it is not fit for the table. The problem that provokes debate among field trial fans is the dog—and it is not a rare occurrence—that catches a live pheasant or pigeon and kills the bird while carrying it in to the handler. It is often argued that this should not be held against the dog because it could never happen in actual hunting. However, others feel that even though the bird is not damaged enough to ruin it for the table, the dog should still be penalized. Most judges follow a middle ground and assess no penalty unless the bird shows considerable evidence of crushed ribs or a crushed backbone—always the true mark of a hard-mouthed dog.

There is some evidence to indicate that the *tendency* toward hard mouth is an inherited trait. This is by no means a certainty, but it has been observed that certain spaniel strains have produced several dogs through several generations that exhibit a tendency toward the fault. For this reason, it would appear that the fault might have some genealogical background. Regardless, the best and only positive cure for a genuine case of hard mouth is to prevent it before it develops. One way to avoid hard mouth is to encourage the dog's best reflexes to get a quick pickup and fast delivery.

Once a dog acquires the fault of crushing the backbone or rib structure of birds while retrieving, it is difficult to overcome. Corrective measures such as using a harness on the bird with carpet tacks protruding may work. The results are never uniformly positive, although this has helped in some cases. Occasionally, a spaniel that has developed the fault will gradually improve his carry if he has lots of game shot for him. Sometimes working the dog in the yard and making it gently hold a taped-wing pigeon will produce positive results if the trainer takes stern action if the bird is injured. Requiring the dog to hold first a dead pigeon and later a live pigeon in his mouth in the yard for five or ten minutes at a time will sometimes produce positive results. Some very patient trainers seem to be able to "talk" the dog into holding the bird tenderly and retrieving the same way.

Force breaking to retrieve can sometimes produce positive results, but this procedure is best used only by a professional or experienced amateur trainer rather than a novice. I am not aware of any 100-percent sure-fire system to correct hard mouth except proper conditioning of the dog's reflexes from the very beginning. It is most interesting that even the earliest writers refer to hard mouth, so it appears that the fault has been around for many years. Fortunately, hard mouth, which makes game unfit for the table, is extremely rare in today's field-bred Springers, and most trainers will never need to be involved in corrective measures.

Acquired Faults in Gun Dogs

Blinking or Bird-shyness

Perhaps the greatest fault that a gun dog can have is the acquired fault of blinking, which is almost always man-made. Blinking refers to a dog's refusal to acknowledge game by flushing it. The dog's behavior may be anything from a slight bit of bird-shyness to an outright refusal to go near a bird. Some blinkers will circle a bird repeatedly, whereas in more severe cases dogs will actually avoid a bird they scent by turning their heads and hunting in the opposite direction.

If a young gun dog exhibits *any* tendency toward bird-shyness (such as a reluctance to flush or circling a bird repeatedly), the danger signals are out and it is time to institute preventive measures. Put the dog in the kennel for a month or two and suspend all training. A complete "lay-off" is important! At the end of the rest period, training may be resumed with taped-wing pigeons. The dog should be encouraged to catch the pigeons and to chase rabbits to his heart's content. When he retrieves the birds or chases a rabbit, he should be made over and petted profusely. If he refuses to give chase, the trainer can set an example by running after the game and exhibiting great animation and excitement.

The taped-wing birds can be thrown for retrieving in the yard. When the bird flutters and attempts to escape, most young blinkers will overcome their fear enough to give chase and show interest. Such action must be encouraged and every opportunity given to the dog to restore his confidence. Sometimes blinking occurs in a very young puppy that is introduced to game too early. The sound or feel of the pheasant or pigeon beating its wings in the dog's face as he tries to catch the bird may frighten a shy, young dog. One solution here is to keep the dog away from game until he is older. Usually by the time the dog is six or seven months old, his self-confidence is stronger and he will be emboldened to chase taped-wing pigeons. Younger dogs should be allowed to mature before they are exposed to game again if they show fright the first time or two they are in contact with a flushing bird. Exposing the young blinker to birds gradually and giving him much praise will serve to build up his confidence. Also, working him with another dog may prove beneficial. Some gun-shy dogs also react to their fear of the gun by blinking birds and thus silencing the guns.

Gun-shyness

The devastating fault of gun-shyness is usually considered a man-made one, although some animal researchers theorize that inherited shyness can predispose a dog to this malady. However, very few experienced trainers agree with this theory. Usually a dog becomes gun-shy when confused or afraid and especially if the dog fails to comprehend why the gun is being fired. If you follow the suggestions outlined in Chapter 5, the chances are high that gun-shyness will never be a problem.

When any hint of the condition is observed, the first thing to do is to stop all work and return the dog to the kennel for a few days' rest. The trainer should think back to recall the events that may have caused the confusion in the dog's mind.

Naturally, repetition of the events that frightened and confused the dog should be avoided at all cost. If the puppy is only six or eight months old, the hand clapping procedure outlined in Chapter 5 should be restarted, mixed with ample kind, reassuring treatment. If the trainer is persistent, this will probably help overcome the dog's fear of the noise. The simultaneous application of two stimuli—in this case, the hand clap with affection—will serve to condition the dog to associate the two. If the dog really loves to retrieve, the trainer can then progress by easy stages and resume use of the cap pistol when the dog is retrieving.

If enough time is taken, and the lessons are carefully and widely spaced, the dog will usually respond as desired. If the prospect is older and exhibits fear or nervousness when the shotgun stage has been reached, he should be taken back to the yard, started over with the hand clapping and worked up progressively through the cap pistol, then the .22 blanks, and finally to the shotgun.

If the gun-shy dog is older or displays an extreme case of gun-shyness, the condition may be very difficult to correct and professional consultation is recommended. Several methods, including gunfire audio tapes, firing a gun at feeding time or, the most extreme, use of tranquilizers to overcome inhibitions are best used only by experienced professional trainers. In severe cases, all remedial efforts are chancy and only infrequently successful.

Hunting Out of Control

Hunting out of control means working out of gun range and usually results from lack of early training. When a Springer works in such a manner, two simple corrective measures are required: 1) he should be worked only into the wind for a month or two and 2) he should be forcefully retaught to turn on the whistle. The training technique to teach both methods is outlined in detail in this chapter. If a dog will turn on the whistle *every* time and has learned the simple hand signals, it is an easy matter to get him to hunt within range. The use of the whistle and the work into the wind alone will usually produce the required pattern of work. The trainer must be sure, however, that the dog knows and understands the whistle signal perfectly and then the trainer must insist that the dog respond every time.

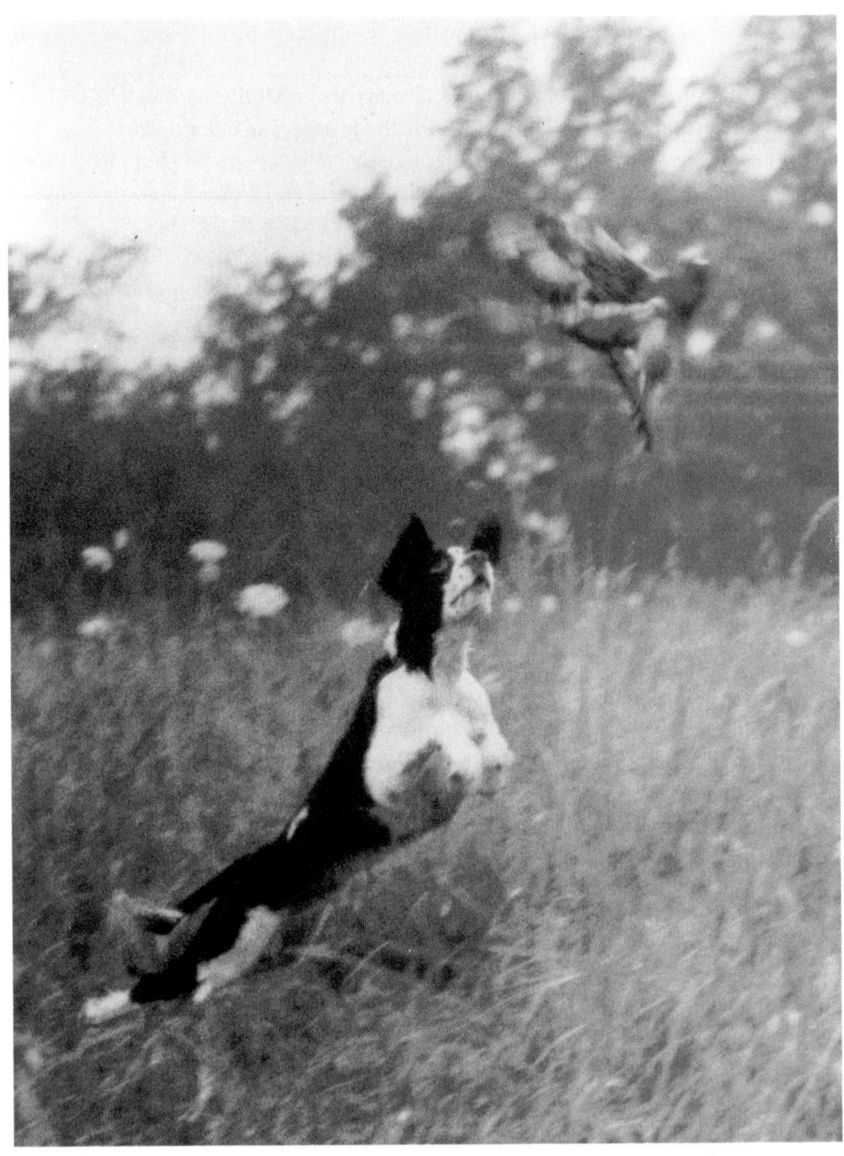

The bold flush, so highly prized by American field trialers, is demonstrated here by FC, AFC, CFC Ru-Char's Quick Shot owned and handled by Ralph Botti of New Jersey. Unfortunately, "Shotsey" died at age six after a short but extremely successful field-trial career. Although Shotsey sired only a few puppies before his death, his progeny have been quite successful. *Botti*

7

Advanced Gun Dog Training

THE TRAINING outlined in this chapter, if successfully completed, will turn the hunter/Springer combination into a polished team able to succeed in the most difficult field situations.

This chapter explains the rationale and methods to:

- Steady the dog to flying birds.
- Help a dog learn to use the wind.
- Instill control that will carry over into the most challenging hunting circumstances.
- Teach the dog to make blind retrieves.
- Teach the "Hunt Dead!" command and when to use it.
- Teach water retrieving.

Steadying the Dog to Wing and Shot

One of the most important requirements of a top quality spaniel gun dog is that he be steady to wing and shot. This terminology, steadiness to wing and shot, means that the dog will stop dead in his tracks and sit (hup) at the instant a bird is flushed or a gun is fired. There are practical reasons for expecting and requiring a dog to react in a steady manner. Charles Goodall's legendary account of a South Dakota hunting trip illustrates this reasoning vividly.

It seems that a veteran hunting party of three long-time friends who owned well-trained steady spaniels were persuaded, at the last minute, to include another hunter and his unsteady spaniel in their hunting trip. The group arrived in South Dakota and decided to push through a field of corn stubble that, in past years, had been fairly alive with pheasants. The dogs were all walked on a leash or at heel to the edge of the field and then the four hunters and their dogs proceeded down the corn rows about fifteen yards apart. About halfway through the field, one of the dogs dived into a pile of corn stubble and flushed a big old cock pheasant that had squatted under some light cover hoping that the hunters would pass him by. The bird flushed out in front of the hunters and was dropped immediately by the center gun. The three steady dogs dropped to shot (hupped) to await orders, but the unsteady Springer raced toward the "fall" to make the retrieve without command. He overran the fall and proceeded down the field, where he bumped into another pheasant that flushed immediately. He gave chase and within three minutes had flushed perhaps forty pheasants out of the corn, none of which came within gun range of the four hunters.

No one had much to say to the owner of the breaking dog, but a great deal of silent swearing took place. Some of the birds that had been flushed were marked down in a slough about a half mile away. The four gunners headed in that direction with their dogs at heel. Upon entering the slough, which was huge, all dogs were turned loose to hunt and as luck would have it, the unsteady dog flushed the first bird and took off on a wild chase. His actions again caused all the birds in the slough to flush out of gun range. This time, not one shot was fired, though dozens of birds had been in the vicinity of the hunters in the corn field and the slough.

A council of war was held immediately and, by vote of three to one, the unsteady dog was banished to his crate in the vehicle for the duration of the hunt. After this had transpired the hunters proceeded to work some other likely covers using the three trained dogs and were able, in the remaining few hours, to take their daily limit.

The Reason for Steady Dogs

A trained Springer, steady to wing and shot and trained to work within gun range, will *not* disturb new and unhunted territory ahead by chasing every hen pheasant that is flushed or every cock that is missed. He will be under perfect control. The most common excuse given by the owner of an unsteady Springer that breaks and chases is that he wants his dog to be there when the bird hits the ground so as not to lose the cripples. This is not a valid argument and has little basis in actual performance. Any spaniel gun dog with an average nose can learn to trail out and retrieve crippled birds that are shot, as well as those that try to avoid being flushed. In addition, dogs that are steady often have a better line of sight on the fall and mark better than the unsteady dog that is crashing through the brush and weeds trying to catch a flying bird. This is especially true on grouse or woodcock.

Note: This steadying process is highly reliable and works very consistently for gun dogs. However, if you are planning to compete in AKC licensed field trials, your dog will be required to have a very bold flush. *In field trials even a very slight hesitation on the flush is severely penalized.* Hence, if your ultimate goal is field trial competition, you should proceed very precisely, and I recommend consultation with local trialers, a local field trial club or a professional spaniel trainer for additional steadying advice.

Teaching the Dog to Be Steady

Understand that steadiness is an *unnatural* act on the part of the dog. His instinct is to flush hard and chase to the horizon. The steadying process is rigorous by virtue of being contrary to the Springer's natural tendency. Therefore, teaching a dog to be steady is a multi-step process that again requires conscientious yard work and adherence to a step-by-step procedure.

First, stand in front of the dog and command him to hup and stay. As the dog faces you (the trainer), his favorite retrieving buck should be tossed over your shoulder (behind you) as you continue to command "Hup! . . . Hup! . . . Hup!" You will probably have to make several quick grabs for the dog to enforce the hup command because up to this time, he has been permitted to chase retrieves and may ignore the command to hup. If the dog is restrained physically several times and scolded in a stern voice, he will usually recall his earlier training and remain sitting as the buck is thrown over your shoulder. This lesson should be repeated several days in succession. As a rule, the dog should now never be permitted to retrieve if he leaves the sitting position without your command to fetch.

Incidentally, the usual command for a retrieve is "Fetch!" At this stage the trainer usually couples the dog's name with the word "fetch," such as "Rover, fetch!" (Many trainers, especially field trialers, gradually drop the word "fetch" and teach the dog to retrieve when only his name is called.

After several days of standing in front of the dog to throw the buck and if he is now reliable, you should begin to toss the buck off to your side, but always be ready and in a position to catch and restrain the dog if necessary. This lesson should be repeated for several days until it is obvious that the dog has learned to wait for the "Fetch!" command before retrieving. You should then change positions to a spot directly behind the dog and throw the buck out in front of the dog. At this point, you can fire the blank pistol every third or fourth throw to create the association of sitting down on the shot. If you have been patient, consistent and diligent, in all likelihood the dog will remain steady most of the time; but when he does break, the trainer must stop him by commanding "Hup!" in a loud voice, catching him and setting him back in his original spot. This often involves the trainer's running out to the dog before it reaches the buck. Some trainers over age fifty try to design an easier method, but younger trainers will find that this practice not only amuses their neighbors, but also is wonderful exercise. Patience and practice will assure solid results. Never fail to pet the dog when he has performed properly, but be sure to withhold petting and verbal praise when he has failed to respond as desired.

The next step is to hup the dog some ten to fifteen yards from you and toss

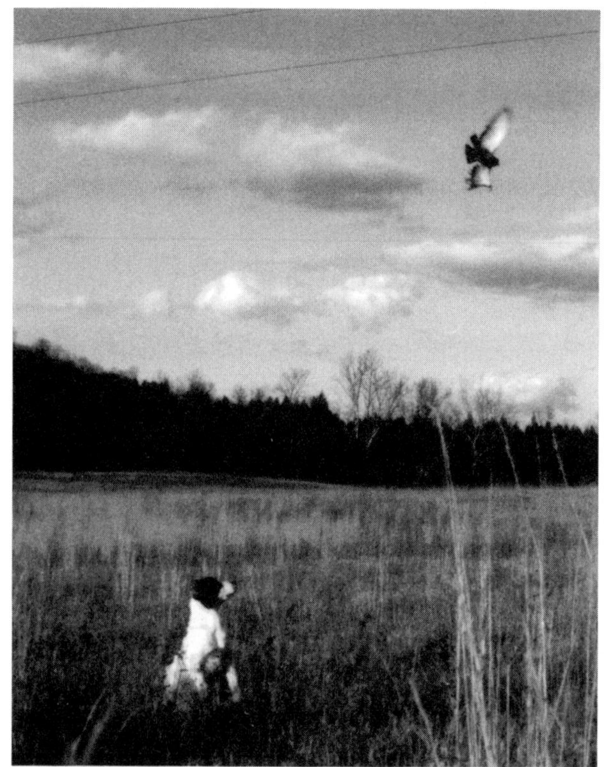

This Springer has learned to "Hup!" instantly when a taped-wing pigeon is thrown while the dog is quartering. This is a very important step in the steadying process. Remember, steadying is a step-by-step process that seldom can be cut short without risk. *Roggenkamp*

Throughout the steadying process, try to keep the dog boldly flushing birds. Here, John Isaacs (Pro) of Ohio teases the young dog with a retrieving buck. Many trainers continue to tease a dog with a live bird before it is tossed. When the bird is thrown the dog is commanded and expected to "Hup!" Instantly! *Friend*

the buck in all different directions—some even in the near-vicinity of the dog. Insist that he be rock steady and make no attempt to retrieve until your command to fetch is given. Gradually increase the distance between you and the dog until it is possible to hup the dog thirty yards away and toss the buck practically under his nose while he remains steady. It is a good idea to walk out occasionally and retrieve the buck yourself in order to teach the dog that he cannot have a retrieve every time. After all, some birds will be missed and the dog must learn very early that he cannot retrieve every time.

It is important that, throughout the steadying process, you continue to work the dog's pattern in the field and allow him to find and catch two or three taped-wing pigeons in every session. This will help retain a bold flush. But be sure there is no wild game or any flyers in the field since this will set back your training program if he breaks and chases.

Once you are completely confident that your Springer Spaniel has learned that he must not retrieve until ordered to do so in the yard, it is time to return to the field. First, cast the dog off to hunt (into the wind); as he approaches from the left, the buck should be thrown to the extreme right. The trainer should step in front of the moving dog and give the whistle or the voice command to hup. In all likelihood the response will be good and the dog will drop after a step or two. Repeat this procedure five times or so, and then let the dog hunt for a while uninterrupted. Next, let him relax in the crate for thirty minutes or more and then hold another identical session before the training day is over.

The lesson described above should be repeated five or six times until the dog is always reliable and steady. Then a dead pigeon should be substituted for the buck. The puppy will exhibit much more interest in the bird than in the buck and may attempt to break the first time or two. If the dead bird is always thrown as the dog approaches, the trainer will be in position to step out *between* the dog and the bird and be able to enforce the command physically. Of course, the verbal and whistle commands to hup should be given each and every time and repeated several times if necessary. When the dog is responding to this situation *every* time, then you may substitute a taped-wing live pigeon for the dead bird. The dog will again be more intense and may try to break for the live bird. The first few live birds will be a real test for you and the dog. Firmness and patience are still the proper attitudes and no transgressions are permitted. As the dog learns that he must obey the command with the live bird, the blank pistol should be reintroduced in the field.

The procedure is to 1) toss the taped-wing bird, 2) yell "Hup!", then 3) fire the blank pistol. This sounds complex, but with a little practice you will soon be able to perform all three actions almost simultaneously. However, your first two or three attempts are sure to amuse your training partners, and even your dog. At this point, you must keep your resolve. Have faith that better days are coming. This fall will be your best hunting season ever and your new gun dog will receive many compliments from your hunting companions.

The next step involves shooting some thrown flyers over the dog as he sits at heel. You can follow this procedure for several training sessions—at least twenty birds—until the dog is thoroughly conditioned to the fact that he must never retrieve until ordered to do so. It's also important to let him retrieve only three or four out of every five birds. You, the handler, should walk out and pick up the other birds while the dog remains sitting in his original position.

After the dog is responding perfectly to all the commands and situations, the next and final step is to work on rolled-in birds. For this you will need two very reliable and disciplined gunners who will follow your directions exactly. Position the gunners about fifteen yards to each side of you and instruct them to shoot the birds *only* at some distance (thirty or more yards) and *only* if the dog hups. Now, as the dog quarters, you should dizzy a bird and throw it into the cover. (Don't let the dog see you do this.) Give him the turn whistle and when the dog races in to flush the bird, you must rush toward him to enforce the hup command. When he sits down, the guns can shoot the bird. You must keep him sitting there for at least thirty seconds (sixty seconds is preferred) before you allow him to fetch. This reinforces your control and his self-control. If it works well the first time, repeat it two more times, then put him away for the day. You must *always be near the dog* to get control if he appears to break when the bird flushes. The whistle command to hup should be given at the exact instant the bird is flushed. If the dog has learned each step well, he will probably be steady on his first flushed pigeon. If he tries to break, you will be in a position to restrain the dog physically. You have both made a lot of progress to reach this point and now it is a matter of ingraining the training through repetition on every occasion possible. Continue to mix flyers with taped-wing birds and gradually make the transition to mostly planted birds.

Most amateurs are able to train only on the weekends, but rest assured there are hundreds of spaniel owners the world over who do it successfully using only weekend training. Don't be discouraged at occasional lapses of memory on the dog's part as the training progresses. Low-flying birds or a bird shot too close may cause the pupil to break. This is the time to refresh the dog's memory by running after him and carrying him back bodily to the point of the flush. He should be placed firmly, and not too gently, back at the point of the flush in the sitting position and scolded in a rough tone of voice.

In rare cases, an incorrigible breaker may force you to turn to a last-resort method. This technique uses a forty- or fifty-foot nylon check cord attached to the dog's collar. When the bird is flushed, the hup! command is enforced by a tight line and a firm pull—not a jerk. The check cord can induce ''pointing'' in spaniels if not properly used. So use it very carefully. This method is not recommended for the first-time trainer who might lack judgment in its use. When all else fails and you have decided, after mature reflection, that this is the only course left, you must be as gentle with the dog as possible. If you ''clothesline'' the dog, you can induce injury or bird-shyness. All slack should be taken out of the line immediately at the instant of flush, so the dog is held steady rather than jerked to a standstill. Also be very careful not to step on the line when he is running. Again, rough treatment here can cause the Springer to become confused and develop into a blinker or pointer—both of which are serious faults. *Note:*

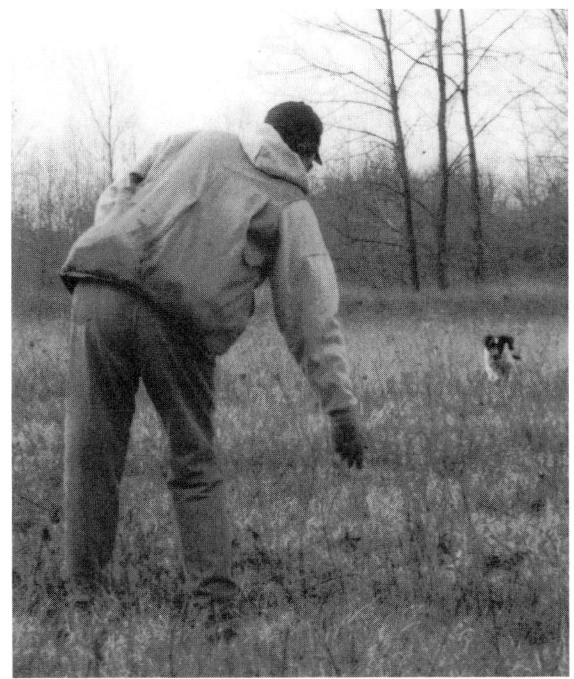

Throughout advanced training the dog must retain its absolute and immediate response to commands. Here, George Wilson of Michigan gives the "Come" hand signal to CFC Rewards of Barney and the dog responds quickly. Most trainers slap the thigh rapidly when teaching young puppies to come. The transition from slapping the thigh to dropping the hand to the knee is gradual but effective. During the steadying process the dog will be called back to the handler on occasion and denied the retrieve. This training comes in handy when a hen pheasant flies away during a hunt in a "roosters only" state.

Roggenkamp

Later in the steadying process birds are flushed close to the handler to allow total control of the dog. Here a Springer flushes a pigeon and hups instantly. Dean Brunn (Pro) of Indiana will watch carefully to be sure the dog is steady before he shoots the bird. He is also very near the dog in case it decides to yield to temptation and "break" to retrieve before it is commanded to do so. In the early stages of steadying it is a good idea to let the dog sit several seconds before it is sent on the retrieve. *Roggenkamp*

During the steadying process, most dogs become somewhat confused, tentative and less self-confident. This generally results in the dog shortening its pattern, watching the handler and running less aggressively. As the dog becomes reliably steady and requires less discipline, he will regain his self-confidence and return to his aggressive hunting style. But give him time to recover.

The Soft Flush

After you are around spaniels for a while, you will hear the term ''soft flush'' used in a derogatory manner. To field trialers, a soft flush is like the plague as it virtually ends a dog's competitive career. What it means is the dog slows down, ''tip-toes,'' hesitates, or flash-points before the bird flushes. For esthetic reasons, field trialers glorify the bold, driving, jump-in-the-air flushes. But for hunting, a soft flush is a minor fault. Many Springers will learn to flash-point during the steadying process if pushed too hard or the process is cut short. Usually this is due to confusion in the dog's mind between flush-then-hup or hup-then-flush. Experience and judgment is the best tool to maintain the hard flush through the steadying process. Too much pressure or discipline during the steadying process is often the root cause of this condition. In England it is not really regarded as a serious fault; hence it is sometimes called an ''English Flush.'' In England, dogs are discouraged from catching unshot game, especially dogs used to flush birds for driven shoots, so a soft flush is more often seen there.

Some hunters purposely seek out field trialers from which to purchase finished dogs termed field trial ''dropouts''—dogs rejected due to a soft flush. This is one way to purchase a world-class gun dog that would rarely be available for sale otherwise.

Pointing Spaniels—A Major Fault

A word about pointing spaniels: Pointing game might seem to be a desirable trait to the novice spaniel owner, but there are several reasons why a Springer can never become a really satisfactory pointing dog. In the first place, a Springer Spaniel does not have the nose or style to hunt like a Pointer or an English Setter.

It is probably true that the early ancestors of both the Springer and the English Setter were the same, and some strains of Springers seem to carry some genes for the pointing instinct. However, the noses of the dogs are very different. Springers have been selectively bred to quarter close to the gun. Springers do not and should not have the instincts to range like a big running pointing dog; no experienced dog person wants a spaniel that points, because it could never be more than a mediocre pointing dog. But remember, even the finest pointing dogs cannot perform the multi-faceted functions of a top Springer Spaniel.

Over the last several hundred years, spaniels have been bred for the type of nose that enables them to trail both fur and feathers and to locate game by body scent as well. Class pointing dogs, on the other hand, rely strictly on body scent when finding game and have minimal ability to trail moving game the way spaniels do. One cannot actually say that a Pointer or English Setter has a better nose than a spaniel, although they seem to be able to locate game by body scent from a greater distance than can a spaniel. It is more accurate to say that the pointing dog's nose is better adapted to its specialized type of hunting, while the spaniel's nose is more suitable for the work that is expected of a multi-purpose dog. It is the opinion of many experienced trainers that each breed's nose is suited to its particular style of hunting.

The Ideal Spaniel Pattern for Different Wind Conditions

To the hunter using a spaniel, the wind (as long as it is not too harsh) is a wonderful hunting partner. As your spaniel grows, gains confidence and acquires bird sense, it too will learn to use the wind to its advantage. Any dog must be downwind of game in order to use its nose to find the bird by scent. Obviously this will radically alter the pattern that an experienced dog runs in different wind conditions.

Normally young dogs are trained to run a flat pattern while you walk directly into the wind—a condition that calls for the simplest pattern of all, the basic windshield-wiper, back-and-forth action. But when you are hunting it is not always possible to walk into the wind. After your dog has mastered all the basics—finding, fetching and obeying—it will begin to acquire wind sense with experience. It is important that you understand how the dog needs to run in different wind situations so you can encourage the dog to run a proper pattern. Be sure you understand the differences in wind patterns so you are not trying to force the dog to hunt incorrectly. The following diagrams offer three key examples.

Example 1 Into the wind: The basic windshield wiper pattern has the dog always in gun range and not unduly covering the same ground twice. The wind is in your face and the dog runs back and forth across your path as you move forward.

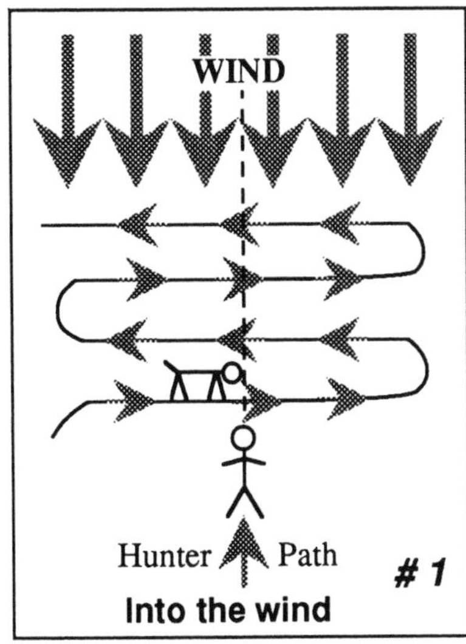

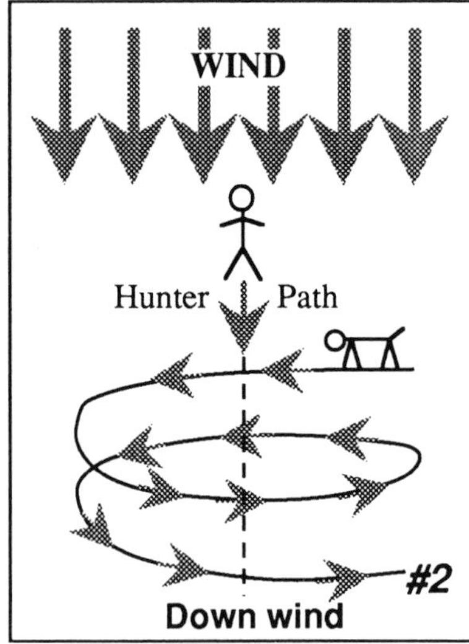

Example 2 Down wind: In a straight downwind hunter path, the spaniel must range out far from you since it must find birds using the wind coming over your shoulder. It is not unusual for experienced spaniels to range out to thirty or forty yards under these conditions. However, since the birds should be found between you and the dog, the dog will be coming back toward you (into the wind) when it flushes the bird. This is very exciting hunting and a spaniel that handles a downwind path well is a pleasure to hunt.

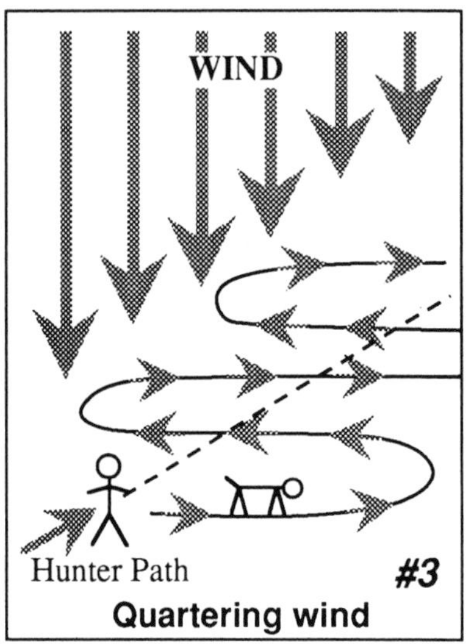

Example 3 Quartering wind: This is an almost everyday hunting situation where the wind crosses the hunter's path at an angle. The experienced dog will always try to run *perpendicular* to the wind wall. The key is to get the dog into the proper flow quickly and allow the dog to properly use its nose.

Ultimate Field Control

A spaniel's utility can be maximized only if it is always under complete and total control. Many hunters never fully enjoy the abilities of their dogs because they are out of control a large part of the time afield. This is true not only of spaniels but of pointing dogs as well.

For several years I have been invited to participate in the Ruffed Grouse Society's National hunt in northern Minnesota. About 100 RGS sponsors from across the country convene to raise funds for the Society. Each day the hunters drive out into the sparsely populated areas to hunt the north woods for grouse and woodcock. Surprisingly, every year several hunters lose many hours or even a whole day of hunting because their dogs simply disappear for hours or days at a time. Most of this can be traced to a lack of control. You go afield to hunt birds, not to hunt for your dog! I have always liked a spaniel's style because he hunts where I go rather than my following him.

Frankly, the key to control in a hunting situation is purely and simply the discipline and respect the dog has for you based on a comprehensive, long-term training program. You cannot and will not retain this if the dog sits in the kennel from one hunting season to the next without training. Not all of this training need be in the field. A rigorous fifteen-minute weekly refresher of "Hup!", "Come!", "Stay!" and "No!" with several steady retrieves, an occasional "Hunt dead!" and some hand signals will work wonders. It is needed not because the dog forgets what it has been taught but because the dog needs its discipline and self-control reinforced.

When training in the field, you can "set up" some situations that tempt the dog to disobey. If he disobeys, you have the opportunity to reinforce your control. Two situations in the field are especially frustrating—dogs that don't come when called and dogs that chase deer or rabbits until they become disoriented. Here are three solutions: 1) When hunting grouse or woodcock, I put a small bell on the dog to help me keep track of his whereabouts in very heavy cover. 2) If you ever do lose the dog in the woods, leave your coat or an article of clothing where your car was parked and stop back every two to four hours. 3) Before I leave on a major hunting trip, I always get in at least two hard-discipline, no-nonsense training sessions where I put the dog through his paces and demand exacting response to every command. This usually makes a strong impression that carries over into the hunt.

But don't suspend discipline *during* the hunt. Some hunters get so overly excited that they fail to maintain control. After a few days, the dog is so hyped up that it is nearly totally wild. If the dog is beginning to get out of control, don't just continue to blow the whistle. Instead, carefully unload your gun, lay it down and mark its location well. Then run, don't walk, to the dog while yelling at the top of your lungs. Grab the dog, discipline him, put him down in the hup position, tell him to stay, then slowly walk back to your gun, reload, call the dog to you and proceed to hunt. That will convince the dog that you are serious about discipline even when excited by the hunt.

How much of this convincing is needed depends on the dog. Some dogs need very little training to stay in control while others need a frequent reinforcement. Only you can determine the level of training needed to keep your dog under total control at all times. This, to a great extent, will determine the enjoyment of your hunt.

Blind Retrieves on Land or Water

Sooner or later in hunting, field trials or hunt tests, the occasion will arise when your dog needs to make a blind retrieve. Often in hunting a bird will pop out of the cover while the dog is deep in a ditch or behind a tree. If that bird is shot, especially if it is a long shot, the dog will be blind to the fall and must rely on you for direction. If the bird is a moving cripple or has fallen across a creek, only the dog will be able to retrieve the game. Hence, the ability to make blind retrieves is a valuable asset.

Teaching a dog to make blind retrieves always involves three factors: 1) the dog must rely on you for direction, 2) the dog must understand what your signal means and 3) the dog must trust you completely and hunt diligently and aggressively whenever you send him on a blind retrieve.

Teaching the dog to make blind retrieves is relatively easy but it is preferable to save it until the later stages of training when the dog is fully steady to wing and shot. First, be sure the dog cannot see, but can hear, what you are doing. For example, use your garage with the dog in a crate and the door open. Now, go around the side where the dog cannot see you and toss the retrieving buck twenty feet—no more—and fire the blank gun. Immediately go and get the dog (preferably on a lead). He will be excited by the shot and anxious to find out why it was fired. Hup him down outside, give him a hand signal and say, "Joe, fetch!" He may take the signal instantly or he may quest around until he stumbles into it. If he is questing aimlessly, give the hand signal and repeat "Joe, fetch!" every few seconds. He will soon associate the signal with finding the buck. Most dogs learn the game in just a few sessions and soon will be excited, eager and anxious to stretch the distance and test the challenges. Next, hide the buck under a bush or behind a tree. Take the dog into the yard and while he is playing, fire the blank pistol. He should hup instantly to the sound of the shot. Now give the hand direction and "Joe, fetch!" Soon he will be doing double blinds and having a great time. Most trainers use several key words at this juncture. "Fetch!" is obvious, "Over!" is to send the dog in a right or left direction and "Go Back!" means quest farther out and directly away from you.

Finally, blind water retrieves require the dog to be willing to swim long distances at your direction. I have always found that dogs who are avid swimmers and eager retrievers are as willing to take direction to blind retrieves in water as on land. Once the dog is fully and avidly retrieving in water, the process for teaching blind water retrieves is exactly the same as blind land retrieves except that, unfortunately, most of us cannot do this training next to our garage.

Hunt Dead

Often when hunting in heavy cover, especially when hunting grouse and woodcock, birds will flush blind to the dog or may even be downed by a gun far out of sight of the dog. In these cases, the downed bird always seems to fall into very heavy brush.

Teaching a dog to "hunt dead" is also relatively easy, but is best delayed until the dog has reached its final level of steadiness. You can start in the yard or park by hiding a dead bird in heavy cover such as the middle of a large shrub or under the branches of a large evergreen. In most cases, real hunt deads will require some special effort on the dog's part, so make the early training a bit difficult. Now take the dog to the general area and let it run free. When the dog is some distance from the spot of the hidden bird and looking away from you, fire the blank pistol once or twice. At this, the dog should hup to shot. Now you must act excited—very excited. Call the dog to you and with great enthusiasm say "Hunt Dead! . . . Hunt Dead! . . . Hunt Dead!" While pointing and shaking your hand at the spot of the fall, force the dog to stay in the area by voice commands until it finds the hidden bird. After a dozen of these sessions, the dog will get the idea that "hunt dead" means there is a bird in the area where you are pointing.

In a real hunt-dead situation, you should mark the fall of the bird, hup the dog, then walk toward the area yourself and mark it well. But don't get directly to the point of the fall because your scent will interfere with the bird scent. Finally, call the dog to you and command to "Hunt Dead!" A dog that handles that command well will save many downed birds.

Water Work

Retrieving from water is one of the most useful functions a Springer Spaniel can perform. Many people think water retrieving applies only with waterfowl hunting, but a surprising number of grouse and pheasants can be retrieved only after a swim across a stream. The dog's performance of this function is a major benefit to the hunter who makes the effort to train and provide the necessary experience.

If your focus is mainly on waterfowl hunting in very cold climates, perhaps one of the retriever breeds is more in line with your needs. The retrievers have the required coat (two of them, in fact) and can stand the grueling conditions that prevail in retrieving ducks and other waterfowl from icy water. However, if you are a typical American hunter who can get in only a few days of waterfowl shooting each year, you will find the properly trained Springer an excellent water retriever as well as a top upland game dog.

Water work should not be started until the dog has developed into a bold and enthusiastic retriever in the yard. Your dog's initial introduction to water is most important, and this is a good procedure to follow: After the puppy is six or eight months old and is retrieving nicely from land, he should be taken to a nearby pond or lake with very gently sloping banks. You should wear waders or a bathing suit, since it will probably be necessary for you both to enter the water. A nice warm sunny day in the late spring or early summer is best for the comfort of both you and the dog.

A familiar boat bumper or canvas retrieving buck should be taken along. At first, let the puppy run up and down the banks of the lake for five or ten minutes, until he feels at home and has investigated all the strange new scents, splashed a little and had a drink. After the puppy has become acclimated and adjusted to this new terrain, call him to you as you walk out a few feet into the water. In all likelihood the dog will follow and frisk around playfully in the water. If he does, let him play and dash in and out to his heart's content. If the trainer remains in water up to a depth of about six or eight inches, the dog will, too, although he may dash in and out playfully. If the dog attempts to swim, so much the better. If he makes no effort to swim, walk out until you are in water

You may find that you need to enter the water with the puppy the first few times to reassure it and help it overcome its initial concern about this new element. However, if you can find a pond or lake with a gradual slope, the puppy will frolic along the edges and will soon be boldly trying to swim in deeper water. Here Roselinde Isaacs (John's daughter) introduces a youngster to the pond.
Friend

How's this for water enthusiasm? The Springer's love for water work is legendary. Here NFC, AFC, CFC Dewfield Brickclose Flint leaps headlong into a lake on his way to a long retrieve.

approximately up to your knees. If the dog does not follow, he should be coaxed (not forced) to venture out this far. If he swims and wades to you, he should be petted and made over as a reward for the effort.

Many young spaniels have an instinctive liking for water and will start to swim immediately. Their first efforts are usually amusingly clumsy and they will splash a good deal with their front feet, which they often lift out of the water with each stroke. Some encouragement from you will help build confidence, and many puppies enjoy the swimming from the very first experience. If, however, the dog exhibits any fear of water, take your time to build up his confidence by making repeated trips to the pond and by letting the dog become adjusted as you wade close to the shore. If you are patient, even the most timid dog will eventually respond to and gain confidence from your encouragement. If your dog shows timidity, a very small, shallow stream can be crossed and recrossed with the puppy following. This is much less intimidating than a large body of water, but once the dog's fear is conquered, you can both return to the pond.

Once the dog appears to have overcome fear and uncertainty, a short retrieve should be tried in the shallow water where it is not necessary for the dog to swim. This may be on the first trip, or the fifth, depending on the dog's response to the experience.

When first sent to retrieve from water, the puppy should be started from very close to the water's edge on a gently sloping shoreline. The buck should be thrown only three or four feet and never into deep water. Because the puppy has been retrieving the buck at home in the yard, he will know immediately what is expected; and it is entirely possible that he will dash into the water, seize the buck and deliver it to hand. If he does so, praise and pet him lavishly.

This retrieve should be repeated five or six times and, if successful, the distance increased gradually so the puppy will have to swim a few strokes to reach the buck. After three or four successful retrieves at this distance, the lesson should be stopped for the day. It is always important to quit while the dog is still enthusiastic and enjoying the work.

The trips to the water should be repeated at frequent intervals and the length of the retrieves gradually extended until the puppy is swimming out twenty or thirty yards. The young dog should, if in the process of being steadied, be required to sit as commanded when the buck is thrown and wait for the command to retrieve. Rest assured after the first two or three lessons that the dog's swimming will improve and there will be considerably less splashing with the front feet.

As the dog gains confidence and is completing thirty-yard retrieves with ease, the next step is to have a friend position himself on a point of land or island or in a boat or raft, thirty or forty yards away but in full view of the dog. The friend should then fire the pistol and throw the buck high in the air, at a distance of about thirty yards from the dog. At the fetch command, the young dog will probably enter the water briskly, swim out, retrieve the buck, and deliver it to you. If the dog attempts to do anything other than return to you, a few calls on the whistle should bring him directly back to you. You can stretch the retrieves a little over time as the dog shows obvious enthusiasm and wants more challenge. Incidentally, especially in hot weather, swimming is the ultimate conditioning

If anyone suggests that English Springer Spaniels of field trial breeding and training are not suitable for an average day of hunting, show them this photo. On a crisp, cold October afternoon of hunting in the northeastern corner of Michigan's lower peninsula, I shot five grouse over these two Springers. They are FC, AFC, CFC Ru-Char's Ruffian (left) 4th and 3rd in 1986 and 1987 National Amateur Championships and FC Reward's Satin Sassy (right) 2nd in the 1985 National Open Championship. I hunted both dogs extensively during the years I owned and trialed them. These grouse fell to my old Lefever Side-by-Side in the photo, which doesn't have a sign of a choke in either barrel nor any bluing left on the outside of the barrels. Most grouse and woodcock are taken at close range, so open chokes work best. *Schirmer*

exercise. However, no lesson should ever extend to the point that the dog gets bored, overtired or loses its keen enthusiasm.

In the early stages of water work, stand close to the water's edge to take the buck from the youngster before he has a chance to put it down. Most young dogs will drop the buck immediately after they are clear of the water in order to shake the water from their coats. It is helpful for the trainer to stand close to the shoreline during the early lessons and accept delivery of the buck before the dog is entirely clear of the water. The distance at which the trainer stands from the water's edge can be increased gradually until he is back some ten or fifteen feet.

All dogs instinctively want to shake to remove water from their coats, so always plan on getting wet during water training! With patience, urging and coaxing, your Springer can be trained to delay the shaking action until *after* delivering the buck. If the dog continues to drop the buck to shake, run back from the water a few yards, as if you are going to leave the area. At the same time, tell the dog repeatedly to "Hold it! . . . Hold it!" This will help overcome the instinct and will speed up the delivery. Continued efforts will instill the idea in the dog's mind that he *must* deliver before shaking. Take care not to let the habit of shaking before delivery become fixed. If a hunting dog drops a crippled duck or goose when it stops to shake, the cripple will take off for the nearest patch of cattails. The dog will, of course, go after the bird, but if it is a strong runner, there is a chance that it could disappear. This wastes time, while the dog is chasing a cripple up and down the bank.

A dog used for upland hunting must learn to retrieve across streams. Start by throwing the buck across a small stream, then work up to wider and wider streams. Spaniels learn this very rapidly. A spaniel used for duck hunting must also learn to work through blocks or decoys without becoming tangled in the anchor lines and without trying to retrieve the decoys. But this phase of the spaniel's education is specialized work that can be taught using the techniques explained in any good retriever training book.

Spaniels can be taught to hunt from a blind or boat very quickly and easily. The key is to have the dog in complete and total control before such training is attempted. Absolute steadiness is a must for this type of hunting. The dog must be fully obedient to the hup and stay commands. The dog can be conditioned to the boat or the blind on dry land and then gradually conditioned to work in the water. Springers get quite excited in either a boat or a blind, so be sure the boat is stable or the blind is solidly constructed.

Electronic Training Aids

Probably the most significant and certainly the most widely advertised training innovation to win approval since 1980 is the electronic training aid. This is commonly referred to as a shock collar, since that is exactly what it does. It allows the trainer to give his dog an electric shock whenever or wherever the dog misbehaves. The dog wears a specially designed radio-controlled collar. The trainer carries the control input device or "hot button." At any time, the trainer can push the button and a harmless but painful shock is administered to the dog. As technology has improved, the devices have gotten smaller, more reliable and less expensive. Some are sophisticated and include beeps or buzzes to warn the dog of an impending shock. Obviously, some trainers consider it a great advantage to be able to administer punishment to a dog that disobeys, even when it is out of reach (up to several hundred yards away).

These collars are especially prevalent among pointing breed and retriever trainers. Because pointing dogs tend to roam for large distances, having a "very long arm" to administer discipline is an asset. Field trial retriever trainers often use electric collars to instill the ultimate level of discipline for the very rigid control standards of retriever trials.

However, in the use of an electric collar on a Springer, caution is the watchword. Most Springer trainers do not use an electric collar in early training stages. Others use them only as a last resort, some not at all. Although these devices have an excellent potential when used judiciously, unfortunately in the hands of a novice trainer, the negatives can override the positives. Let me emphasize that I am not against electronic collars, but you must recognize the complexity of the situation.

First, the field-bred Springer is a very smart, very sensitive, very soft animal. It is not unusual for a dog to learn that a collar equals discipline and therefore he may "shut down" or refuse to hunt or even leave the trainer's side when wearing an electronic training collar.

Second, it is very easy to hit the button at the wrong time and hence punish the dog inappropriately or in a way that could actually ruin a fine dog. What if you accidentally hit the button just as a dog raced in to flush a bird? Would it begin to point or avoid game altogether? Or what if you bumped the button as the dog carried a retrieve to you? Would it suddenly associate retrieving with punishment? These are not common situations, but accidents can and do occur. Finally, if you tend to flare up or lose your temper, it is very easy to over-discipline. Punishment is just a button-push away.

I know several trainers who do use electronic training collars very successfully, but sparingly on Springers. A novice trainer should proceed cautiously. If I were new to dog training, such a device would be far down on my list of needs and one of the things I planned to acquire only after I'd learned a lot about dog training and my own temperament. It is common practice today to use a collar after the dog is fully trained as a correction device when the dog willfully disobeys the handler.

Conclusion

Now that you have completed the advanced training outlined in this chapter, you can rest assured that few dogs, when taken afield, will ever perform as capably as your Springer. You have trained for, practiced for and are ready to handle almost any situation that might arise. It is now time to enjoy what you have been working so diligently to achieve—a finished, advanced gun dog. *Good hunting! Enjoy!*

8

Why Field Trials and How They Work

INDIVIDUALS in the market for a solid, consistent Springer gun dog often struggle to understand the relationship between field trials and their own hunting interests. If one carefully analyzes how any breed is developed, standardized, sustained and nurtured, one realizes that some overriding process shapes the progress of that breed over time.

In the case of Springer Spaniels, we are lucky that a very insightful group of early breeders were inspired to carefully design a simple but exacting field trial format that has endured virtually unchanged for more than sixty years. Field trial Springer breeders have certainly been the influential group shaping the field strain of this breed. Field trial enthusiasts can take most of the credit for keeping the field qualities of the Springer at its highest apex. Unfortunately, in some other breeds such as the American Cocker, the field attributes of the breed quickly disintegrated once the field trial set disappeared.

Springer Spaniel field trials, by definition, are a close replica of "a typical day in the field." Hence the dogs that excel at the field trial sport are well suited to the average hunter. However, why so many of us choose to spend our weekends in pursuit of ribbons, trophies and championship titles often to be frustrated is harder to explain. Actually, most of us find it an intriguing competitive pursuit—no more outlandish than playing golf or tennis, sailboat racing or waxing an antique car. The major appeal is that trialing extends our primary interests—bird hunting and dog work—from a four-week hunting season to an eight-month competitive season and a twelve-month training season.

A Springer field trial championship is built primarily on dog talent, but with strong dependence on training acumen, handling skill and to some extent on tenacious and diligent effort on the part of the owner. Making a champion imparts a great sense of accomplishment, considering that in an average year fewer than forty dogs from the more than 20,000 Springers registered each year reach this pinnacle of success.

In the end, it is a consuming hobby for the devoted trialers across the nation. They have developed a broad network of friendships and welcome newcomers who are willing to pursue the sport in a manner consistent with the highest levels of decorum and sportsmanship. Certainly, one of the factors that appealed to me was the high level of sportsmanship and civility at Springer trials. No yelling at the officials is tolerated in this game.

Years ago, spaniel trials were populated by wealthy, landed gentry able to pursue the sport in a very luxurious manner. Most of the dogs were trained and handled by professionals in extensive private kennels, much like the big Kentucky horse farms.

Over time, the sport has broadened. Today people from all walks of life participate. Although campaigning one or several dogs on a broad geographic basis is not an inexpensive hobby; it ranks somewhere near owning a cabin cruiser or belonging to an exclusive country club. Competitors today include doctors, lawyers, executives, dentists, veterinarians, entrepreneurs, airline pilots, retirees, men and women.

Field trialers pursue excellence in performance and biddability far in excess of any possible monetary reward. It is members of this group who journey to England in search of new talent, fly a female cross country to be bred to just the right male and train four puppies from a litter just to better evaluate the talent and temperament of a particular combination of bloodlines.

How Field Trials Work

Field trials for spaniels are competitive hunting contests, in which released game is substituted for native game in order to provide each dog with equal opportunity. The dogs are worked in braces on parallel courses, but do not cooperate with each other. The handler of each dog is accompanied by an official gunner and a judge. Birds are found, flushed, shot and retrieved in a near perfect manner. All dogs that perform creditably in the first series are called back for further testing in a second series (under a second judge); in Championship All Age stakes, the top dogs are called back for a third series, with both judges observing one dog simultaneously.

The spaniels are scored on their ability and desire to hunt and find game; nose; the quality of their hunting pattern and the way they cover the ground; the degree to which they work with the handler and their response to hand, voice or whistle commands; their ability to flush and mark the fall of shot game; their steadiness to flush and shot; and their ability to find and retrieve with a soft mouth all shot game.

The Springer Spaniel field trial format closely resembles actual hunting. The competing dogs must find and flush birds within gun range and then retrieve the downed game to hand. Every effort is made to find natural cover that normally holds game. The gallery is always allowed to follow along and watch the action. *Friend*

Here the dog has found and flushed a bird. The handler is shown on the far left, the judge is in the center and the right-hand gunner prepares to shoot. *Friend*

John Eadie of British Columbia and his multiple champion FC/AFC/CFC Kaymac's Kiltie (by Saighton's Scud) is shown with the symbols of victory for one of the most successful dogs of her generation. Kiltie accomplished the seemingly impossible feat of winning the High Point Canadian Award in 1987 at age seven, High Point U.S. Open dog in 1988 at age eight and High Point U.S. Amateur dog in 1989 at age nine. These three accomplishments and the age at which they were completed is a testament to her talent, mental stability and longevity.

FC/AFC Pondview's Windy Acres Yankee created quite an impact when he won seven trials in a single year. Yankee is owned and handled by Don Cande of New Hampshire. Mr. Cande is a former President of the ESSFTA. Yankee has been bred extensively since his victory streak, so his puppies will be showing up across America. Yankee is the offspring of two National Champions, Top Sire NFC Sunrise Zinger and NFC Wind Riding Streak. *Cande*

Proving the breeder's belief in the talent of his or her puppies is a key motivation for many field trial advocates. Note the physical resemblance of Windbourne's Classic Design (left)—1992 High Point U.S. Open dog—to his sire, FC Reward's Genuine Charter (right). Class is owned by Lea Ames of Chicago and handled by professional Ben Martin.

FC Reward's Genuine Charter is shown here in full winter coat. Note that his coat is not as long or as thick as a show Springer's coat. "Charlie" is owned by Joe and Frances Ruff of Connecticut and is proving his ability as a sire. *Ruff*

FC/CFC Canspan's Magnum D-2 (Tyler) is shown with one weekend's worth of trophies and ribbons. "Tyler" is owned by Roy and Billie Joe Hopkins of Ontario and was handled to his championships by Oklahoma professional Barney Zeigler. Americans and Canadians compete actively back and forth across the border; however, points won in Canada do not count toward American championships and vice versa.

Three very successful West Coast dogs that, in turn, became solid sires. Left to right: FC Fetchfeather's Valiant—1984 High Point Open Dog, CNFC/FC Patchwood's Trapper and FC/AFC Samson of Saighton. Valiant and Trapper are owned by Dick and Sylvia Lane of Los Angeles, California. Samson is owned by Andy Shoaf of Santa Ana Heights, California. All three dogs were handled by Dick Vermazen (Pro). *Vermazen*

The events normally scheduled during any of the AKC licensed spaniel trials in the United States are a Puppy Stake (up to two years of age), an Amateur All Age Stake (open only to amateur handlers), and an Open All Age Stake (open to professionals and amateurs alike). Both of the All Age Stakes carry championship points toward the title of either Amateur Field Champion (AFC) or Open Field Champion (FC).

Ribbons and AKC points are awarded to the dogs receiving 1st, 2nd, 3rd or 4th place in All-Age events. Puppies receive ribbons but no AKC points. Most clubs present beautiful trophies to event winners, and numerous other trophies (e.g., the Eastern high point dog trophy) are awarded for special achievements. Canada does not have an Amateur All-Age classification, only an Open All-Age.

If you are interested in seeing a field trial, contact your local club or *Spaniels in the Field* magazine for a schedule of events. Even if you have absolutely no interest in competitive field activities for Springers, you owe it to yourself to attend a trial and see the best in action. After all, it is these people who set the standards and maintain the excellence of this noble breed.

This crew of top-quality gunners was invited to gun at a recent National Championship. They are (standing left to right): Dick Vermazen (CA); Dave Lorenz, Jr. (IL); John Meyer (WI); Roger Houk (WI); (kneeling left to right): Lea Ames (IL); Dan Hale (CA); and Paul Van Houten (NJ). *Cande*

9

The National Field Championships

SHORTLY AFTER WORLD WAR II, a group of dedicated spaniel fanciers conceived and initiated a major annual competitive event, the National Championship. The first national trial was held in 1947 at Crab Orchard Lake Game Area in southern Illinois after an intense and dedicated effort on the part of several key individuals, including Charles Goodall, Henry Ferguson, Bob Becker, Robert Bishop, William Kirkland, Dr. Charles Sabin, Harry Ceasar, Conway Olmsted, Claude Jasper, James Simpson and Harry Shoot. The talent of this founding core of enthusiasts is validated by the fact that the format remains virtually unchanged to this day. Today the National is an accepted tradition, but without the work of these unsung leaders, it might never have happened.

A list of the National Open winners follows:

WINNERS OF THE NATIONAL OPEN FIELD TRIAL CHAMPIONSHIPS FOR ENGLISH SPRINGER SPANIELS

Year	*The Springer*	*The Handler*	*The Owner*
1947	Russet of Middle Field	Roy Gonia	Dr. Chas. Sabin
1948	Stoneybroke Sheer Bliss	Clifford H. Wallace	Mr. and Mrs. P. D. Armour
1949	Davellis Wager	Martin J. Hogan	David B. Silberman

A Nationals competition requires several hundred acres of prime pheasant habitat. By late fall the weather has usually turned brisk and cool, so serious field gear is appropriate. Here a fairly small gallery follows the action of a rainy series. *Friend*

Here the winners of the first-ever National Amateur Championship (1963) display their trophies and ribbons. They are (left to right): George Webster, London, Ontario, Canada, with the winner, 1st Place dog NAFC Pam's Aphrodite of Camden; Roy French, Gridley, Kansas—Judge; Larry Gillingham, Milwaukee, Wisconsin, 2nd Place dog Gypsy Joy; John Pirie, Chicago, Illinois—Judge; Mrs. Jean Hutchenson, Greenwich, Connecticut, 3rd Place dog Staindrop Hiwood Spider. *Craig*

1950	Whittlemoor George (Imported)	Steve Studnicki	Mr. and Mrs. P. D. Armour
1951	Flier's Ginger of Shady Glen	Arthur Eakin	C. M. Kline
1952	Stubbliefield Ace High	Stanley Head	W. R. Gibson
1953	Micklewood Scud (Imported)	Steve Studnicki	Mr. and Mrs. P. D. Armour
1954	Ludlovian Bruce of Greenfair (Imported)	Larry McQueen	Joseph C. Quirk
1955	Ludlovian Bruce of Greenfair (Imported)	Larry McQueen	Joseph C. Quirk
1956	Micklewood Scud (Imported)	Steve Studnicki	Mr. and Mrs. P. D. Armour
1957	Staindrop Breckonhill Chip	Elmer Chick	Rux-Roy Kennels
1958	Staindrop Breckonhill Chip	Elmer Chick	Rux-Roy Kennels
1959	Brackenbank Tangle (Imported)	Elmer Chick	E. W. Wunderlich
1960	Carswell Contessa (Imported)	Julia Armour	Mr. and Mrs. P. D. Armour
1961	Armforth's Micklewood Dan	Steve Studnicki	Mr. and Mrs. P. D. Armour
1962	Kansan	Lem Scales	Roy E. French
1963	Waveway's Wilderness Maeve	Clarence Wingate	Mr. and Mrs. William Lane
1964	Gwibernaut Ganol (Imported)	David Lorenz	John T. Pirie, Jr.
1965	Gwibernaut Ganol (Imported)	David Lorenz	John T. Pirie, Jr.
1966	Wivenwood Willie (Imported)	Larry McQueen	Dean Bedford
1967	Brackenbriar Snapshot	David Lorenz	Brackenbriar Kennels
1968	Tillan Ticket	Elmer Chick	Charles Mee
1969	Dansmirth's Gunshot	Daniel K. Langhans	Daniel K. Langhans
1970	Saighton's Sizzler (Imported)	Clifford H. Wallace	John M. Olin
1971	Saighton's Sizzler (Imported)	Clifford H. Wallace	John M. Olin
1972	Dot of Charel	David Lorenz	Charles T. Curdy

1973	Dewfield Brickclose Flint (Imported)	Dr. C. A. Christensen	Dr. C. A. Christensen
1974	Saighton's Ty Gwyn Slicker (Imported)	John W. Buoy	John W. Buoy
1975	Dewfield Brickclose Flint (Imported)	Dr. C. A. Christensen	Dr. C. A. Christensen
1976	Saighton's Ty Gwyn Slicker (Imported)	John W. Buoy	John W. Buoy
1977	Joysam's Solo Sam	Walter Retzlaff	Walter Retzlaff
1978	J-J Chelese Sara J	John Hiller	John Hiller
1979	Burcliff's Brandi	Dean Brunn	Dean Brunn
1980	Saighton's Scud (Imported)	Janet Christensen	Dr. and Mrs. C. A. Christensen
1981	Far Ridge Request	Dean Brunn	Carl R. Smith
1982	Wind Riding Streak	Dr. Mark Schinderle	Dr. Mark Schinderle
1983	Saighton's Scout II (Imported)	Jess Sekey	Jess Sekey
1984	Wind Riding Streak	Dr. Mark Schinderle	Dr. Mark Schinderle
1985	Sunrise Zinger	Daniel Langhans	Gordon Madsen
1986	Pine Island Patches	Jim DeVoll	Dr. George Cherewan
1987	Pondview's Left in the Light	Ray Cacchio	L and R Cacchio
1988	Denalisunflo's Bandita	Ralph Palmer	R. E. French and Ralph Palmer
1989	Windbourne's Militant	Ben Martin	John M. Spengler
1990	Morgan's Agatha Brodrick	Brenda Falkowski	Brenda Falkowski
1991	Ru-Char's Country Boy	Ray Cacchio	Ken Nesky
1992	Denalisunflo's Ring	David Maike	Roy French

The annual National Championship spawned a level of competition, interest and intensity that resulted in several competitors' decision to import the highest quality English dogs available for this event. The above list of winners shows that many were successful here. This importation of top-quality dogs has, in retrospect, been very good for the breed since it broadened the gene pool and provided more top bloodlines in North America.

National Championships are also noted for demanding a high level of consistent performance and mental stability in a winning dog. Because a National takes place over several days and includes five land series and two water series,

Safe, reliable, consistent gunning is a key to the success of a National Championship. Only the best, proven shooters are invited to shoot for a National. This "gun crew" for the 1992 National Open Championship wears winter gear at the cold Pittsburgh, Pennsylvania, site. Top row (left to right): John Isaacs (Gun Captain, Ohio), Pat Fisher (Wisconsin), Dan Hale (California), Paul Van Houten (New Jersey), Al Osborne (Ohio), Rick O'Brien (Ohio), Don Alexander (Michigan). Front row (left to right): Ed Faraci, Jr. (Connecticut), Bob Sanchez (California), Marshall Lussen (Connecticut). Only two-barreled guns, over and unders or side by sides, are legal here—for safety reasons.

NAFC BJ's Copper Penny was handled to a National Amateur Championship by Marshall "Jim" Lightfoot. Jim and his wife, Beverly, labor long and hard in many capacities on behalf of the English Springer.

the winning dog must be able to handle the intensity of excitement and still keep its head.

The National Amateur Championship

In 1954 a second major event open only to amateurs was initiated that was ultimately to have an equally stimulating effect on the breed. From 1954 to 1962, the National Amateur Shooting Dog Stake was held and was largely the brainchild and work effort of James R. Dodson. However, after eight successful years, the level of interest and participation was so high that the concept was totally revised to become the National Amateur Championship in a format very similar to the National Open Championship, except that *only amateur handlers* would be eligible. The first National Amateur championship was an immediate success and was supported by amateurs from all sections of the United States.

In 1967, Mrs. Janet Christensen of Portland, Oregon, became the first handler to place in both the Open and Amateur Nationals in the same year. Daniel K. Langhans's sensational winning of both the Open and the Amateur Nationals in 1969 established the fact that the level of competition in the National Amateur was on a par with the National Open. Since that time, many dogs and amateur handlers have placed in both championships and many amateur handlers have won a National Open handling their own dogs.

WINNERS OF THE NATIONAL AMATEUR FIELD TRIAL CHAMPIONSHIPS FOR ENGLISH SPRINGER SPANIELS

Year	*The Springer*	*The Owner/Handler*
1963	Pam's Aphrodite of Camden	George Webster
1964	Denalisunflo Sam	George Webster
1965	Saighton's Swank (Imported)	Jack Redman
1966	Juliet Eb-Gar	Curtis Killiane
1967	Gwibernant Gefni (Imported)	Dr. Jack Riepenhoff
1968	Gwibernant Gefni (Imported)	Dr. Jack Riepenhoff
1969	Dansmirth's Gunshot	Daniel K. Langhans
1970	Misty Muffet	Janet Christensen
1971	Saighton's Signal (Imported)	Dr. C. A. Christensen
1972	Burtree Maverick	John Buoy
1973	Sunray of Chrishall (Imported)	Dr. Warren A. Wunderlich
1974	Sunray of Chrishall (Imported)	Dr. Warren A. Wunderlich
1975	Joysam's Solo Sam	Walter Retzlaff
1976	Coginchaug Shine	John J. Mangine
1977	Sheila of Sherwood	Denny Crick
1978	Cathy's Kris of Burnsget	Albert D. Beedie, Jr.
1979	Saighton's Scud (Imported)	Janet Christensen
1980	Saighton's Scud (Imported)	Janet Christensen
1981	Far Ridge Revere	Wayne Kilpatrick
1982	Sherwood's Best Chance	Denny Crick

A. Ewen MacMillan, veteran trialer from Vancouver, British Columbia, is shown with his 1988 Canadian National Champion CNFC/FC Sherwood's Ace in the Hole. Mr. MacMillan's dogs have had great success in the past decade and have garnered numerous championships and two Canadian National Championships.

Two-time National Open Champion Wind Riding Streak, owned by Drs. Mark and Aileen Schinderle. Streak produced several fine litters including one by NFC Sunrise Zinger that yielded FC/AFC Pondview's Windy Acres Yankee.

1983	Saighton's Scout II (Imported)	Jess Sekey
1984	Conklin's Bandit	Doc Conklin
1985	Marshfield's Tucker	Les Girling
1986	Kwi Wy Chas Jodi	G and L Leach (O)/G. Goodman (H)
1987	Windy Acres Luck Penny	Dr. Mark Schinderle
1988	Glenrock Raeven	Jamie Armour
1989	Orion's Arch Rival	Gene Falkowski
1990	B. J.'s Copper Penny	Jim Lightfoot
1991	Wild Irish Kelly	John Hall
1992	Major's Black Magic	Russ Verkamp

The Canadian National Championship

In 1960, George Webster and Ted Haggis were leaders in organizing the first Canadian National field trial, which was held each year until 1964. Then, because of organizational difficulties, the trial was canceled until 1972, when under the leadership of Jim Abbey, Les Girling and others the Canadian National Trial was revived and has been held successfully ever since. Today, with easy air travel to even the farthest reaches of the Provinces, the Canadian National always draws a large and excellent entry from across Canada and the USA.

WINNERS OF THE CANADIAN NATIONAL FIELD CHAMPIONSHIP

Year	*The Springer*	*The Owner/Handler*
1960	Apache Magic Clipper	Julian Collins
1961	Trent Valley Andrea of Athlorne	Thomas Atherton
1962	Apache Clipper's Gay Lady	Julian Collins
1963	Apache Clipper's Brown Ghost	Julian Collins
1964	Rogue O'Rock Acre	William Watt
1972	Cactus Of Camden	Millard Tewell
1973	Marshfield Tagger	Les Girling
1974	Tara VI	Frank O'Grady
1975	Joysam's Solo Sam	Walter Retzlaff
1976	Tara VI	Frank O'Grady
1977	Marshfield's Gary	Jack Williams
1978	Schlitz Real Gusto	Craig G. Endsley
1979	Chevrier's Scarlet Quince	Bob Palmer
1980	Saighton's Scud	Janet Christensen
1981	Far Ridge Request	Carl Smith (O)/Dean Brunn (H)
1982	Sherwood's Best Chance	Denny Crick
1983	Canvasback Mike	Doug Day
1984	Whisper Pine's Starter	Brian Mooney
1985	Patchwood's Trapper	Dick Lane (O)/Dick Vermazen (H)
1986	Royal's Best Maggie	Fred St. Clair (O)/Ben Martin (H)
1987	Whitlock's Warrior	Terry Pellow
1988	Sherwood's Ace-in-the-Hole	A. Ewen MacMillan
1989	Winnimac's Widgeon	Chas. Anderson (O)/Dan Langhans (H)

Janet Christensen of Oregon and Talbott Radcliffe of the famous Saightons Kennels in Wales both hold the Breeders' Trophy, now presented annually to the breeder of the National Open Champion. The trophy itself was donated to the ESSFTA at the 1983 National Championship in Washington state. The Saighton Breeders' Trophy is now a most prestigious award. Mr. Radcliffe is a legend in the breed and Saighton dogs can be found around the world and in a significant percentage of field-bred American Springer pedigrees. Also shown in the photo (left) Jim Collins, well-known East Coast gunner and (right) Beverly Lightfoot, long-term secretary of the National Open Championship.

Jamie Armour, Esq., journeyed from his home in Nova Scotia, Canada, to California with NAFC/FC/AFC/CFC Glenrock Raeven to win the 1988 National Amateur Championship. Mr. Armour is an avid trialer and also an accomplished falconer. In the off-season he uses his Springers to flush game for the falcons in the ancient style.

1990	Windmillwood Storm	A. Ewen MacMillan (O)/Terry Pellow (H)
1991	Northern Thunder's Rupert	Roger Doliff (O)/Dan Langhans (H)
1992	Pel-Tan Roly	Jeff Miller

The British National Championship

The Kennel Club (England) holds its Championship Field Trial each January for spaniels of any variety except Cocker Spaniels. This trial is emblematic of the British National Championship. To qualify, spaniels must place first in a trial held durig the current shooting season.

WINNERS OF THE BRITISH NATIONAL FIELD CHAMPIONSHIP

Year	*The Springer*	*The Owner/Handler*
1914	Champion Denne Duke	C. Eversfield
1915 to 1921—*No trials were held because of World War I*		
1922	FC Flush of Avendale	The Duke of Hamilton
1923	FC Dan of Avendale	The Duke of Hamilton
1924	FC Firecall	Dr. Wilson
1925	FC Reece of Avendale	The Duke of Hamilton
1926	FC Banchory Bright	Mrs. Quintin Dick
1927	FC Banchory Bright	Mrs. Quintin Dick
1928	FC Rivington Rollo	C. A. Phillips
1929	FC Nithsdale Rover	Col. C. Brooks
1930	FC Peter O'Vara	Selwyn Jones
1931	FC Banchory Boy	Lorna Countess Howe
1932	FC Bee of Blair	G. Clark
1933	FC Maida of Barncleuch	Lorna Countess Howe
1934	FC Dalshangan Maida	H.H. The Maharaja of Patiala
1935	FC Spy O'Vara	Selwyn Jones
1936	FC Beeson of Blair	G. Clark
1937	FC Style O'Vara	Selwyn Jones
1938	FC Sally O'Vara	Selwyn Jones
1939	FC Bobble	Cadet Calvert
1940 to 1947—*No trials were held because of World War II*		
1948	Breckonhill Bee	G. Curle
1949	Rivington Glensaugh Glean	E. and M. Ainsworth
1950	FC Spurt O'Vara	Selwyn Jones
1951	Criffel Daisy Belle	T. B. Laird
1952	FC Ludlovian Darkie	W. G. Sheldon
1953	FC Acheron Pat	R. N. Burton
1954	FC Scramble O'Vara	Selwyn Jones
1955	FC Scramble O'Vara	Selwyn Jones
1956	FC Gwen of Barnacres	H. Jackson
1957	FC Griffle Snip	T. B. Laird
1958	FC Willie of Barnacres	H. Jackson
1959	FC Micklewood Slip	Capt. R. W. Corbett
1960	FC Harpersbrook Reed	F. George
1961	FC Markdown Muffin	F. Thomas
1962	FC Ruffin Tuff	J. M. Kelvey
1963	FC Berrystead Freckle	Charles Williams

1964	FC Saighton's Stinger	Talbot Radcliffe
1965	FC Meadowcourt Della	Ronald Weston-Webb
1966	FC Hamer's Hansel	B. Dalton
1967	*No trial held*	
1968	FC Joss of Barnacres	H. Jackson
1969	FC Layerbrook Michelle	Mike Scales
1970	FC Layerbrook Michelle	Mike Scales
1971	FC Coppicewood Carla	C. Lawton-Evans and Capt. C. Owens
1972	FC Robbie of Barnacre	Selwyn Jones
1973	FC Harwes Silver	D. Bovill
1974	FC Crowhill Raffle	P. Stewart
1975	FC Nell of Bellever	R. J. Hill
1976	FC Sport of Palgrave	D. F. Cock
1977	FC Kimble Kim	R. A. Longville
1978	FC Ashley Buster	C. R. Burgoyne
1979	FC Judy of Runwell	B. J. De'Ath
1980	FC Macsiccar Mint	R. S. Knight
1981	FC Inler Harryslin	J. Orr
1982	FC Sandvig Triumph	I. Bateson
1983	FC Parkmaple Jolly	Mrs. M. Gosling
1984	FC Dandelion of Gwibernant	Miss J. Carter
1985	FC Cortman Garry	R. L. M. Black
1986	FC Cortman Lane	A. M. Erlandson
1987	FC Drury Girl	J. D. Pope
1988	FC Simonseat Slip	M. Rock
1989	FC Penny of Housty	M. J. Shefford
1990	FC Tops of Castlings	S. E. H. Block
1991	FC Rytex Racine	D. J. A. Openshaw
1992	FC Tanya's Bass Special	N. Blake

The Modern Nationals

Today the National Championships have become a significant annual event where field trialers from across the United States and Canada converge to compete and then see a new National Champion crowned. Not only are the Nationals the major annual competition, but they are also a major social and business event. Socially, it is a chance for trialers from across the nation to renew old friendships, swap stories and see great dog work. From a business standpoint, several key meetings of the ESSFTA are held during this event.

By the time the dates of the US Nationals roll around (it is traditionally held starting the weekend after Thanksgiving), the dogs are in peak condition from a fall season of hunting and field trial competition, hard frosts have left the cover in superb condition, scenting is usually excellent and the crisp temperatures invigorate the dogs and the trialers. The smell of the Nationals is in the air. The locations change every year and vary from as far east as New York or Nova Scotia to as far west as California or Alberta.

Once you have become involved in field-bred Springers and the excitement of Springer gun dogs, you should plan to attend a local trial and then a National Championship. It is an exciting way to broaden your knowledge of the sport and see the best display their talent.

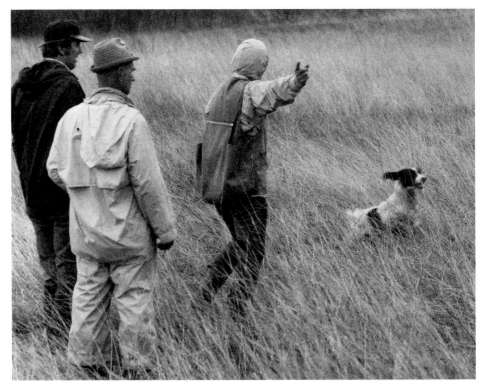

Field trials, like horse races and football games, "go on" rain or shine. Here, two well-known veteran judges, Larry Frankovich of Pennsylvania and Mel Wolfe of Ontario, observe as Marilyn Watkins of Ohio directs Turtle Creek Tac in the third series of an Open All-Age trial. Spaniels relish inclement weather and hunt with no noticeable change in style or enthusiasm. Quality rain gear is a must for avid field trialers. *Friend*

Art Rodger, editor/publisher of *Spaniels in the Field* magazine is shown with AFC South Chase Steele. Art has done a masterful job of developing this magazine into one of the best specialized publications in the dog world. The magazine focuses on field-bred Springers in trials, hunt tests and hunting but also covers all spaniel breeds and all field activities for them.

10

The People, the Clubs, the Kennels and the British Connection

---

The Springer People

The English Springer Spaniel owes its success not only to the great dogs but to the many people who own, breed and protect it. Much credit also accrues to the many people who enthusiastically and tirelessly labor on organizational matters, serving on the ESSFTA Board or Committees or managing a National Championship or holding a local field trial. This chapter acknowledges those people who formerly and currently put their influence on this sport. Through their hard work, the field-bred English Springer Spaniel has become the finest all-around gun dog in North America.

I compile the following list with great concern and extreme trepidation. There certainly is not space to list everyone; and regardless of how carefully I pore over my name lists, I am bound inadvertently to omit some loyal, dedicated and active enthusiast who has contributed mightily to the breed and the sport. This list is based mainly upon current, active participation in local, regional and national competitive events as well as involvement in club activities, hard work on committees or major events and years of continued involvement.

To anyone I've missed, please accept my apologies.

Historically Significant Contributors to the Breed

ESTABLISHED FIRST TRIALS UNITED STATES:

Walton Ferguson, Jr., Samuel Allen, Reg Halladay, William Sinclair, William Hutchison, Henry Ferguson and Alfred Ferguson

PAST PRESIDENTS OF THE PARENT CLUB (ENGLISH SPRINGER SPANIEL FIELD TRIAL ASSOCIATION):

Samuel Allen, Walter Ferguson, Jr., William J. Hutchinson, David Wagstaff, Henry L. Ferguson, Robert McLean (10 years), Charles Greening (6 years), Ed Whitaker (8 years), Joe Angelovic, Don Cande, George Cacchio, David Hopkins

KEY WRITERS:

Charles Goodall, Evelyn Monte, Ken Roebuck, David Duffey, Larry Mueller

PUBLICATIONS:

Spaniels in the Field *(formerly* On the Line *magazine): Ron Baldwin, Founder; Vance Van Laanen, former Publisher; Roger Houk, former Editor; Art Rodger, current Publisher/Editor.* Springer Bark *(now defunct): Evelyn Bui.*

The "Interclub" Structure

All field trial competition is scheduled and monitored through a series of five regional groupings called "interclubs." The following is a list, by interclub and by state, of well-known and currently active participants. This list will help the newcomer find the folks who are currently involved in field-bred English Springer Spaniels in their area of the country.

Eastern Interclub

Maine: *Dennis Quinn, Peter Dalfonso, Don Chisholm, Robb and Kelly Cotiaux*—Portland area

New Hampshire: *Don Cande*

Vermont: *Casey Sajdak*

Massachusetts: *Bob King, Kathy Goddu, Ron Belanger*—Boston

Connecticut: *Bernie Castellani, Ed and Esther Faraci, Joe and Francis Ruff, Forsythe Kineon, Dan Lussen, John and Francis Mangine*

Drs. Mark and Aileen Schinderle of Norway, Michigan, are shown with their fine bitches FC/AFC/CFC Windy Acres Zip Dang and her mother NAFC/FC/AFC Windy Acres Lucky Penny. The Schinderles have been very successful in the trialing sport, completing championships on four dogs and winning three National Championships with two.

Russ Smith, widely traveled Ohio field trialer, is shown with his very successful string of five field trial dogs. In 1992 Russ was able to place all five dogs and won several trials. In addition, two of the dogs earned ribbons in the National Championships. To top it off, Russ entered several of the dogs in state-wide Pheasant Championships and won every event he entered.

New York: *John Lamendola, Robert Ryan*—NY metropolitan area; *George (Bobby) Cacchio, Ray (Jerry) Cacchio (Pro), Karen Stone*—Dutchess County; *Gary Wilson (Pro), Roger Schenone*—Elmira area; *John Spengler, Dick Maturski, Harry Merrill*—Buffalo area

New Jersey: *Ruth Greening, Paul and Gloria Van Houten, Ralph Botti, Glenn Ferrara, Frank MacKinson, John Whitaker, J. C. Shannon, Paul Harris*

Pennsylvania: *Ed Whitaker, Bob Daum (Pro), Ed Berger, Bob Delaney, Mary Taylor*—Philadelphia area; *Tom Aungst, Larry Frankovich, Mike Wintersteen*—Danville area; *Val and Ruth Walsh*—Pittsburgh area

Mideast Interclub

Virginia: *Mike Wallace (Pro), Steve MacNaughton, Julie Hogan*—Washington, D.C., area

Ohio: *Russ Smith, Dr. John Riepenhoff, Rick O'Brien, John Isaacs (Pro), B. B. and Evelyn Flick, Fred St. Clair, John Friend, Al Osborne, Carol Cramer, Ken Willis*—Columbus area; *Bill Zipp (Pro), Al Hric, Ralph Williamson, Rudy Linhart, Mr. and Mrs. Tom Vail, Phil Baird*—Cleveland area; *Art Rodger, Ben and Rita Martin (Pro), Russ Verkamp, Mike and Diane Elsasser, Marilyn Watkins, Bill Cosgrove, Mark Brookshire, Paul Rupert, Melanie Titanic*—Cincinnati area

Indiana: *Dean Brunn (Pro), Ed Finn*

Michigan: *George and Delores Wilson, John and Jessie Blanock, John Dallas, Garry Findley*—Detroit area; *Al Ringenberg, Don Alexander*—Out State; *Mark and Aileen Schinderle, Bob Sansom, Carl and Lori Stein*—Upper Peninsula

Midwest Interclub

Illinois: *David Hopkins, Jim and Beverly Lightfoot, Al Beedie, Carl Smith (Pro), Brud and Kaye Prock, Bob Mueller, John and Phyllis Buoy, Dan and Marie Langhans (Pro), Dave Lorenz (Pro), Dave Lorenz, Jr. (Pro), Lea Ames, Bonnie Beedie, Nancy and Ron Smith, Bob Gasper, Bob Shambaugh, Doug Miller, Fred Smalarz, Norb Jamnik, Al Scharlow, Tom Brisbin, Bronwyn Vernau, David Bailey, John Hall, Bob Krause*—Chicago area

Wisconsin: *Bob and Gerry Sommer, Dean Reinke, Don Brunn Jr., Roger Houk, Jim and Kim Naber, Steve Sebestyen, Rich and Cookie Csanda, Pat Hempel, Karen Hopper (Pro), Ron Baldwin*—Milwaukee area; *Pat and Janet Fischer, Fred and Sue Neville, Ralph Sheldon*—Green Bay area

On the West Coast, Dick Lane (left) has been a stalwart of the sport since 1955. He has owned a series of very successful dogs, including Canadian National Champion CNFC/FC Patchwood's Trapper, and has been instrumental in trial activity in the Los Angeles area. With Mr. Lane is his wife, Sylvia, and the late Paul Ruddick, who, for many years, was a well-known West Coast professional trainer and handler.

Illinois trialers John Buoy (left) and Dr. Brud Prock (center) and Wisconsin veteran Bob Sommer (right) were in the gallery enjoying the 5th and final series of a National Amateur Championship.
Roggenkamp

Dean Reinke had outstanding success during the 1991 season when his FC/AFC Raintree's Sassy Lady earned more combined points in Open and Amateur competition than any other Springer in the United States in that year.

Minnesota: *Kevin Martineau (Pro), Mike McGinty, Tom Meyer, Kermit Gillund, Dr. Elmer Kasperson, Peter Anderson, Craig Chilstrom, Bill Boeckman, Terry Sworsky, Jack Carlson*—Minneapolis/St. Paul area; *Harry Henriques*

Rocky Mountain Interclub

Nebraska: *Jim DeVoll (Pro), Jim DeVoll, Jr. (Pro), Ralph Palmer*—Omaha area

Kansas: *Roy French, Gene Falkowski, Brenda Falkowski, Chad Betts, Don Bramwell, Randy Curtis (Pro), David Maike (Pro)*

Oklahoma: *Barney Zeigler*

Texas: *Mark Hairfield (Pro), Steve Kane, George Keiller, Bill Winney, Donna Meyers, David Jones (Pro)*—Houston area

Colorado: *Robert Fink, Tim DeGroff, Cindy Goode, John Phillips, Dwight Such, Mark Tholen*

Far West Interclub

Washington: *Jeff Miller (DVM), Al DeFalco (MD), Lyn Madigan, Dominique Savoie*—Seattle area; *John Prideaux*—Spokane area

Oregon: *Janet (DVM) and Chris (MD) Christensen, Bob Bullard (DVM), David Miller*—Portland area

California: *Dick Vermazen (Pro), Danny Hale, Orville Oie, Gordon Breitbarth*—Sacramento area; *Wayne Kilpatrick, Doc Conklin, Archie Whiting*—San Francisco area; *Dick and Sylvia Lane, Dave Anderson, Willie and Sue Howell, Mike Knudson, Oliver Woods, Ron Carlson (Pro), Bob Stockmar, Andy Shoaf, Bob Sanchez, Gene and Rosemary McKusky, Nick Campanelli, Eva Hanks, Art Perle*—Los Angeles area

Utah: *Danny West, Gary Riddle, Terry Pippin*

Nevada: *Jerry and Cheryl Sligar, Steve Abbate, Alfie Knudson*—Las Vegas area

Idaho: *Ed Feller, Jerry Livingston*

Canada

Maritimes: *Dr. David McCurdy, Jamie Armour, George Hickox (Pro), Gil White, Don Warner, Jim Warner*

Ontario: *Chris and Ernie Barriage, Jack Williams, Roy and Billie Joe (Pro) Hopkins, Mel and Millie Wolfe, Tony Paravaro, Wray*

Cincinnati area trialers (left to right) Russ Verkamp, Mike Elsasser and Bill Cosgrove. These three have achieved great success in the sport including Nationals wins and placements and a national high point amateur dog. They have consistently fielded very competitive dogs through the years and through several dog generations. *Roggenkamp*

Veteran Pittsburgh area trialer Val Walsh (left), successful newcomer Ken Willis (center) of the Columbus, Ohio, area and Dr. John Riepenhoff (right), also of Columbus, are shown at the 1993 Euclid Club spring trial. Mr. Walsh and Dr. Riepenhoff are experienced trialers with many years of success and many victories. Mr. Willis has several very fine young dogs and has achieved some immediate success in the field trial sport.

	Upper, Frank and Bonnie O'Grady, Alex Smith, Laverne Forwell, Drew Goldsmith, Wes Nesbitt, Norm Mongahan
Western Provinces:	*Terry Pellow, Les Girling, Alex Stewart, Jack Porter, Blaine Mooney, Henry Ens, Wally Stewart, Bob Palmer, Dan McIntosh (Pro), Mark Knibbs (Pro), Dan Porter*
British Columbia:	*John Eadie, A. Ewen McMillan*

Kennel Names

Anyone who begins to study pedigrees, magazine articles or field trial catalogs will begin to recognize certain common first names on numerous dogs. These are Kennel Names. The AKC has a formal kennel name procedure, which stipulates a substantial fee for registration of a name, but most spaniel kennel names are not registered. However, it is considered very poor form to use a known and respected kennel name without permission. The purchaser of a puppy should be sure to discuss the use of the kennel name with the breeder.

A high percentage of all competing spaniels have the kennel name as a part of their formal AKC registered name. Unlike race horses where every horse has a unique (and often humorous) name, in the spaniel world most have a kennel identifier. That is not to say that some owners don't choose brief or whimsical names—three very competitive dogs are named Buck, The Iceman and Willie the Tasmanian Devil. But generally, it is names like Ru-Char's Country Boy, Windbourne's Militant, Denalisunflo's Bandita or Sunrise Zinger that win the Nationals; and it is by the kennel name that experienced breeders know the exact source of the dog.

From east to west, some of the most well-known kennel names are:

East	*Brackenbriar, Butterfield, Mountain View, Pondview, Ru-Char, Salmy, Sunrise, Windbourne*
Mideast/Midwest	*Bluff Creek, Chaloruva, Dal-B, Dansmirth, Denalisunflo, Findaway, Guadiara, High Plains, Kane, Majors, Melchris, Midlands, Northern Thunder, Orion, Raintree, Rewards, Royal, Sanquest, Shoreline, South Chase, Southaven, Strong, Tridon, Turtlecreek, Westphal, White Oak, Windy Acres*
Rocky Mountain/Far West	*Arrow Point, Bishop Creek, Black River, Burcliff, Fetchfeather, Greenbriar, Kwi-Wy-Chas, O.W., Sherwood, Patchwood*
Canada	*Bimidan, Breezy Points, Canspan, Glen Rock, Grouse Wing, Springville*

There are many, many great dogs in America that do not bear any of these kennel names, but usually, somewhere back in the pedigree, one or more of these familiar logos will be present.

In 1979 FC Findaway's Luck of Burnseget, "Lucky," owned by Tom and Iris Vail of Ohio, earned the National High Point Open Dog Award. In 1982 FC Findaway's Bon Chance, a daughter of Lucky, won the High Point Open Dog Award. Bloodlines often breed true! Lucky is shown here with his trainer/handler Dave Lorenz (Pro) of Illinois.

In the last twenty years, perhaps no spaniel trainer/breeder from the United Kingdom has been more visible and outspoken than Keith Erlandson of Gwibernant Kennels in Wales. Mr. Erlandson is able to back up his strong opinions with success in the field trial and breeding arena and was the breeder of Hales Smut, arguably the most important sire of the last thirty years. Erlandson once explained that the main difference between the speed and pattern of English dogs (when running over there versus running here) is due to the extremely heavy, dense cover in England. This would preclude shooting opportunities if the dog were to run as big in England as here. Erlandson is shown on his property in Wales with EFC Cortman Lane. *Rodger*

Spaniel Field Trial Clubs

Many spaniel owners will find membership in an AKC field trial club to be a very helpful and rewarding experience. Every club I have belonged to included both active field trialers and active hunters. This membership allows each to profit from the experience and efforts of the other. Since spaniel field trial training is simply a very precise version of gun dog training, the hunter is able to work with, train with and share ideas with the field trial trainer. The spaniel world is unique in that the field trial format is so realistic and applicable to hunting; therefore, many of the clubs exist as much for the hunter as for the field trialer.

Most clubs hold regular training sessions where new owners are welcome. Hunters are frequent participants in the AKC *sanctioned* trials. Sanctioned trials are less formal and less rigid than AKC *licensed* trials and often include a gun dog stake. Clubs also hold the AKC hunting tests, which most hunters will find to be a very exciting off-season pursuit.

Currently there are more than sixty active clubs in the USA holding trials or hunt tests in twenty-four states. In addition, there are fourteen active clubs in Canada. In the United States, clubs are active in Maine, New Hampshire, Connecticut, New York, New Jersey, Pennsylvania, Virginia, Ohio, Michigan, Illinois, Wisconsin, Minnesota, Iowa, Nebraska, Kansas, Oklahoma, Texas, Colorado, Utah, Nevada, California, Oregon and Washington.

In Canada active clubs exist in Nova Scotia, Prince Edward Island, Quebec, Ontario, Manitoba, Saskatchewan, Alberta and British Columbia.

For a complete list of clubs, addresses and activities write to *Spaniels in the Field* magazine, 10714 Escondido Drive, Cincinnati, Ohio 45249, or call (515) 489–2727. This publication is the bible of the sport and is very valuable to any spaniel activist.

Today's British Connection

Although the original bloodstock for the American strain of the English Springer Spaniel has been in this country for more than ninety years and has been recognized as a breed by the AKC since 1910, there is still a consistent yearly flow of English stock to America. Several of the top performing dogs in the United States every year are English imports. Unfortunately, this is a one-way flow of dogs since very restrictive British import laws, designed to shelter that island nation from rabies contamination, virtually preclude the shipment of American dogs back to England. At a recent National Open Championship, seventeen of the eighty-seven entries had been imported from England—some as puppies, others as yearlings and a few as finished English field champions.

A dog registered in England will show the designation UK in its pedigree, a sure sign that it is an import. By far the most familiar English kennel names to be seen in the United States today are: Saighton, Bricksclose, Windmillwood, Badgercourt, Housty, Cortman, Gwibernant, Gorsty and Rytex.

It is a well-known fact that American field trialers tend to favor a different style of dog than the ideal estate-type dog used in England. We Americans want our dogs to run bigger, wider and faster. Also, the English format is based on absolute, instant control—always close to the handler and thoroughly covering the ground. To them control is critical. We Americans also have a very high regard for control, but it is not the definitive factor here that it is in England. We also focus to a great degree on the *bold flush*, the spectacular jump-into-the-air driving flush that you will see in most American trials. The British say we "hot-up" our dogs, fire their enthusiasm and boldness, whereas the British style tends to subject the dogs to rigorous discipline and control. British cover tends to be heavier than American cover, making control their key factor. That is not to say the dogs we favor are out of control, just less rigidly controlled and less mechanical than the British. In fact, most people attending their first United States field trial are in awe of the control and solid discipline of the dogs.

Which is better, a dog with mostly American parentage or a recent British import? Most knowledgeable people feel there is little difference between the two; in fact, the bloodlines are so intermingled in most pedigrees as to be indistinguishable. There is no single physical type among the imported dogs. Not even the most experienced eye can see whether this dog is American and that dog is English.

The importation of dogs from England will most likely continue as long as the quality of dogs available meets the needs of American enthusiasts. The British do seem to be willing to sell high-quality, mature prospects, whereas really competitive and winning American dogs rarely change hands during their prime competitive years.

A major factor in a passing score for either an AKC Hunting Test or a UKC Retriever Test is staying under control. Here a Springer flushes a hen pheasant well within gun range. At the AKC Senior Hunter level, the dog must restrict its chase on missed birds. At the AKC Master Hunter level, the dog must be completely steady to wing and shot as is this dog. *Craig*

Water retrieving is a key objective in the AKC Hunting Tests and the focal point of the UKC retrieving tests. In the higher levels, the dog must be completely line steady, i.e., must remain at the handler's side until sent into the water to retrieve. *Lightfoot*

11

Other Hunting Events and Tests

HUNTING AND FIELD TRIALS are not the only way to enjoy your Springer. Two very interesting, noncompetitive but challenging testing programs exist that can extend your hobby several months of the year and validate your belief in the attributes of your dog.

AKC Hunting Test

A few years ago, the American Kennel Club recognized the growing interest in recreational-hunting test programs. Nationwide, the levels of participation in local hunting contests and retriever tests proved that a broad base of enthusiasm was just waiting to be cultivated. Hence the AKC developed the Hunting Test format.

To be sure, this testing idea was not met with universal enthusiasm in the field trial community. Some veteran field people believed that the ultimate hunting tests already existed in the form of licensed field trials and that a hunting test program would only serve to weaken a very strong and successful field trial format. However, these same people also recognized that field trialing is a very expensive and time-consuming sport that excludes many people because of the rigors of participation. Gradually, veteran field people have worked with the AKC to develop a testing format that fairly and rigorously tests spaniels and makes a hunting title something to be proud to earn, especially at the higher levels.

The tests are designed to fully evaluate the skills the dog demonstrates in a variety of hunting situations—and these are tests, not competition. In fact, at the end of the test there are no winners, just pass or fail scores. The lack of competition was a carefully considered part of the test concept.

Dogs are tested on three levels:

Junior Hunter is a very basic test for beginner-level dogs;

Senior Hunter requires a higher level of ability and training, and a dog that passes should be a solid hunting dog;

Master Hunter is a very rigorous test of ability. A considerable amount of training and experience is necessary to reach this level of competence. Even proven field trial dogs are challenged to complete some of the most difficult parts of this test. A dog that passes this test should be a top-notch hunting companion in almost any situation. (See Chapter 4 for more details.)

Incidentally, the same test format is used for all AKC spaniel breeds except the Irish Water Spaniel, which competes as an AKC retriever. If you decide to try your hand, you may see Cockers or Clumbers or Welsh Springer Spaniels trying the same test the same day. Before you enter competition, you should contact the AKC for a current rule book and test format.

Again, the American Kennel Club or *Spaniels in the Field* magazine is the source for the competitive calendar of events. For more information, contact the American Kennel Club, 51 Madison Avenue, New York, New York 10010.

UKC Retriever Trials

Some spaniel owners are beginning to broaden their scope of competition by testing their little Springers against the big Labrador and Golden retrievers in retriever tests.

These events are sponsored by the United Kennel Club and are open to English Springer Spaniels. In the highest levels of competition, the dogs must also be registered with the UKC. The main focus of this competition is on retrieving in a variety of water and land situations. Although the competition is relatively new, the few Springers in evidence are faring quite well. What Springers lack in size, they certainly make up in desire, intensity and natural ability. Two of the first handlers to enter their dogs in this format were Stanley Latreille and Dave Bowman, both of Michigan. The results were very positive, and Bowman's dog Justamac Riley achieved a "Started Hunting Retriever" title from the UKC in short order.

For further information, contact the United Kennel Club, 100 East Kilgore Road, Kalamazoo, Michigan 49001-5598, telephone (616) 343-9020.

12

Hunting with Your Springer

A SPRINGER SPANIEL, from my viewpoint, is the most versatile, flexible and broadly useful bird dog available in the world. He can, and should, be the ultimate all-around hunting dog. Some people might argue that retriever breeds or continental pointer breeds can also function extremely well in a variety of situations. But I have never seen one of those breeds actually perform with the broad base of skills that is consistently available in a Springer—at half the size.

One of the reasons for my Springer enthusiasm is that it allows a hunter to own and train one dog that can handle almost any game bird in any area of the country. Over the years I have hunted pheasant in Iowa, the Dakotas and Michigan; grouse and woodcock in Minnesota, Michigan, Indiana, New York and New Jersey; valley quail and pheasant in California; bobwhite quail in Indiana and Iowa; ducks and geese in Michigan, Iowa, New York and New Jersey; doves in Indiana and California; plus numerous preserve hunts in several states. I did all of this with one typical little liver-and-white Springer.

How you control and modify the action of your Springer for each quarry varies, and your ability to adapt your dog to the circumstances will determine your success. Each game bird requires a different modus operandi, which I will explain here.

Pheasant

The well-trained Springer Spaniel is the pheasant dog par excellence, the crème de la crème. Over the last several years, pheasant hunting has improved in a number of states as a result of agricultural programs such as the Conservation Reserve Program (C.R.P.) set-aside acreage and the introduction of Sichan strains into Michigan. The key to success is knowing where to find the birds and then controlling the dog so that it works the cover in a way that forces the birds to fly within gun range. This involves careful observation and development of a strategy for hunting the property in a way that uses the cover, terrain and wind to find birds, then uses bare ground as a barrier to pressure the birds into the air. Because pheasants are notorious runners, you will have more success if you can stop your dog when trailing a moving bird to allow you to catch up and gain the advantage.

Controlling the dog's actions to match the property is also a key to success in pheasant hunting as you sweep the cover using natural breaks in the cover to force the birds to fly rather than run ahead and flush wild. Often that can mean pulling the dog in tight to work out just a small finger of brush or a fence row. At other times, it means letting the dog run big, fast and wide to sweep a large section of thick set-aside acreage. The diagram on page 140 shows an example of the proper way to hunt an Iowa slough with a serpentine path for the hunter and an appropriate wind pattern and ground coverage from the Spaniel around the hunter's path. Retrieving is also a key factor. Usually 25 percent of all pheasant retrievers will require special effort, such as tracking a crippled bird.

Grouse and Woodcock

With grouse and woodcock, ground strategy is relatively unimportant, but dog control is paramount. The objective is to get into likely habitat and then control the dog so birds are flushed within gun (and sight) range. This is especially true early in the season, before the foliage drops, when spotting flushed birds is difficult. Because the cover is usually thick and dense, you cannot allow the dog to work more than twenty yards from you. The density of the cover often limits the dog's range but being able to turn the dog on the whistle is a valuable tool. I always put a bell on the dog's collar in these circumstances so I can track its path.

Although you hunt grouse and woodcock in a very similar manner, when you hit a patch of really top woodcock cover, with the tell-tale ground splash, hack the dog in tight and be ready for some really fast shooting action. Much has been written about some dogs' reluctance to retrieve woodcock, but I have never hunted with a Springer that wasn't an eager and enthusiastic woodcock retriever.

A last reminder for grouse and woodcock hunting: always wear glasses as protection against an eye injury from a limb or brush whip, and take your porcupine pliers along just in case.

A well-bred and well-trained English Springer Spaniel is an extremely versatile dog. Here, I take the liberty of using photographs of my own AFC Ru-Char's Genuine Risk, "Genny," to photographically demonstrate this versatility. I was often able to hunt and field trial her in the same week, and she was able to adapt her style to a wide variety of situations. Here she retrieves a grouse from a Minnesota reforestation area. *Roggenkamp*

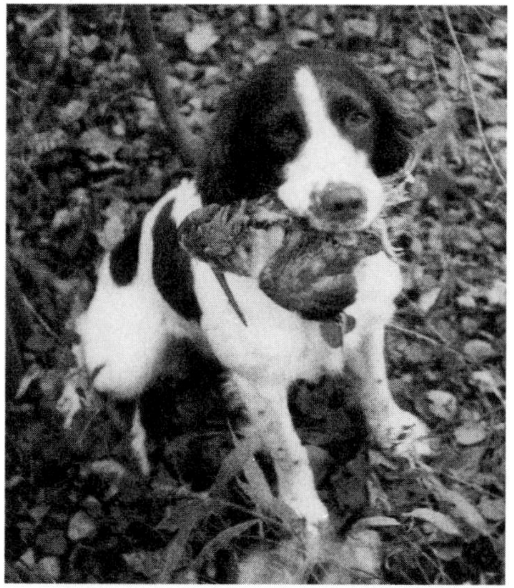

Here, Genny presents a woodcock she retrieved in New York's Adirondack Mountains. Control is the key to both woodcock and grouse hunting with a Springer. Quick response to fundamental training is the key. *Roggenkamp*

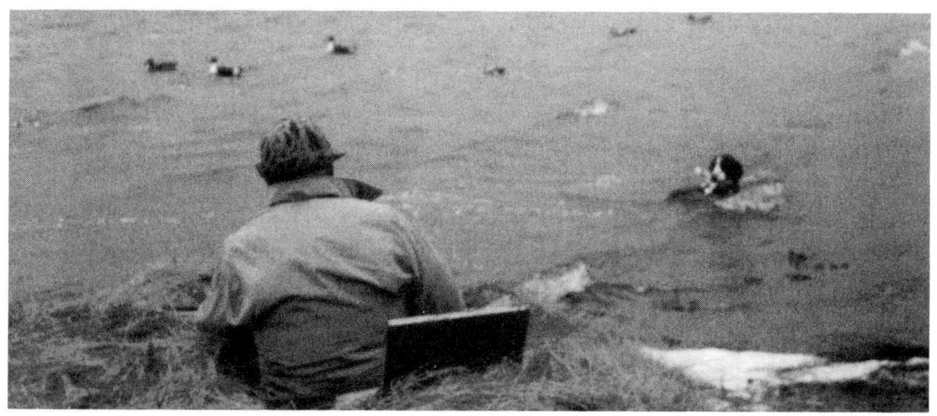

Hunting New Jersey's legendary Barnegat Bay for ducks and brant out of sneak boxes is a special thrill. Here Genny retrieves a black duck. Incidentally, we even towed along a small sneak box for her to sit in. *Roggenkamp*

Quail

Bobwhite quail hunting with a Springer is a wild, fast game requiring lightning reflexes and good bird sense. Usually I hunt quail as a bonus bird found accidentally as part of an Iowa pheasant hunt. Springers are not good covey dogs and usually put up the covey while in the process of looking for pheasants. However, once the covey explodes, you can have a ball chasing singles with a Springer. The key is to watch the covey rise carefully and mark down the areas where they land as precisely as you can. Usually quail peel off in many directions on the covey rise, so either shoot fast or hold your fire while marking birds as they land. Next, if possible, circle the landing area and hunt into the wind since quail singles give off very little scent. Then hunt through the area hacking the dog in close, loaded with 8's and 9's and get ready for some fast action.

Other types of quail, such as the valley, desert or Gambel's varieties, are running birds that seldom fly without serious pressure from the dog. Though the terrain is awesome, the shooting can be fast and furious with a Springer forcing the birds into the air. A steady dog is important here since the birds never lift very high off the ground.

Duck and Goose

For the most part, this is retrieving work for the dog so it involves marking, trailing out or swimming after cripples and the obedience to sit quietly in the blind for hours. Frankly, the toughest part of hunting waterfool with Springers is the discipline required of them to sit in the blind. Here, their enthusiasm becomes a frustration as they whine and fidget. However, once the retrieving starts, you will recant and show pride as your bold and aggressive Springer tackles the most difficult of retrieves as if it were an everyday occurrence. You will also need strong *No*! and *Come*! commands. On occasion, a duck or goose will be so slightly wounded that no dog can swim fast enough to catch it. If you can't call the dog off game and back to you, the dog could be in peril. I recall being quite relieved when, at dusk on a very cold winter evening on Lake Ontario, Genny responded to my *No*! command and came swimming back empty-mouthed from what seemed to be the horizon.

Geese are an interesting challenge for a Springer. The dogs can handle the job, but it is a royal battle if the bird is only slightly wounded. Remember: a goose in water is in its own element, but a goose in a corn field is in the dog's element.

Springers are bright dogs that quickly learn the rules of the new game. They soon learn to ignore decoys and hunker down at your side under a cedar tree as you wait for wood ducks to whistle past or crash through cattails in search of a wing-tipped mallard. No book can address every hunting circumstance, but if you have laid the basic training foundation the dog will adapt its knowledge to the hunting situation.

I remember this day as if it were yesterday. It rained hard all day, but hunting days in Iowa are too precious to waste, so we pressed on. By closing hour, I had bagged two roosters and both Genny (AFC Ru-Char's Genuine Risk) (right) and Old Rocky (Ru-Char's Rocky Creek, dam of Top Sire Ru-Char's Roger Jr.) (left) were tired, wet and cold. But it was a great day of hard hunting, fine dog work and special memories. *Vaughn*

I've heard estimates that there are more Canadian Geese in America today than at the time of the American Revolution. A good blind, a few decent decoys, a solid 12-gauge and a good Springer gun dog can add this species to your game list. On this day we were shooting over decoys in a cornfield and the gunning was fast and furious. This was Genny's first goose. *Anger*

This is how a 34-pound Springer carries a Canada Goose. *Anger*

Dove

A Springer's nose, retrieving talents and enthusiasm really show in the dove field. Without a dog, as much as 50 percent of all fallen doves are lost. However, with a good dog, nearly 100 percent will be found. This is hunker-down-in-a-fence-row shooting where dog control is important and where a willingness to take hand signals will save many birds. Since no dog can mark more than two or three falls, you will need to guide the dog to the area of the fall, then let his nose handle the rest. Always try to handle the dog to a position downwind of the fall. Here, many hunters simply tie the dog to a tree or post so they can concentrate on the shooting, which is always a challenge.

Preserve Hunting

Today, in order to extend their season by several months, many hunters belong to preserves or hunting clubs. The usual game species in those hunts are pheasant, chuckars and quail. The Springer's animated body English and flushing style enhance the excitement and challenge of this sport. Preserve properties are usually dotted with patches of heavy cover that hold game even under heavy hunting pressure. Such cover is often standing sorghum or heavy brush stands where the birds move around and elude pointing dogs. Your Springer will excitedly crash through this cover following the scent until it worries the bird into flushing. Meanwhile, you're out in the open for the shooting action.

Rabbit

Some people love to hunt rabbits with a Spaniel. I'm not one of them. Even though rabbits greatly excite a Springer, I call my dogs off rabbits to preserve their bird steadiness.

However, in England the Springer is a premier rabbit hunter. The Springer will work rabbits boldly and start them running for your gun. But take extreme care in your shooting, since the rabbit and the dog are both on the ground. A spaniel, if so trained, will find, flush and fetch rabbits with alacrity.

Hunter Style

Upland game hunting with a Springer is not a spectator sport! You are an active player in this game. Unlike hunting over pointing dogs, where you can amble down a logging road hoping to get a glimpse of your dog on point so you can go in for a shot, with a Springer you will need to be in the cover working with the dog. You will also need quick reactions for snap shooting. The Springer style of hunting will challenge your skills. You'll be proud that you worked for your game and honored it with your efforts.

Most of my Springer friends are very physically active people. These are robust, athletic individuals who often hunt, ski, hike and fly fish into their

Many field trialers hunt their dogs. Here Dr. Mark Schinderle (left) and Frank Guzowski show the results of a productive hunting trip to northern Wisconsin. Dr. Schinderle was hunting with his fine field champion FC/AFC Braw Bagpiper of Burtree, and Mr. Guzowski was using well-bred Windy Acres Ocajawia. Mark frequently hunts his trial dogs in the great grouse and woodcock cover near his northern Michigan home.

The range of a Springer is critical to your hunting success. Here, during a field trial, FC Bricksclose Sprigg flushes a pheasant well inside gun range. The judge was the late Larry McQueen and the handler, John Isaacs. *Friend*

Springers with experience and training can become avid waterfowl retrievers. Minnesota professional hunting guide and outfitter Harry Henriques and his young dog Wild Wings Max crouch in the blind as the ringneck ducks work to the decoy rig.

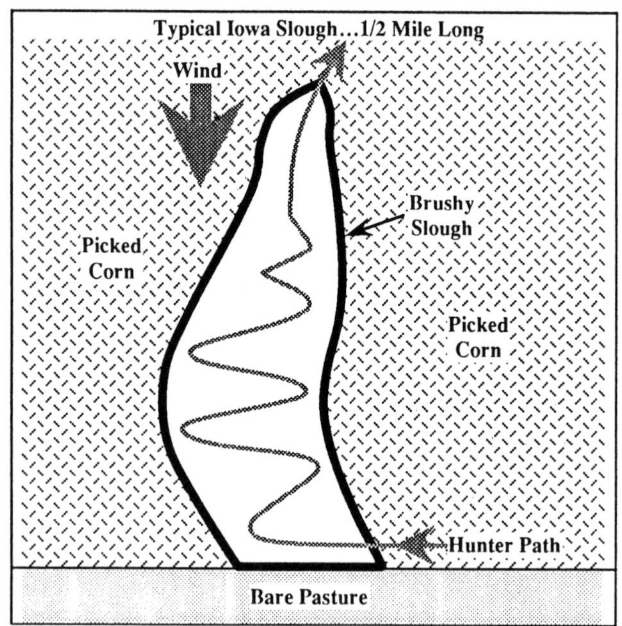

In the Midwest pheasant range, the birds are generally found in the big weedy sloughs that bisect the giant grain fields. How you hunt these large tracts of cover will, to a great extent, determine your success. This diagram suggests a serpentine path for the hunter, while directing the dog to run an appropriate wind pattern to cover the area. Working your dog into the wind when hunting is less unsettling to game and hence the quarry tends to set tighter and run less. Your voice, your whistle and the noise of you and your dog's movement through the cover alerts the birds to your presence. In the case of grouse and pheasant, excessive noise can cause them to run from your approach. To prove the noise difference between upwind and downwind, first stand downwind and then upwind as your partners work their dogs during a training session. You will find the difference in the noise level surprising. *Ellis*

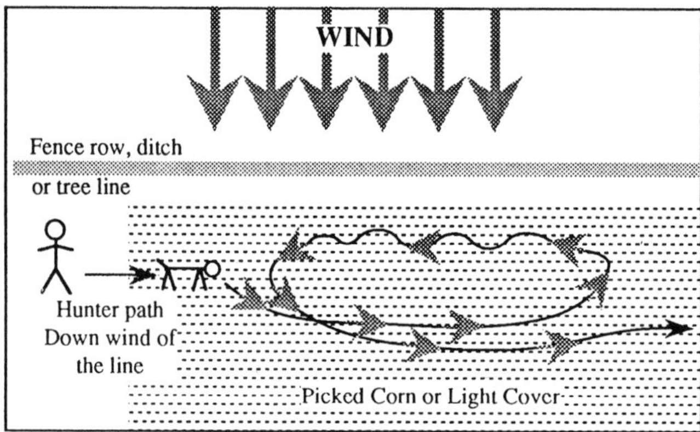

When hunting a fence row, deep ditch or wide tree line, always try to work the dog on the downwind side of the cover. Direct the dog to loop out into the surrounding light cover then work back toward you along and through the heavy cover. This holds birds in a pincers movement between you and the dog. It also forces the dog to quickly search the light cover downwind of the fence row. If, instead, the dog were to work the fence row straight away from the handler, the dog would quickly get out of range and any birds that choose to run ahead would be pushed farther and perhaps out of range of the gun. *Ellis*

eighties. That is the style of the dog too. I have, on occasion, hunted with dogs that were twelve or thirteen years old and were still very active and aggressive with amazing stamina.

The gun you use is a personal choice, of course, but most spaniel hunters tend to use lightweight, fast-action double guns, either over-and-unders or side-by-sides, which are easy to carry and quick-handling.

Range

No discussion of bird dogs of any breed would be complete without an open and honest coverage of the subject of range. Range has caused an extreme rift in the pointer and setter communities: the field trialers bred horizon runners for horse-back handlers, while the foot hunters opted for close-working dogs, some now bred to work so close that they remind me of non-slip retrievers—real boot polishers.

In the world of Springer Spaniels, range is also a debate but the discussion is between twenty yards and forty yards. The field trialers naturally want a dog that runs with great style, speed and a wide pattern past each of the two official gunners. However, even the boldest field trial dog will generally adjust and reduce its range when hunting with a single gunner. This smaller pattern is obviously more suited to the hunter. The excitement of a field trial also stimulates the dog, and every dog I have ever owned ran bigger, wider and faster when entered in a trial than when hunting or training.

In a hunting situation, a Springer that is out of control is useless; but at the opposite end of the spectrum, a boot polisher will not find much game for you either. The key is always control. If the dog will turn when you two-toot the whistle, you will have a great hunt. Personally, when I hunt pheasants in Iowa or grouse in Minnesota, I like the dog to run a wider pattern than some hunters might prefer chiefly because I want to know if there is game in the area. Even if the dog bumps a bird at the edge of gun range (which is surprisingly quite rare), I then know there is game in the area and I can hack the dog in and follow-up for a second shot.

The training chapters of this book apply equally to any spaniel, from an easy-going, close-working estate-type dog to a wide-running, fast and flashy field trial prospect. If you have done the training well, you will be rewarded in the woods or fields.

Physical Capabilities and Conditioning

Dogs have inherent physical attributes. Some have an easy-running, fast style. Some have tremendous lung capacity and endurance and can run all day seemingly without effort. Others are slower moving and less agile. The dog's inherent physical attributes are determined by genes—not by training.

However, your dog should be conditioned properly prior to the start of the hunting season. Unfortunately, many dogs waddle out of the vehicle on opening day. They are overweight, out-of-condition and need refresher training. Several methods of conditioning are available even to the busiest hunter. In the hottest summer weather, long swimming retrieves are excellent aerobic exercise. In the fall, I run my dogs alongside my ten-speed bicycle. Several bike runs a week plus two rigorous weekend training sessions for six weeks leading up to opening day will do the trick. Also, carefully monitor the amount of food during this period to trim excess weight. All of these efforts will result in more enjoyable hunting and allow your dog to display its real talent as a superbly conditioned athlete.

Summary

The true enjoyment and value of your Springer as a hunting companion is a direct result of your training for ORFFF (Obedience–Range–Fetch–Find–Flush).

The key questions are: Does the dog respond to your obedience commands promptly? Does the dog turn on the whistle, look for you and work within gun range? Does he quest boldly in cover using his nose to find game? When he scents game, does he track it out and push it into flight with an aggressive effort? When birds are shot, does he retrieve promptly?

If the answer to all of these is *yes*, you have trained a valued and valuable hunting partner. Now it's time to go hunting.

On a crisp, clear, spring morning outside Sedona, Arizona, this Gambel's quail's song was so loud and clear that I searched for his location. I was surprised to find him in a tree, calling to the covey (do you see him?). The range of hunting for you and your Springer is limited only by the training of your dog and the adventure in your soul. On this morning we weren't hunting . . . just hiking. *Roggenkamp*

13

Professional Training Assistance and Advice

THE SPORT of Springer trialing has long been home to the professional trainer/handler. Indeed many of the most successfully campaigned dogs have reached their zenith under the careful tutelage of one of the many pros who specialize in Springers. However, there are many reasons why a hunter may also wish to seek the assistance of a trainer. These can include:

- A lack of available time or facilities to properly train the dog.
- A lack of knowledge or ability to train the dog.
- A dog with so much potential that the owner wants to give it the best opportunity possible.

No one should ever be hesitant to seek the help of a professional trainer. After all, it is standard practice in race horses. We all seek the help of a pro to train our own children, whether teachers, tutors or coaches. However, you must be willing to properly compensate the trainer for services rendered. Always ask, up front, about the costs, time required and the potential of your dog. Using a professional trainer is not inexpensive but it can be a very reliable way to maximize the potential of your dog.

In many cases the busy hunter hires a professional trainer to lay a solid foundation in a young gun dog to prepare the dog for a lifetime of consistent performance. Normally, once the basic training is firmly grasped, a little refresher training by the owner on a limited but consistent basis will keep the dog in tune.

A dozen of the top professional trainers in the United States and Canada

Jim DeVoll, Sr., and his wife LuAnn base their training operation in Omaha, Nebraska.

Mark Hairfield trains Springers and operates a shooting preserve just south of Houston, Texas, but competes in field trials nationwide.

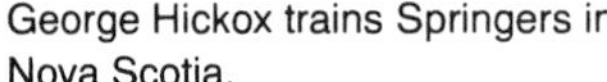

George Hickox trains Springers in Nova Scotia.

were asked to give some very brief advice on how to handle a simple training situation with a young dog. Their replies follow:

James E. DeVoll, Sr., Midland's Kennel, Omaha, Nebraska:

Question: How do you introduce gunfire to the puppy?

Answer: Once your puppy is retrieving to hand, you may begin shooting the blank pistol while he is at the fall, just about to pick up the buck or clipped-wing bird. He will be so excited about the retrieve that the shot will go almost unnoticed. If all goes well, begin to shoot a little sooner, but watch his ears and tail; for if the shooting bothers him at all you'll notice them go down. Continue to shoot only the blank until you are certain he's comfortable with the report, then carefully shoot a small-bore shotgun in the opposite direction as he reaches the fall. Never shoot directly over a young dog's head, as the muzzle blast will turn him off to the gun.

Mark Hairfield, Southaven Kennel, Rosharon, Texas:

Question: How do you introduce a young dog to water?

Answer: There are several factors to be considered when introducing a young dog to the water. The ideal situation would be a warm sunny day with access to a small farm pond with gradual, sloping sides. Steep banks should be avoided. I prefer to wait until the pup is four to six months of age and it should be retrieving enthusiastically. The initial contact with water should be voluntary. The pup will want to cool off and/or drink at the edge. I then enter the water a few feet and encourage the pup to do the same. At this point, I introduce the pup's favorite retrieving dummy, which I throw for a few short retrieves of about four to five feet and very near the bank. I lengthen the retrieves as the pup becomes more confident. With a little encouragement and lots of patience, your dog will soon be swimming.

George Hickox, Grouse Wing Kennels, Berwick, Nova Scotia, Canada:

Question: How do you keep a dog in gun range?

Answer: Staying in gun range is a function of control. Always demand an immediate response to any command. A proper foundation in yard training and quick response to *Hup*!, *Stay*!, and *Here*!*(Come!)* is mandatory. In training, always plant birds to the left and right of the handler, not down the field. Don't let the dog learn to run straight down the field and find birds. Then demand immediate response to the turn (two toots) and come commands, consistently reinforced by repetition. That is the key to success.

Billie Jo Hopkins, Canspan Kennel, Bailieboro, Ontario, Canada:

Question: How do you teach *Hup*! in the yard?

Answer: I teach *Hup*! in the yard starting between five and nine months of age with on-lead basic obedience training. Start the dog walking on lead on your left. When you stop, the hup command is given with slight pressure on the dog's rump to achieve the sit position. Repetition and praise reinforces this. As soon as the verbal command is understood, the whistle is introduced (one toot equals the verbal hup command). Most dogs pick up this lesson in two or three sessions. Next, start by putting the dog in the hup position and move away. If the animal gets up or moves, go back to him and correct him by putting him back in the hup position where he should have stayed. Now go back to your original position. Return to the dog to praise rather than calling him to you. This reinforces the hup command. The exactness in teaching *Hup*! in the yard saves many future steps. This command is the foundation for steadiness.

John C. Isaacs, Guadaira Kennels, Amanda, Ohio:

Question: How do you enforce commands?

Answer: Most Springers are not tough dogs so you should develop a lot of patience. Start with a light punishment (a shaking or scolding) and work toward a tougher chastisement until you reach the point where the dog knows that you mean business. Also, develop a reward system, even if the reward is only a "good dog" or a pat on the head. That makes training simpler. The more the dog enjoys the reward, the less punishment that will have to be given.

David G. Lorenz, Hogan Kennels, Ingleside, Illinois:

Question: How you get a puppy to stop dropping retrieves and deliver them promptly?

Answer: When the puppy is three or four months old and successfully carrying a paint roller or small retrieving dummy, take him out on the lawn with a light line attached to his collar. Throw a small dummy, then cheerfully coax and whistle and pull him into you even if he drops the dummy. If he comes in without the dummy, pick it up and throw it again. When he does bring it to you without dropping it, praise him and give him a dog cookie. Don't become discouraged if this takes a while for the puppy to learn.

Carl Smith, R-Quest's Kennel, Morris, Illinois:

Question: How do you teach a dog to hunt heavy cover?

Answer: Once a puppy is fully trained and steady to wing and shot in light cover, you can take the youngster to heavier cover and train with him there. After becoming accustomed to training in these denser areas, he will learn to hunt heavy cover for his master. Springers are smart and learn readily to hunt in heavy cover.

Richard L. Vermazen, Arrowpoint Kennel, Woodland, California:

Question: How do you teach a dog to use the wind?

Answer: Breeding, breeding, breeding—desire and ability derived from genetics is of *prime* importance. There's no making a silk purse from a sow's

Billie Joe (B.J.) Hopkins (right) is shown here with Don Cande of New Hampshire when they judged the 1991 Canadian National Championship. Ms. Hopkins became a professional trainer in 1991 and now trains in Ontario, near Toronto.

John Isaacs with FC Pinewarren Warloan and FC Bricksclose Sprigg. In several trials this pair placed first and second in the Open All Age. Sprigg's owners are Vince and Elana Bolling, and Warloan is owned by Steve and Esther Ujhelyi. John trains south of Columbus, Ohio.

David Lorenz, veteran trainer from the Chicago area, has trained many champions.

Carl Smith, who bases his training operation in Morris, Illinois, is shown here with Radar's Rooster Raiser.

Dick Vermazen is a well-known West Coast professional and trains near Sacramento, California.

Barney Zeigler started in Ohio but moved to Oklahoma and trains near Tulsa. He is shown here with FC/CFC Canspan's Magnum D-2, "Tyler," a dog that won many trials while handled by Barney.

Gary Wilson, now based near Elmira, New York, is well known for training many successful puppies. He is shown here teasing a puppy with a bird to keep the dog's flush bold during the steadying process. *Sharon Parks*

Ben Martin trains near Dayton, Ohio. Ben is shown here when he judged a National Championship in Washington state. Ben has trained and handled both a Canadian National Champion and an Open National Champion.

Well-known East Coast professional trainer Ray "Jerry" Cacchio is shown here with National Champion NFC Pondview's Left in the Light. Jerry's training operation is about seventy-five miles north of New York City.

ear. K.I.S.S. (**K**eep **I**t **S**imple, **S**tupid)! Let the dog develop by being a winner every time. Start with birds planted into the wind in light cover. Let the dog find its birds without control. Control comes later. Let God-given instincts develop with positive influence from the trainer. (Have fun!) Dogs with natural talent learn from experience!

Barney Ziegler, High Plains Kennels, Chouteau, Oklahoma:

Question: How do you teach a dog to turn on the whistle?

Answer: Two short, sharp toots is what most handlers use as a turn whistle. While your young dog is quartering, blow two sharp toots. Then when it looks at you to see what you want, you take a few steps in the opposite direction and give it a hand and arm signal to quarter in the other direction. Through repetition during training sessions, it will learn that the two sharp toots mean turn and follow your direction.

Gary Wilson, Sunrise Kennel, Canisteo, New York:

Question: What steps are necessary before you try to steady a dog?

Answer: Before steadying your pup, he must be ready. First, the pup must be bold and outgoing. He needs to develop his natural desire to run and hunt, which may be accomplished by daily walks in the woods inhabited by wild game. After the pup learns how to hunt, let him flush and chase several planted pigeons to develop a bold flush. When I decide the pup is ready for steadying, I take him out of the field and start a rigorous program of obedience followed by a program of steadying in the yard.

Training a dog is like building a house. You must have a good foundation. After several weeks of obedience work, I yard-steady my pups at eight to twelve months of age (depending on the dog's progress and readiness). Using a progression of temptations and assistance of a short check cord, I steady the pup to clipped-wing pigeons. It is very important to create movement by teasing the pup before you throw the pigeon. Never harshly punish a pup at this stage for breaking in yard steadying.

Ben A. Martin, Royal Kennels, Franklin, Ohio:

Question: Which basic commands are most important to a hunter?

Answer: The stop (hup) and heel (come) commands are the most valuable to a hunter. You must be able to stop a flushing dog when he is tracking game and is getting too far out in front. This way you can catch up to him and be in gun range when game is flushed.

The heel (come) command is also of great value when hunting a flushing dog because there are many situations when a hunter will encounter areas (such as standing corn) where a flushing dog and hunter can't stay in touch with each other. I usually bring the dog to heel rather than lose him or have game flushed

Dean Brunn bases his training in Milltown, Indiana, near Louisville, Kentucky. Dean, son of the late trainer Don Brunn, has trained and handled several National Champions and is shown here with FC Denalisunflo's Lady owned by Ed Bideau.

Dan Langhans, a well-known Chicago-area trainer, is shown with Canadian National Champion NCFC, FC Windmillwood Storm, owned A. E. MacMillan. Dan has trained and handled several National Champions.

out of range. In preserve hunting, you sometimes have eight or ten pheasants in a single area. Being able to heel the dog mainly allows a little more control. Control is the name of the game with a flushing spaniel.

Ray Cacchio, Pondview Kennels, Staatsburg, New York:

Question: How do you encourage natural retrieving instincts?

Answer: When I start out with young pups (eight weeks to eight months), I *never* ask them to sit on a retrieve. I let them chase the dummy or bird as fast as they can go. Just before they get to the retrieve, I whistle to get them to pick up the dummy quickly and this encourages a prompt return.

Keep it simple and fun in the beginning—no sitting on a retrieve in the beginning; that can be done at a later date after you have built up their desire. Always keep a lesson fun.

Dean Brunn, Dal B Kennels, Milltown, Indiana:

Question: How do you introduce dogs to game and at what age?

Answer: I like to introduce pups to birds at the young age of three to six months. Older dogs (age ten to fourteen months) that haven't previously had birds often develop problems such as being bird-shy or having a hard mouth.

Start a young pup by teasing it with a bird wing on a line and/or by a retrieving buck with a wing taped on it. This gets him used to the smell and feel of feathers. Next, use a dead bird (pigeon or quail) for retrieving practice. If any indication of hard mouth surfaces, use a frozen bird.

Now move on to a shackled or taped-wing pigeon for retrieves. If after several retrieves the puppy shows enthusiasm, you can move on to a strong, live taped-wing pigeon. If that goes well, move to full-winged birds. It is not unusual to have a dog fully introduced to live birds by six months of age.

Dan Langhans, Dansmirth's Kennel, Harvard, Illinois:

Question: How do you develop a hunting pattern?

Answer: Developing a hunting pattern is one of the easiest aspects of dog training. Wind direction is most important! Always work the pup directly into the wind. With the help of two assistants (positioned as guns), work the pup in a figure-eight pattern, quartering from side to side. The assistants can encourage the dog by shaking their hands or waving their hats at knee level. It is to the handler's advantage to spend as much time as possible with the young dog to perfect this pattern as it will retain this training forever.

14

Top Field Sires: Bloodlines and Natural Talent

AN IMPORTANT PART in the making of any excellent bird dog is competent training. However, even the most capable trainers are constrained by the dog's inherited genetic capabilities. For that reason, most knowledgeable hunters and field trialers are very careful to select a puppy with proven field breeding in its pedigree *to improve the odds*. This is not to say that a puppy out of unrenowned parentage will not someday win the National Field Trial Championship—but don't bet on it. The odds are long and your chances of success are greatly enhanced when you start with proven stock. If you read *Spaniels in the Field* magazine, you can review many four-or five-generation pedigrees, and any competent breeder will be glad to give you a copy of the pedigree for any puppy you may be interested in.

Some sires have made a major impact on the field-bred side of the English Springer Spaniel in recent years. This chapter reviews some of the names you can expect to encounter frequently in field pedigrees.

Years ago, when my interest in competitive field trialing became very intense and my trial schedule very active, I decided to research which dogs were siring the most field trial winners. I assumed that by studying progeny performances, I could increase my chances for picking puppies with a potential to win. However, when I looked for the statistics on English Springer Spaniel field sires, I was surprised to learn that no such statistics were either compiled or published. I immediately set out to remedy that by keeping a summary and supplying the data on Springers to *On the Line* magazine (now *Spaniels in the Field*). Every year since 1983 the data has been compiled and published and is now computerized. However, what follows is my own summary of the sires that have made a significant difference in the breed since 1980. Their names will show up prominently in the pedigrees of thousands of field-bred Springers well into the next century. *Note:* I focus on sires rather than dams because, although I personally believe the dam is as critical as the sire, in her lifetime a dam will produce perhaps thirty puppies, while a popular sire may produce 150. Hence a sire can have more long-term impact on the breed.

Approximately thirty sires have been significant since 1980. I have included a background on the top ten. In doing this I may offend a few owners of good sires, but that can't be helped. There are many great dogs that were either bred infrequently or whose puppies were never given the real chance to compete at a level necessary to earn for their sire a place on the Top Sires list.

The following are dogs with proven siring performance:

NFC/NAFC/NCFC
Saighton's Scud
(called "Scud")
Sire: *Saighton's Seeking*
Dam: *Sophie of Saighton*

Bred in England by Talbot Radcliffe, imported to the United States by Janet Christensen and field trial–campaigned and –handled in the United States by Janet Christensen, Scud won several national championships. He was a marvelous dog that performed great feats with flawless consistency. The fact that this great dog was trained and handled by such a talented owner only served to enhance his success. Fortunately for the breed, Scud was bred frequently and to some very high-quality bitches. Hence his get earned and held for him the Top Sire ranking for several years. Scud also sired many dogs that have made the Top Sires list.

The following is a justifiably proud review of Scud's achievements by his owner and handler Janet Christensen:

> Scud was a big, well-built, athletic dog with great stamina and jumping ability. He had a broad head and a kind eye. He was an exceptional dog in that he excelled in most aspects of trialing—excellent nose, great marker, good mouth, all above average. He ran hard and used the wind well but he was not a flashy dog so could, on occasion, be beaten by a flashier running dog. He had an ability to do extremely difficult feats so easily that, at times, the judges may not have given him sufficient credit for it.
>
> As a sire, Scud was able to pass along most of his great characteristics and his puppies often resembled him physically. I knew he was a special sire when he was able to produce field trial champions out of average bitches.
>
> He sired eleven FCs, eight AFCs, and five CFCs. Ten of those offspring garnered

Janet Christensen, D.V.M., of Oregon with Top Sire and multiple National Champion NFC/NAFC/NCFC Saighton's Scud. For many years Mrs. Christensen has been one of the most successful trainers and handlers in the United States. She has handled dogs to numerous National Championships.

Ruth Greening, veteran trialer from New Jersey, is shown with Top Sire FC/AFC Ru-Char's Roger Jr. Mrs. Greening has continued to campaign field trial dogs very successfully at an age of "over 80." In 1991 she personally handled her dog AFC Ru-Char's Autumn Mist to five Amateur victories in a row, a feat never before accomplished in field trialing. Mrs. Greening truly demonstrates that this is an ageless sport where youngsters and senior citizens compete on an equal footing.

twenty national placements including four national championships (NFC/NAFC Saighton's Scout II, NAFC Ky Wy Chas Jodi, CNFC Patchwood's Trapper.) One female offspring, FC/AFC/CFC Kaymac's Kiltie was high point dog in all three categories, U.S. Open, U.S. Amateur and Canadian Open. Others: FC Braw Bairn of Suthron Glen—High Point Open dog 1984; FC/AFC Freckles Flash of Scud—High Point Open dog 1985 and High Point Amateur dog 1986; and AFC/CFC My High Hope—top producing female in 1991 and 1992.

Scud threw many many good animals and one of the significant things was that he often had a dozen of his offspring placing and winning in any given year, most handled and trained by amateurs. Scud went sterile by age seven so all his winning progeny were produced in a relatively short time.

FC/AFC
Ru-Char's Roger Jr. (1977–1991)
(called "Junior")
Sire: *FC & AFC Ru-Char's Roger*
Dam: *Ru-Char's Rocky Creek*

Bred, owned and handled by Ruth Greening of Ru-Char Kennels, Junior was the son of Old Roger—himself a pretty solid sire. Junior was high point amateur dog in the United States in 1981 and continued to win trials until he was nine years old. Junior was handled to most of his wins by Ruth herself, but because of health problems and the death of her husband Charles, Ruth turned Junior over to several handlers, professional and amateur, who continued to place and win with the dog. I myself handled Junior in a few trials so I had the pleasure of hunting and trialing him. He was a talented animal with an almost-human thought process. His natural talents, nose, marking and retrieving ability were superb. He could run effortlessly hour after hour. He was a gentle dog with a loving temperament and spent most of his life as Ruth's house dog. Junior produced winning dogs out of many different bitches. His progeny include many field champions and several National placements.

Liver and white, mostly white; wide face blaze; lots of ticking; weight of 45–50 pounds. Junior's noteworthy progeny included: FC/AFC Ru-Char's JR. Regent; NFC Ru-Char's Country Boy; FC/AFC Ru-Char's Rise & Shine (1987 High Point Amateur Dog); FC/AFC Ru-Char's Quick Shot; FC/AFC Sunrise Rebel Cause; and many more.

FC
Badgercourt Druid (England) (born 4-28-79)
(called "Druid")
Sire: *FC Don of Bronton*
Dam: *FC Badgercourt Susan*

This dog never set foot in the United States, but as many as a dozen of his puppies were imported, campaigned and won here in the states. Druid is now the second top-producing sire in English history with twelve English champions to his credit and probably another five or six in America. Druid was bred and owned by R. P. Coombes of England. The Druid dogs I've seen are often distinctly marked by an all-liver head. Perhaps the most noted of his offspring trialed in the United States is FC/AFC Brickclose Matchwood (Badger), which was imported as a puppy and trained by the Texas pro Mark Hairfield. Later, Badger was sold to Mike Elsasser, who handled him to High Point National Amateur dog in 1988. Badger was later sold back to Hairfield, who then handled the dog to High Point National Open dog in 1990. Druid also sired AFC Badgercourt Shot and AFC Buzz of Noarhill. Some Druid offspring have a reputation for running for the sheer love of running; thus, Druid is noted for adding *drive* to his progeny.

Denalisunflo's LuMox (1975–1990)
(called "Lump")
Sire: *Denalisunflo's Buddy*
Dam: *Denalisunflo's Snow*

This dog, a grandson of 1962 NFC Kansan, was bred and owned by Roy French of Gridley, Kansas. LuMox was bred to only one bitch, Denalisunflo's Duchess, also owned by French. This combination produced three litters. From these puppies came many champions (in the first litter five of six became champions), several national placements and the 1988 National Champion, Denalisunflo's Bandita. Lump himself was never trialed but was hunted extensively, and French could see great potential in the dog. French then decided to test Lump's talent as a sire, and his faith was well founded. Some of Lump's get included these champions: Denalisunflo's Lady, Denalisunflo's Hunk, Denalisunflo's Kan, Denalisunflo's Darkey. Two of Lump's grandchildren are doing well—Denalisunflo's Ring became the 1992 National Open Champion and Denalisunflo's Thurnelda is already a champion.

FC/AFC/CFC
Windbourne's Try Two
(called "Try Two")
Sire: *Rush of Harwes*
Dam: *Windbourne's Thumbprint*

AFC/CFC
Springjoy's Act II
(called "Nugget")
Sire: *FC/AFC/CFC Windbourne's Try Two*
Dam: *CFC Winnamac's Cinnamon Sue*

This father and son act have both been on the Top Sires list. Both were owned and trialed by and stood at stud with Joe and Frances Ruff of Connecticut. Try Two sired many champions, including my own FC/AFC/CFC Ru-Char's Ruffian, which placed third and fourth in National Amateur Championships. Act II sired FC/AFC Windbourne's Militant, the 1989 National Open Champion. Both sires were liver and white and although the father was of average size, the son was one of the largest dogs ever to achieve success on the field trial circuit—weighing over 60 pounds through his competitive years. Try Two also sired FC Rewards Genuine Charter. Nugget's progeny also includes FC/CFC Windbourne's Loyal, CFC Rewards of Barney, AFC Saxon's Shot (4th in the 1992 National Amateur) and CFC Windbourne's Surf Rider.

Roy French, legendary Kansas field trialer, with Top Sire Denalisunflo's LuMox (right) and dam Denalisunflo's Duchess. This pair produced numerous field champions.

FC/AFC/CFC Windbourne's Try Two, owned by Joe and Frances Ruff of Connecticut, is a Top Sire and sired a Top Sire.

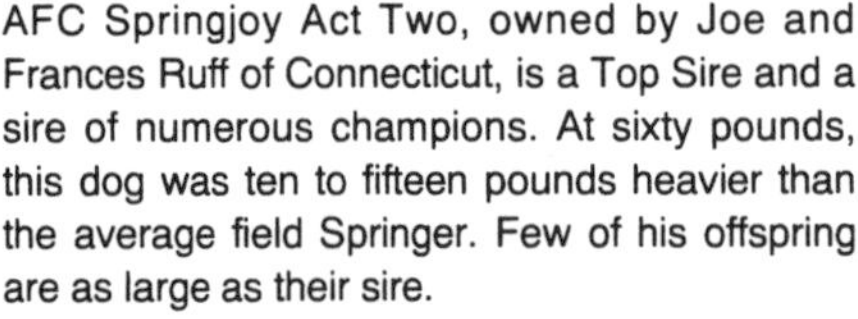

AFC Springjoy Act Two, owned by Joe and Frances Ruff of Connecticut, is a Top Sire and a sire of numerous champions. At sixty pounds, this dog was ten to fifteen pounds heavier than the average field Springer. Few of his offspring are as large as their sire.

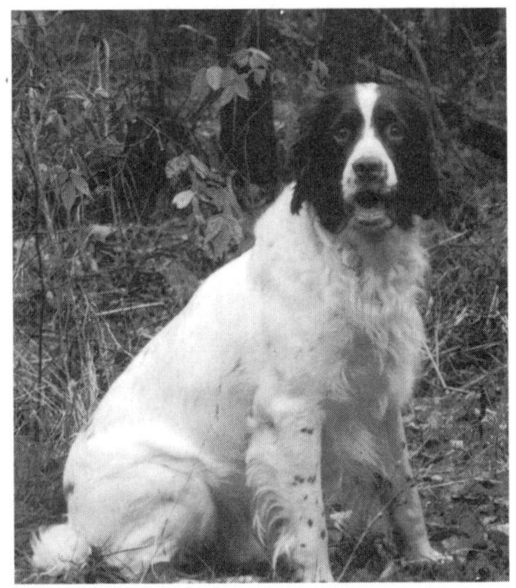

FC
Saighton's Stat
(called "Stat")
Sire: *FC Slattery of Saighton*
Dam: *Saighton's Glenrock Regent*

Saighton's Stat was bred by Talbot Radcliffe in Wales, imported to the United States by John Riepenhoff, M.D., then was owned and trialed by John Isaacs and stood at stud at his Guadara Kennel in Amanda, Ohio. Stat was consistently on the Top Sires list for six years and produced many top dogs with a couple of the most noteworthy being FC/AFC Ivanhoe's Abigail (2nd in the 1989 National Open), owned and handled by Bill Cosgrove, and FC/AFC King George of Westfall, which was owned and handled by Russ Smith and was a consistent performer that continued to win and place in trials until age eleven. George probably showed as much longevity as any trial dog in the history of the sport. Stat's puppies were widely dispersed across the United States and his influence was strongly felt over a wide area. Stat was liver and white and weighed about 42 pounds. He also sired FC Dansmirth's Leprechaun, owned by Bob Shambaugh and handled by Dan Langhans; FC Saight, owned by Steve McNaughton and handled by John Isaacs; and FC/AFC Chaloruva's Lancelot, owned and handled by Val Walch (2nd in the 1985 National Amateur).

NFC/AFC
Sunrise Zinger
(called "Zinger")
Sire: *AFC Sunrise Zachary*
Dam: *Breakwater Bess*

Sunrise Zinger was bred by Tom Ackerman of Maine and owned originally by East Coast professional Gary Wilson. However, at age two he was sold to Gordon Madson of Minnesota and from then on was trained and handled by professional Dan Langhans of Illinois or by Madson himself. In 1985, Zinger won the National Open Championship. Dan Langhans describes Zinger as "an excellent bird finder, and an uncanny marker, very stylish along with good conformation." Like many National Champions, Zinger's breeding schedule increased dramatically after his National Championship victory and his progeny have really come of age in the 1990s, especially FC/AFC Pondview's Windy Acre's Yankee, an extremely successful dog with seven wins in a single year; AFC K's Surfire Zack (3rd in the 1990 National Amateur); FC/AFC KB's Sir Coach (3rd in the 1992 National Open); AFC Zinger's Oakhills Bandito; FC/AFC/CFC Northern Thunder's Bocephus; and two National Champions: NAFC Wild Irish Kelly (1991) and CNFC Northern Thunder's Rupert (1991).

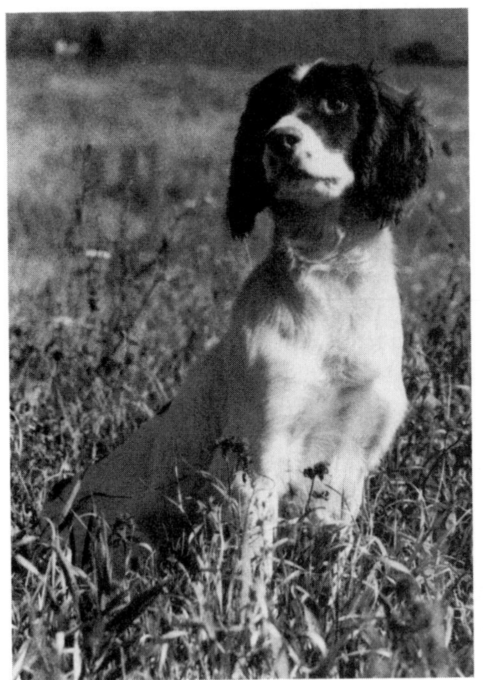

FC Saighton's Stat was imported from Saighton Kennels and was first owned by John P. Riepenhoff, M.D., and handled to five first place All Age wins. John Isaacs bought Stat in the spring of 1979 and won two Open All Age trials and eight more placements, including fourth place in the 1980 National Championship. Stat sired eight field champions, including the legendary FC King George of Westphal.

NFC/AFC Sunrise Zinger and professional trainer Dan Langhans. Zinger, owned by Gordon Madsen of Minneapolis, Minnesota, was handled to his National Championship by Langhans. Afterward, Zinger sired numerous field champions. Zinger was also the 1985 High Point Open Dog.

FC/NAFC/CNFC
Sherwood's Best Chance
(called "Chance")
Sire: *NFC/AFC/CFC Dewfield Brickclose Flint*
Dam: *NAFC/FC/CFC Sheilla of Sherwood*

Sherwood's Best Chance was owned and campaigned by Denny Crick of Oregon. In 1982, Chance was National Amateur & National Canadian Champion. He was also 2nd in the National Open on two occasions. He then began to stand at stud to several high-quality bitches. Chance himself was sired by NFC/AFC/CFC Dewfield Brickcloses Flint who was owned by Chris Christensen. Chance in turn sired NCFC/FC/CFC Royal's Best Maggie. So the chain holds true again. National Champion Flint sires National Champion Chance who sires National Champion Maggie. Incidentally, Chance's dam, Sheilla, was also a National Champion, and she was sired by a National Champion, NAFC Saighton's Signal.

FC/CFC
***Strong's Seamus* (1979–1990)**
(called "Seamus")
Sire: *Saighton's Strong*
Dam: *Saighton's Chama*

Seamus was owned by Strong Kennels of Victoria, Texas, and handled by professional trainer David Jones to High Point Open dog in 1986. Since the dog's passing, many of his progeny continue to win big. Seamus was a big, leggy dog and imparted his physical size and legginess to several of his offspring, which include: FC/CFC Grousewing Swaps, 1992 Canadian High Point Dog; FC/CFC Grousewing Britches; and FC/AFC Redcoat's Request.

Several Other Significant Sires

CNFC/FC **Patchwood Trapper**, is owned by Dick and Sylvia Lane of Los Angeles, California, and was handled to his Canadian National Championship by Dick Vermazen. Trapper has thrown several fine offspring and has been on several years' Top Sires lists.

NETC **Cortman Lane** was bred by Peter Onslow and campaigned in England by Keith Erlandson. Several of his offspring have been imported to the United States and are doing well, including NCFC Pel-Tan Roly, 1992 Canadian National Champion, owned by Jeff Miller.

FC/AFC **Solomon of Saighton** and FC/AFC **Samson of Saighton** are litter mates; Solomon is owned by Wayne Kilpatrick and Samson is owned by Andy Schoaf.

NFC **Pondview's Left-in-the-Light**, winner of the 1987 National Championship, owned by Leslie Cacchio and handled by East Coast professional Jerry

Cacchio is throwing some fine young dogs at this writing, including FC/ACF Raintree's Sassy Lady (two Nationals placements) and CAF Bar-Dan's Drift.

EFC **Brickclose Masterpiece** was English-bred and owned by Mrs. M. Pratt. He was never imported to the United States but several of his puppies were brought to this country by enthusiasts Jack Riepenhoff, Pat Fischer and Jeff Miller.

TOP SIRES: PAST, PRESENT AND FUTURE

Many other fine studs produced outstanding offspring—many before the 1980s and the advent of the Top Sires list. The following dogs truly made an impact on the breed in recent generations.

NFC ***Burcliff's Brandi***, owner Dean Brunn; 1979 National Open Champion.
FC/AFC ***Bluff Creek Shadow***, owner Tom Meyer; 2nd, 1982 National Open and National Amateur Championships.
Whispering Pine's ***Ebony Rebel***, owner Stan Beckner.
NFC/AFC/CFC ***Dewfield Brickclose Flint***, owner C. A. Christensen.
FC **Slattery of Saighton,** owner John Buoy; sire of *Saighton's Stat.*
FC/CFC ***Canspan's Magnum D-2***, owner Roy and Billie Jo Hopkins.

At this writing (1993), the following dogs are beginning to throw some very successful progeny, and it is my prediction that they will soon make their mark strongly on the breed. It will be interesting to see if time proves me right.
FC ***Reward's Genuine Charter***, owner Joe and Francis Ruff; sired the 1992 High Point Open dog.
FC/AFC ***Brickclose Matchwood***, owner Mark Hairfield; sire of several solid young performers.
PC ***Housty Samson***, owner Dick Turner.
FC/AFC ***Ru-Char's Rise & Shine***, owner Ruth Greening; sire of several high-performing young dogs.
FC/AFC ***Braw Bagpiper of Burtree***, owner Mark Schinderle.
FC/AFC ***Pondview's Windy Acre's Yankee***, owner Don Cande.
FC/AFC ***Kane's Rocky Road***, owner Steve Kane; sired 1992 NAFC Major's Black Magic.
Midland's Maker, owner Jim DeVoll; sired 1992 NFC Denalisunflo's Ring.

WHO WAS HALES SMUT?

If you study the pedigrees of successful field trial Springers, you will find that the name Hales Smut appears in most. As I researched this book I decided to find out more about this dog, which obviously had such a strong impact on the breed. Inquiries to Janet Christensen, Ed Whitaker and Art Rodger all led

FC/AFC Bricksclose Matchwood (Badger) was sired by Top Sire EFC Badgercourt Druid and then imported to the United States. Badger was the 1988 United States High Point Amateur dog and the 1991 United States High Point Open dog. Badger shows the normal dark head of Druid offspring.

CNFC/FC Patchwood's Trapper, son of "Scud," owned by Dick and Sylvia Lane of Los Angeles, California, and handled by Dick Vermazen (Pro).

me to the source of information and in fact the breeder of Hales Smut, Keith Erlandson of Wales. My special thanks go to Mr. Erlandson for his kind and articulate reply to my questions.

Hales Smut was whelped in Llangollen, Wales, on July 14, 1960, at Erlandson's Gwibernant Kennels. Smut was sold as a puppy to Arthur Cooke, an employee of the Hall family of Shropshire. Mr. Cooke then added the kennel name "Hales," which is the Hall family estate name.

Smut ran trials in 1961, '62, '63 and early '64, always handled by Mr. Cooke. Surprisingly, he never completed his field championship, though he did earn two seconds and two thirds, plus two diplomas in the English National Championships and several certificates of merit.

Reportedly Smut had such drive and enthusiasm that, to quote Erlandson, "often, after running a brilliant trial, he would boil over and come unstuck in the run off." On a few occasions he "ran in," or broke, as we say in America.

Hales Smut was bred extensively during his seventeen-year-life and in the end produced thirteen champions in Great Britain and reportedly thirteen more in the United States. A few of those are well known, such as Jonkit Joel, Wivenwood Willie and Sunray of Chrishall (a dog that once won five Open All-Age stakes in a row). Offspring of Smut were all bred extensively in the United States. As a result, the genetic influence of Hales Smut is most strongly felt in American dogs.

Hales Smut had a tremendous impact on the breed. His popularity as a stud put him in virtually every pedigree. His tremendous drive and energy was imparted to most of his offspring and may be the fountainhead for much of the enthusiasm we see in the field Springers of today.

The legendary producer Hales Smut (far left) is said to be one of the most important sires of field-bred Springers that ever lived. Born in 1960, he exerted an enormous influence on the breed and his name will be found in the background of many outstanding champions. Shown with him are his dam, Breckenhill Brando (center), and his half-sister Gwibernant Garreg Wynn.

15

Dog Things

A TOP-QUALITY gun dog, trial dog or hunting test dog quickly becomes the basis for an avocation of consuming interest. You will most probably want and need additional information and equipment to fully enjoy and pursue your sport. From personal experience, I recommend the following:

Magazines

Spaniels in the Field
10714 Escondido Drive
Cincinnati, Ohio 45249
Tel.: (513) 489–2727
Fax: (513) 489–4105
Information on hunting, training, trialing and hunt tests for spaniels.

Gun Dog Magazine
P.O. Box 350948
Des Moines, Iowa 50315
For subscription, call toll free: 1-800-435-0715
General hunting and gun dog information.

Books

Recommended books for additional training insight:

1. *Gun Dog Know How: Expert Advice on Gun Dog Training*, by David M. Duffey, published by Winchester Press.
2. *Hup! Training Flushing Spaniels the American Way*, by James B. Spencer, published by Howell Book House.
3. *Gun-Dog Training Spaniels and Retrievers*, by Kenneth Roebuck, published by Stackpole.

4. *Gundog Training*, by Keith Erlandson, published by Popular Dogs Publishing Co., Ltd.

These books are available through *Gun Dog Magazine* (1-800-767-4868) or Upland Sports listed below or can be ordered at your local bookstore.

Dog Food

I suggest a high-quality, name-brand food with a high-energy/nutrient-dense content, especially during hunting season. Scrimping on food is a very short-sighted way to save money. Most hunters feed dry dog food.

There are numerous high-quality brands of dog food on the market, but the top of the line is Purina Hi-Pro or Purina Pro-Plan.

Purina also has a valuable supply of free brochures on a wide variety of valuable-topics. For copies, write to:

Ralston-Purina Co.
1 Checkerboard Square
St. Louis, MO 63164
Attn: Mary Fuller (3RN)

Kennels

A good dog run is a life saver for you and the dog. I use Mason's—they are built to last forever. They are also easily portable if you move or change configuration.

Mason Kennel Company
260 Depot Street
Leesburg, Ohio 45135
(513) 780–2321

General Equipment

The following are sources for whistles, leads and other necessary items. Most spaniel trainers use either a buffalo-horn "peeper" whistle or the old standard orange "Roy Gonia" whistle. Either works fine; I use both.

Upland Sport
P.O. Box 288
Mukwonago, WI 53149
(414) 363-4595

RC Steele
1989 Transit Way, P.O. Box 910
Brockport, NY 14420–0910
1-800-872-3773

Drs. Foster & Smith, Inc.
2253 Air Park Road
P.O. Box 100
Rhinelander, WI 54501-0100
1-800-826-7206

Dunns, Inc.
Highway 57E
P.O. Box 449
Grand Junction, TN 38039-0449
1-800-223-8667

Travel is much easier when your dog is safely locked in a travel crate. These low-cost airline crates are available at many pet-supply outlets and serve a triple purpose: as travel crate, in-the-house bed and house-breaking aid. *Roggenkamp*

Some hunters or field trialers use dog trailers, which, on occasion, are towed by customized vans or suburbans. *Roggenkamp*

Some dog owners prefer wire crates, especially in hot weather. Many Springers can be doubled up in crates or kennels so long as they have enough room and ventilation. *Roggenkamp*

Collars: I *always* hunt a dog with a suitable collar and identification. I highly recommend using a strong, blaze-orange nylon collar with an attached brass nameplate giving your name, address and phone number. A good example is the Reflexite model sold by Nite Lite Company, P.O. Box 8210, Little Rock, Arkansas 72221-8210, 1-800-648-5483. They cost about $6.00 and seem to last forever.

Crates: I use ''Vari-kennel 300'' (fiberglass) airline crates, which are inexpensive, durable, easy to clean and provide some privacy. The ''300'' size is correct for 99 percent of all Springers. Other hunters prefer wire crates like ''Kennel-aires.''

Tattooing: It is a good idea to tattoo an identification number in your dog's ear. Your veterinarian can handle the job very easily.

Leads: I buy plain old nylon leads from a variety of sources. (I tend to lose them.)

Pliers: This item may surprise you. When hunting grouse or woodcock in the north woods, *always* carry a pair of needle-nose pliers. If your dog ever encounters a porcupine, you will need them.

Pedigrees: Pedigrees for your dog are available from various services such as Angell Pedigree Service, 1-800-468-0882.

Clubs: English Springer Spaniel Field Trial Association (ESSFTA). This is the parent club of the breed, meaning it is the governing body that, together with the American Kennel Club, sets the breed standard and rules of competition, which the AKC then administers. For more information write:

Marie Anderson (Corresponding Secretary)
ESSFTA
29512-47th Avenue South
Auburn, WA 98001

Glossary of Spaniel, Hunting and Field Trial Terms

Blink: An extremely serious fault in which a dog deliberately avoids game, often the result of too much pressure in training.

Bolter: A spaniel that leaves his handler and goes self-hunting (hunts for himself and not for, or with, his handler).

Cast: Has several meanings, but usually means the distance or depth to which a hunting spaniel penetrates the cover when quartering.

Cover: Grass, weeds or vegetation in the area where one is hunting or working his dog.

Fall: The spot where the game falls when shot.

Hard mouth: The fault by a dog of injuring game while in the act of retrieving.

Heel: The traditional command ordering a spaniel to walk at the handler's left heel if handler is a right-handed gunner.

Honor: Steadiness to both wing and shot when game is flushed by brace mate in trialing or hunting.

Hup: The traditional command ordering a spaniel to sit.

Pattern: The ground coverage that a spaniel demonstrates while quartering.

Potterer: A dog that lingers or remains too long on old or stale scent.

Quartering: The desirable back-and-forth, windshield-wiper-like path, covering both sides of the handler, run by a hunting spaniel.

Range: The distance a dog hunts from the handler.

Runner: Game that runs rather than flushes; often a cripple with a broken wing.

Steady to wing or to flush: Describes a spaniel that stops instantly and remains motionless when it flushes game, or when a flying bird passes overhead.

Steady to shot: Describes a spaniel that stops instantly (preferably sits) when a gun is fired.

Wild flush: A bird that flushes some distance out in front or to the side of a dog, and often out of gun range, before the dog gets to the bird.

Work a line, trail out, etc.: The action by a dog of following the body or foot scent in cover or on ground to locate moving game.

II

The English Springer Spaniel in the Show Ring and Obedience Competition, and as a Family Companion

by Julia Gasow (with Kellie Fitzgerald)

Ch. Inchidony Prince Charming, owned and bred by Becher and Dorothy Hungerford, one of the breed's most memorable sires. He produced fifty champions, including six Best in Show dogs out of six different bitches.

To my husband,
Fred,
to whose unselfish love, continual encouragement and ever-dependable help I owe whatever success I've enjoyed in the sport of dogs—and who, more than anyone else, has helped keep it fun for me.

JULIA (MRS. FRED H.) GASOW

Mrs. Gasow and the English Springer Spaniel have been synonymous for over sixty years, and during that tenure each has benefited from the other in many ways. Mrs. Gasow's Salilyn prefix has been attached to the names of a host of English Springer show dogs. Included among them are many of the breed's most distinguished producers, Specialty winners and all-breed Best in Show dogs. Throughout a life in dogs laden with honors in the ring and from her peers, Mrs. Gasow remains a breeder at heart and totally devoted to the well-being of her breed above all.

The Author

JULIA GASOW and English Springer Spaniels are inseparably linked in the minds of conformation dog sport enthusiasts. And no breed ever had a truer friend. Since the early 1930s Mrs. Gasow has owned, bred and shown English Springers under the celebrated "Salilyn" prefix, pursuing a program of highly effective linebreeding. The success of her efforts is a matter of history, and she is a towering presence not only in her own breed, but for all who know what it means to breed fine dogs consistently, one generation after the other.

Twice named "Dog Woman of the Year" (1971 and 1980) and "Dog Breeder of the Year" by *Kennel Review* magazine (1970 and 1975), she was also one of the first women to be named an American Kennel Club delegate. Hers has been a profound and happy influence and the dog sport is better for her participation.

From her breeding expertise has come such unforgettables as King Peter, Citation, Hallmark, the super-sire Aristocrat and, of course, "Robert," Ch. Salilyn's Condor, Best in Show at the 1993 Westminster KC show, the top-winning show Springer of all time! There have been other notables and there will be more, but when one breeder can account for hundreds of champions and numerous top winners and producers, little else needs saying.

Through all of this Julia Gasow has never lost sight of what is best for the dogs and her breed. Even after six decades of wonderful dogs and wonderful achievements, Mrs. Gasow maintains a perspective that so many others would probably lack.

In coming through with yet another "Show Section" for this perennial classic, Julia Gasow further extends the greatest gift that can be made to the fancy—breed knowledge.

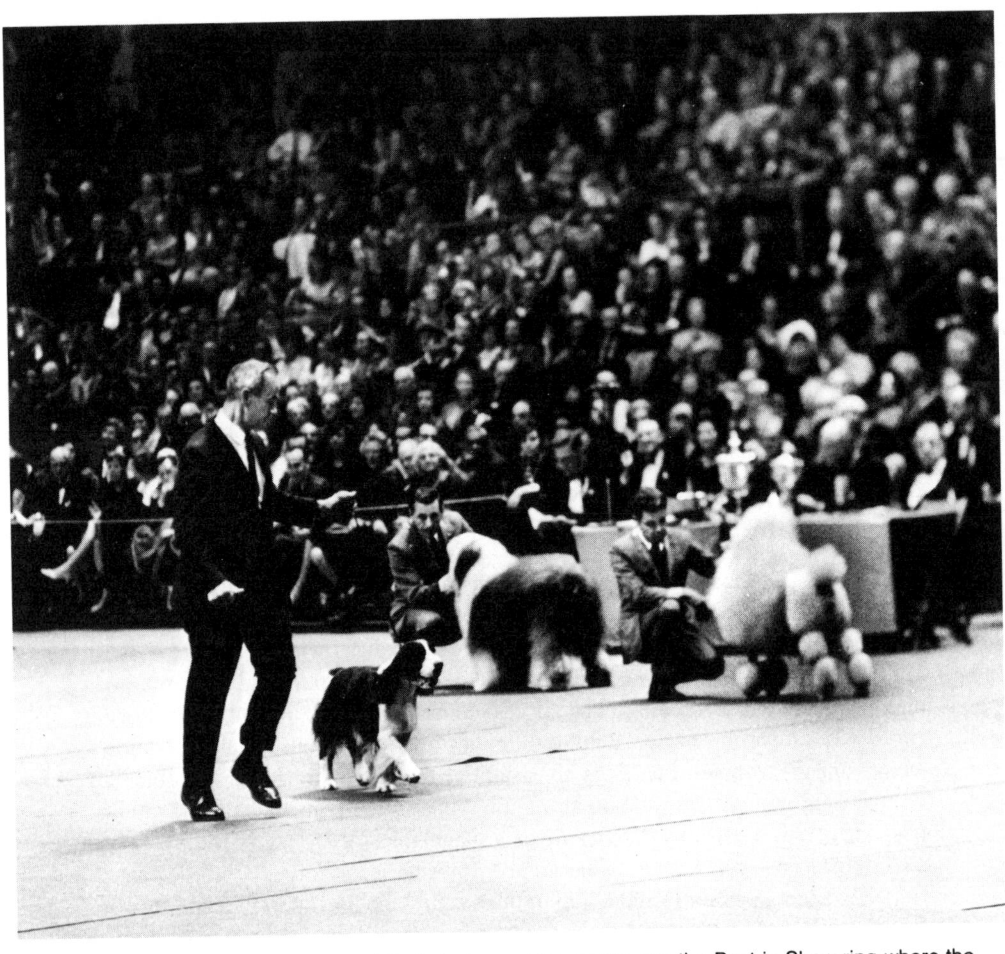

The year was 1967. The show was Westminster and the scene was the Best in Show ring where the unforgettable "Risto"—Ch. Salilyn's Aristocrat put his best foot forward as the representative from the Sporting Group. Dick Cooper handled him in this final that included some of the most acclaimed and accomplished show dogs of the day.

Preface

It is a great pleasure to embark on the third edition of *The New Complete English Springer Spaniel.* I first want to express my appreciation to Charles Goodall for his contributions to the previous editions. Edd Roggenkamp, an active member on the Board of Governors of the Parent Club, now adds his knowledge to the book. The relationship between the field trial enthusiasts and the bench show enthusiasts has now been accepted by both components of the sport; old animosities have been resolved, and all accept the fact that each side has made its own contribution to the completion of the English Springer Spaniel.

It is important that we concentrate on individuals and bloodlines not only that establish top winners but that can also produce future generations of them. There is now more emphasis on the Sire and Dam section in the book to show the importance of particular dogs that not only are show winners but can continue to produce top progeny. Any accomplishments we have achieved at Salilyn are due completely to consistent line breeding that is based on sixty years of breeding the English Springer Spaniel.

I would like to take this opportunity to thank Kellie Fitzgerald for her work in helping with the material and information; Nancy Siver for her contribution of the Parent Club's Statistics; and Marcia Gillett and Kerrie Frederick for their book *The Directory of the English Springer Spaniel.* Special thanks go to Mary Grill for her typing of the manuscript and to all the Springer breeders and owners for their cooperation in sending me their pictures and pedigrees.

—Julia Gasow

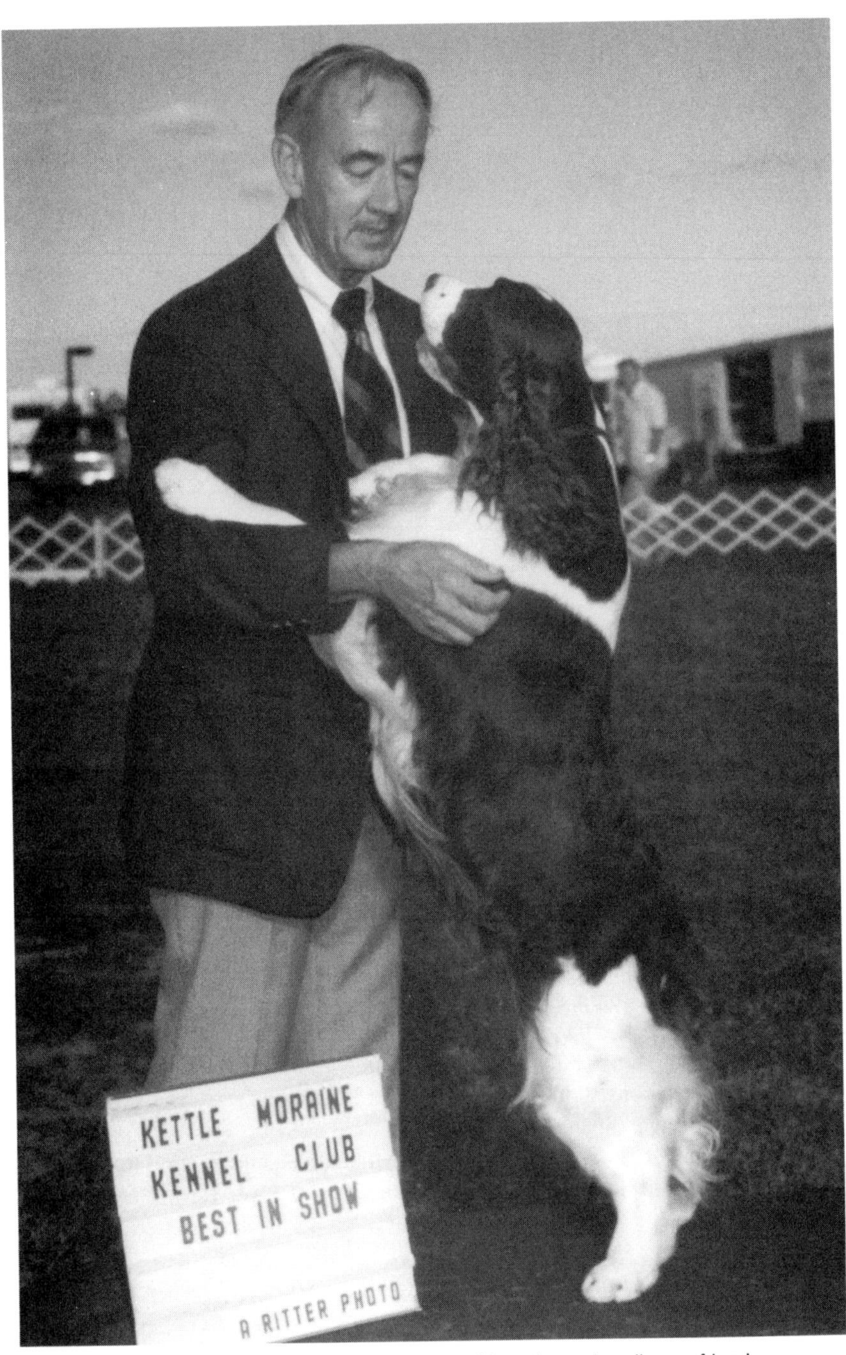

Dick Cooper with Ch. Salilyn's Hallmark. More than a handler—a friend.

Special Acknowledgment

There have been many top professional handlers in our sport, but, in my opinion, one man stands above all. One of the greatest sporting dog handlers of all time is Dick Cooper of Barrington, Illinois.

A second-generation professional handler, Dick has been showing dogs for nearly sixty years. He has been awarded eleven Ken-L-Ration Show Dog of the Year titles as winning handler in his groups; seven of those awards were with English Springer Spaniels from Salilyn Kennels. He was inducted into the Ken-L-Ration Hall of Fame in New York on February 6, 1993.

Dick was much more than a handler—he made the dog game fun for me. I could depend on his information or suggestions. He always had the dog's welfare in mind and knew the importance not only of his winning record but also of the dog's ability to produce so that that particular dog would leave a mark on the breed.

This gathering of Springer pioneers took place at the first Specialty show in America for English Springer Spaniels. This historic photo records the 1922 event in Englewood, New Jersey. Among those pictured are W. J. Hutchinson (third from right), a pioneer of American interest in the breed, and Freeman Lloyd (far right), famous writer and breed advocate. Rudolph Tauskey took this photo and later presented it to Mrs. Gasow.

16

Bench Springers in America

THE FIRST SPECIALTY SHOW for English Springer Spaniels in the United States was held at Englewood, New Jersey, in 1922. The exhibits were field trial dogs and their owners great sportsmen, to be remembered for their contribution to both bench and field.

These gentlemen ran their dogs in a field trial one day, combed out the burrs, and then the following day showed them for conformation. However, this first Specialty touched off a spark of enthusiasm for the joy of winning on Springer beauty as well as field ability.

Fanciers continued to run and show their dogs successfully as late as the early 1930s. But more and more they became critical of the overall appearance of the "non-conformist" field trial Springer, whose owner was interested in only that one phase of the sport. They became aware of the importance of coat and feather in the ring, and a show-minded individual no longer cared to subject his prospective winner to the general hazards of field work.

This was the beginning of a division in Springer type, represented by two distinct sports within the breed. Over the years, these groups have grown farther apart, with some resulting friction along the way.

Many felt that this division would be the ruination of the breed, but results have proved quite the contrary. Each of the two phases has become so highly specialized that we now have English Springer Spaniel superiority on two fronts, as it were: ability unsurpassed by any other breed in field trials, and a bench record unmatched by any other breed since 1967.

Eng., Am., Can. Ch. Springbok of Ware (left) and Dual Ch. Flint of Avondale (right), whelped 1921. These two were the most prominent Springers imported to America by Eudore Chevrier of Canada.

Eng., Am. Ch. Nuthill Dignity, imported from England by E. deK. Leffingwell, was a Best in Show winner in 1930.

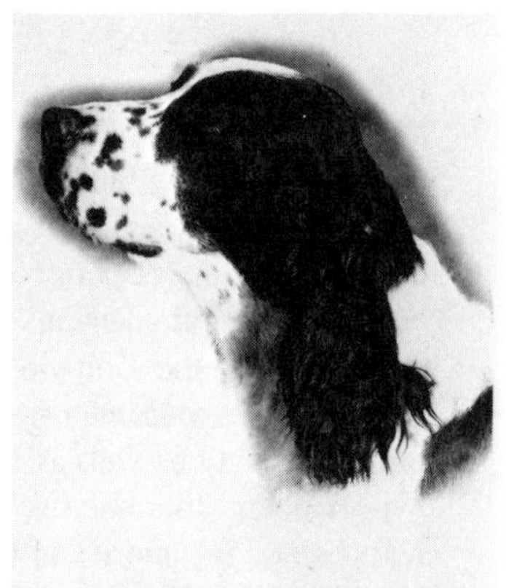

Ch. Woodelf of Breeze, a Nuthill Dignity daughter, appears in the backgrounds of many important Springers that followed.

Am., Can. Ch. Norman of Hamsey, owned by Blue Leader Kennels, was the first English Springer to win the Sporting Group at Westminster. The year was 1933.

Today field trial enthusiasts and bench enthusiasts are pretty much agreed that each dog does best within its own sphere, and that neither does well the work of the other. It is also agreed that the field trial dog is too high strung to make a good house dog.

From personal experience I can advise against crossing these two strains if your aim is to produce a show-winning Springer that can compete creditably in field trials. From the first breeding of such a cross it would take at least four generations back to bench breeding to have a show dog. By this time, naturally, the speed and field ability gained would be lost. It is easy to produce an excellent hunting dog from bench breeding, but almost impossible to breed a show Springer from field trial stock.

Significant Show Dogs of the 1920s and Early 1930s

Most active in the importation of many English Springer Spaniels that began in the early 1920s was Eudore Chevrier of Canada. Mr. Chevrier bought extensively, and did well with the breed in Canada under the banner of "Avandale." Most notable of the many he imported were Dual Ch. Flint of Avandale, bred by the Duke of Hamilton, and Eng. Am. & Can. Ch. Springbok of Ware. But Mr. Chevrier's dogs were a heterogeneous lot. He was basically an importer—not a breeder—and established no set line.

In 1928, E. de K. Leffingwell, a Californian, imported Ch. Nuthill Dignity from England. Dignity became a tri-international champion. He had an outstandingly beautiful head—good enough to outweigh the fact that he was, reportedly, somewhat spindly, with weak pasterns and a curly coat. He was a fine showman, and did top winning on both coasts through the early 1930s, including Best of Breed at Westminster in 1930.

Dignity was an important sire as well. Mrs. Betty Buchanan of Breeze Kennels, Denver, Colorado, bred her Dilkusha Darkie to him to produce the ever-remembered bitch Ch. Woodelf of Breeze, the dog behind so many winning Springers of today.

Robert Elliot also used Nuthill Dignity to advantage at his Elysian Kennels. Dignity is the grandsire of the famous Elysian quintuplets, one of which—King Lion—became the first dual champion in America.

Tragically, Nuthill Dignity got loose one day and ran to the mountains and was never seen again.

One of the important English imports, although a somewhat controversial one, was English, American and Canadian Champion Showman of Shotton, brought over in 1939 by Paul Quay of Chagrin Falls, Ohio.

Showman's winning career started immediately upon his arrival. He was shown exclusively by one of the leading handlers in the country, Billy Lang, who later became a licensed all-breed judge, and then an American Kennel Club field representative. Billy campaigned Showman extensively, piloting him to many Best in Show wins in an era before the Springer's great popularity as a Group dog.

Eng., Am., Can. Ch. Showman of Shotton, imported from England in 1939 by Paul Quay.

Ch. Clarion Rufton Tandy (at nine months) is said to have been the model for the 1932 Standard revision.

Ch. Runor's Agent, owned by Norman Morrow.

Though outstanding in the show ring, Showman's influence on the breed remains questionable. The West Coast profited by establishing his powerful rear movement in their bloodlines. In the East, Norman Morrow's best winner, Ch. Runor's Agent, a great moving dog, was sired by him. But Norman himself said of his dog, "Agent was short in foreface and neck and had a somewhat harsh expression."

Well after Showman's retirement Billy Lang wrote, "Showman of Shotton was a mean-eyed rascal and contributed nothing in the way of soft expressive eyes to the breed." Edward Dana Knight, well-known breeder-judge, wrote: "Let's face it—Showman is the greatest disaster that's ever happened to American Springers. There were many things to like about him, but he sired a high percentage of shy dogs and an astonishing number with bad feet."

Mr. Charles Toy, whose Clarion Kennels was named for the county in which he lived—about sixty miles from Pittsburgh—was doing much to improve the breed with his English imports during this whole period. Such Springers as Clarion Rufton Trumpet and Clarion Rufton Tandy were great then, and I think would look good today. As a matter of fact, the latter was used as a "model" for the revision of the English Springer standard in 1932.

Mr. Toy's close friend, R. E. Allen of Provo, Utah, a highly respected breeder of champions, did well for the Springer cause with his Timpanogos dogs. Possibly his best were Ch. Melinda, Group winner at Westminster in 1942, and Ch. Timpanogos Radar.

And I must certainly mention George Higgs, whose Boghurst Springers were winning then and are still in the rings today.

There were many other winners at the time, but they have left little, if any, imprint on the breed. The dogs, generally, were longer in body than our present Springer. They were short on legs with poor fronts. Most were heavily ticked.

Above: Ch. Elysian Emissary, a 1934 Best in Show winner. Right: Ch. Timpanogos Melinda, owned by R. E. Allen, was first in the Sporting Group at the 1942 Westminster show. Her handler was the celebrated Harry Sangster.

Eng., Am. Ch. Rufton Recorder (Boss of Glasnevin ex Rufton Flirt), whelped on May 11, 1926, and imported to the United States by Fred Hunt in 1933, initiated the beginnings of the modern English Springer Spaniel as it is now seen in the American show ring.

17

The Recorder Influence

ENGLISH and American Champion Rufton Recorder had the greatest impact of any single dog on our show Springer of today. He was purchased by Fred M. Hunt directly from his English breeder, R. Cornthwaite, and imported to this country in 1933.

Fred Hunt was well known to the dog world long before this date. He had established his Green Valley Kennels in the beautiful farm lands of Devon, Pennsylvania, had produced several show champions, and for years had taken an active and enthusiastic part in field trials.

Fred had purchased Recorder strictly for breeding purposes. The dog was seven years old at the time and therefore an unlikely show prospect. But Recorder was an English show champion, and his sire—Boss of Glasnevin—had been a field trial winner, at one time considered the top prospect in England. Thus Recorder had everything to offer Fred's breeding program.

Very shortly after this great dog's arrival in America it became evident that he was not too old for the show ring, after all. He was active, gay, in good physical condition—in fact, Fred felt that he was the best Springer he had ever seen.

Accordingly, he entered him in several shows and Recorder immediately created a sensation. Many exhibitors were highly critical of him—not surprising, really, for he was very different from the dogs they were producing. He represented change—a "new model" Springer that some refused to accept. But the more serious breeders recognized in him quality and style not to be surpassed during the era.

He was taller than his competitors and far more compact, standing on well-

Dual Ch. Green Valley Punch, a Recorder son, was the last of the breed to gain the title in the ring and the field. One of an all-champion litter of six, he became a dual in 1938. He was owned by Fred Hunt.

Ch. Dunoon Donald Dhu, owned by Janet Henneberry, was Best of Breed at Westminster 1938 and sired Ch. Rodrique of Sandblown Acre.

boned, perfectly straight forelegs that offered great breed improvement. And his feet were excellent. Though plain in head, his appearance was enhanced by a collar and markings of pure, sparkling white, making him stand out against the heavily ticked dogs of the day.

I am grateful to have seen him shown in 1934 at the English Springer Spaniel Club of Michigan's first Specialty Show, where he was Best of Breed from the limit class (now extinct) of over 104 entries. The judge was Freeman Lloyd. Recorder finished his championship in record time.

Since names of Rufton Recorder's direct descendants appear many times in the pedigrees of our current winners, it is interesting to know how they came about, remembering, of course, that we can only touch the high points in the space allowed us here.

Fred Hunt leased Woodelf of Breeze, a Nuthill Dignity daughter for two breedings to Recorder. The first produced the most famous litter in Springer history, consisting of six bench show champions. One was Green Valley Punch, who also achieved a Field Trial Championship in 1938. We have not had another dual champion Springer in America since. The other five bench champions were all important winners and all good producers.

One bitch in the litter was never shown. Her bone was fine, and her head unattractive. Her eyes, small and slanting, suggested the name given her—"Orientia." But although not herself show material, Orientia is significant because of her progeny.

In 1935, Fred bought Dunoon Donald Dhu from Andy Dunn in Canada, and did well with him in the States. He was a short, well-balanced dog, though large and lacking in angulation.

While resting on his laurels at Green Valley Kennels, his championship certificate hanging on the wall, Donald Dhu took a fancy to our ugly duckling Orientia and, when no one was looking, jumped the fence and bred her. A black male puppy from this litter was sold to William Belleville of Langhorne, Pennsylvania, and was registered "Rodrique of Sandblown Acre." As we shall soon see, Rodrique was to be the first of a line of top winning and producing dogs for this well-known kennel.

Dunoon Donald Dhu was soon sold to Janet Henneberry of Golf, Illinois, who loved him so dearly that she named her kennel for him: "Donnie Dhu."

Fred Hunt brought over another bitch from Mr. Cornthwaite in England named Rulton Rosita, and bred her to Recorder to produce Ch. Green Valley Hercules. Hercules, bred to his half-sister Orientia, produced Tranquillity of Well Sweep, who became the dam of Ch. Tranquillity of Melilotus, Mrs. R. Gilman Smith's outstanding bitch.

Recorder was bred to his granddaughter, Ch. Green Valley Dinah, to produce Ch. Green Valley Oak. Oak, bred to his half-sister, Ch. Green Valley Judy, a Recorder daughter, produced Ch. Green Valley The Feudist.

Recorder was the sire of Ch. Field Marshall, the foundation of Bob Morrow's Audley Farm Kennel, and when linebred through Green Valley Oak, gave Norman Morrow the foundation for his Runor Kennel, Ch. Audley Farm Judy.

Ch. Green Valley Oak, an important producer.

Ch. Tranquility of Melilotus, owned by Mrs. R. Gilman Smith (Mrs. Frederick Brown).

Am., Can. Ch. Rodrique of Sandblown Acre (Ch. Dunoon Donald Dhu ex Green Valley Orientia).

Recorder and his offspring are behind Walpride Springers, Rumack, Charlyle, Kaintuck, Wakefield, Inchidony, Frejax, Salilyn and others.

Fred Hunt personally handled Recorder to his championship, as he did most of his Springers. He also ran Green Valley Punch, exclusively, for his Field Trial Championship. Fred seldom entered a dog in the Specials class, having little interest in campaigning a dog for Group winning.

In 1941 he was transferred to Detroit, Michigan, so closed Green Valley Kennels. But in a span of ten years, he had finished fifty-six champions!

Important Sires Following Recorder

In the wake of Recorder, two sires above all others can be credited with leaving their imprint on top-winning Springers of today. They are Am. & Can. Ch. Rodrique of Sandblown Acre and Ch. Inchidony Prince Charming.

Bred at the Green Valley Kennels of Fred Hunt, Rodrique was sold to William Belleville as a puppy. For Mr. Belleville, Rodrique represented an exciting new interest—the dog game. He became the foundation of Sandblown Acre Kennels, named for the Bellevilles' sandy acre of land in Pennsylvania. He was the sire of twenty-eight champions, most of them outstanding producers, including Ch. Co-Pilot of Sandblown Acre with twenty-eight champion get.

Mr. Belleville was the head tomato grower for Campbell Soup Company at the time, and although fairly well along in years and completely inexperienced in dog breeding, bred a good number of winners—all descendants of Rodrique. Unfortunately, this success was short-lived. He found that his theories for breeding bigger, better tomatoes were not applicable to breeding dogs.

Just as Rufton Recorder was the link connecting Mr. Goodall's early history in this book to our modern Springers (with Rodrique of Sandblown Acres as the stepping stone in between), Ch. Inchidony Prince Charming stands as the solid beginning of today's winners.

Life moves at such a fast pace around us that it is natural to expect to find many changes in our breed during the past twelve-year period. Some of the "Modern Greats" of yesterday are no longer found prominently in pedigrees today.

We all want to know the Springers that are in the winning circle today—those making Parent Club records by achieving recognized awards and that are generally in the public eye. Most interesting of all, we want to find the dogs that have produced them and continue to remain prominent in current pedigrees.

One statistic remains unbroken: Ch. Green Valley Punch, bred and owned by Fred M. Hunt, in 1938, is still the last English Springer Spaniel Dual Champion.

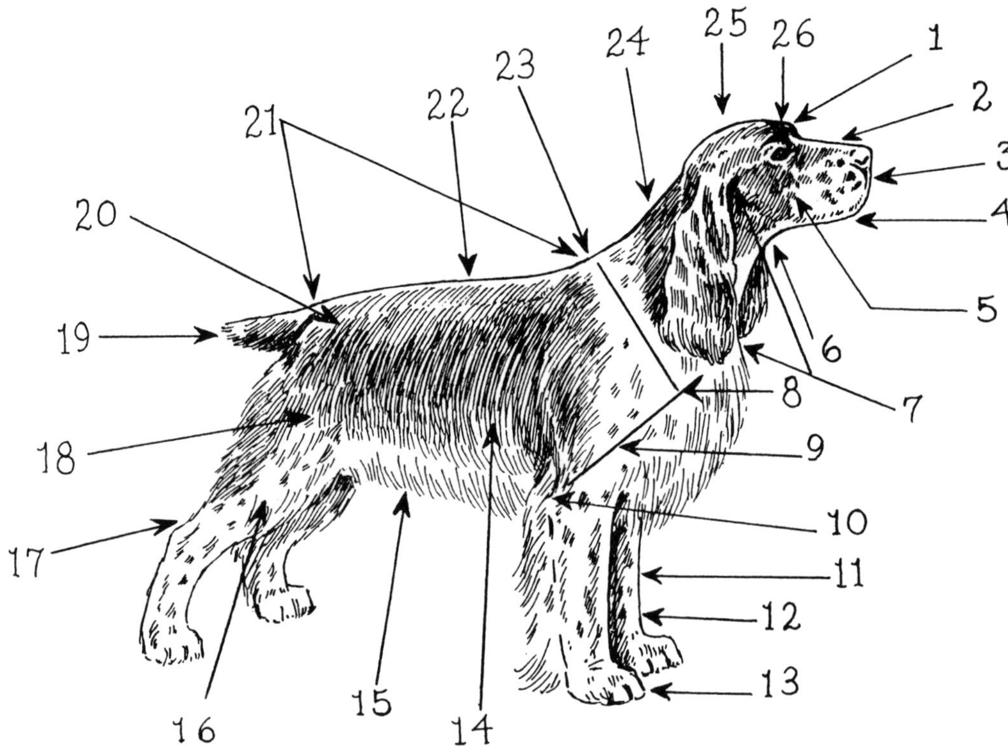

1—Stop, moderate; eyebrows, well developed
2—Nasal bone, straight
3—Muzzle, fairly square
4—Jaws, strong, even
5—Chiseling under eyes
6—Not too throaty
7—Ears, set low, falling close to head
8—Sloping shoulders
9—Brisket to elbow
10—Elbows, close to body
11—Forelegs, straight with good bone, slightly flattened
12—Pasterns, strong
13—Feet, strong, compact, toes arched, pads thick
14—Body, deep, ribs well sprung
15—Not tucked up
16—Stifle joint, strong, moderately bent
17—Hock joint, rounded, moderately bent, well let down
18—Thighs, broad, muscular
19—Tail, set low, carried horizontally with merry action
20—Hips, nicely rounded
21—Distance withers to base of tail, slightly less than shoulder height
22—Back, strong, no dip or roach
23—Shoulder blades, fairly close
24—Neck, arched
25—Occiput bone, rounded, inconspicuous
26—Eyes, dark, friendly, tight lids

18

Official Standard for the English Springer Spaniel

General Appearance—The English Springer Spaniel is a medium-size sporting dog with a neat, compact body, and a docked tail. His coat is moderately long and glossy with feathering on his legs, ears, chest and brisket. His pendulous ears, soft gentle expression, sturdy build and friendly wagging tail proclaim him unmistakably a member of the ancient family of Spaniels. He is above all a well-proportioned dog, free from exaggeration, nicely balanced in every part. His carriage is proud and upstanding, body deep, legs strong and muscular with enough length to carry him with ease. His short, level back, well developed thighs, good shoulders, excellent feet, suggest power, endurance, agility. Taken as a whole he looks the part of a dog that can go and keep going under difficult hunting conditions, and moreover he enjoys what he is doing. At his best he is endowed with style, symmetry, balance, enthusiasm and is every inch a sporting dog of distinct spaniel character, combining beauty and utility. *To be penalized*—Those lacking true English Springer type in conformation, expression, or behavior.

Size, Proportion, Substance—The Springer is built to cover rough ground with agility and reasonable speed. He should be kept to medium size—neither too small nor too large and heavy to do the work for which he is intended. The ideal ***shoulder height*** for dogs is 20 inches, for bitches, 19 inches. *To be penalized*—Oversize or undersize specimens (those more than one inch under or over the breed ideal). Length of topline (the distance from top of the shoulders to the root

Heads–Front View

1. A bad head—Eyes too prominent—Narrow, pointed skull
2. Heavy skull—Cheeky—High-set ears
3. A well-proportioned head

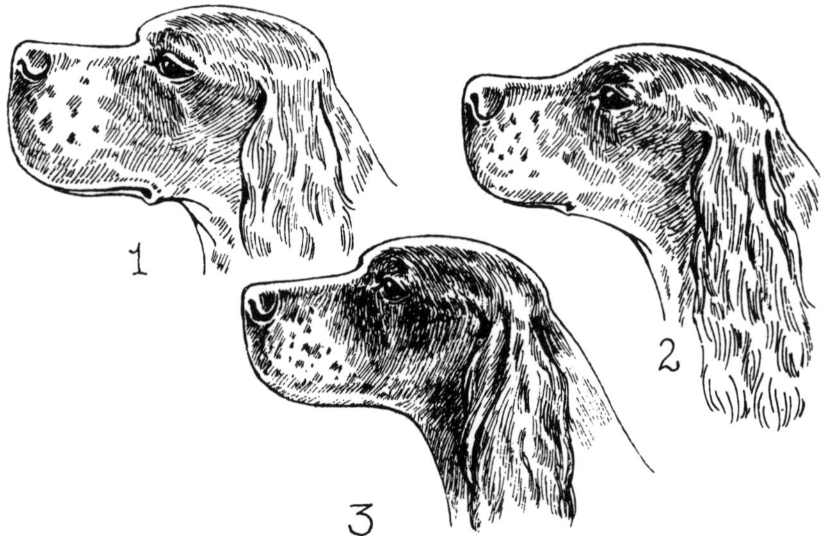

Heads–Side View

1. Too much stop—Heavy lips—Loose-lidded eyes
2. Too little stop—Muzzle too short for skull
3. A good head

of the tail should be approximately equal to the dog's shoulder height—never longer than his height—and not appreciably less. The dog too long in body, especially when long in loin, tires easily and lacks the compact outline characteristic of the breed. Equally undesirable is the dog too short in body for the length of his legs, a condition that destroys his balance and restricts the gait. ***Weight*** is dependent on the dog's other dimensions: a 20-inch dog, well proportioned, in good condition should weigh about 49–55 pounds. The resulting appearance is a well-knit, sturdy dog with good but not too heavy bone, in no way coarse or ponderous. *To be penalized*—Over-heavy specimens, cloddy in build. Leggy individuals, too tall for their length and substance.

Head—The head is impressive without being heavy. Its beauty lies in a combination of strength and refinement. It is important that the size and proportion be in balance with the rest of the dog. Viewed in profile the head should appear approximately the same length as the neck and should blend with the body in substance. The stop, eyebrow and the chiseling of the bony structure around the eye sockets contribute to the Springer's beautiful and characteristic expression. The ***expression*** to be alert, kindly, trusting. ***Eyes***—More than any other feature the eyes contribute to the Springer's appeal. Color, placement, size influence expression and attractiveness. The eyes to be of medium size, neither small, round, full and prominent, nor bold and hard in expression. Set rather well apart and fairly deep in their sockets. The color of the iris to harmonize with the color of the coat, preferably a good dark hazel in the liver dogs and black or deep brown in the black and white specimens. The lids, tight with little or no haw showing. *To be penalized*—Eyes yellow or brassy in color or noticeably lighter than the coat. Sharp expression indicating unfriendly or suspicious nature. Loose droopy lids. Prominent haw (the third eyelid or membrane in the inside corner of the eye). ***Ears***—The correct ear set is on a level with the line of the eye; on the side of the skull and not too far back. The flaps to be long and fairly wide, hanging close to the cheeks, with no tendency to stand up or out. The leather, thin, approximately long enough to reach the tip of the nose. *To be penalized*—Short round ears. Ears set too high or too low or too far back on the head. The ***skull*** (upper head) to be of medium length, fairly broad, flat on top, slightly rounded at the sides and back. The occiput bone inconspicuous, rounded rather than peaked or angular. The foreface (head in front of the eyes) approximately the same length as the skull, and in harmony as to width and general character. Looking down on the head the muzzle to appear to be about one half the width of the skull. As the skull rises from the foreface it makes a brow or "stop," divided by a groove or fluting between the eyes. This groove continues upward and gradually disappears as it reaches the middle of the forehead. The amount of "stop" can best be described as moderate. It must not be a pronounced feature; rather it is a subtle rise where the muzzle blends into the upper head, further emphasized by the groove and by the position and shape of the eyebrows which should be well developed. The ***cheeks*** to be flat, (not rounded, full or thick) with nice chiseling under the eyes. Viewed in profile the topline of the skull and the

Toplines

1. Sway back
2. Roach back
3. Correct topline

muzzle lie in two approximately parallel planes. The nasal bone should be straight, with no inclination downward toward the tip of the nose, which gives a downfaced look so undesirable in this breed. Neither should the nasal bone be concave resulting in a "dish-faced" profile; nor convex giving the dog a Roman nose. The nostrils, well opened and broad, liver color or black depending on the color of the coat. Flesh-colored ("Dudley noses") or spotted ("butterfly noses") are undesirable. The ***jaws*** to be of sufficient length to allow the dog to carry game easily, fairly square, lean, strong, and even (neither undershot nor overshot). The upper lip to come down full and rather square to cover the line of the lower jaw, but ***lips*** not to be pendulous nor exaggerated. *To be penalized*—Oval, pointed or heavy skull. Cheeks prominently rounded, thick and protruding. Too much or too little stop. Over-heavy muzzle. Muzzle too short, too thick, too narrow. Pendulous slobbery lips. Under- or overshot jaws—a very serious fault, to be heavily penalized. The ***teeth*** should be strong, clean, not too small; and when the mouth is closed the teeth should meet in a close *scissors bite* (the lower incisors touching the inside of the upper incisors). *To be penalized*—Any deviation from the above description. Irregularities due to faulty jaw formation to be severely penalized.

Neck, Topline, Body—The ***neck*** to be moderately long, muscular, slightly arched at the crest, gradually blending into sloping shoulders. Not noticeably upright, nor coming into the body at an abrupt angle. *To be penalized*—Short neck, often the sequence to steep shoulders. Concave neck, sometimes called ewe neck or upside-down neck (the opposite of arched). Excessive throatiness. The ***topline*** slopes *very gently* from withers to tail—the line from withers to back descending without a sharp drop; the back practically level; arch over hips somewhat lower than the withers. The *body* to be well coupled, strong, compact; the ***chest*** deep but not so wide or round as to interfere with the action of the front legs; the brisket sufficiently developed to reach to the level of the elbows. The ribs fairly long, springing gradually to the middle of the body, then tapering as they approach the end of the ribbed section. The bottom line, starting on a level with the elbows, to continue backward with almost no up-curve until reaching the end of the ribbed section, then a more noticeable upcurve to the flank, but not enough to make the dog appear small waisted or "tucked up."

The ***back*** (section between the withers and loin) to be straight and strong, with no tendency to dip or roach. The ***loins*** to be strong, short, a slight arch over loins and hip bones. Hips nicely rounded, blending smoothly into hind legs. ***Croup*** sloping gently to base of tail; tail carried to follow the natural line of the body. The Springer's *tail* is an index both to his temperament and his conformation. Merry tail action is characteristic. The proper set is somewhat low following the natural line of the croup. The carriage should be nearly horizontal, slightly elevated when dog is excited. Carried straight is untypical of the breed. The tail should not be docked too short. *To be penalized*—Topline sloping sharply, indicating steep withers (straight shoulder placement) and a too-low tail set. Body too shallow, indicating lack of brisket. Ribs too flat sometimes due to

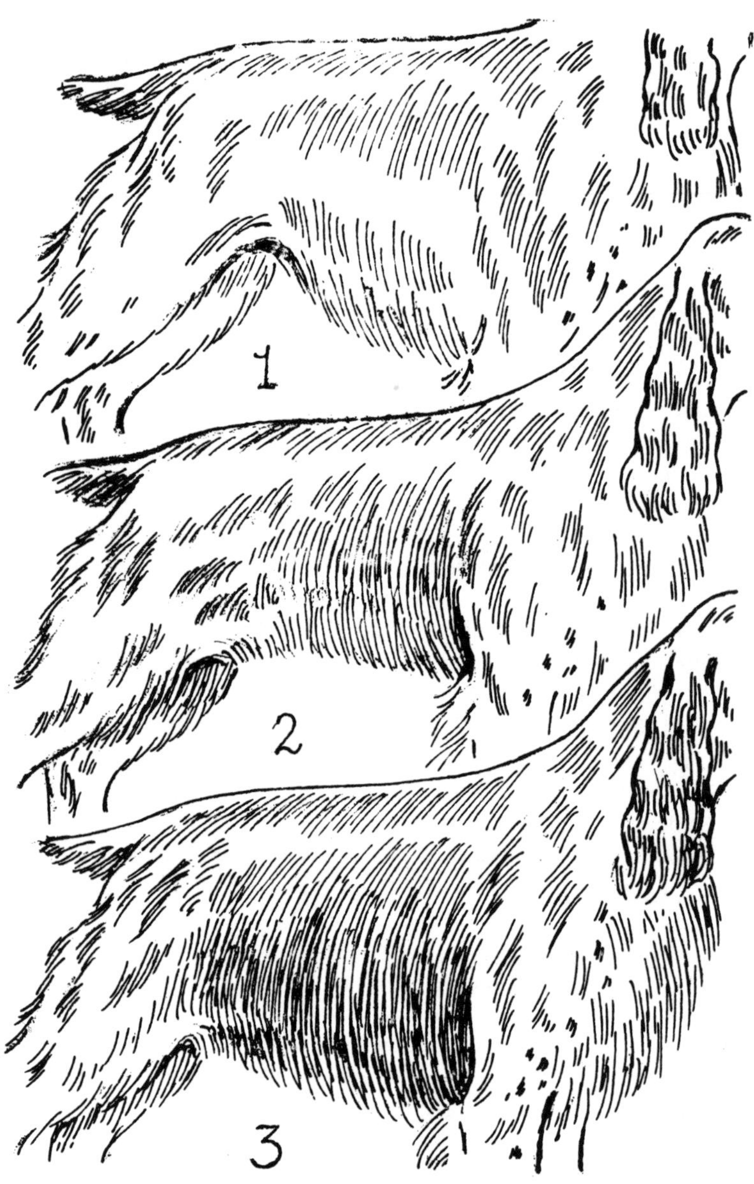

Bodies

1. Exaggerated tuck-up
2. Narrow rib section—Shallow
3. Good bottom line—No tuck-up

immaturity. Ribs too round (barrel shaped), hampering the gait. Sway back (dip in back), indicating weakness or lack of muscular development, particularly to be seen when dog is in action and viewed from the side. Roach back (too much arch over loin and extending forward into middle section). Croup falling away too sharply, or croup too high—unsightly faults, detrimental to outline and good movement. Tail habitually upright. Tail set too high or too low. Clamped-down tail (indicating timidity or undependable temperament, even less to be desired than the tail carried too gaily).

Forequarters—***Shoulders*** (fairly close together at the tips) to lie flat and mold smoothly into the contour of the body. Efficient movement in front calls for proper shoulders, the blades sloping back to form an angle with the upper arm of approximately 90 degrees which permits the dog to swing his forelegs forward in an easy manner. ***Elbows*** close to the body with free action from the shoulders. The ***forelegs*** to be straight with the same degree of size to the foot. The bone, strong, slightly flattened, not too heavy or round. The knee, straight, almost flat; the ***pasterns*** short, strong. *To be penalized*—Shoulders set at a steep angle limiting the stride. Loaded shoulders (the blades standing out from the body by overdevelopment of the muscles). Loose elbows, crooked legs. Bone too light or too coarse and heavy. Weak pasterns that let down the feet at a pronounced angle.

The ***feet*** to be round, or slightly oval, compact, well arched, medium size with thick pads well feathered between the toes. Excess hair to be removed to show the natural shape and size of the foot. *To be penalized*—Thin, open or splayed feet (flat with spreading toes). Hare foot (long, rather narrow foot).

Hindquarters—The Springer should be shown in hard muscular condition, well developed in hips and thighs and the whole rear assembly should suggest strength and driving power. The ***hip joints*** to be set rather wide apart and the hips nicely rounded. The ***thighs*** broad and muscular; the stifle joint strong and moderately bent. The ***hock joint*** somewhat rounded, not small and sharp in contour, and moderately angulated. Leg from hock joint to foot pad, short and strong with good bone structure. When viewed from the rear the hocks to be parallel whether the dog is standing or in motion. *To be penalized*—Too little or too much angulation. Narrow, undeveloped thighs. Hocks too short or too long (a proportion of 1/3 the distance from hip joint to foot is ideal). Cowhocks—hocks turning in toward each other. Flabby muscles. Weakness of joints. Feet as in front.

Coat—On ears, chest, legs and belly the Springer is nicely furnished with a fringe of feathering of moderate length and heaviness. On head, front of forelegs, and below hocks on front of hind legs, the hair is short and fine. The body coat is flat or wavy, of medium length, sufficiently dense to be waterproof, weatherproof and thornproof. The texture fine, and the hair should have the clean, glossy, live appearance indicative of good health. It is legitimate to trim about head, feet, ears; to remove dead hair; to thin and shorten excess feathering, particularly from the hocks to the feet and elsewhere as required to give a smart,

Fronts
1. Too wide in front
2. Bowed and pigeon-toed
3. A good front

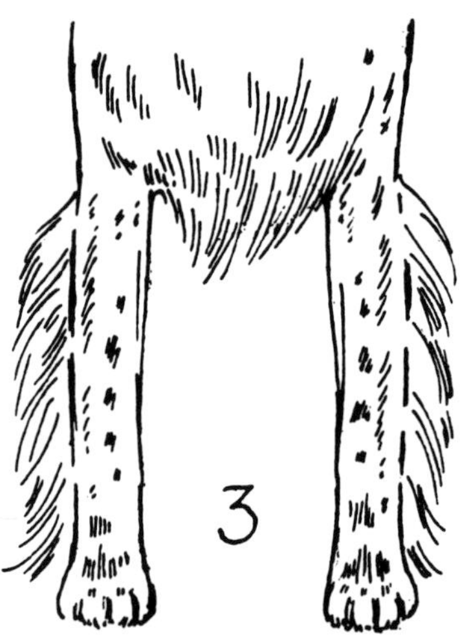

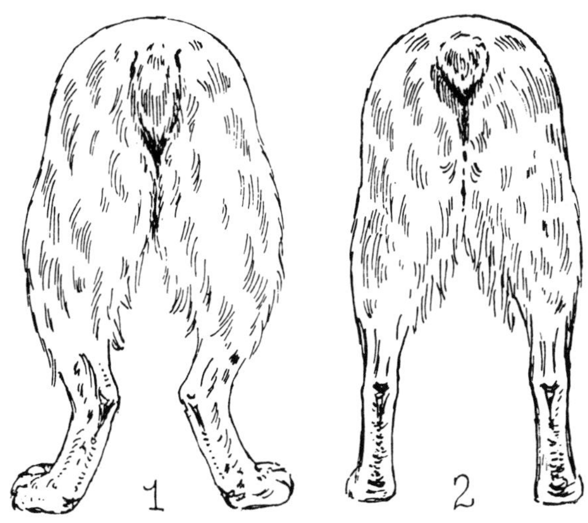

Rears
1. Cowhocks
2. Good rear

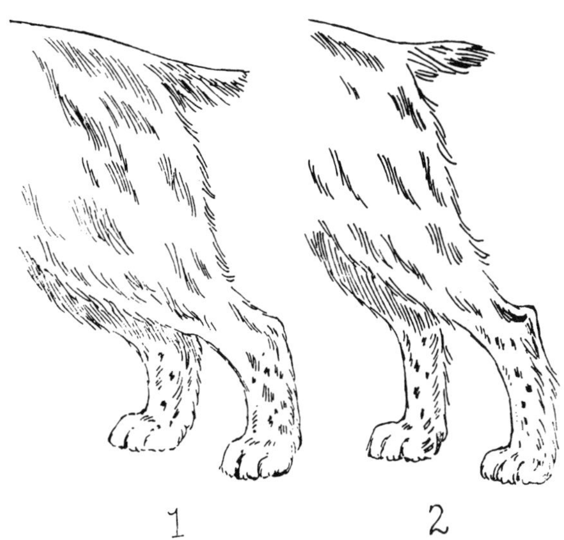

Rears–Side View
1. Good rear from the side
2. Thigh too narrow—Lacking angulation. Hocks too long and sharp

clean appearance. Tail should be well fringed with wavy feather. It is legitimate to shape and shorten the feathering but enough should be left to blend with the dog's other furnishings. *To be penalized*—Rough curly coat. Overtrimming, especially of the body coat. Any chopped, barbered or artificial effect. Excessive feathering that destroys the clean outline desirable in a sporting dog.

Color—May be black or liver with white markings or predominantly white with black or liver markings; tricolor; black and white or liver and white with tan markings (usually found on eyebrows, cheeks, inside of ears and under tail), blue or liver roan. Any white portions of coat may be flecked with ticking. All preceding combinations of colors and markings to be equally acceptable. *To be penalized*—Off colors such as lemon, red or orange not to place.

Gait—In judging the Springer there should be emphasis on proper movement, which is the final test of a dog's conformation and soundness. Prerequisite to good movement is balance of the front and rear assemblies. The two must match in angulation and muscular development if the gait is to be smooth and effortless. Good shoulders laid back at an angle that permit a long stride are just as essential as the excellent rear quarters that provide the driving power. When viewed from the front, the dog's legs should appear to swing forward in a free and easy manner, with no tendency for the feet to cross over or interfere with each other. Viewed from the rear, the hocks should drive well under the body following on a line with the forelegs, neither too widely nor too closely spaced. As speed increases there is a natural tendency for the legs to converge toward the center line of gravity or a single line of travel. Seen from the side, the Springer should exhibit a good, long forward stride, without high-stepping or wasted motion. *To be penalized*—Short choppy stride, mincing steps with up-and-down movement, hopping. Moving with forefeet wide, giving roll or swing to body. Weaving or crossing of fore- or hind feet.

Temperament—The typical Springer is friendly, eager to please, quick to learn, willing to obey. In the show ring he should exhibit poise, attentiveness, tractability, and should permit himself to be examined by the judge without resentment or cringing. *To be penalized*—Excessive timidity, with due allowance for puppies or novice exhibits.

SUMMARY

In judging the English Springer Spaniel, the overall picture is a primary consideration. It is urged that the judge look for type which includes general appearance, outline and temperament and also for soundness, especially as seen when the dog is in motion. Inasmuch as the dog with a smooth easy gait must be reasonably sound and well balanced he is to be highly regarded in the show ring; however, not to the extent of forgiving him for not looking like an English Springer Spaniel. A quite untypical dog, leggy, foreign in head and expression, may move well. But he should not be placed over a good all-round specimen that has a minor fault in movement. It should be remembered that the English Springer Spaniel is first and foremost a sporting dog of the Spaniel family and he must look and behave and move in character.

Approved June 13, 1978
Reformatted February 14, 1989

Correct Springer movement.

Ch. Chinoe's Eminent Judge, CDX, and his son, Chuzzlewit's MacHeath. *Jean Jasinsky*

19

Breeding Better Dogs

THIS CHAPTER offers a number of practical suggestions for establishing a successful breeding program. You must know, first, that this writer never studied genetics. I use my own experiences, the methods that have built Salilyn.

I also emphasize that you must "understand" the English Springer Spaniel Standard. It is not enough that you can recite it word for word. The Standard is a pattern. Its purpose is to help you form a picture in your mind of the ideal English Springer Spaniel. Every artist has a model: yours is a clear picture created from your interpretation of the breed Standard and stamped so indelibly in your mind that you see it as if the actual dog were standing before you. Without a positive idea of what you want, you cannot breed good dogs.

We must be ruthless in faulting our own dogs, constantly and consistently trying to breed out faults. This means we must know and face up to the blemishes in our stock in order to be able to discard them. If we can't see the bad points, we can't breed better dogs; nor can we trim dogs properly or show dogs to advantage. To do either well, we must try to minimize faults as much as possible. There has never been a perfect dog, but, working toward this goal, we must always choose a male to overcome the faults in our bitch and that is also strong in the features where the bitch excels. True, we want to breed for the beautiful things too, but first we must see our bitch's faults and try to overcome them. Of course, we will probably pick up a new set of faults in the process of breeding out the old ones, but we keep on striving to improve, and to do this we must clearly see what needs improving.

Three different paths are open to us for breed improvement—linebreeding, inbreeding or outcrossing. All three have their place, but each must be followed only for a specific reason. Though I have on occasion used all three of these breeding methods, my kennel is founded on linebreeding—that is, breeding within a family. One must always bear in mind that breeding to a relative doubles up on the bad points as well as the good, so it is of the utmost importance never to use a dog carrying the same faults as your bitch. Moreover, the closer the relationship the greater the chances are of intensifying faults. So, unless a breeder is extremely knowledgeable and has kept very careful records of many litters over several generations, he had best forget about inbreeding. This does not imply that inbreeding is wrong; but I feel that the same results can be accomplished through linebreeding far more safely, though not as quickly.

Linebreeding

Linebreeding, as previously stated, means breeding within a family using individuals further removed than one generation. The important thing is they must be tied to a common ancestor, an individual that represents a type nearest our "ideal." It is this dog that is going to influence our program. Each time we breed to a dog that carries this dog prominently in his pedigree, we will increase the number of genes in the progeny. And with each such breeding we can depend more on what to expect in coming litters.

Inbreeding

Inbreeding is exactly what it says, breeding dogs more closely related within a family, or incest: mother to son, daughter to father or sister to brother, which is the closest breeding of all. We are doubling more and more on the same genes, unfortunately the bad as well as the good. However, this breeding method is also very important. Our finest strains of cattle have been developed in this way, but working with cattle offers an entirely different set of circumstances regarding numbers and records and housing; most dog breeders cannot afford to follow the methods of cattle breeders in order to achieve success safely. Breeders frequently say, "I inbreed because I want to establish type." Often they are making their decisions on a litter that has produced one top winner. Suppose there were eight puppies in that litter. What about the seven puppies that were sold as pets? Inbreeding is extremely important to "test breed" for serious faults.

Inbreeding concentrates on one or more particular individuals and reduces the overall number of possible different hereditary contributions. It is the quickest way to establish a line, though perhaps a line one may not want. Should luck be with us the progeny is good; but the next generation may regress and be equally as bad.

Inbreeding is not for the novice breeder. Our interest is to be able to hew to our plan and keep in mind what we have started out to get.

Outcrossing

Outcrossing is exactly what it says—breeding out of our family. We do this to bring in new genetic material and with it added strength and vigor. But then we must go right back into our own line, never losing sight of the characteristics we are striving to keep.

Ch. Salilyn's Aristocrat (Ch. Inchidony Prince Charming ex Ch. Salilyn's Lily of the Valley), owned by Julia Gasow, was one of the great modern pillars of the breed. *Booth*

Ch. Salilyn's Colonel's Overlord (Ch. Salilyn's Aristocrat ex Ch. Salilyn's Radiance), owned by Col. Forrest Andrews and Julia Gasow, was a top winner and a producer of great merit.

20

The Aristocrat Influence

"ON DECEMBER 19, 1964, a little liver and white puppy was born, and the Springer world would never be the same." This is a quote taken from *The Directory of the English Springer Spaniel*, written by Marcia Gillett and Kerrie Frederick, which adequately describes the affect on the breed of Ch. Salilyn's Aristocrat. Unlike his ancestors, he overcame some of the outstanding faults that had been associated with the breed over a long period of time. He was an overall balanced dog, beautifully proportioned with a desirable head and typical spaniel expression. His temperament was flawless; he was a dog who loved everyone and assumed everyone loved him.

In 1967, "Risto" set an all-breed record with forty-five Bests in Show and seventy-one Group Firsts in one year, and was also the Quaker Oats all-breed dog of the year. In mid-December of 1967, on the last dog Show weekend of the year at the Western Reserve Kennel Club Show, Risto broke the Best in Show record held by the famous Pekingese, Ch. Chik T'Sun of Caversham. Twenty-six years later, it would be at that same show that Risto's great-grandson, Ch. Salilyn's Condor, would break another long-standing record and become the top-winning Sporting dog of all time. This distinction was previously held for some forty years by the memorable English Setter, Ch. Rock Falls Colonel.

Even with all the fanfare of the great records that are made, it is the record of 188 champions out of ninety-six different dams that will be the lasting effect of Ch. Salilyn's Aristocrat.

The first offspring to leave a lasting impression was Ch. Chinoe's Adamant

Ch. Chinoe's Adamant James (Ch. Salilyn's Aristocrat ex Ch. Canarch Inchidony Brook), owned by Dr. Milton E. Prickett, was one of the breed's most celebrated winners. DJ was the last dog to date to have won back-to-back Westminster Bests in Show. He was bred by Ann Roberts and handled throughout his stellar career by Clint Harris, who is shown with DJ in the second Westminster presentation (1972) under judge W. W. Brainard, Jr. (left).
William P. Gilbert

Ch. Loujon Executor (Ch. Chinoe's Adamant James ex Ch. Loujon Jennifer), owned by Jo Ann Larsen and bred by Karen Prickett Miller, shared his family heritage for top winning and producing. He is shown here with Ms. Miller, who handled him throughout his career. *Booth*

James. "D.J." was a Best in Show and National Specialty winner, but best known for his back-to-back Best in Show wins at the Westminster Kennel Club in 1971 and 1972. He retired at the age of three and a half with sixty-one Bests in Show and 113 Group Firsts. D.J. was one of only four dogs to win the National Specialty and sire a son Ch. Loujon Executor, who also won the National. The other three were D.J.'s sire Aristocrat, Ch. Salilyn's Classic and Ch. Telltale Author. D.J. was a top producing sire with twenty-five champions out of twelve dams. He was bred by Ann Roberts and owned by Milton Prickett.

Another Risto son, Ch. Salilyn's Colonel's Overlord, "Andy," was the number-one Springer in 1969 and in the top ten Sporting dogs for that year. In 1970 he was runner-up Springer of the Year to his half brother, Adamant James. Andy sired forty-two champions out of twenty-seven dams, including Ch. Salilyn's Encore, a top winner and producer of twenty-nine champions and Ch. Salilyn's Exclusive, sire of nineteen champions. Andy was bred and owned by Col. Forrest Andrews and Julia Gasow.

Ch. Telltale Author is another outstanding Risto son who has made his mark not only as a top winner but also a top producer. His show record included five Best of Breed wins at the Michigan English Springer Spaniel Specialty from 1977 to 1981, and he is only the third dog in history to win the prestigious Eastern English Springer Spaniel Specialty three times. He won in 1977 and 1979, and in 1982 as a veteran. Also as a veteran, "Lumpy" won the 1982 National Specialty, making this his final win to cap a brilliant show career. As a sire, Lumpy produced seventy-seven champion offspring out of thirty-six dams, and is the fourth-highest producing sire of all time. Among those many champions is Ch. Telltale Royal Stuart, the 1986 Springer of the Year and Quaker Oats award winner for the Sporting Group. Author was bred and owned by Delores Streng of Farmington Hills, Michigan.

Some other Aristocrat sons include Ch. Loresta's Storm King, Springer of the Year in 1972 and again in 1973, and Ch. Springcrest Declaration, CD, the sire of twenty champion offspring. Ch. Chinoe's Applause and Ch. Felicia's Wescot Justin were both Best in Show winners as was Ch. Devan's Galliano of Tantramar who was owner-handled to his top honors.

Ch. Salilyn's Condor, owned by Robert and Donna Herzig and Julia Gasow (his breeder), established new records for his breed and for all Sporting dogs. Best in Show at Westminster, 1993, he is shown here winning the first of three consecutive Bests in Show at the American Spaniel Club, with handler Mark Threlfall. *Dave Ashbey*

21

Top Winning and Producing Sires

IT IS MY THEORY that you breed to a dog to overcome faults rather than breed to a dog for his virtues.

The dogs on the following pages fit what I call the two-pronged qualification of having established great show records themselves and of siring get that were likewise outstanding winners and producers.

It is particularly interesting to note that the dogs that are dominant in the ring today stem from the dogs presented in this chapter.

CH. SALILYN'S CONDOR
(Ch. Salilyn's Dynasty ex Ch. Salilyn's Emblem)

''Robert'' is a result of sixty years of linebreeding. With limited breeding, due to his extensive show career, he has produced fourteen champion offspring, including several Specialty winners.

Robert's show career was a spectacular one, making history by winning Best in Show at the American Spaniel Club Specialty for three consecutive years in 1991, 1992 and 1993. Not only was he the only English Springer to accomplish this but the only spaniel to do this since 1930.

The winning team of Robert and his handler, Mark Threlfall, catapulted Robert into the record books as the top-winning English Springer Spaniel of all time as well as the number one Sporting dog in history. Robert's lifetime record stands at 102 All Breed Bests in Show and 243 Group Firsts. Among Robert's

Ch. Salilyn's Dynasty, owned by Julia Gasow and bred by Steve and Jane Stewart, made a number of good wins in the hands of Dick Cooper. His greatest impact on the breed, however, has been as a highly successful sire.
Petrulis

Ch. Kay N Dee Geoffrey, CD, WD, owned by Deborah Kirk and Mary Gibbs, had a good show career and was ESSFTA Sire of the Year for 1983 with ten champions finished for that year.

numerous achievements was the coveted Best in Show at the Westminster Kennel Club in 1993, a spectacular finale to a great show career. He was also Show Dog of the Year, awarded by the Parent Club in 1991 and 1992. He is every inch a Springer, especially in the wonderful temperament so evident in his showmanship as well—and, most important, passed on to his offspring. With all the fanfare and excitement of his winning, it is his mark as a sire that will leave a lasting legacy of Condor.

CH. SALILYN'S DYNASTY

(Ch. Telltale Author ex Ch. Stepney's Cinderella)

"Blake" is the result of the first breeding between Author and Cinderella. His show career began at an early age, when he received Specialty majors, including Best of Winners at the 1983 National Specialty from the nine- to twelve-month puppy class. He then began a short Specials career handled by Dick Cooper and garnered four all-breed Bests in Show and multiple Group wins.

Blake's influence as a sire has been very evident during the past few years. He was named runner-up Sire of the Year by the Parent Club in 1990 to his brother, Royal Stuart, and in 1991 was Sire of the Year while Stuart was runner-up. Blake's offspring include many top winners such as Ch. Salilyn's Condor, the top-winning English Springer Spaniel of all time as well as the number-one Sporting dog of all time. Another son, Ch. Keswicke Gadabout Grandee is a multiple Best in Show and Group winner; Ch. Genuwin's Million Dollar Baby, a multiple Group-winning bitch and Ch. Wil-Orions Foreign Affair a Top Ten winner. Blake has also produced many offspring that have had important wins at major Specialty shows, including many sweepstakes.

Blake was bred by Steve and Jane Stewart and owned by Julia Gasow.

CH. KAY N DEE GEOFFREY, CD, WD.

(Ch. Salilyn's Classic ex Ch. Judge's Pride Jennifer, CD)

The foundation for Kay N Dee Springers, Jennifer, was bred to Ch. Salilyn's Classic and the first homebred champion produced, "Geoffrey," was the result of a repeat of this breeding. He was a multiple Group winner and in the Top Ten in breed and Group competition in 1979 and in 1980. As a sire, Geoffrey produced fifteen champions out of three dams, ten of which finished their championships in 1983, making him Parent Club Sire of the Year. He was owned by Deborah Kirk and Mary Gibbs and handled by Kathy Kirk.

CH. SPRINGERLANE'S RIDGEWYN

(Ch. Kimet's Khristopher Robin ex Springerlane's Royal Flush

Owned by Patti Nelson, Don Kelley and Cherrie Zayac, "Jackson" was named the Best of Opposite Sex Springer by the Parent Club in 1988, while his brother Ch. Springerlane's Churchill was runner-up. The following year, he became the 1989 Show Springer of the Year, always handled by Gary Zayac.

CH. KIMET'S KHRISTOPHER ROBIN

(Ch. Filicia's Bequest ex Ch. & OT Can. Ch. Salilyn's Radiant Taunya)

During his show career, "Khris" won twenty-five all-breed Bests in Show, over 100 Group Firsts and eleven Specialty Bests of Breed including the 1983 National Specialty. In that same year, Khris was awarded Parent Club Springer of the Year honors. He was ranked in the Top Ten Springers from 1982 through 1985.

As a sire, he has produced eighteen champions thus far out of eleven dams. When bred to a Canadian bitch, Springerlane's Royal Flush, three champions were produced. Ch. Springerlane's Churchill, Fenwick and Ridgewyn, all of which are Group and Specialty winners. Two other littermates have also distinguished themselves: Ch. Marjon's Magnificent Westoak, a Top Ten winner, and Ch. Marjon's New Years Toast, a Best in Show winner.

Khris was bred and owned by Nona Butts of Kimet Springers and handled throughout his career by Gary Zayac, with whom he lived upon his retirement.

CH. WINAKO'S CLASSIC REPLAY

(Ch. Salilyn's Classic ex Canarch Yankee Tea Party)

"Herbie," as he is known, was the winner of three all-breed Bests in Show, sixteen Group Firsts and three Specialty Bests of Breed, two of which were won from the Veterans Class. As a producer, Herbie sired sixty-six champions, making him the top-producing, black-and-white sire in breed history. His offspring have been awarded multiple Best in Show and Group wins and include four Specialty Best of Breed winners. He has sired five top producers himself, including Ch. Ocoee Living Proof, sire of twenty-five champions, many of which have major Specialty wins. The Parent Club awarded Herbie Sire of the Year in 1981 and 1983, and he was also the runner-up to Sire of the Year in 1978 and 1980. Herbie was bred by David Morman and owned by Kathy and John Lorentzen.

CH. SALILYN'S PRIVATE STOCK

(Ch. Filicia's Request ex Ch. Salilyn's Sonnet)

Here is an excellent example of a dog that fits the "winner and producer" title.

"Stock's" show record stands at twenty-one all-breed Bests in Show, 104 Group Firsts and eleven Specialty Bests of Breed, including the 1981 National Specialty. He was the Parent Club Springer of the Year in both 1981 and 1982, as well as number one Sporting Dog in 1982, winning the Quaker Oats award for the Sporting Group.

Ch. Springerlane's Ridgewyn.

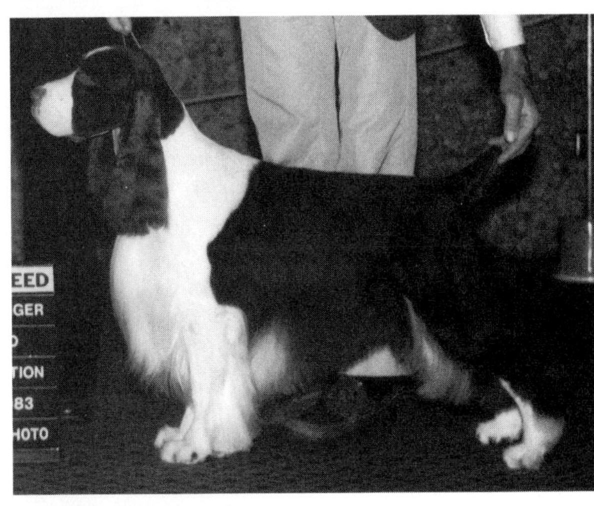

Ch. Kimet's Khristopher Robin.
Morrissette

Ch. Winako's Classic Replay.
Martin Booth

Stock has also been a top-producing sire, with eighty-two champion offspring out of thirty-nine dams. Stock has been awarded Parent Club Sire of the Year six times from 1981 to 1991 and was the runner-up to Sire of the Year twice during this time. His son, Ch. Filicia's Dividend, was the number one Sporting Dog in 1983 and 1984. He has produced many top-winning and -producing daughters, including the Best in Show winner, Ch. Monogram's English Garden, Ch. Canamer High Fashion, who was Best of Opposite Sex Springer in 1986, and Ch. Palindrome's Pathfinder. Stock was handled throughout his show career by George Alston for his owners, Robert Gough and Julia Gasow.

CH. TELLTALE ROYAL STUART

(Ch. Telltale Author ex Ch. Stepney's Cinderella)

Stuart finished his championship with all majors and began a winning specials career. He broke the Best in Show record of sixty-six wins held by his paternal grandfather, Aristocrat. In 1989, Stuart won his sixty-seventh all-breed Best in Show, making him the top-winning springer of all time until, in 1992, Stuart's half-brother, Ch. Salilyn's Condor, took over this honor. As someone once said, "It's all in the family."

Following in his father's footsteps, Stuart is the sire of seventy-five champions. He was awarded Sire of the Year by the Parent Club in 1987; in 1988 tied with his sire, Author: and in 1990 was Sire of the Year. He was runner-up in 1989 to his grandfather, Private Stock, and runner-up again in 1991 to his brother, Dynasty. His first champion, Ch. Salilyn's Desert Tempest, owned by Charles Lox, was a multiple Group and Specialty winning bitch and was Best of Opposite Sex at the 1986 National Specialty. A son, Ch. Brendon's Royal Command, was Best of Winners at the 1987 National Specialty to finish his championship. Stuart was bred by Steve and Jane Stewart and owned by Celie Florence and Delores Streng. He was handled throughout his winning career by George and Maryanne Alston.

CH. TELLTALE AUTHOR

(Ch. Salilyn's Aristocrat ex Telltale Victoria)

Author is another dog whose record as a winner and top producer has put him in the history books.

"Lumpy," as he was known throughout his lifetime, was the winner of multiple Bests in Show and Specialty Bests of Breed, but his importance as a sire is still evident today. He is the sire of seventy-seven champion offspring, including such Best in Show winners and sires of merit Ch. Donahan's Mark Twain and Ch. Salilyn's Dynasty. Together with Ch. Stepney's Cinderella, fourteen champions were produced. Among those offspring is Ch. Telltale Royal Stuart, the number one Sporting Dog of 1986.

Author was awarded Parent Club Sire of the Year in 1988 in a tie with his

Ch. Salilyn's Private Stock, with handler George Alston.

Ch. Telltale Royal Stuart, owned by Celie Florence and Delores Streng and bred by Steve and Jane Stewart, shown here winning the Sporting group at the Lancaster Kennel Club under the late Ed Dixon; handler Maryanne Alston. *Bernard Kernan*

Ch. Telltale Author, owned and bred by Dolores Streng, was a multiple Specialty and Best in Show winner and a sire whose influence is still being strongly felt throughout the breed.

Ch. Loujon Black Label, owned by Karen and Lillian Gough and bred by Karen Prickett Miller, was yet another memorable Springer who shone in competition and as a sire of great ability. *Kim Booth*

Ch. Keswicke Gadabout Grandee, owned and handled by Laurin Howard.
Luis Sosa

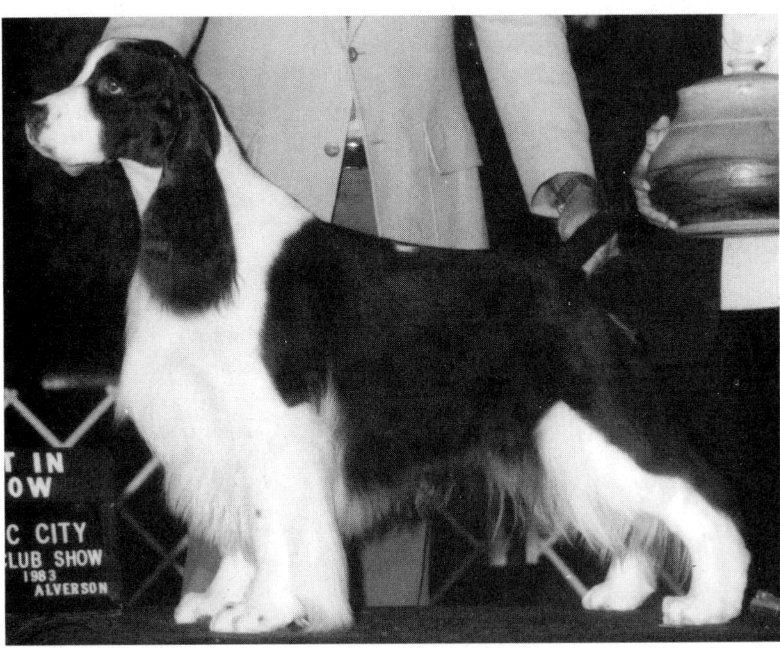

Ch. Filicia's Dividend, owned by Sonny and Alan Novick and bred by co-owner Ann Pope, established a glittering record of top wins during the early 1980s and was handled to this record by Houston Clark. *Alverson*

son Royal Stuart and has been runner-up Sire of the Year five times, each time to Ch. Salilyn's Private Stock, who is Royal Stuart's maternal grandfather.

Author was bred and owned by Delores Streng of Telltale Springer Spaniels.

CH. LOUJON BLACK LABEL
(Ch. Salilyn's Design ex Ch. Loujon Heritage)

"Jack" is the eighth of ten champions for his dam, Ch. Loujon Heritage, a sister to the top-winning Ch. Loujon Executor. During his show career, Jack won eight all-breed Bests in Show and forty-eight Group Firsts and in 1984 was Best of Breed at the National Specialty. He won the 1986 Michigan Specialty the day before the National, a win that made Jack the top Specialty winner in the history of the breed. He is the sire of sixteen champions out of ten dams, two of which were Top Ten winners. Jack was bred by Karen Prickett Miller and was owned by Karen and Lillian Gough.

CH. KESWICKE GADABOUT GRANDEE
(Ch. Salilyn's Dynasty ex Ch. Keswicke Promise the Wind)

Grandee finished his championship at thirteen months at the 1990 National Specialty. Always bred, owned and handled by Laurin Howard, his record stands at ten all-breed Bests in Show and thirty-one Group Firsts, with several Specialty wins. Being used at stud on a limited basis, Grandee has produced a Group-winning bitch, Ch. Quailwood's Paper Tiger, who was the 1992 National Specialty Sweepstakes winner.

CH. FILICIA'S DIVIDEND
(Ch. Salilyn's Private Stock ex Ch. Danaho's Lalique of Stanton)

"Zoot" finished his championship in 1982 and became the number one Sporting Dog in 1983 and again in 1984, which made him a back-to-back Quaker Oats Award winner. The Parent Club awarded him runner-up Springer of the Year in 1983, and in 1984 he was Springer of the Year. Zoot represents the culmination of the Filicia bloodline of Ann Pope, which was established by combining the Kaintuck bloodlines with Ch. Charlyle's Fair Warning. When that foundation was crossed with Salilyn, four Best in Show dogs were the result, and Dividend was one of them. He was handled by Houston Clark for his owner Alan Novick and breeder/owner Ann Pope.

22

The Importance of a Quality Bitch

SO, LET'S START a breeding program. Our primary interest is in the selection of a worthy bitch. As it is said, "a kennel is no better than its bitches." We will not throw away money, time and effort on trying to upgrade a bitch only because her pedigree boasts winners in its background. True, she should come from a good family; though she need not be a glamorous show winner herself, she must not have objectionable faults. We will choose a bitch for her lack of faults rather than for a few outstandingly good characteristics. She must have a good temperament, be sound and compact. Overall size is easier to control than an imbalance of body. A long body, for instance, may be passed down through several generations. The same thing is true of the short-legged characteristic. But we can make a coming litter (or at least most of the puppies in a litter) either larger or smaller through proper linebreeding.

The stud we decide upon must complement our bitch. He must be strong where she is lacking. But he must be linebred for the characteristics we want to improve. That is, both his sire and grandsire and his dam and granddam must carry the same characteristics.

Four things should be noted here: 1) Never breed on paper alone. As Kyle Onstott says in his enduring classic book *The New Art of Breeding Better Dogs*, "We must never let the pedigree wag the dog." 2) Never breed to a dog just because he is a top show winner. He may be the one to use, but only if he and his ancestors cross well with our bitch. 3) If we get a "click" stay with it! I repeated one mating four times and had a Best in Show dog from each litter.

Some people urged me to try the bitch on another dog, but I saw no reason to. 4) We must never allow personalities to interfere with our breeding program.

There are many characteristics we can change quickly with thoughtful breeding. My first Best in Show dog, Sir Lancelot, had bad feet. I was a complete novice and failed to realize this until the fact was dropped on my head like a bomb by a conversation I overheard at ringside. I had assumed that, of course, having won a Group, everyone agreed he was an absolutely perfect Springer! The criticism troubled me deeply, but I finally realized that Lance had poor feet. I tried everything under the sun to improve them. I exercised him behind a station wagon for several miles a day. I even stood him in four coffee cans of alum water every night but, naturally, nothing changed the feet at all. Lance was born with bad feet. So, I made up my mind I would breed dogs with good feet no matter how many years it took, and it did not take long. Some characteristics are difficult to change. It is easier to change an entire head than its individual parts; for example, an undershot jaw or poor markings are difficult to overcome once established.

Once we have a bitch and have decided upon the stud for her, when is the right time to breed her? This depends on how old she is at her first heat period, or season, and on how well developed her physical condition and her temperament are at that time. Generally, we breed a bitch on her second season. If she handles her litter easily and soon returns to tip-top shape, we may breed her again on her third season. But from then on, she is bred only every other season. We would rather retire our brood bitches one season or one litter early for their own sake. Our theory is that it is better to breed bitches when they are young as they may at some time have nursing problems as they get older.

In this chapter we honor those English Springer bitches that have written their own pages in the history of the breed. We hope you enjoy these accounts of their successes.

CH. JESTER'S LIL' LIMERICK

(Ch. Filicia's Woodlyn Poet ex Ch. Jester's Woodlyn De Gegar

"Midget," as she is so well known in the Springer world, has the honor of being the top-winning bitch in the history of the breed. Throughout her illustrious career, she won a record thirty all-breed Bests in Show and over 100 Group Firsts. In 1987 and again in 1988 she became only the second bitch to be awarded Parent Club Springer of the Year. Midget is also a two-time National Specialty Best of Breed Winner, the second time winning from the veterans class. She also had the honor of being awarded Best of Breed and Group 2nd at the 1988 Westminster Kennel Club show. She is the dam of several champions including Best in Show and Group winners. Midget was bred and owned by Andrea Glassford of Jester Springer Spaniels.

Ch. Jester's Lil' Limerick, owned, bred and handled by Andrea Glassford, is the top-winning English Springer Spaniel bitch in history. A multiple Best in Show winner, she is shown being presented with Best of Breed at the Eastern English Springer Spaniel Club's 1991 Specialty under judge D. Roy Holloway.

CH. ALPINE'S ROYAL PARK

(Ch. Telltale Royal Stuart ex Ch. Alpine's Back Ali)

"Parksey" is one of only a few bitches to be awarded Parent Club Springer of the Year honors. This distinction came in 1990. She was Best of Opposite Sex Springer of the Year in 1989. Her show record stands at one all-breed Best in Show, twenty-two Group Firsts and fourteen Specialty wins, including two Bests of Opposite Sex at the National. Parksey was handled throughout her show career by Jaque Whidden for breeder/owners Roberto and Sarah Munoz.

CH. MONOGRAM'S ENGLISH GARDEN

(Ch. Salilyn's Private Stock ex Ch. Monograms English Ivy)

"Heather" completed her championship in April 1982; from there, her specials career began. She was the top-winning Springer bitch in breed and Group competition in 1982 as well as in 1983, and was honored by the Parent Club as top bitch for both years. Heather's record stands at one all-breed Best in Show, eight Group Firsts and two Specialty Bests of Breed as well as seventeen Specialty Bests of Opposite Sex awards. Heather was bred and is owned by Maggie Madden.

CH. STEPNEY'S CINDERELLA

(Ch. Salilyn's Private Stock ex Ch. Salilyn's Delight)

In 1982, "Cindy" was Best of Winners at the American Spaniel Club Specialty. From then on she became a top producer. She was bred to Ch. Telltale Author five times, and this happy pairing resulted in a total of fourteen champions. Among them were many outstanding winners and producers such as Ch. Salilyn's Dynasty and Ch. Telltale Royal Stuart, both Best in Show winners and top producers and Ch. Salilyn's Stepney Alicia, the youngest Springer bitch to win a Best in Show—this at thirteen months. Cindy received the Parent Club Dam of the Year Award in 1984. Cindy was bred and owned by Steve and Jane Stewart.

CH. LOUJON SARAH

(Ch. Salilyn's Encore ex Ch. Loujon Heritage)

"Sarah" is a multiple Group and Specialty winner. In 1981 she was awarded Best of Opposite Sex Springer of the Year by the Parent Club and was the number one bitch in Group competition as well as being in the Top Ten in breed competition in 1982. Sarah was bred and owned by Karen Prickett-Miller.

CH. GILCHRIST BRIGHTWATER TABOO

(Ch. Rainheir's Foxridge Kodiak ex Ch. Gilchrist Charade)

"Megan" finished her championship in nine straight all-breed shows before her second birthday. She received the Parent Club Dam of the Year Award in

Ch. Alpine's Royal Park, owned and bred by Roberto and Sarah Munoz.

Ch. Monogram's English Garden, owned and bred by Maggie Madden.

Ch. Stepney's Cinderella, owned and bred by Steve and Jane Stewart. *William Gilbert*

Ch. Loujon Sarah, owned and bred by Karen Prickett Miller.
Martin Booth

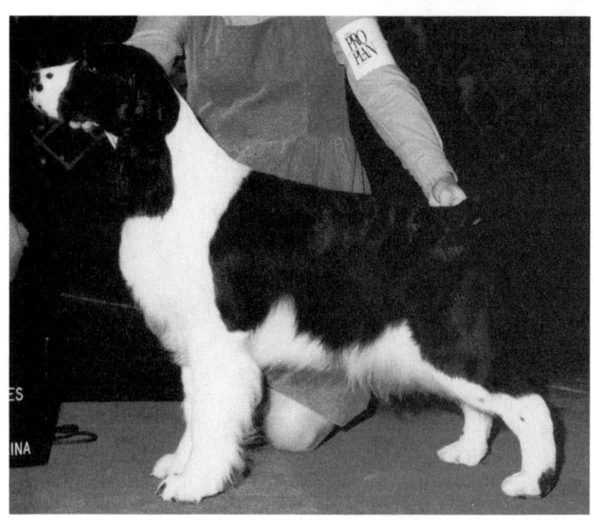

Ch. Gilchrist Brightwater Taboo, owned by Ruth Kirby and Nancy Siver. *Earl Graham*

Ch. Berwick Look of Lear, owned by Donna Duffy.
Alverson

1990 with five champion offspring. Included among them was Ch. Gilchrist Renegade, sire of ten champions; Ch. Gilchrist Hollidae Roulette, a multiple Group winner; and Ch. Gilchrist Alibi, a winner at several Specialty shows. Megan was bred by William and Ruth Kirby and is owned by Ruth Kirby and Nancy Siver.

CH. BERWICK LOOK OF LEAR
(Ch. Salilyn's Private Stock ex Ch. Willowbanks Second Look)

"Fey" is the foundation bitch for Donna Duffy's Berwick English Springers. She finished her championship at just over a year, winning Best of Opposite in the Sweepstakes at the 1985 National Specialty along the way. Fey has received runner-up Dam of the Year honors in 1988 and in 1989 was awarded Dam of the Year with a total of seven champions from two litters.

CH. NORTHGATE'S AMANDA LASS
(Ch. Somerset Saga's Sirius ex Northgate's Enchantress)

"Mandy" was named Parent Club Dam of the Year in 1991. She has a total of ten champion offspring, eight of which are sired by Ch. Stepney's Bustin' Loose, CD, a brother to Dynasty and Royal Stuart. Six of her get are Specialty winners, including Top Ten winner Ch. McScott's That's Life, Best of Opposite Sex winner at the 1991 National Specialty. Mandy was bred by Maurisa Paddock and owned by Don and Nancy McCarthey Scott.

CH. CANARCH LULLABYE
(Ch. Almanac's Autograph ex Telltale Punctuation)

"Eva" was acquired from the Canarch Kennels of Charles and Mary Lee Hendee in 1980 by Janice Johnson of Cambrian English Springers. She went on to become Parent Club Dam of the Year in 1986 as the dam of ten champions, including Best in Sweepstakes winner, Ch. Cambrian's Lyracist.

CH. SALILYN'S PRIMA DONNA
(Ch. Salilyn's Design ex Salilyn's Preference)

"Donna" finished her championship easily and was then bred to Ch. Salilyn's Private Stock. From that breeding came a bitch, Ch. Salilyn's Emblem, dam of the top-winning Springer of all-time, Ch. Salilyn's Condor. Donna became the Parent Club Dam of the Year in 1987 and has a total of eleven champion offspring, which also includes the Best in Show winner Ch. Jester's Spotlight and several other Specialty winners. Donna was bred by Salilyn Kennels and owned by Janice Johnson.

Ch. Northgate's Amanda Lass, owned by Don and Nancy McCarthey Scott. *Stephen Klein*

Ch. Canarch Lullabye, owned by Janice Johnson and bred by Charles and Mary Lee Hendee.

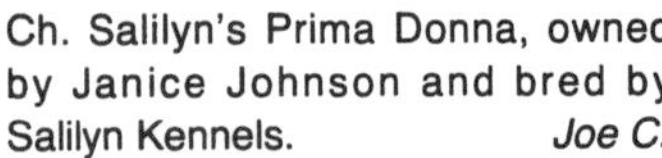

Ch. Salilyn's Prima Donna, owned by Janice Johnson and bred by Salilyn Kennels. *Joe C.*

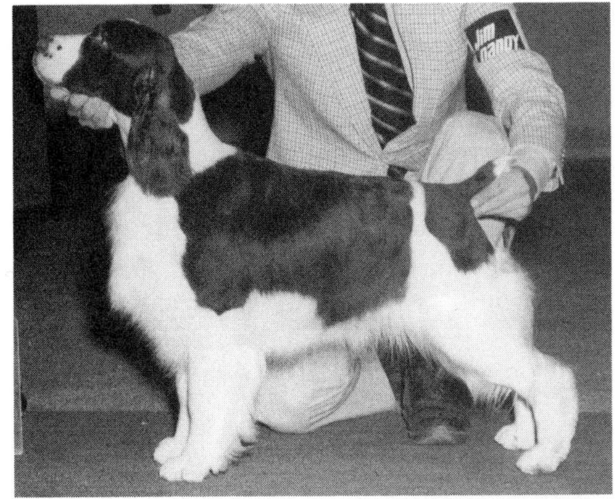

Ch. Willowbank Second Look, owned by Kathy and John Lorentzen and bred by Mary Roberts and Julia Merriman. *Martin Booth*

Ch. Wil-Orion's Freedom Choice, WD, owned by Steven and Janice Johnson. *Lloyd Olson*

Ch. Glen-Lovic's Merry-K, owned and bred by Joseph Agelovic. *John Ashbey*

CH. WILLOWBANK'S SECOND LOOK

(Ch. Winako's Classic Replay ex Willowbank Armars Mirage)

In 1980, "Matilda" was runner-up to the Best of Opposite Sex Springer of the Year. Her record as a producer stands at eight champions by three sires—a tally that earned her Parent Club Dam of the Year in 1985. One daughter, Ch. Berwick's Look of Lear, went on to become Dam of the Year in 1989. Matilda was bred by Mary Roberts and Julia Merriman and owned by Kathy and John Lorentzen.

CH. WIL-ORION'S FREEDOM CHOICE, WD

(Ch. Krystal's Exclusively Thomas CD ex Ch. Neogahbow's Lola of Tyrol)

"Sophie" is a multiple Group placing bitch. In 1987 she was awarded Dam of the Year, with four champions sired by Ch. Salilyn's Nomination finishing that same year. Sophie was bred and owned by Steven and Janice Johnson of Wil-Orion Springers.

CH. GLEN-LOVIC'S MERRY-K

(Ch. Linbrooks Pound Sterling ex Glen-Lovic's Medea)

Bred and owned by Joseph Angelovic, "Merry" was the only bitch in a litter of six puppies. She became a champion in 1982, during which time she was Best of Opposite Sex in Sweepstakes and Reserve Winners Bitch from the Bred by Exhibitor class at the 1981 National Specialty. As a producer, she was bred to two different studs and produced a total of seven champions. She was named Parent Club Dam of the Year in 1985.

CH. KAY N DEE GORGEOUS HUSSY

(Ch. Kay N Dee Geoffrey ex Ch. Kay N Dee Maginna Gibson Girl CD)

"Dotty" was the Parent Club Dam of the Year in 1986. She has produced six champions out of two sires. Among these champions are multiple-breed Group and Specialty winners. Dotty was bred and owned by Mary B. Gibbs and Deborah Kirk.

CH. KAY N DEE MAGINNA GIBSON GIRL, CD

(Ch. Vernon's Marco Polo ex Ch. Maginna's Loujon Victoria)

Bred by Helen Maginnes, "Gigi" was selected and purchased by Kathy Kirk to breed to Ch. Kay N Dee Geoffrey. She was bred twice to him producing a total of twelve champions, eleven of which finished in 1983, making her the Parent Club Dam of the Year while Geoffrey was the top sire in that same year. Gigi was owned by Mary B. Gibbs and Deborah Kirk.

Ch. Kay N Dee Gorgeous Hussy, owned and bred by Mary B. Gibbs and Deborah Kirk. *Luis Sosa*

Ch. Kay N Dee Maginna Gibson Girl, CD, owned by Mary B. Gibbs and Deborah Kirk and bred by Helen Maginnes. *Martin Booth*

CH. RIDGEWYN'S RACHEL RACHEL
(Wescot's Joe Thomas ex Fanfare Flourish, CD)

"Rachel" was bred to Ch. Springerlane's Ridgewyn and also to Ch. Kimet's Khristopher Robin. These breedings resulted in a total of fourteen champion offspring to make her the 1988 Parent Club Dam of the Year. Rachel is owned by Cherrie Zayac and Joene Kelly.

Ch. Ridgewyn's Rachel Rachel, owned by Cherrie Zayac and Joene Kelly. *Callea*

23

Showing Your Springer

ALTHOUGH the main purpose of dog shows is to promote the breeding of purebred dogs, the showing of dogs has become a sport of major importance. It offers what is for many the opportunity of achievement as meaningful as the Olympics, and competition as exciting as the World Series.

Fundamentally, when you pay an entry fee at a dog show, you pay for the judge's opinion of your dog. His decision will be based upon how closely your dog conforms to the official Standard of the breed, in comparison to the others in his ring. The American Kennel Club suggests a time allowance of less than three minutes for the judging of each dog, so it is essential that you have your entry looking his best and showing to advantage whenever the judge's glance happens to come his way.

This calls for homework. Ring manners can be taught fairly easily. For instance, any dog can learn to walk on a leash—but the important thing is how he does it. A top show dog loves the ring and therefore moves with style and spirit. To accomplish this end result you must have patience, and be willing to take things slowly, never making a "duty" of his lessons. The secret of making a showman is to keep the illusion, forever, that this is a fun game.

Training the Puppy for Show

A puppy's training can begin as soon as he is able to walk steadily. Stand him on a table and, while you hold his head up with your right hand, use your left hand to *very gently and slowly* distribute his weight evenly on all four legs. In a surprisingly short time, he will learn to hold this pose alone with merely a touch of your finger under his chin and his tail.

By the time he is seven weeks old, your puppy should be acquainted with a show lead. Use a soft 1/4-inch Resco variety. Children do well leash-breaking puppies. However, they must be emphatically cautioned never to pull or jerk the leash. The puppy must enjoy what he is doing and as soon as he begins to tire, the lesson must end.

I cannot emphasize too strongly the benefits of entering your dog in licensed matches and conformation classes, and of getting him accustomed to riding with you in the car, and to crowds and noises of all kinds. Last, but far from least, it is important to introduce him to a dog crate, for remember, at dog shows he must live in one.

Coat

To be able to build a strong, healthy coat, you must have the following:

1) *A healthy dog*. Coat is a mirror of the health and condition inside your dog.
2) *Proper diet*. Good food in adequate quantity is essential for prime condition, which is reflected in blemish-free skin and soft, shining hair—winter and summer.
3) *Sufficient exercise*. Also, it is necessary for your dog to have plenty of fresh air and sunshine. This calls for judgment under severe changes in the weather. For instance, the direct rays of the summer sun can be the ruination of a show coat. Not only will the liver dogs fade when subjected to constant sunlight, but the blacks, under the same conditions, will take on a henna hue that is most undesirable, and the body coat of both will become dry and harsh.

Bathing

Cleanliness is next to Godliness. Contrary to some advice, we feel that frequent bathing with the best-quality shampoos render health to a dog's skin and hair coat. Frequent applications of water, bathing once a week, enlivens the skin and removes scale. A good-quality conditioner, diluted with water, should follow every bath. It is suggested that a coat oil be applied to the coat through the week to prevent tangles and hair breakage. We use Pro-Gro, manufactured by the Pro-Line Company.

It is essential to bathe and blanket the dog twenty-four hours before trimming.

Time Schedule for Show Trimming

If a dog is completely untrimmed, the work should be done in three stages, starting two full weeks before the show.

Otherwise, trim your Springer about two or three days before a show. The hair on his head and clippered areas will have grown out sufficiently to give him a natural look and to enable you to even out any marks or lines you may have left.

TRIMMING THE SPRINGER FOR SHOW

It must be remembered that there has never been a "perfect" dog, but it is possible to greatly improve any dog with proper trimming. By studying the official standard you can form a picture of the Springer *you* like and trim accordingly, using the Standard as your guide.

People who are skilled in show trimming have their own methods for obtaining the desired effects. As a matter of fact, a good trimmer can be recognized by the individual style he puts on a dog. We do not contend here that our way of trimming is the "right" way—only that it gives us the effect we like best.

In the past fifteen years there have been changes in grooming. Better ways have been developed for getting that look or effect we want. But the overall picture remains the same. The real purpose is to cover up all faults and accentuate every virtue.

Tools Needed:

Straight scissors
Thinning shears (single-bladed)
Resco medium tooth steel comb
Oster clipper with #10 blade
Stripping knives—fine, medium, coarse
Pin brush
Toenail clippers

When the pressure is greatest, a cool head is the most valuable asset. Eldon McCormack and Ch. Magill's Patrick, CDX, in the Best in Show ring at the 1969 Westminster KC show. Patrick was owned by Wayne Magill. *William Gilbert*

Head (Photo #1)
This area is the most important part of trimming the Springer. The trimmer can accentuate the chiseling around the eyes and cheeks, thereby bringing out the dog's expression.

1

Ears
Start 1/3 of the way down. Trim against the grain up to the top of the ear. **(Photo #2)** Repeat the same procedure on the inside of the ear, allowing it to lie as close as possible to the head. **(Photo #3)**

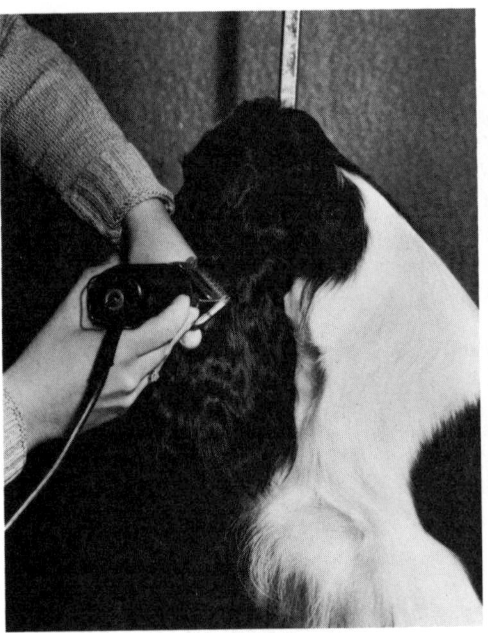
2

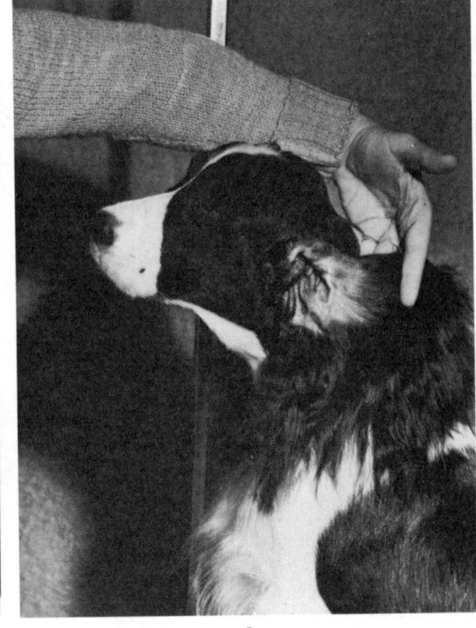
3

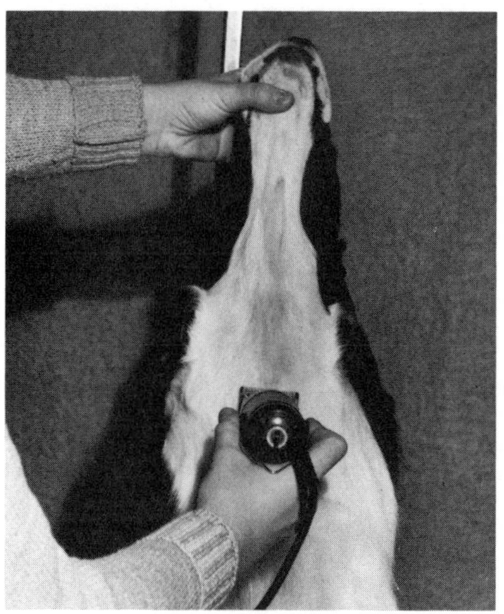
4

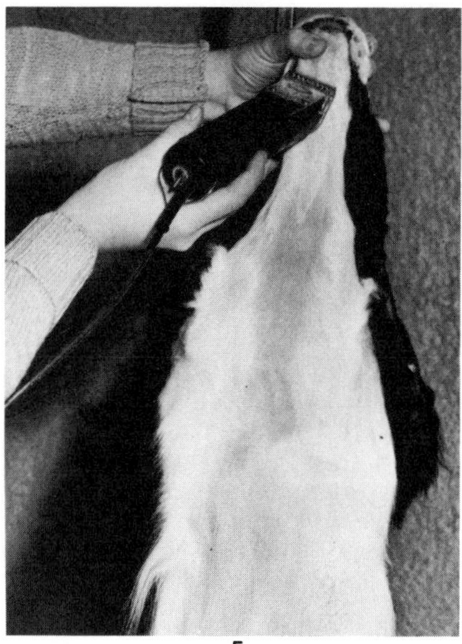
5

Throat

Start about 2 inches from the breastbone **(Photo #4)**, trimming against the grain, up to under the chin. **(Photo #5)** Under the ear, with the grain, take the clippers down to your starting point. **(Photo #6)** Clean out the hair in between by going against the grain up under the lip. **(Photo #7)**

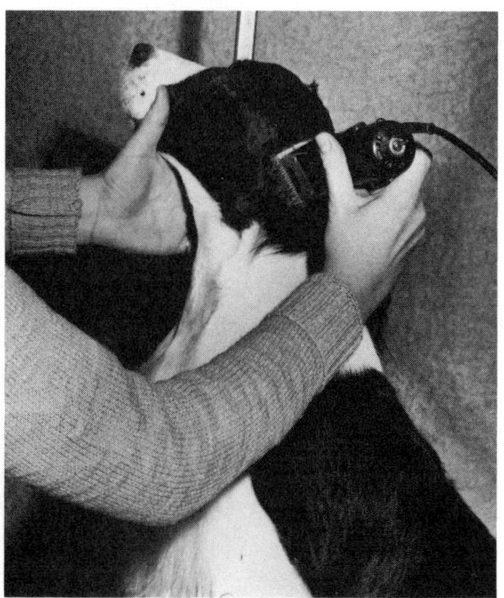
6

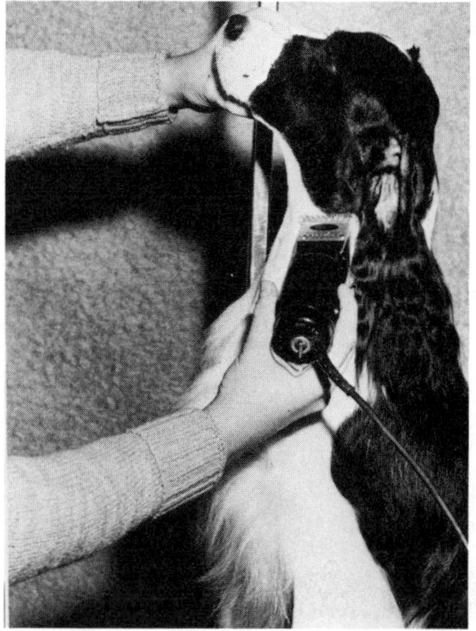
7

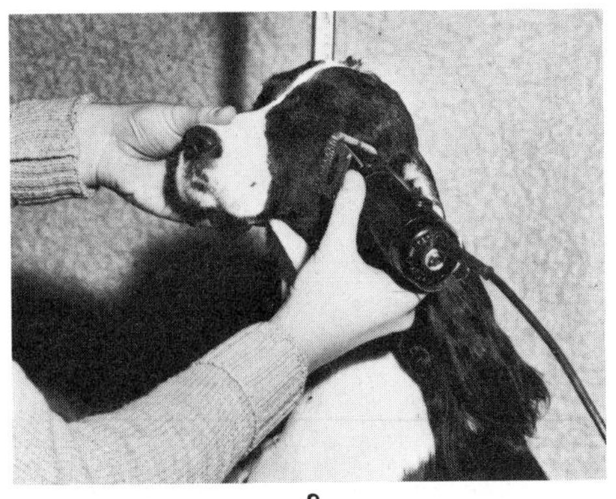

8

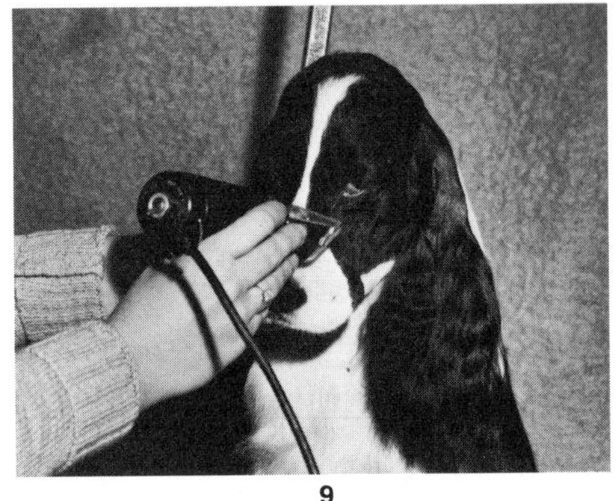

9

Lower face and cheeks

Clip closely against the grain to show chiseling around the eyes—all in order to bring out expression. **(Photo #8) The stop**—Using the corner of the clipper, go with the grain into the groove, and proceed over the skull, making it as flat as posssible, to the occipital bone. **(Photo #9)** Then pull the skin forward with your thumb, and with the clippers smooth over the occipital bone. **(Photo #10)** Continue the clippers with the grain over the sides of the skull, being careful to leave the eyebrows. Blend the line that you made when the ear was finished. **(Photo #11)** The whiskers should be removed with the straight scissors or lightly with the clippers. **(Photo #12)**

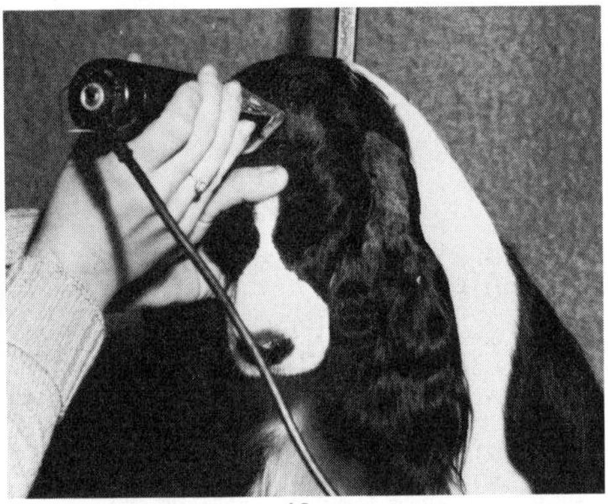

10

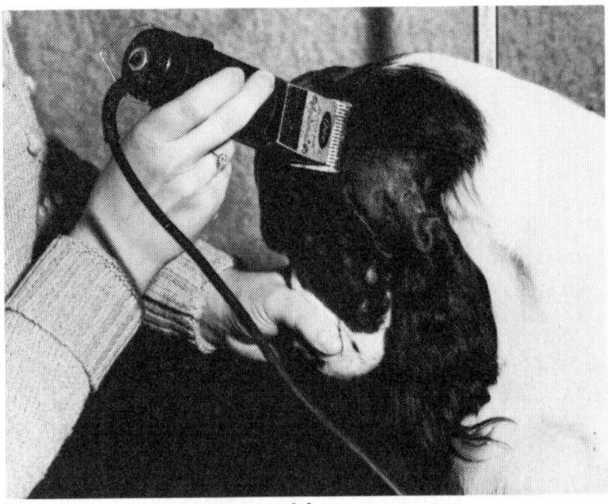

11

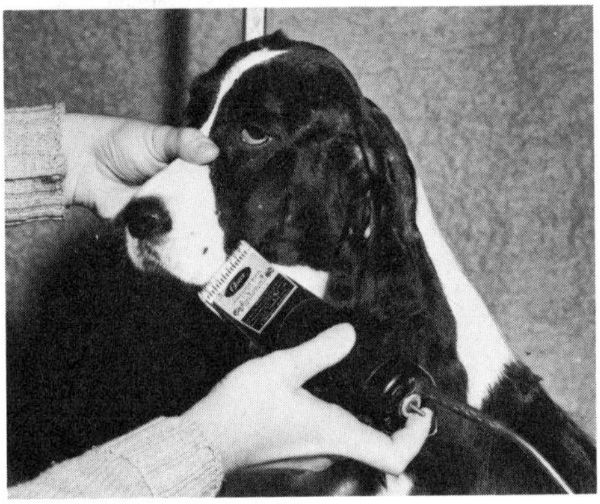

12

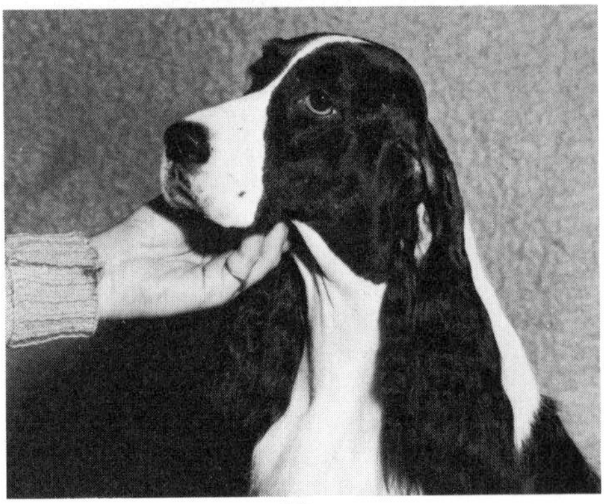

13

The neck and shoulder

With the dog's chin held upward in your left hand, trim the hair with the thinning shears to the line made by the clipper. **(Photo #14)** *Thinning Shears*—Use of this tool requires practice for perfection. A medium-weight, single-blade thinning shears gives best results and should be handled as if you were a barber trimming the back of a man's head. Hold a "medium" tooth steel comb in your left hand and lift up the hair. As you move the comb upward against the grain, cut the ends of the hair above the comb. Comb the hair back down after each cutting. Repeat the procedure until the hair is the desired length. **(Photo #15)** The hair on the top of the neck should be left longer so there is no apparent break to show where the neck ends. The hair should be left long enough on the neck to give the appearance of the neck blending into the shoulders. Blend in the clipper lines behind the ear at the occipital bone, into the neck. **(Photo #16)** Beware of the white hair—it can easily show scissor marks.

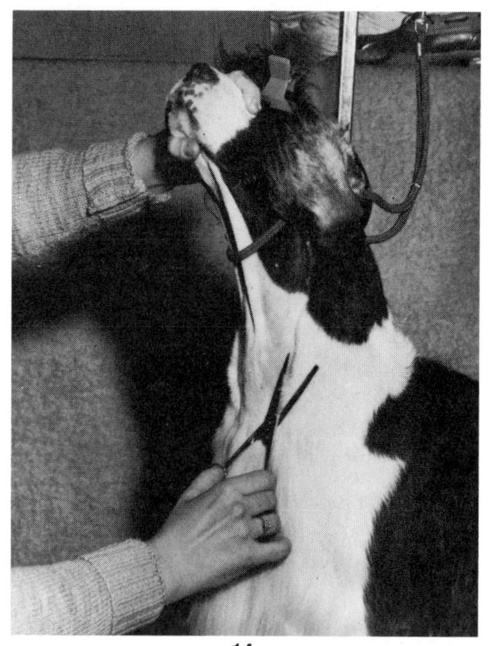

14

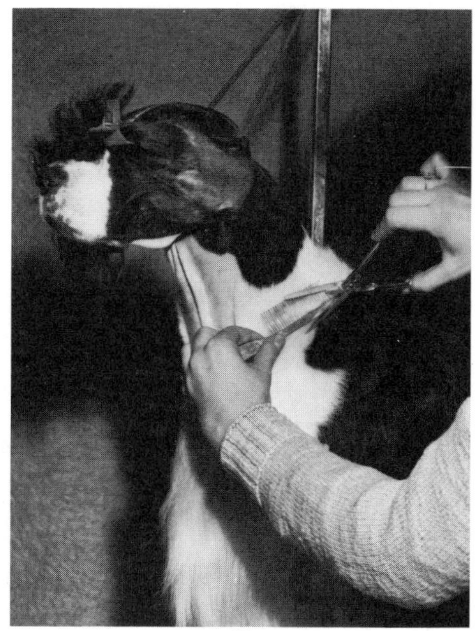

15

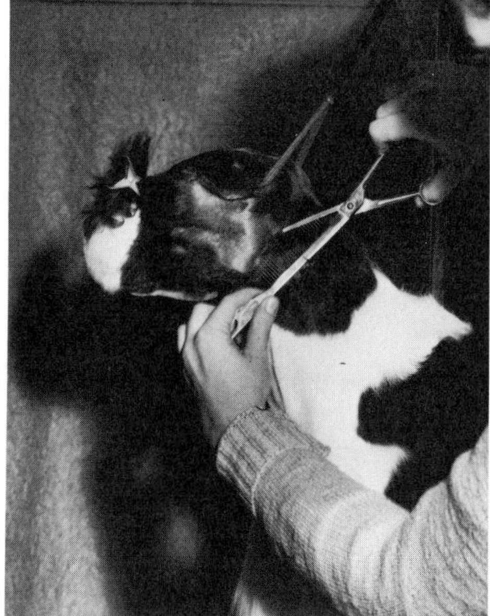

16

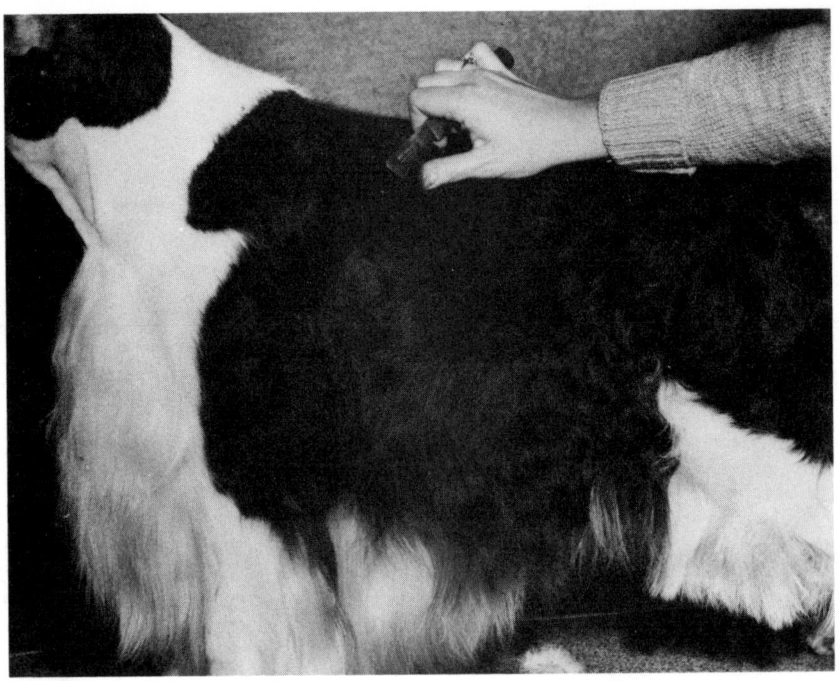

17

The Body Coat

The following procedure is used to give the coat a naturally flat look. In order to do this, you must thin the undercoat by pulling it out with a stripping knife, as opposed to scissoring the top coat.

Hold the knife in your right hand. Keeping in mind it is the softer of the two coats you want to take out *(the undercoat)*, gather a small amount of hair between your thumb and the blade and pull in the direction you want the hair to lie in. **(Photo #17)**

It is important to be sure not to ''pluck'' the coat as with a terrier, but to ''pull'' to avoid damaging the top coat.

We are thus able to improve the outline and the contour of the dog and at the same time keep the natural, unbarbered look as stated in the Standard.

Trimming the Tail

This is the second and only other area where the clippers must be used. Starting from under the tail, take your clipper with the grain of the hair to the tip of the tail—do *not* go over the tip. **(Photo #18)** Any hair on the tip may be carefully taken off with the thinning shears. **(Photo #19)**

Now, with the thinning shears, blend the hair into the upper thigh **(Photo #20)** Your stripping knife may be used here alternately with the thinning shears to blend for a more natural look. **(Photo #21)**

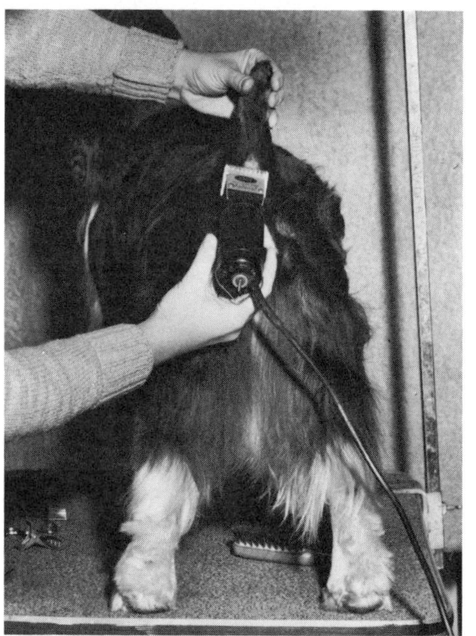

18

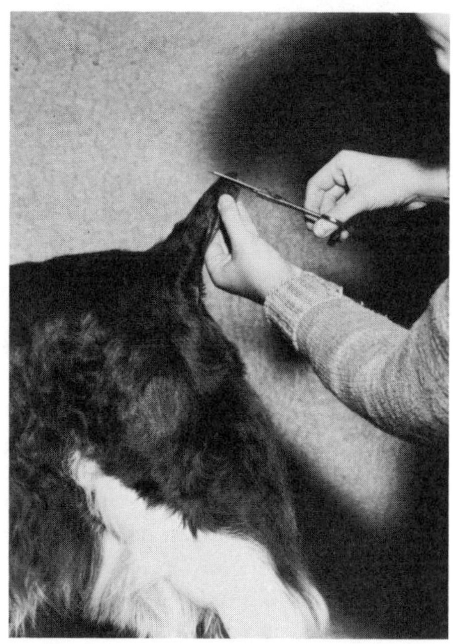

19

Stand back and look at your work frequently. If possible, trim in front of a mirror.

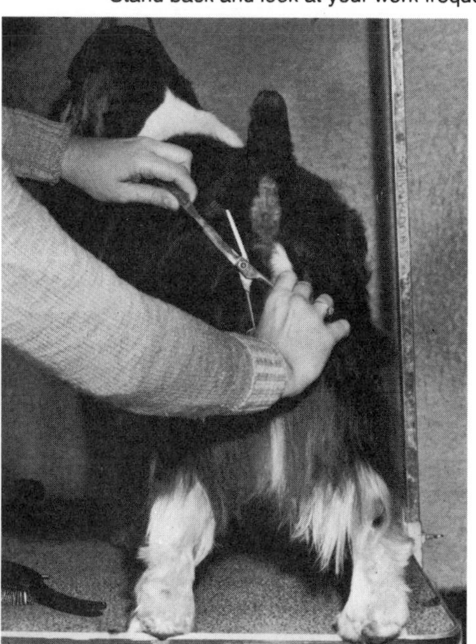

20

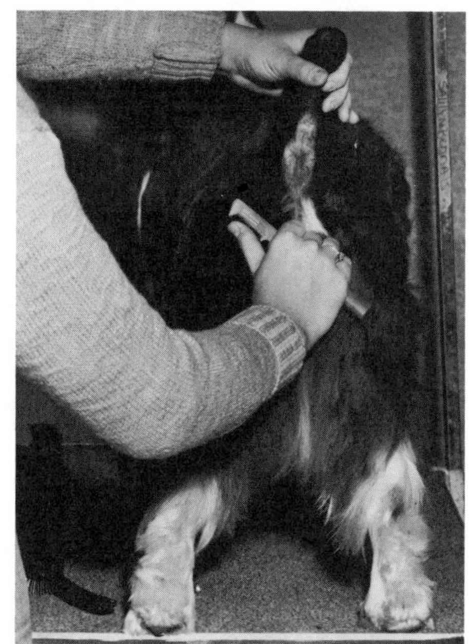

21

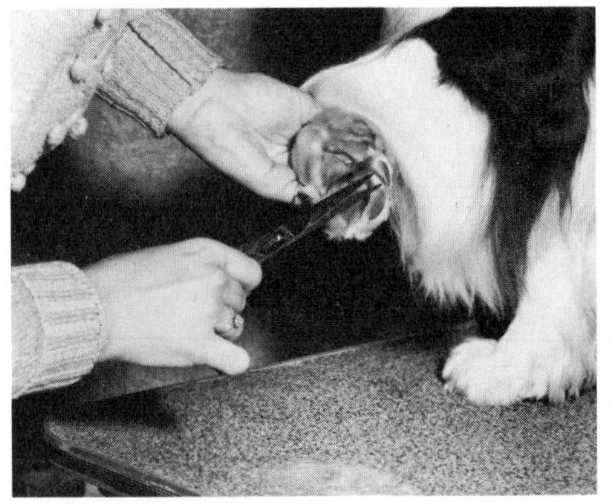

22

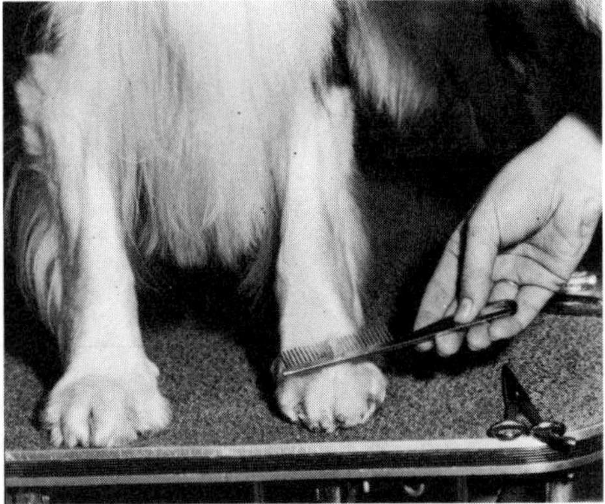

23

Trimming the Feet

Now to finish off that well-groomed appearance. Your goal is to make the foot appear as tight, compact and clean as possible. This is one area that calls for extensive use of the scissors.

With your straight scissors, pick up the foot and trim off the hair underneath and around the pads. **(Photo #22)**

Place the foot back on the table. Again, with straight scissors, trim around the foot to give a round outline.

After combing the hair up, on and in between the toes **(Photo #23)**, take your thinning shears and gradually scissor from the bottom up, to the arch. **(Photo #24)** Scissor only the hair you have combed up. Be careful not to remove any hair in between the toes. This helps give you your full compact look. **(Photo #25)**

To be penalized: Thin, open or splayed feet (flat with spreading toes). Hare foot (long, rather narrow foot).

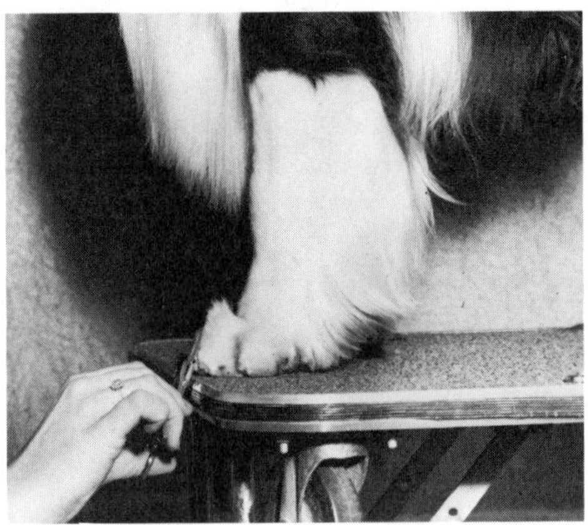

24

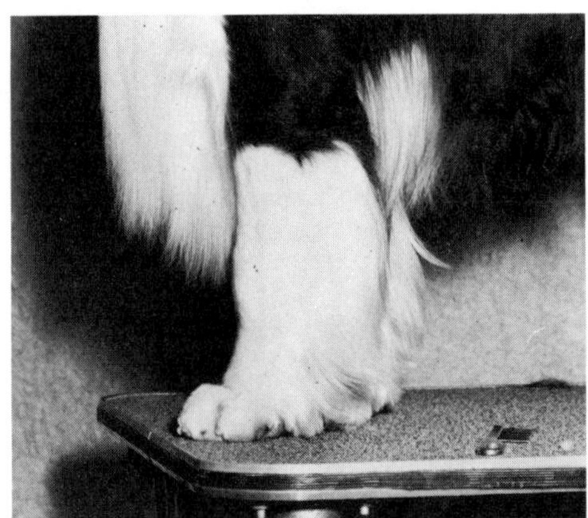

25

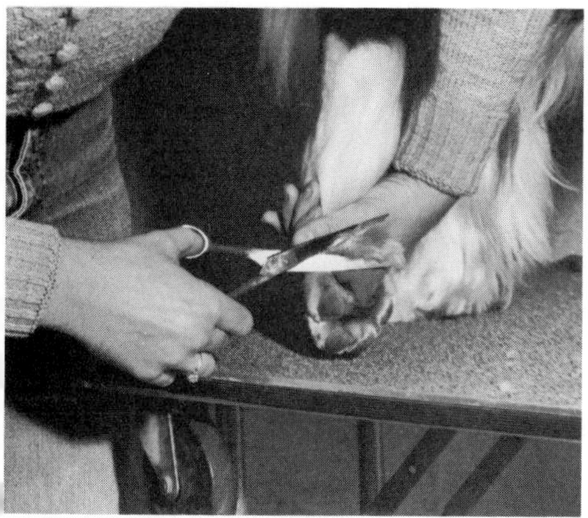

26

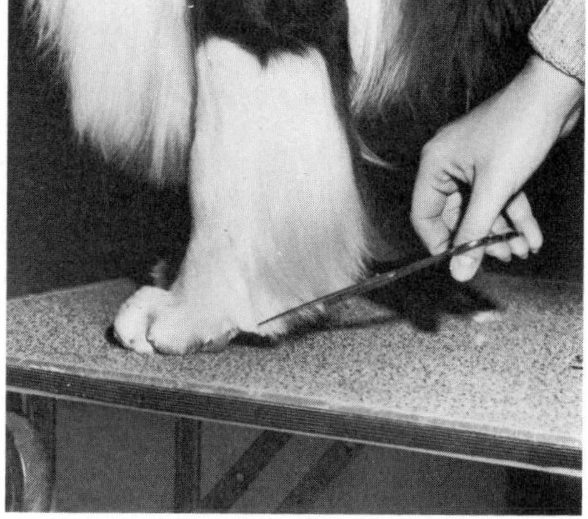

27

Pasterns

The pastern requires careful attention because if trimmed incorrectly, it can ruin the tight compact trim you have just finished on the front foot.

Comb out the feathering on the front leg. Gather the hair in your left hand and cut a straight line across. **(Photo #26)** In keeping with the neat appearance you have just given the foot, trim the feathering at an angle so that the hair isn't touching the ground. **(Photo #27)** It is important to be sure not to cut too far into the back of the foot, but softly blend it into the feathering to give it a natural, strong look, as stated in the Standard.

Hocks

The trim on the hocks can give the dog the effect of more or less angulation and more or less length of body.

Comb out the hair on the hock and, as done with the pastern, gather the hair down to the top of the pad and cut a straight line. **(Photo #28)**

Comb the hair up again. Now comes the time to determine whether your dog needs more or less angulation, leaving more or less hair at the top of the hock accordingly. **(Photo #29)** The point of the hock should be softened to make it less obvious to the eye—to take away from the sharp, unattractive point. If possible, allow a small amount of feathering to fall softly over the top.

28

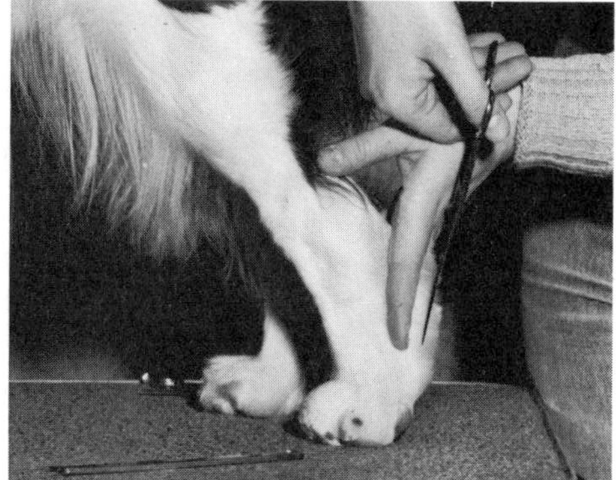

29

Blanketing a Springer

For blanketing our dog, we will need a bath towel and three blanket pins. The towel, or terry cloth jacket, should be of medium weight and wide enough to go around the dog's body. Some jackets fasten with tapes that cross underneath and tie on top; I do not care for these because they leave a line when the dog is dry.

Blanket pins are to be found at the notions counter in most variety stores and in hardware stores as well.

Fold the towel back, collar fashion, and pin under the neck. Carefully smooth hair once more on the back before laying towel down to tail. Pull snugly around rib cage and pin underneath. The last pin is used up under the loin to hold the towel tight over the back.

When the blanket is removed in the morning, your dog will have a smoothness and sparkling sheen that will delight you. **(Photo #30)**

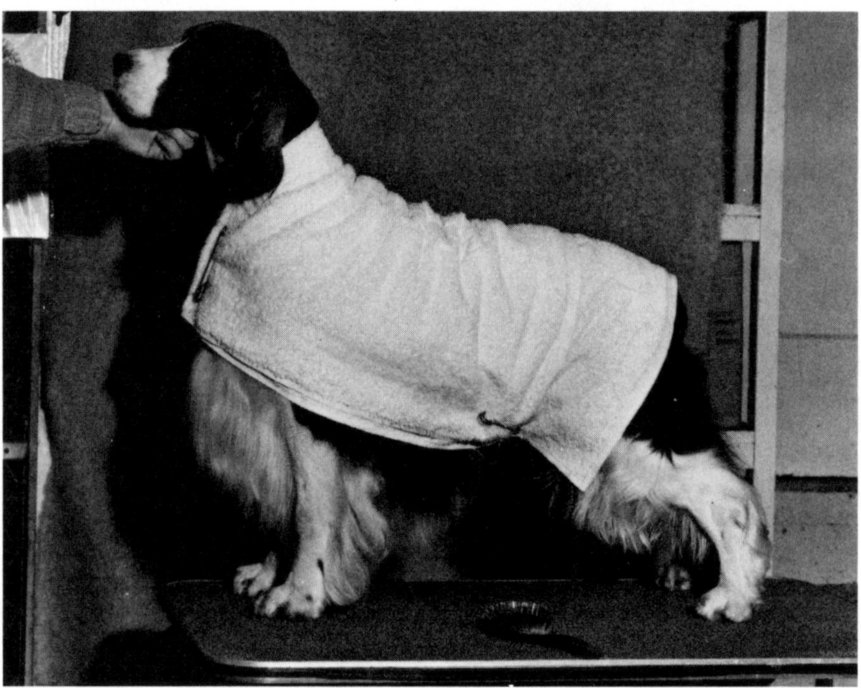

30

The End Result!

"What is worth doing, is worth doing well" applies to show trimming a Springer Spaniel. We strive for a clean, natural, neat appearance that gives a stylish effect—without any signs of the scissors.

Ch., OTCH Foxwood's Piece of the Rock, owned and bred by George A. Burburan and Peggy L. Manker, Obedience Springer of the Year for 1990 and 1991, is the first of the breed to earn championships in conformation and obedience. "Chip" put together an outstanding record that includes four Highs in Trial, thirteen high combined scores and 172 OTCH points. Burburan, an AKC obedience judge, attributes this success, in part, to the training program designed to complement this talented dog's particular personality. Sired by Ch. Coventree's Allegro ex Ch. Woodlyn's Triumphant, UD, Chip's litter brother and sister, Ch. Foxwood's Sparkler, UDT, owned by Peggy Manker, and Ch. Foxwood's Tingle Valley, UD, owned by Whitney Lang, were also top obedience Springers. Brains obviously run in this family. Chip is shown here completing the required point totals for his OTCH title under judge Christine Wright; George Burburan handling. *Luis Sosa*

24

The Springer in Obedience

THE SPRINGER'S high intelligence and merry temperament make him a top-working Obedience dog. Obedience training offers many advantages not the least of which is making your dog a more enjoyable, well-behaved companion. It also holds tremendous appeal and fascination in that, if properly trained, you can enter him in the exciting competition of the Obedience trials. Before starting on an Obedience program, bear in mind that the English Springer Spaniel has an essentially soft temperament and, as a rule, will not take severe corrections. Avoid punishment, be lavish with praise. The techniques effective in training larger Working breeds are not applicable to the English Springer Spaniel.

Enroll in an Obedience training club or school, preferably one for Springers only. Today there is scarcely an area that does not have some group with the common objective of training dogs to be better behaved companions, or of working toward the coveted AKC Obedience degrees. These are: Companion Dog (C.D.), Companion Dog Excellent (C.D.X.) and the Utility Dog (U.D.).

The degrees are earned by receiving three "legs" (which are earned by qualifying scores of 170 to the perfect 200 points at each level) for each degree. The degrees must be earned in order, starting with the Novice Class (C.D.), which has the following exercises: heel on leash, stand for examination, heel free, recall, long sit (one minute) and the long down (three minutes). Next comes the Open Class (C.D.X.), and the exercises for this class are: heel free, drop on recall, retrieve on flat, retrieve over the high jump, broad jump, long sit (three

Marjon's Happy Thing, UD, High in Trial at the 1976 ESSFTA Nationals, "Utility Springer of the Year" and tied for "Obedience Springer of the Year." Whelped in October, 1970, "Happy" was bred by Peggy and Vern Johnson, and owned by Art and Sharon Stewart. She earned her CD in three straight shows in 1971 with an average of 194, and her CDX in 1972 with an average of 193. After a time out for puppies, she came back to obtain her UD with a 192 average. "Happy " was a member of the top dog team in 1972, 1973 and 1976, representing the Santa Ana Valley Kennel Club.

O.T. Ch. Chuzzlewit's Favorite Son, the first English Springer Spaniel to earn the Obedience Trial Champion title. The parent club "Obedience Springer of the Year" for 1977, he carries a lifetime cumulative score of 195.966, and was a six-time High in Trial winner. Of his 36 Obedience class placements, 15 were first-place wins. "Sonny" was bred by F. Nelson and Mr. and Mrs. G. Dahlberg, and owned by Clayton and Patricia Berglund. He was trained and handled throughout his career by Clayton Berglund. *Josinsky Studio*

minutes) and the long down (five minutes). Both the sit and down for the Open work are done with the handler out of the dog's sight. Then we come to the Utility Class (U.D.) with the challenges of: hand signal exercises, two scent discrimination tests (leather articles and metal articles), directed retrieve, directed jumping and group examination (a long stand).

The ultimate title in Obedience is the Obedience Trial Champion (O.T.Ch.). Once you have obtained your U.D. degree then you may go out and try to win this challenging and exciting title. You must receive the required 100 points by wins that include a first place in Utility (or Utility B) with at least three dogs in competition; a first place in Open B, with at least five dogs in competition; and a third first place, in one or the other of these classes. The three first placements must have been under three different judges. The point schedule is based on how many dogs were in competition on the days that your dog won; usually either first or second in your class counts. If it is your intention to enter your Springer in Obedience trials, send for the booklet "Obedience Regulations," which will explain the necessary details and requirements as set down by the American Kennel Club. A copy may be obtained (single copies are free) by writing to the American Kennel Club, 51 Madison Avenue, New York, N.Y. 10010.

Of obvious assistance in the training of your dog is a good book on the subject, and there are several that we recommend. One of the best is "Training You to Train Your Dog" by Blanche Saunders, founder of Obedience training as we know it in America today. An excellent book is "The Pearsall Guide to Successful Dog Training" by Margaret E. Pearsall. The Pearsall methods are particularly interesting in that they are based on keeping in mind the dog's physical capabilities and limitations, and of what dog psychology has taught us of his behavior patterns. (Both of these books are available from the Howell Book House, 866 Third Avenue, New York, N.Y. 10022). Howell Book House publishes a large number of outstanding training books. A free catalog is available on request.

Some knowledgeable people insist that Obedience training will interfere with showing your Springer in conformation. Rather, if properly trained, the dog will handle more confidently in a show ring with the other dogs. However, it is vital that prime consideration be given to the temperament. Too heavy a training hand will subdue the spirit so essential in a winning show dog, be it in the conformation or Obedience ring. Even the smartest, best performing Springer will leave a bad impression if he is dirty and untrimmed. Too often we hear, "Oh, he is only entered in Obedience." Never forget that there are often as many people watching the Obedience ring at a show as the conformation ring. All Springers should be groomed before competition, and the handler should demonstrate pride in his own appearance. These are psychological advantages. The English Springer Spaniel as a breed is being judged by the public in both rings and should be well represented.

Nancy's Fancy Lady, UD, "Obedience Springer of the Year" for 1972. Owned by Mr. and Mrs. Larry Libeau. Pictured here doing the Utility glove retrieve, she is the only Springer to earn the four Parent Club Obedience awards: "Novice Springer of the Year," "Open Springer of the Year," "Utility Springer of the Year" and "Obedience Springer of the Year."

O.T. Ch. Ruleon's Sir Dandy of Belmar, ESSFTA "Obedience Springer of the Year" for 1978 and 1980 (runner-up in 1979). Whelped in 1974, Dandy was bred by Billy and Elmer Marlin, and was owned and trained by Stephen G. Dreiseszun. (He was Steve's first dog, and the first he trained in Obedience.) Dandy became a UD at two years of age, completing his CD, CDX and UD within 12½ months. Only the second Springer to earn the O.T. Ch. title, Dandy consistently ranked in the top four Springers in the national Obedience rating systems, including 1st in the TSR Phillips and Schuman systems for 1978 and 1980. He has been "High in Trial" 8 times, including the 25th anniversary ESSFTA National Specialty, and had over 100 qualifying scores with 50% placements, including 24 1st placements.

OBEDIENCE SPRINGER OF THE YEAR

Each year the English Springer Spaniel Field Trial Association, parent club of the breed, awards a Certificate of Merit to the "Obedience Springer of the Year," won by the dog with the highest average of scores for the preceding year.

To qualify for this prestigious award all dogs with five or more qualifying scores are considered. The average of the five best scores of each eligible dog is determined, and then the one with the highest average is named "Obedience Springer of the Year." If one studies the breeding of these winners it is evident that they are from widely different areas and completely different breedings. Unlike the conformation competition, the Obedience Springer competition is not dominated by a few big-name kennels. It would seem that no line has a monopoly on Springer intelligence.

Here are the dogs honored as "Obedience Springer of the Year" since inauguration of the award in 1959:

1959: Fleishman's Spectacular, U.D.
owned by (Mr. and Mrs. A. Fleishman, Spokane, Wash.)
1960: Pussy Willow Sir Skeeter
(R. G. Leonard, Adrian, Mich.)
1961: Bal Lakes Lady Patricia, U.D.
(Edson Bahr, Edmonds, Wash.)
1962: Bal Lakes Lady Patricia, U.D.
1963: Bal Lakes Lady Patricia, U.D.
1964: Bal Lakes Lady Patricia, U.D.
1965: Tie: Loujon Deuce of Charlemar, C.D.X., W.D.
(Kay Crisanti, New Richmond, Ohio)
and La Belle Don Mitzi
(Judy Lundbeck, Fargo, N.D.)
1966: Tie: Ch. Walpride Karrie of Charlemar, C.D.X., W.D.
(Kay Crisanti, New Richmond, Ohio)
and Loujon Deuce of Charlemar, C.D.X., W.D.
1967: La Belle Don Mitzi, C.D.X.
1968: La Belle Don Mitzi, U.D.
1969: Tigaria Pamper, U.D.
(Ruth Wallace, Riverdale, Ill.)
1970: Loujon Lord Kelvin, U.D.
(Theresa Luley, Indianapolis, Ind.)
1971: Ch. New Dawn of Marjon, U.D.
(C. Thistel, Annapolis, Md.)
Note: New Dawn won her C.D., C.D.X. and U.D. in one year.
1972: Nancy's Fancy Lady, U.D.
(Laurence J. Libeu, Garden Grove, Calif.)
1973: Naia's Molly Malone, U.D.
(Laurence J. Libeau, Garden Grove, Calif.)

1974: Naia's Molly Malone, U.D.
1975: Naia's Molly Malone, U.D.
1976: Tie: Marjon's Happy Thing, U.D.
(Art and Sharon Stewart, Irvine, Calif.)
Endeavor's White Frost, U.D.
(Doris Peppers, Broomfield, Colo.)
1977: Chuzzlewit's Favorite Son, U.D.
(Patricia and Clayton Berglund, Bloomington, Minn.)
1978: Ruleon's Sir Dandy of Belmar, U.D.
(Steve Dreiseszun, Phoenix, Ariz.)
1979: Jessica Imp of Whimsy, U.D.
(Martha Leonard, Montclair, N.J.)
1980: O.T.Ch. Ruleon's Sir Dandy of Belmar
1981: O.T.Ch. Jessica Imp of Whimsy
1982: Ch. JD's Short-N-Sweet, U.D.
(Jean Lucas, Renton, Wash.)
1983: Kaleros Fat Boy Beaujangles, U.D.
(Debbie Parks and Bill Lee)
1984: O.T.Ch. Kaleros Fat Boy Beaujangles, U.D.
(Bill Lee, Greenville, S.C.)
1985: Tie: O.T.Ch. Bethellen Cane's Taylor-Made, U.D.
(Brenda Roe, Rossville, Ga.)
and O.T.Ch. Kaleros Fat Boy Beaujangles, U.D.
(Bill Lee, Greenville, S.C.)
1986: Windwards Bie Bye, U.D.
(Roland Speck, Indianola, Iowa)
1987: Lee Vee's Tail Wind, U.D.
(Marilyn J. Massey, Rockwell, Tex.)
1988: Canyonwood's Benediction, U.D.
(C. Shedd, Long Beach, Calif.)
1989: Frierpats Arthur, U.D.T.
(Joanna Lewis, Northville, Mich.)
1990: O.T.Ch./Ch. Foxwoods Piece of the Rock
(George Burburan and Peggy Manker, Coral Springs, Fla.)
1991: O.T.Ch./Ch. Foxwoods Piece of the Rock
(George Burburan and Peggy Manker, Coral Springs, Fla.)
1992: Sulo's Ledgewood Gypsy, U.D.
(Sandra Davis and Lois Cutler, El Paso, Tex.)

OBEDIENCE TRIAL CHAMPIONS

Chuzzlewit's Favorite Son (P. and C. Berglund)
Ruleon's Sir Dandy of Belmar (S. Dreiseszun)
Jessica Imp of Whimsey (M. Leonard)
Kalero's Robust Ricochet (L. Schwartz)

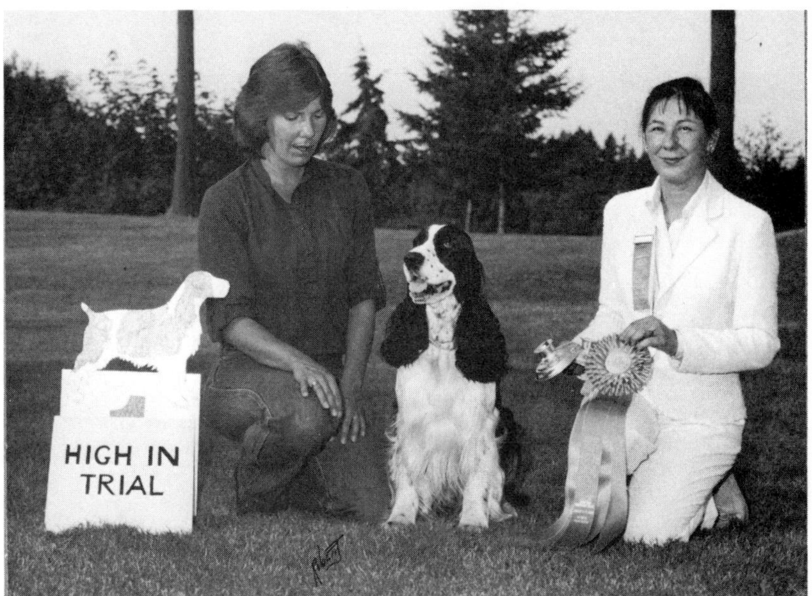

Am., Can. Ch. JD's Short-N-Sweet, UDT, WD, Can. CD. ESSFTA "Obedience Springer of the Year" for 1982, and High in Trial at the 1982 Specialty. ("Utility Dog of the Year" in 1981, with scores averaging 196 plus.) Whelped in 1976, "Shorty" was bred by Don and Jean Lucas, handled to championship by Don, and is Jean's first Obedience dog. He earned his American championship in 1980 with four majors and three BOBs from the classes. In Canada, he earned championship with a Group fourth from the classes, and his CD with wins including two Highs in Trial.

Canarch Madeira, CD, High Scoring Dog in Trial at the 1983 ESSFTA National Specialty, with a score of 199 from the Novice B class under judge Emma Brodzeller. Madeira was bred by Bill Davidson, and was owned and handled by Francie Nelson. Madeira achieved a *Dog World* Award of Canine Distinction for her Novice work; her average for her three CD legs was 197.5.

A distinguished Obedience trio, owned by Doris and Larry Peppers. At center is Endeavor's White Frost, UD, WDX. Whelped in 1971, bred by S. M. and M. L. Hite, Susie was handled to her CD by the Peppers' son Larry. Mother Doris took over the training to take her to CDX in just four shows, and to UD in seven shows. Susie earned the WDX at the tender age of nine in 1981. Ch. Ozark Princess Susanna, UD, achieved both her UD and conformation championship in 1979. Good-Will Happy Go Lucky, UD, WDX (at right) completed his UD in 1982.

Canarch Contemplation, at left at age of nine, was the foundation bitch for Fanfare (formerly Chuzzlewit) Springers, owned by Frances Nelson. "Tempo" was dam of three champions, several Obedience/Tracking title holders, and of three Working Dog title holders. At center is her daughter, Ch. Chuzzlewit's Polonaise, and at right, her granddaughter, Canarch Madeira, CD, High Scoring Dog at the 1983 ESSFTA National Specialty.

Jessica of Wentworth Manor (M. Becker)
Kalero's Fatboy Beaujangles (B. Lee)
Winward's Bie Bye (R. Speck)
Hillslik Candy Kiss (L. Hill)
Bethellen Cane's Taylor-Made (B. Roe)
Brandy Valentine Velvet (R. and K. Kahler)
Frierpats Arthur (H. and J. Lewis)
Lee Vee's Tail Wind (M. Massey)
Ch. Foxwood's Piece of the Rock (G. Burburan and P. Manker)
Valimar's Bustin Out All Over (R. Speck)
Whimsy's Ghostwriter (B. Parrott)
Valimar's Busy Bee (R. Speck)
Sulo's Ledgewood Gypsy (S. Davis and L. Cutler)
Valimar's Oreo (D. Schempp)

TRACKING AND ENGLISH SPRINGER SPANIELS

by James M. Eadie,
AKC TD and TDX Judge

In reviewing the AKC Gazettes for the period January 1974 through June 1993, it is noted that 289 Springers have passed their TD test, and since the TDX test was approved in 1979, 35 Springers have accomplished this very difficult test to earn their TDX title.

In tracking, we acknowledge the dog's natural scenting abilities (which is well demonstrated when we see newborn puppies find their way to the dam's teat for nourishment) by training the dog to follow a track scent and find the article at the end of the track.

Not much equipment is needed in tracking considering the magnitude of this adventure. A non-restrictive harness, a forty-foot tracking lead, tracking stakes, articles, brush and comb, a field and a dog—preferably an English Springer Spaniel!

The AKC has published specific regulations regarding tracking tests. The dog has to pass only once to earn its title; however, a dog must be "certified" ready to take such a test by an AKC judge sometime prior to the dog's being entered in a licensed test. This is to make sure that the dog is "ready" in the opinion of a judge, and such certification must be attached to the entry form or the entry will not be accepted.

All AKC tracking tests are judged by two AKC approved judges who have plotted and laid out the tracks the day before the test for each individual dog entered. On the day of the test a tracklayer, a stranger to both the dog and handler, walks the individual test track leaving an article at the end of the track.

A TD test track is 440 to 500 yards in length, has two starting flags placed approximately 30 yards apart, at least two right angle turns and one article at the

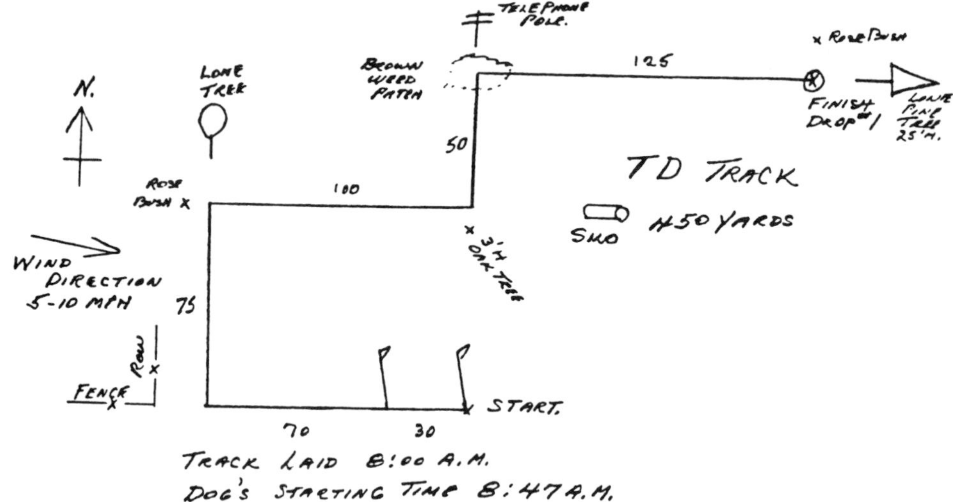

T.D. track — 450 yards.

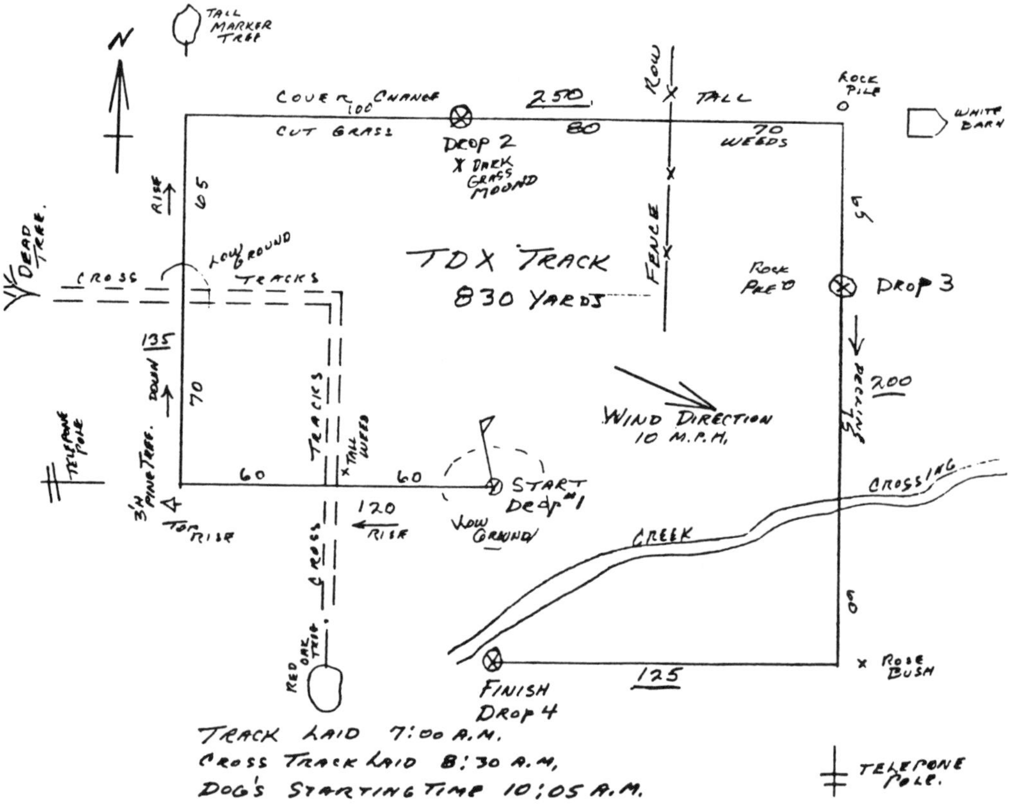

TDX track—830 yards.

end of the track. The track is aged thirty minutes to two hours before the dog is run on the track. The dog must complete the track and retrieve or indicate the article at the end of the track.

Tracking is a noncompetitive sport with dog and handler working as a team in the field. The handler is to make no corrections, give no directions and neither scold nor chastise the dog while it is "working" a track. The only command the handler will give his dog is at the starting flag, when he downs or sits his dog for approximately thirty seconds to enable the dog to pick up the track scent and then commands the dog to "track" or "go find," or whatever starting command he may wish to use. When the dog has taken the direction of the track, which is between the two starting flags, the handler will wait at the first flag while feeding out the tracking lead, always keeping tension on the lead.

After feeding out thirty to forty feet of tracking lead, the handler will follow his tracking dog—observing his actions, being able to read and understand them, knowing when he is investigating a turn or about to make one, when in trouble or off the track, patiently waiting for the dog to work out his problems. Remember, the terrain and track are new to all participants, except for the two judges who will pass or fail the tracking entry based upon the dog and handler performance.

The TDX test track is considerably more difficult, being 800 to 1,000 yards in length. It has one starting flag, two cross tracks at various intervals walked by two tracklayers and at least two obstacles must be overcome—road crossing, creek crossing, fence rows, embankments, etc. There should be changes in ground cover, at least three right angle turns and four article drops—one at the start, two articles at intervals along the track and also one article at the end. The dog must indicate or retrieve all four articles which are to be presented to the judges upon completion of the track.

It is a great challenge to a dog and handler to successfully complete a TDX test with all the many variables. When passed, it is a very proud moment not only for the dog and handler, but for the judges, tracklayers and the spectators.

Springers who have attained their tracking titles have proved that they can be used very effectively on search teams, serving their communities when called upon to help locate children who may have wandered off in forest areas, or elderly people who have become confused and lost. Here, of course, they are trained to pick up human scent, working ahead of their handler and controlled by voice command and whistle.

The age of the Springer makes little difference in its tracking abilities, so long as the dog is healthy. An ideal time to start a Springer in tracking is at four months of age, as a puppy is very receptive to training.

In training your Springer to track you will develop a very close bond with him, for in tracking the dog is boss and you must learn how to read and understand him.

His . . .

. . . and Hers.

Ten-year-old Heather Schaefer and her Springer companion, "Trapper," winners of the 1983 "Search for the Great American Dog" contest sponsored by Purina Dog chow. The win carried a $25,000 prize and an appearance in New York's Macy's Thanksgiving Day Parade. It was also tremendous positive publicity for all that's good about dogs and dog ownership.

25

The Springer as a Pet

NOW PERHAPS you have no interest in field trials or dog shows, nor the patience to train a dog for Obedience. You might only be looking for a dog to be a member of your family—a pal, one that wants to please you, go wherever you go and do what you want to do, that will be good with the children and can be easily housebroken. You might also enjoy taking him hunting once or twice a year, though you have no time to actually train him for the field.

Then an English Springer Spaniel fills your bill. He is a natural in the field and can hunt all day with enthusiasm; yet, being of medium size, he is ideal in the home or car, and can easily adjust himself to any mode of living. Many Springers live in apartments, getting their exercise on leash or in the park.

This is a sturdy breed. Usually they are good eaters and can live indoors or out. But to thrive, a Springer must have human companionship. He is a happy fellow with a merry tail, eagerly anticipating your next move so that he can please you. Feed him well, love him, and he will repay you tenfold.

Buying a puppy is a thrilling and exciting experience, but for some it is a frightening responsibility as well. We have compiled some of the questions most frequently asked us by new owners, and perhaps answering them can help smooth the way for others.

But first, some general suggestions. Be prepared when you buy your Springer puppy to devote two or three days to properly orienting him. His habits must be established the first day you bring him home. It is far easier to *train* him than to *untrain* him.

Gentleness and repetition do the trick. No slapping, please. No newspapers. Just one word—"No!"—in a sturdy, I-mean-it tone of voice.

A crate of suitable size is a wise investment, whether it is the folding wire variety or plywood. Feed and sleep him in it. This comes to be his own secure domain, greatly facilitates housebreaking him, prevents him from chewing or causing damage when left alone and is the answer to rainy days when he comes in with muddy feet!

Play ball with your puppy from the beginning, coaxing him to bring the object back to you. He will love the game and be getting the best kind of exercise, particularly if he lives in an apartment. Moreover, this teaches him to retrieve. He can soon be taught to come when called and, later, to lie down. It is a pleasure to own a well-mannered house dog.

Don't give him bones. They cause too many kinds of trouble much beyond their worth. But by all means give the puppy something to chew; any rawhide toys are good, particularly chew bars.

Now let us answer some of the questions most often asked by new puppy buyers:

How much do I feed my puppy? How often do I feed him? What do I feed him?

An eight-week-old Springer puppy should eat one and one-half to two pounds of mixed food a day, divided into three meals, plus one-half to one can of evaporated milk.

2 parts dry food
1 part meat
1 part water
(Meat and water weigh the same)

Cover the dry food with very hot water and soak fifteen minutes. Add meat and mix thoroughly. The consistency of the mixture is important. If too stiff or dry it will stick to the puppy's mouth, but if too sloppy it will have a laxative effect. The mixture should be soft and almost fluffy.

When the puppy has finished his meal, or most of it, pour some *undiluted* evaporated milk in the same pan.

Feeding time should be regular—as close as possible to the same time each day.

Between nine weeks and three months, your puppy should consume two and one-half pounds of mixed food a day. Shortly thereafter, three pounds of food a day. As you increase his morning meal he will show less interest in his noon meal, at which time you may divide the full amount into two meals instead of three a day.

Never decrease the amount of food. Growing dogs need food more than do adults. Some active young dogs at the ages of between ten months and two years will eat four pounds of wet food to satisfy their calorie requirement for show condition. Your puppy will love all table scraps and they may be added to his regular diet, particularly bits of fat and gravy. Cooked eggs and cottage cheese are excellent foods for him.

How often should he have a bath?

Whenever you think he needs one. Use a shampoo for people, rinse him thoroughly, dry him well and keep him out of drafts.

What about distemper and other vaccines?

We can indeed boast about the effectiveness of our immunization program for canine distemper, hepatitis, leptospirosis, parainfluenza (kennel cough) and parvovirus. The first vaccine should be given at age six weeks, followed by the same treatment three weeks later, and a third dosage in another thirty days. It is a mistake to bunch the injections at closer intervals because of maternal immunity. Mothers understand maternal immunity in their children. A long maternal immunity in puppies renders early vaccines less effective.

Ask your veterinarian to issue a certificate and request that he or she remind you to return for yearly booster vaccines of distemper, hepatitis, leptospirosis, parainfluenza and parvo to keep high immunity against those diseases.

Has the puppy been wormed?

Yes, three times. At five weeks, six weeks and seven weeks of age. However, it is advisable to have your veterinarian run a fecal check in about three months. All worms (except tapeworms) produce characteristic eggs or ova readily detected under a microscope.

Tapeworm eggs are voided in small segments or packets passed on the outside of the stool. Sometimes the dried tapeworm packets are found on the hair underneath the tail.

Specific vermicides or vermifuges are available for each of the parasites we wish to eliminate. They must be administered with judgment. If used injudiciously they could be toxic, causing dizziness, coma, diarrhea, kidney and liver damage. Use under the supervision of your veterinarian.

Should I take any precaution against heartworm?

Heartworm infestation in dogs is now a national concern. Details concerning the life cycle and *spread* of this parasite are readily available from veterinarians and veterinary literature for the asking.

Heartworm infestation in years past was considered primarily a warm-climate or tropical disease, but today, dogs in every area are being infected with this parasite and protection is important.

A blood examination by your veterinarian each spring during the months of March or April is certainly to be recommended. In the northern states, some areas show a very low incidence of heartworm—for example, possibly 1.5 percent of the dog population. The disease is endemic in other areas, and infestations of over 25 percent of the dog population are reported.

Administration of daily or monthly preventative medication must be decided upon between you, as the owner, and your veterinarian. Treatment of infected dogs is possible, and veterinarians approach these cases with care and consideration.

Is it true that Springers have ear problems?

Springers have pendant ears, and consequently less ventilation than in a short-eared or prick-eared dog. The ear canal of your puppy should be whitish-pink, free from debris and wax, and free from odor. The dark wax which sometimes accumulates in puppy ears can be removed with Q-tips dipped in baby oil. Dogs have long ear canals and the eardrum is situated around the side of the ear canal. Consequently, the applicator can be inserted to its full length without causing injury. This point must be emphasized to mothers who, of course, use extreme care in cleaning their baby's ears. Ear infections are caused by bacteria, by parasites, and by fungus infections. Treatment of these more serious problems must be handled by a veterinarian.

What should I know about eye problems?

Retinal examinations must be made by a veterinary ophthalmologist on animals seven weeks of age and older. Here we are at the mercy of the examining specialist. Retinal dysplasia is said to show folds in the eye grounds or punched out areas. This condition usually does not cause complete blindness. Dogs do not have to read a newspaper and individuals so afflicted will make satisfactory pets. It probably would be best not to use such individuals for breeding. Dogs with detached retinas are blind and should be euthanized.

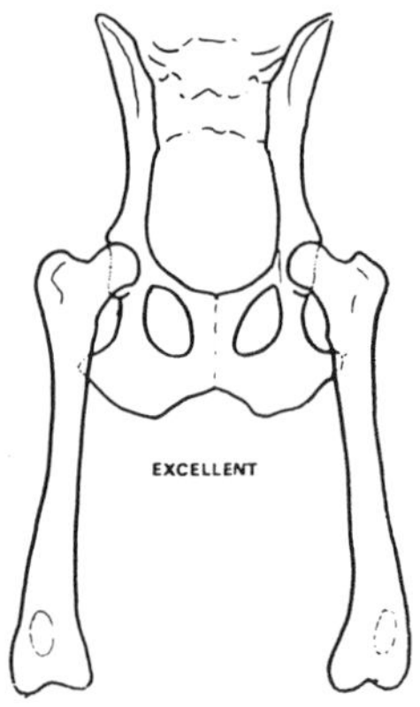

What is hip dysplasia?

Normal hip joints should show on a properly taken radiograph a deep, round cup for a socket or acetabulum and a round and closely or tightly fitting femoral head. There are varying deviations from this normal condition, classified from a taint to grade I through IV. Dysplastic dogs have shallow hip sockets appearing as saucers instead of deep cups. Laxity in hip joints results in abnormal wear, causing the femoral heads to remodel and to lose the round character; the femoral heads flatten. Laxity of hip joints also causes arthritic changes to be evident on the radiograph but not necessarily lameness. It is my opinion that some variations from the completely normal state may be tolerated. Radiographs taken at six to eight months of age may give some clue as to hip conformation, but a dependable judgment cannot be made until the animal is past one year old and, of course, the OFA requires a two-year age limit.

I have observed cowhocked Springers, animals with poor rears, showing perfect hip joints on x-ray. Conversely, I have seen show dogs with some degree of radiographic abnormalities with the most perfect angulation and leg placement and ideal gait. Some tolerance is needed in the judgment of hip dysplasia.

Is it true that Springers shed a great deal?

Shedding is a problem that dog owners of all breeds experience to some degree. Hair growth in animals is not a constant process, but a phasic one. In the first part of the phase, the hair is actively growing. In the second part, the growth stops and the hair goes into a resting stage. The resting hair is sooner or later shed and the follicle is left empty in preparation for the next growth phase.

Typically the dog goes through two growing and resting phases each year. More obvious is the resting phase associated with the spring shedding. Since dogs are now often kept inside most of the year, the cycles become less distinct until the animal sheds all year around.

Illness or stresses such as pregnancy may cause a dog's hair to go into a resting stage and shed. Regrowth will occur when the hair enters the next growth phase if the underlying stress is gone.

Excessive shedding may just be a variation of the normal, but should be checked as a sign of possible skin disease. Good health, a well-balanced diet and brushing all help.

We could not housebreak our last puppy because of constant diarrhea. Have you any suggestions?

We have two suggestions, depending upon the age of the puppy. For puppies age two to three weeks: A particular condition occurs occasionally in our puppies. The stool is yellow and of watery consistency. Puppies are wet and greasy in appearance and this is usually caused by an infection. Coating agents such as Kaopectate and/or Pepto-Bismol are *not* effective. Give a few drops of tetracycline syrup, approximately 20 milligrams, three times a day for two or three days.

For puppies six weeks old: First eliminate parasites such as roundworm, hookworm and Coccidiosis. Treat with appropriate amount of broad spectrum antibiotic and feed a bland diet. Eliminate milk and heavy dog meal. Feed KD (prescription diet), one half can liquefied with one quarter cupful of water and add one to two tablespoonsful of ground beef. Other suggestions: several slices of whole wheat toast moistened with water to which raw beef has been added is helpful, or try Shredded Wheat biscuit or shredded Ralston. Our Springers love scrambled eggs. Prepare a nice, big, well-cooked omelet.

When will my female have her first heat period?

Heat cycles vary. Generally our Springers come in season for the first time at about nine months (it can be as early as six or as late as eleven months). The heat period lasts about eighteen days and occurs again at six-month intervals for the remainder of her life. There is no menopause in dogs.

When should I breed her?

We suggest breeding a bitch for the first time on her second heat period unless the bitch has come in season late, is well developed and in excellent health. It is best to skip a season before breeding her again.

A bitch in estrus shows us and tells us that she is in heat. Her vulva is swollen and she has a discharge of a bloody secretion. When she twists and flags her tail and does not object to having us touch her at the rear, she is telling us she is in estrus and wishes to be bred. A vaginal smear is helpful in making a decision as to the stage of her heat cycle. A female in estrus shows red blood cells of varying amounts, from a few to loaded (90 to 100 percent cornified epithelial cells and no white blood cells, or at least very few). Breed her—she is ready.

Is it wrong to consider spaying her?

If you have no desire to raise a litter of puppies, or to ever show your female—if she is intended strictly to be your pet and companion—we urge you to have her unsexed. This is better than risking the likely possibility of a mismating to some roaming neighborhood male, adding to a sad surplus of unwanted animals.

What is an acceptable age for a stud dog?

A prospective stud dog should be given his first opportunity at the age of eleven months. It is best to introduce him to an older bitch who is friendly and has had at least one litter of puppies. We should hold the bitch by the head and let him approach her and often, happily, we will notice him accomplishing his purpose very soon.

My dog came back from a boarding kennel yesterday and seems to have a bone caught in his throat. He is feeling fine—full of pep, eating well and his stools are good—but he sometimes raises a little mucus or liquid when he coughs. Do you think this is serious?

Your dog has symptoms of what we commonly call ''kennel cough,'' properly *trachea-bronchitis* (an upper respiratory disease) or *parainfluenza*. Ani-

Your dog looks to you for all its material needs and that makes your lives together better and personally more rewarding. Properly meeting those needs is what being a responsible dog owner is all about.

mals infected with this virus usually recover in about two weeks. You should refer the matter to your veterinarian.

In answering the above questions, we have tried to pass on what we have learned as a long-time dog breeder and raiser. But in no way do we advocate the administering to your puppies and adult dogs as a do-it-yourself operation. Let your veterinarian be your dependable guide.

TAIL DOCKING AND THE REMOVAL OF DEWCLAWS

Tail docking, an important procedure, is best performed by a professional, namely, a veterinarian. The proper age is three to six days after birth, but the most important consideration is the health of the puppies and the behavior of the mother dog. We wish to have the puppies warm and healthy with fully rounded bodies. The mother dog should be calm, happy, adjusted to caring for her litter and willing to leave them at intervals to relieve herself. Puppies are transported to the veterinarian in a box covered by a towel or blanket to maintain warmth and protect them from drafts. A hot water bottle or a heating pad may be used in the puppy bed to supply a degree of warmth in winter months. If the puppies are heated too much, they will protest loudly with distressing cries. When a litter is brought to us and we recognize these sounds of discontent, we remove the heat source; immediately there is silence or simply low sounds, and all is serene. The mother should be brought to the veterinary office with the baby pups or conned into taking a breather in an outside pen during the puppies' absence.

The tails are clipped and cleansed with antiseptic soap routinely prior to docking. A ruler is used on each tail to insure uniformity. Some slight variation is allowed for a very small pup as opposed to a whopper, but using the ruler is generally advisable. A dog has to live with his tail all of his life and a stubby tail detracts from his style. We use a tail docking instrument which cuts the tail in the shape of a V as shown in the accompanying illustration. The flaps of skin, top and bottom, are closed with three interrupted sutures of cotton or nylon thread #50. Cat-gut absorbable sutures will not do. The licking of the mother soon unties the knots or dissolves the sutures and we have an open end which must granulate to close. Suturing tails insures a proper skin covering over the amputation and also controls the bleeding which, unchecked, could result in a puppy's death.

Springer puppy tails are cut one inch from the body at age three to six days. If the age is ten or fourteen days, we cut them at one and one-quarter inches. Variation in size is, of course, taken into consideration.

The owners of field Springers usually desire a long tail. Removal of only one-third of the tail is customary. A consultation is held and a judgment made according to the field trialer's wishes. A long tail and a flag on the end seems to be most desirable.

The front dewclaws on the Springer puppies are routinely removed at the

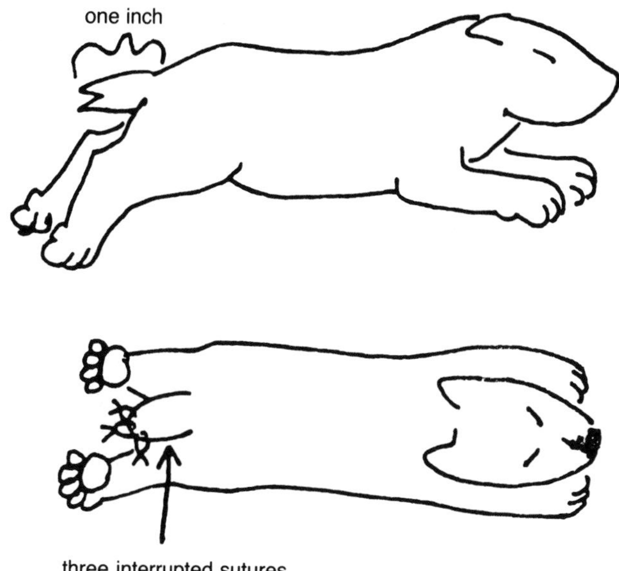

time of tail docking. These extra toes are snipped with scissors and closed with one or two interrupted cotton sutures. The cut is deep enough to remove the entire toe and sutured securely to control the hemorrhaging. As for rear dewclaws, always examine the puppies for these extra appendages. They are present on 25 percent of the Springer puppies. You will note that there is a variation of these rear toes in size and position on the leg. Some are very tiny. Others are large or even double and extend almost to the level of the other four toes. When we encounter a rear foot like this, we count the four toes and then go about removing the dewclaw.

When the litter is returned to its home, puppies should be placed with the bitch immediately. She will be very busy licking and cleaning for a few minutes, but within a short time nursing begins and the little ordeal has been accomplished and forgotten.

Am., Can. Ch. Salilyn's Mac Duff (Ch. King William of Salilyn ex Shercliff's Lady Debby), bred by Robert E. Gibson and James Mitchell and owned originally by Mrs. F. H. Gasow and later by William and Elaine P. Randall, was Springer of the Year 1958–1960.

Ch. Wakefield's Black Knight (Ch. Kaintuck Christmas Carol ex Ch. Wakefield's Fanny), owned and bred by Mrs. W. J. S. Borie, Springer of the Year for 1962 and 1963. "Danny" was the first of the breed to go Best in Show at Westminster; this was in 1963 under judge Virgil Johnson. The handler was D. Lawrence Carswell.

APPENDIX

English Springer Spaniel Field Trial Association Annual Award Winners

Year	*Springer of the Year*	*Best of Opposite Sex*
1958	CH. SALILYN'S MAC DUFF owner, Mrs. F.H. Gasow	CH. GYPSY'S BLACK MAGIC owner, Ed Hollister
1959	CH. SALILYN'S MAC DUFF owner, Mrs. F.H. Gasow	CH. SCHWEDEKREST LO AND BEHOLD owner, Lucille Schwede
1960	CH. SALILYN'S MAC DUFF owner, Mrs. F.H. Gasow	CH. SCHWEDEKREST SENSATION owner, Lucille Schwede
1961	CH. LEE VEE'S HIGH TRUMP owner, Vivian Diffendaffer	LOUJON LIGHTNING'S CAMEO owner, John R. Greeno
1962	CH. WAKEFIELD'S BLACK KNIGHT owner, Mrs. W.J.S. Borie	CH. PAXTON'S MERRY RHYTHM owner, Mrs. Richard Walters
1963	CH. WAKEFIELD'S BLACK KNIGHT owner, Mrs. W.J.S. Borie	CH. SCHWEDEKREST SPECIAL EVENT owner, Mrs. E.A. Klocke
1964	CH. WAITEROCK ELMER BROWN owner, Juanita Howard	CH. SCHWEDEKREST SPECIAL EVENT owner, Mrs. E.A. Klocke

1965	AM., CAN., MEX. CH. MULLER'S BLAZING KANE owner, Mrs. Hazel Westlund	NOT KNOWN
1966	CH. CHARLYLE'S FAIR WARNING owner, Anne Pope	CH. KENLOR LILAC TIME owner, Joyce Morin
1967	CH. SALILYN'S ARISTOCRAT owner, Mrs. F.H. Gasow	NOT KNOWN
1968	CH. CHARLYLE'S FAIR WARNING owner, Anne Pope	CH. JOYMORE BRIGITTE owner, Joyce Morin
1969	CH. SALILYN'S COLONEL'S OVERLORD owners, Forrest Andrews & J. Gasow	CH. WAKEFIELD'S DEBORAH owner, Mrs. W.J.S. Borie
1970	CH. CHINOE'S ADAMANT JAMES owner, Dr. Milton Prickett	CH. SALILYN'S SOPHISTICATION owner, Mrs. F.H. Gasow
1971	CH. CHINOE'S ADAMANT JAMES owner, Dr. Milton Prickett	CH. WESCOT'S BONNIE BALLAD owners, Herbert Albrecht & R. Partyka
1972	CH. LORESTA'S STORM KING owners, Edward & Lillian Stapp	CH. EL REY'S REINA OF WHITNEY owners, Eli & Frances Franco
1973	CH. LORESTA'S STORM KING owners, Edward & Lillian Stapp	CH. EL REY'S REINA OF WHITNEY owners, Eli & Frances Franco
1974	CH. SALILYN'S CLASSIC owners, Mrs. F.H. Gasow & Barbara Gates	CH. JA-HILL'S ANGELICA owners, James & Hilda May
1975	CH. SALILYN'S CLASSIC owners, Mrs. F.H. Gasow & Barbara Gates	CH. DANAHO'S BALLET RUSSE owner, Dana Hopkins
1976	CH. SALILYN'S HALLMARK owner, Salilyn Kennels	CH. SPRINGCREST WINDSONG owner, Bonnie Besse
1977	CH. SALILYN'S HALLMARK owner, Salilyn Kennels	CH. LOUJONS FEMININITY owners, Maureen Brady & Patty Alston
1978	CH. ASPENGROVE'S DU BONNET owners, Dr. Patrick & Barbara Baymiller	CH. EL REY'S BONANZA owners, Eli & Frances Franco
1979	CH. PRELUDE'S ECHO owners, J. Gasow & Jacqueline Tousley	CH. AMY WINDSOR O'WINGSHOT owners, Richard & Suzanne Burgess
1980	CH. PRELUDE'S ECHO owners, J. Gasow & Jacqueline Tousley	CH. AMY WINDSOR O'WINGSHOT owners, Richard & Suzanne Burgess

Ch. Charlyle's Fair Warning (Ch. Inchidony Prince Charming ex Charlyle's Nanette), bred by Charles R. Clement and owned by Anne Pope, Springer of the Year for 1966 and 1968, was a multiple Best in Show and Specialty winner and the sire of many champion sons and daughters. He is shown here with his handler, D. Lawrence Carswell.

1981	CH. SALILYN'S PRIVATE STOCK owners, Robert Gough & J. Gasow	CH. LOUJON SARAH owners, Karen Prickett & Edna Randolph
1982	CH. SALILYN'S PRIVATE STOCK owners, Robert Gough & J. Gasow	CH. MONOGRAM'S ENGLISH GARDEN owner, Maggie Madden
1983	CH. KIMET'S KRISTOPHER ROBIN owner, Nona Butts	CH. MONOGRAM'S ENGLISH GARDEN owner, Maggie Madden
1984	CH. FILICIA'S DIVIDEND owners, Sonnie & Alan Novick	CH. SALILYN'S JOY OF PHYLWAYNE owners, Wayne & Phyllis Magill
1985	CH. LOUJON BLACK LABEL owners, Lillian Gough & Karen Prickett	CH. JESTER'S 'LIL LIMERICK owner, Howard Groffoths
1986	CH. TELLTALE ROYAL STUART owners, Celie Florence & Delores Streng	CH. PALINDROME'S PATHFINDER owner, Melodie Hanke
1987	CH. JESTER'S 'LIL LIMERICK owners, Dani Rosenberry & Andrea Glassford	CH. TELLTALE ROYAL STUART owners, Celie Florence & Delores Streng
1988	CH. JESTER'S 'LIL LIMERICK owners, Dani Rosenberry & Andrea Glassford	CH. SPRINGERLANE'S RIDGEWYN owners, Cherrie Spring & Don & Patti Kelley
1989	CH. SPRINGERLANE'S RIDGEWYN owners, Cherrie Spring & Don & Patti Kelley	CH. ALPINE'S ROYAL PARK owners, Nancy Siver & Roberto & Sarah Munoz

Beginning in 1990 the ESSFTA changed the name of these annual awards to *Show Dog of the Year* and *Show Bitch of the Year*. A double asterisk (**) in the tabulations below indicate *Show Springer of the Year* for that year.

	Show Dog of the Year	*Show Bitch of the Year*
1990	CH. ALPINE'S ROYAL PARK ** owners, Nancy Siver & Roberto & Sarah Munoz	CH. SALILYN'S CONDOR owners, Donna & Roger Herzig, MD & J. Gasow
1991	CH. SALILYN'S CONDOR ** owners, Donna & Roger Herzig, MD & J. Gasow	CH. JESTER'S 'LIL LIMERICK owners, Andrea Glassford & the Reuben Hortas
1992	CH. SALILYN'S CONDOR ** owners, Donna & Roger Herzig, MD & J. Gasow	CH. GENUWIN MILLION DOLLAR BABY owners, Tom & Laura Burke & Karen Nicholas

Ch. Aspengrove's Dubonnet (Ch. Goodwill Aspengrove Q. T. ex Salilyn's Lady Kaye), owned by Dr. and Mrs. Patrick Baymiller, Springer of the Year for 1978, was one of only three bitches that has earned this distinction. She boasted an excellent show record and was also a noteworthy producer.
Joan Ludwig

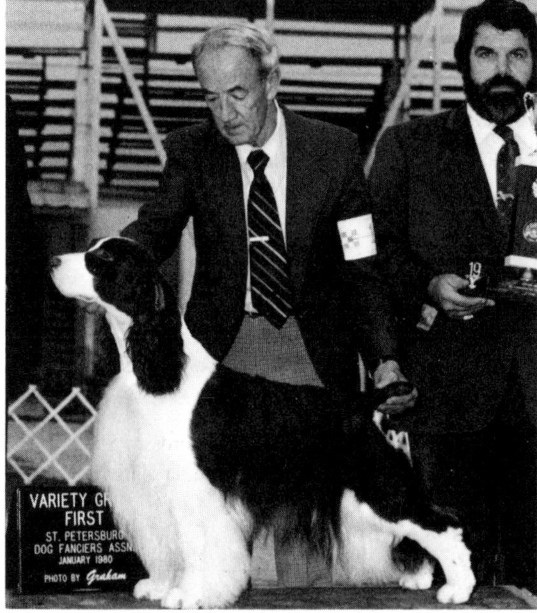

Ch. Prelude's Echo (Ch. Salilyn's Colonel's Overlord ex Ch. Salilyn's Debutante II), owned by Julia Gasow and Jacqueline Tousley, Springer of the Year for 1979 and 1980, won the Quaker Oats Award as Top Sporting Dog for the same years. A very successful show dog and producer, he is shown here with his handler, Dick Cooper.
Graham

r of the Flannery O'Connor Award for Short Fiction

THE NATURE O

Win

THE NATURE OF LONGING

Stories by Alyce Miller

The University of Georgia Press   Athens & London

Published by the University of Georgia Press,
Athens, Georgia 30602

Designed by Sandra Strother Hudson
Set in 10 on 14 Sabon by Tseng Information Systems, Inc.
Printed and bound by Maple-Vail
The paper in this book meets the guidelines for
permanence and durability of the Committee on
Production Guidelines for Book Longevity of
the Council on Library Resources.

Printed in the United States of America
98 97 96 95 94 C 5 4 3 2 1

Library of Congress Cataloging in Publication Data
Miller, Alyce.
The nature of longing : stories / by Alyce Miller.
p. cm.
"Winner of the Flannery O'Connor Award for short fiction"—P.
preceding t.p.
Contents: Tommy—Off-season travel—A cold winter light—The
nature of longing—Color struck—What Jasmine would think—
Summer in Detroit—Dead women.
ISBN 0-8203-1674-1 (alk. paper)
I. Title.
PS3563.I37424N3 1994
813'.54—dc20 94-7582
British Library Cataloging in Publication Data available

Some of these stories first appeared in the following publications:
"Tommy" in the *Southern Review;* "What Jasmine Would Think"
in *American Fiction: The Best Unpublished Short Stories by
Emerging Writers,* number 4; "A Cold Winter Light" in *North Dakota
Quarterly;* "Color Struck" in the *Los Angeles Times Magazine;* and
"Summer in Detroit" in the
High Plains Literary Review.

For Stephen, and for all my families

CONTENTS

TOMMY

There are people who remain connected to us throughout our lives, who seem to follow a similar trajectory, more often through accident than design. It was that way with Tommy Pendleton and me: all those years since we'd both left Fields, Ohio, right up until last week when I got the call from his sister Betty. Strange how quickly I placed her: regal brown Betty Pendleton, four grades ahead, the school's first black homecoming queen. I hadn't seen her in over twenty years. Now, Betty's tone was pleasant and matter-of-fact, with the familiar flattened vowels and slow drawl of our hometown. She'd just flown in to San Francisco, she started off in a chatty way. I knew better than to think this was just a social call.

Her voice softened ever so slightly as she asked if I'd heard about Tommy. That he'd died—this past Wednesday—and his funeral service was going to be held day after tomorrow in Oakland. Did I think I could make it? When I recovered myself, Betty said sweetly, "I'm so sorry, Marsha," as if she'd done something wrong.

My "yes" got lost in my throat. I jotted down the address of the chapel in someone else's shaky handwriting.

"I'm glad you can come," Betty said. "You were one of his best friends. The Lord bless you."

When I hung up, I realized that when I'd asked, "How?" Betty had avoided the word "AIDS." Instead, she said, "Pneumonia." I cursed myself for not having figured out that Tommy was sick. Of course he wouldn't have told me, not the way he was about these things, always so clever about protecting himself. But it would explain his conversion to religion, the final wedge between us that made it so difficult to communicate much at all the last couple of years. "Best friend," I thought bitterly. Tommy and I were never best friends. I don't cry often, but I let myself go on this one.

Back in Fields, all through junior high and high school there were only three of us in the advanced classes. Me, Diane McGee, and Tommy, a regular triumvirate of color, toting around our accelerated literature anthologies and advanced trig textbooks, along with the other college placement kids.

The Tarbaby Triplets, Diane used to joke, loud-talking in her more audacious moods, just to make the white kids turn red. In that snowy dominion, we did manage to quietly flourish, three dark snowflakes alighting on the ivory pile like bits of ash. We ran the spectrum from light to dark—Tommy the color of a biscuit, me cinnamon brown, and Diane bittersweet dark chocolate—handpicked from our 40 percent of the population there in Fields and carefully interspersed among the white kids for that slow-fizzling illusion known in our liberal town as racial harmony. Other than that, we had little to do with one another. Me, Diane, and Tommy, someone's proof of something, all going our separate ways, Diane with the black kids, Tommy with the white, and me floundering somewhere in between.

It was in junior high that Diane indignantly informed our stunned English class that *we* were no longer "colored," nor "Negro," but "*black*." She spat out the word with proud anger that reverberated distantly within a part of an as-of-yet undiscovered me. I quickly seconded her outburst, conscious of the puzzled looks of my white classmates. Hadn't they guessed, I thought, sitting there year after year, tolerating us and taking their own privilege for granted? Hadn't it ever occurred to them that beneath our agreeable demeanors there was more than just a faint rumble of discontent? Diane held out one long, thin ebony arm. "Can't you see?" she demanded. "I'm not colored. Everybody's *colored*. I'm *black*."

The whole time she talked, her voice trembling and passionate, Tommy Pendleton sat stiffly in his seat, never saying a word. I didn't have the nerve, but Diane did. "You too, Tommy Pendleton," she needled. "You too, *brother*." There was a barely perceptible flutter of movement in his left jaw.

The Pendletons owned a small horse farm on Lincoln Street not far from Mt. Zion Baptist Church. There were four boys and Betty, Tommy being the youngest. Mr. Pendleton was a cripple, his body hunched and crumpled like an aluminum can. Years before, he'd been the victim of a horrible riding accident. Everyone said the crippling had affected his mind, as if twisted limbs could spawn a meanness of spirit. You could catch him out back in his icy field in the most inclement weather, staggering among his horses, as if daring another one to kick him.

Tommy's mother was known as "the invisible woman." She was a Jehovah's Witness, spent all her time inside praying. Rumor had it that Mrs. Pendleton was so weak she let Tommy's father padlock the refrigerator so Tommy and his brothers wouldn't eat him out of house and home.

"That man is downright stingy and hateful," Diane informed me once. She lived just down the street from the Pendletons. "He treats those boys something awful. Beats them—those grown boys, too. That's why Tommy's *that way,* you know."

Back then, I hadn't a clue what she meant. Diane knew so much, but I was too caught up in myself to understand.

Tommy never seemed troubled. Every morning he sauntered

good-naturedly up the school's circular walkway with the boys in our advanced classes, or goofed off with white girls at their lockers.

Tommy, never pretending one thing while being another, eventually slipped through the cracks of rebuke and after a while the black kids seemed to forgive him for his betrayal and left him in peace. He was so determined in his position that people quit linking him to the Toms and Oreos who faked it on both sides. It was as if, at least in our minds, Tommy had ceased to be black, or even white. He was just Tommy, handsome Tommy Pendleton ("Mr. *Too* Fine Tommy Pendleton, some of us girls used to concede enviously), even in his downright square clothes: long-sleeve cotton button-down shirts, pressed slacks, and lace-up Hush Puppies from J.C. Penney's in Elyria. When the other black kids were growing their hair, Tommy kept his short and cropped like a newly mowed lawn. You wouldn't have caught him dead with a cheesecutter in his pocket or a braid in his head.

Instead, he walked off with the highest test scores and model essays, posing solemnly for yearbook photos of the Speech, Drama, and Chess Clubs, the only poppyseed in the bunch. His best friend was a white egghead named Paul Malloy.

"The Pendletons must be so proud," my mother used to say wistfully of Tommy's top grades. "Watch, that boy ends up at Harvard."

Big deal Harvard, I grumbled to myself, let him go ahead off with a bunch of peckerwoods and see if anybody cared. Tommy aroused in me all my own uncertainty, about myself, about my awkward friendship with a shy white girl named Mary, about militant Diane acting like everyone's conscience, about my goody-twoshoes boyfriend Phil Willis, and the accompanying push and pull of contradictions. I used Tommy as proof that I was more acceptable.

Though we saw each other daily all through grade school and junior high, we rarely spoke. High school was no different. Even now I can remember only little incidents, like the time he broke a piece off the black frames of his glasses during silent reading and I wordlessly took them from him and repaired them with a piece of masking tape from my bookbag. As the weeks wore on, he never bothered to have his glasses fixed. I derived an odd and private satisfaction from seeing the piece of masking tape there. Too bad, I used to think, too bad he's so fine and so peculiar.

Social divisions run all latitudes and longitudes, and we were all mostly too busy worrying about black and white and on which side of the racial borders romance was flowering to give much attention to what Tommy Pendleton might actually be.

After high school, turned upside down by racial tensions and old pains, I went off to college in the rolling hills of southern Ohio; Tommy predictably left for Harvard on a scholarship, though his father had loudly protested. But our lives, oddly enough, remained entangled long after Diane McGee turned to drugs, my old boyfriend Phil Willis married a white girl named Ellen, and I had moved as far away from Ohio as I could get.

The morning of Tommy's funeral service I canceled my classes in San Francisco and drove over the East Bay Bridge to the Chapel of the Chimes where Tommy's body lay. I took a seat on a wooden pew in the very back of the chapel. It was an odd bunch, to say the least—mourners taken from someone else's life, I couldn't help thinking. Half the pews were filled with formally dressed Japanese business people from a company Tommy had done legal work for. The other half were occupied by mostly well-scrubbed white couples who looked as if they might want to sell me insurance. There was a sprinkling of single men, what Tommy used to in his rare candid moments jokingly refer to as "friends of Dorothy." The front row was packed with a conspicuous group of black women in silk dresses and oversized hats, obviously relatives. There were a couple of men as well, portly and graying. All I could see were the backs of their heads, but I had a feeling Betty and Mrs. Pendleton were among them.

Viewing the corpse was a shock. I had never looked at the dead body of someone my own age, pasted and glued together with heavy makeup, worn out from the ravages of a devastating disease. It didn't look like Tommy at all, too pale, too thin. I turned away, ignoring the woman next to me who was murmuring, "Doesn't he look just wonderful?"

I was both stunned and angered by the simplistic explanation of Tommy's death which, according to the minister, was "part of God's wonderful plan to call his son Tommy home, because Tommy had special business with God." Still no mention of AIDS. It was as if Tommy's "special business" was the reassurance we all needed to pacify us against the senselessness of his death. Easier to believe God chose Tommy than to believe Tommy had slept with many men. I thought about one of the last conversations I'd had with him. I'd accused him of choosing this religion as a way of turning his back on himself. He was smart enough to know what I meant, and he looked pained. Now I wanted to yell, "It's not true!" Somehow, deep inside, I think Tommy might almost have approved.

I kept waiting for someone else to object. I looked to the front row; not so much as a feather on those wide-brimmed hats trembled. As the minister talked on about Tommy's talents (he'd directed the church youth choir), I wondered which one, if any, of those starchy looking white men present had caused him to grow sick and die. I studied the bowed heads, the impassive faces, the soft "Praise the Lord's," and I knew that no one here, except maybe me, was really part of Tommy's past.

The gravesite was three blocks away up a green hill. I parked my car and stood on the periphery, feeling anxious. An overly polite white couple in shades of gray and black and moussed hair accosted me. "We're Bill and Cynthia, friends of Tommy's from church. Are you a *relative?*"

I shook my head. "We grew up together, back in Ohio."

"Oh!" they cooed, "isn't that nice?" I was suddenly being introduced around to strangers. "This is Marsha. She grew up with Tommy in Ohio."

In a way it was true, I thought, truer than anyone could imagine, the growing-up part, I mean. The words rebounded unexpectedly like a heavy fist. I moved back along the edges of the mourners. As the preacher prayed over Tommy's casket, I wandered a ways up the cemetery hillside and looked out over the Bay, the stunning view from Tommy's gravesite, which he would never see, now that his eyes would soon be six feet underground.

The Christmas dance of 1969—such a silly thing, but a turning point of sorts. Tommy and I had never talked about it. Not when we ran into each other one summer on Harvard Square, not when we stumbled on each other in the Cleveland Art Museum one wintry afternoon during Christmas break. And not even when Tommy moved to San Francisco and shared my apartment for six months, shortly after I'd finished graduate school and he was studying for the California bar exam. I knew better than to think Tommy had actually forgotten. Perhaps it was why he felt comfortable inviting me as his "date" to subsequent law office parties and events, even holding my hand sometimes when we were among strangers.

Tommy could be so peculiar about his private life. I mean, one minute he and I would be laughing about the baths and red rooms and glory holes and the games boys used to play, and the next he'd draw back, like a crab in its shell, and say disapprovingly, "MAR-sha," as if I'd said something too personal for him.

Even when Tommy shared my apartment and I'd go to tease him about one of his occasional tricks I'd passed that morning in the hallway, he'd tell me sternly, "It isn't what you think."

"Then what is it?" I'd ask him.

"It's too complicated," he answered. "Don't try to figure it out."

Actually, one night I did broach the subject of the 1969 Christmas dance. Tommy and I were sitting around the kitchen table eating fried egg sandwiches and laughing about the old days in Ohio. We were laughing about Fields, about Diane McGee, about the time gay Terence Lords put on makeup and ran down the school hallway shouting, "I'm ready for my close-up, Mr. DeMille!"

"Tommy . . ." I began, still convulsed with laughter. "Tommy, do you remember that stupid dance we went to?" It slipped out before I knew it.

He looked up at me in such a way that the laughter died on my lips. And then the phone rang. Tommy went to answer it, and from the other room I heard him say cheerfully, "Hi, Jeff." A pause, followed by a low soft chuckle, and then the door of his bedroom closed. A terrible pang cut through me. I had underestimated, as I often did with Tommy, the ways I could offend him.

The 1969 Christmas dance happened like this. In tenth grade I broke up with Phil Willis because, in my teen arrogance, I decided he was a nobody. His only future was to inherit his father's bakery, one of two black-owned businesses in town, and I couldn't picture myself behind the counter for the rest of my life wearing a white baker's apron and serving up dozens of oatmeal cookies to local kids. His parents were what we used to call "siddity." They were extremely fair people, with pink skin and curly sandy hair, the kind of "good Negro that, oh, if only the others could be like, we wouldn't have such problems." Mrs. Willis headed the Boy Scout troop, composed mostly of little white boys, Phil being the exception. Oh, how people like the Willises kidded themselves! Black is black, no matter how white.

I myself had found this out the hard way when, the summer after tenth grade, my friend Mary's family became "concerned." They thought Mary ought to be relating more to her own "peers," and stopped finding it convenient to have me over. Finally, when confronted, Mary's mother informed us gently that we were too old now to continue our friendship, that there would be too many problems. I knew exactly what Mary's parents believed to be in store for Mary: tall, jet-black friends of my boyfriends with hair like tumbleweed sidling up to their front porch asking for porcelain Mary in silky whispers; parties on the east side of town where Mary might dance a hairsbreadth from dark-skinned boys in Ban-Lon shirts and smelling of hair oil.

I started hanging out with other black girls, Camille Hubbard and Monica Pease, who lived on streets named for presidents. We'd meet after school for our singing group and practice in the choir room, and then accompany one another home. I now bypassed the streets named for trees, avoiding the route Mary and I used to take.

Just after Halloween, Camille and Monica and I sneaked into a college dance on borrowed ID's. It was that night I fell in love with Calvin Schumate, a student majoring in political science. Calvin was the kind of boy who gets under your skin and keeps you restless every second of the day. He was, in the opinions of Camille and Monica, just about the *finest, toughest, bossest* thing that ever set foot on the college campus, *ooooh, girl.* Tall and chocolate brown. His hair was thick and wild, and added softness to his angular face. He was a full three years older than I, an abyss I leaped with pure frenzy.

That first night I danced every record with Calvin. He danced New York, I danced Detroit. "You've got some moves there," he said admiringly. Afterwards, dripping sweat, we wandered into the moonlight, fanning ourselves with paper napkins. I suffered from that delicious exhaustion when one is beyond caring. Calvin clasped my hand in his, walked me out to the square, and kissed me so deeply I thought he'd sucked my heart out.

I accepted his ring. My parents heard about this through the grapevine and confronted me immediately.

"He's a full-grown man," said my father, "and you're still a young girl. He's much too old for you."

"He'll pressure you," worried my mother. "He'll expect things of you. I don't understand for the life of me why you broke up with Phil. Now those were nice people, the Willises, whatever could you be thinking?"

I could explain it: Calvin came from the mean streets of Harlem, which was about as exotic as you could get for a sheltered middle-class black girl from a tiny Ohio college town. And he was brilliant and tough. He had grown up in a neighborhood where streets were numbered, where everybody had a hustle, and junkies shot dope in the alleys. He'd shot it himself, he told me, and gambled, and hung around prostitutes until his fed-up father finally dragged him around to the nuns at a Catholic boarding school and insisted they and their God "do something with my wild boy before he gets himself killed."

I thrilled to these stories of the precocious street hood turned scholar, wise and sassy beyond his years, full of himself, and not fooled for one minute by me and what he called my "bourgeois thinking."

My parents and I fought terribly about Calvin. Raised voices and slammed doors were not acceptable at our house, yet the subject of Calvin provoked both.

"He's not even Catholic," my mother fretted.

"He went to Catholic school."

"Not the same," said my mother. "Phil's Catholic."

"I don't love Phil!"

"You don't love this boy either. You're too young. You'll thank us later," my mother went on. "We have only your welfare in mind."

My father warned me, "I want to see you go on to college and get a good education. A boy like Calvin could get you involved in things . . ." His voice trailed off at that intersection of truth where what he really wanted to say lay well beyond what a man can comfortably say to his own daughter.

Little did my parents know that their cryptic, anxious warnings came too late. I did not mean to be careless, but Calvin had a man's ways and a man's ideas. He told me the most compelling things a man can tell a woman, and I was a foolish, lovesick girl with my nose open a mile wide.

We pursued a ritual of clandestine meetings in his dorm room, dangerous and heated congresses, where under sagging fishnets suspended from the ceiling a red strobe light whipped over our bodies with the force of fireworks and stern-faced posters of Malcolm X and Huey Newton observed our tussles grimly. Jasmine incense burned ceremonially in a small ceramic holder by the bed. Now, I was still cautious about certain things and refused Calvin the final token of romantic commitment, but we played at everything else, tumbling around in his sheets, even showering together after in his yellow-tiled shower stall, with me soaping up his thick gorgeous hair. He'd lie naked in bed and read me Harlem Renaissance poetry and essays by Baldwin. We listened over and over to the Last Poets, memorizing together the rhythms of our own lives and talking about "the struggle," Calvin explaining to me earnestly what it meant to be part of a revolution. When he was out on the town square, megaphone in hand, railing against "the Man," I stood on the edge of the crowd, reading his passionate appeals as a secret message directed to me.

At Calvin's urging I took the straightener out of my hair and grew a curly 'fro. I talked more and more about the Revolution, and took to wearing dashikis and brass bangles and the African elephant-hair bracelet Calvin gave me. In my sophomore speech class I expounded on such subjects as "The Role of the New Black Womyn" and the necessity for black students to bear arms. I was Calvin's mouthpiece, his right hand. I was frightening even to myself, uncovering decades of rage my parents had covered over with their prosperity.

"Girl, where the hell do your folks think you are all the time?" Camille wanted to know as she waited for me outside Calvin's dorm room one afternoon.

"Aren't you afraid of . . . *you* know . . . ?" Monica asked.

"Calvin and I don't do that," I informed them self-righteously. Virginity was still a big deal back then, and I wore mine like a badge. "I love Calvin and he loves me, but *that* is out of the question."

I believed what I offered Calvin was enough for any man. I believed Calvin when he said we were two lost halves who'd made a whole, destined to leave our mark on the world together, and that our grapplings in the dark were a natural extension of the sublime communion that passed between us as two exceptional lovers.

And so the Christmas dance approached. I was crazy with wanting to bring Calvin, just long enough to stroll through the door with him and let everyone who'd ever snubbed me, black and white, see me with my fine college brother on my arm. I wanted to set their ignorant tongues to wagging.

It was out of the question.

My mother began pestering me about making up with Phil. She even went so far as to drop hints about having seen Mrs. Willis at Sparkle Market and letting me know that Phil had looked longingly at her when she stopped in the bakery to buy a pie. "You need a date for the dance," she pressed.

And that's when I seized on the idea. In a moment of pure inspiration I became the architect of a crafty plan: I couldn't stand Phil, but I could, yes, I would, invite Tommy Pendleton. The perfect camouflage. My parents, content to think I was finally out with a "nice boy," would extend my curfew, and after I'd pleaded the flu and rid myself of the unsuspecting Tommy, the remaining hours would be spent in rapture with Calvin.

Camille's only comment, when I told her, was "You might as well invite a white boy as invite Tommy Pendleton."

Frostily I approached Tommy outside of English class a day or two later. It felt more like a business proposition than a party invitation, but I said my piece in a casual, upbeat tone I had rehearsed in front of the bathroom mirror.

Tommy studied me a moment, fingering the masking tape on his black-framed glasses. For a moment I thought he might say no, a possibility that had not occurred to me. "Okay," he said simply, as if it were about time a black girl like me showed interest. Perhaps it was relief I saw in his face, more than expectation. "Thank you," he added. I walked off feeling strangely sad.

I bought a new orange minidress and matching fishnet stockings and T-strap, sling-back heels. I even roamed the lingerie department and selected a silk bra-and-panty set, with Calvin and Calvin alone in mind. This would be the night, I thought, my entire body radiating the heat of anticipation. I would be sixteen in the spring; it was time.

"Why doesn't Tommy pick you up?" my mother asked over an early dinner.

"He doesn't drive," I explained, which was conveniently true. "You know how weird and strict the Pendletons are, with that crippled dad and all their crazy religion that's gone to their heads."

"Now that's no way to talk about folks," said my mother, the devout Catholic. "Make sure you two stop by here so your father and I can get a peek."

They were suspicious of my sudden interest in Tommy Pendleton, but I could read the one word in their minds: *Harvard.*

I drove my father's blue Buick LeSabre across Main Street to Tommy's house. When I pulled into the dark driveway and honked, the headlights picked up Mr. Pendleton's twisted silhouette out near the small barn behind the house. He might have been a crooked, leafless tree. A shiver ran through me as though I'd had a premonition. Then the porch light flashed on and Tommy's father vanished into wintry darkness. Mrs. Pendleton stood foregrounded on the porch, her arms clasped across her chest to ward off the chilly December night. She motioned me to come in. Reluctantly, I cut off the motor and got out of the car.

It was the first time I'd ever seen Mrs. Pendleton up close. She was a plain woman, but not severe. She wore her hair pulled back in a loose bun, and a long, brown flowered housedress. She had been pretty once.

"Hello, Marsha," she greeted me with warmth and drew me by my arm into the stale house. "I've heard so much about you. Tommy says you're in all his classes."

"Except P.E.," I clarified nervously. The house was overheated and the smell of cooking grease hung in the air.

Mrs. Pendleton offered to take my coat and insisted I join her for a cup of tea. I had no choice. The house was uncannily silent. Tommy was nowhere in sight. I took a tentative seat on the sofa under a triple portrait of Martin Luther King and the Kennedy brothers. Just knowing they hovered above disturbed my conscience.

"So, Tommy tells me your father teaches at the college." She seated herself across from me, her eyes bright in that smooth, serene face.

"Administration," I corrected her. "He works in administration."

"Isn't that wonderful!" She asked me all about my mother, my brothers, and the exact location of our house. "Of course," she said, "that lovely big white one on the corner of Pine. And I know who your mother is too. Pretty woman, has all that nice thick hair."

She prattled on, appraising me with her eyes as if I were an article of clothing she was assessing for a good fit. Guilt made me overcompensate. I had what folks call good home training, and I didn't hold back. Each courtesy seemed to please her more, until I realized my politeness would be my own undoing.

Her smile was broad now. "I'm just so pleased you two are going to this dance. I don't normally let Tommy go to such things, but I know what a nice girl you are."

I glanced nervously at my watch. When I looked up, Tommy was standing in the doorway in a dark brown suit, his hair parted on one side. We exchanged cautious hellos.

Mrs. Pendleton had a camera ready and she insisted we pose before the fireplace. "Turn this way, you two," she cooed. "Now, give me a big smile. I can't see your eyes, Tommy."

Tommy removed his glasses and held them behind his back as he squeezed awkwardly beside me. We stared dutifully into the blinding flash.

"Oh, the flowers!" Mrs. Pendleton disappeared into the kitchen and I heard the refrigerator door open and close. Too quickly, I thought, for her to have undone a padlock.

She'd seen to it I had a corsage, something frilly and white, with perfume and ribbons, which she pulled from the chilled box. She handed the corsage to Tommy and then photographed him pinning it to my chest ("Oh, I wish I'd known you were going to wear orange!"), cautioning him when he came too close to my breasts ("Careful now, you don't want to stick your little girlfriend!"). I could see how hard she was trying, how important this moment was to her. She wanted to make things right.

Tommy was flustered under the pressure. Beads of sweat broke out over his forehead.

"Now put your arm around Marsha's waist," insisted Mrs. Pendleton. "There, now don't you make a lovely looking twosome? Praise the Lord."

The flash went off three or four more times. I finally pleaded sensitivity to bright lights.

"Look at me keeping you all to myself. I wish the others were around. I'm so sorry Tommy's father wasn't here tonight to see you two off."

I was still at an age when a lie from an adult startled me. Mrs. Pendleton followed us to the door, her eyes bright as a child's: her son Tommy was off to a dance with a girl, and a black one at that, and now she had the pictures to prove it. She stood on the porch clutching the camera as if she'd just photographed Our Lady of Lourdes.

"My parents want us to stop by," I explained dully to Tommy as we came down the driveway.

"*Quid pro quo,*" he said agreeably, but I had no idea what he meant.

Fortunately my parents seemed satisfied just to have us stand in the living room and be viewed. Tommy was not Phil, but my mother made over him just the same. Coatless, she and my father braved the cold and followed us onto our front porch.

"So, will it be Harvard or Princeton?" my father asked Tommy, already joining the two of us in his mind's eye.

"Let them go, Ralph. Have a nice time," said my mother. "Don't worry about hurrying home. Take your time."

We piled back into the LeSabre, and I backed out of the snowy drive. By now it was almost nine, and I was frantic. Calvin's face loomed before me; I felt the irresistible pull of his soft lips on my neck.

"I need to stop by the college for a minute," I said on impulse. "I have to drop something off to a friend."

Tommy didn't object. Instead, he sat stiffly in the passenger seat, staring out the window.

We drove the few blocks to Calvin's dorm. I left the engine running and my maxi coat flung across the back seat: a promise that I would return quickly.

Adrenaline swelled my pulses. Every joint in my body throbbed as if badly bruised. I scampered quickly in my thin-soled T-straps through the darkness, feeling the cold on my half-naked feet and in my bones. Calvin was a hot fire in my brain.

I took the stairs two at a time, coming up through the propped-open fire-exit door. I was Cinderella from the ball. I tapped at his door. No answer. I tapped again. Then again.

"Who're you looking for?" asked a boy poking his head out from the room next door.

"Calvin." My tone implied privilege.

"He's gone."

I should have left it at that and headed for the dance with Tommy. I should have realized that the fever and chills alternately coursing through me signaled danger. But I couldn't resist one more knock, and then the knob was in my hand, turning much too easily, and the sudden chill of my own body startled me in the wake of damp heat that poured toward the open door.

It was like entering a sauna. First the dimness, then the steam rising from Isaac Hayes's brooding *Hot Buttered Soul* album and mingling with the essence of jasmine incense. The air was thick and moody, the candlelit walls alive with ambiguous shadows.

A motion from the corner of the room caught my eye, and then it became two separate motions I saw: one was Calvin rising up from the sheets, with nothing but his medallion around his neck; the other was the silhouette of a long dark body with large tubular breasts and a huge halo of black hair unfolding itself with knowing insolence.

Someone exclaimed, "Oh, my God!" There was a sudden flurry of sheets and pillows and brown limbs, then a woman's voice cried out, "Calvin, what the hell is going on here?" and I realized it was me speaking, using the tone of voice I had imagined only a woman capable of.

"Marsha!"

I didn't recognize my own name. I yelled, "Bastard!" and ran out, twisting my ankle when one of my heels caught on the carpet.

I was too stunned to cry. My chest threatened to cave in on itself. As I ran back out the fire exit, I found I could not catch my breath. Panic set in. It took several minutes of standing in the outside stairwell below, pulling in the frosty air with lungs so tight I thought they would explode.

I had never suspected, because I lacked the experience to suspect.

I stuffed my fist in my mouth and bit down hard until I tasted salt. I shook my hand free and thrust it into a thin layer of snow to stop the pain. And then there was nothing to do except walk back around to the other side of the dorm and get into my father's car next to Tommy Pendleton as if nothing had happened. My voice had disappeared somewhere deep in my throat. As if mutually agreed upon, I said nothing and Tommy said nothing. We went grimly on to the dance at the school gym, my heart as hard as a rock.

The gym was decorated with Christmas tree boughs and ribbons. An inflatable Santa-and-reindeer set hung from the ceiling. A huge fir tree stood in the middle of the floor, lit up and covered with red balls and silver tinsel.

After we'd gotten ourselves settled and I'd managed to swallow some punch, Tommy asked me to dance. We moved stiffly around the floor, nodding to people we knew. "You look very nice," he told me. "You really do."

His touch left me cold inside. I kept my face turned.

We joined Tommy's red-haired friend Paul Malloy and his date, a pale white girl named Lisa from Firelands. Tommy and Paul immediately began whispering together. I made a point of ignoring them all, including Lisa, who was feeling ignored by Paul. She kept trying to show off her corsage that seemed to have taken root right there on her wrist.

"So are you and Tommy going together?" she asked.

"No," I told her and turned my head. Monica and Camille appeared then in jovial moods with dates they'd gotten from a Catholic school in Cleveland. They were both dressed and perfumed and oiled, looking like Cheshire cats.

"How's your health?" asked Monica boldly, with a meaningful look at the clock.

Camille flashed a wicked smile. "Feeling a little sick, Marsha?"

Sitting there with them all, my surroundings melted away and I realized how alone I was, nursing my grief in this empty space. I was seized with panic, afraid I could never dare desire again. Cold terror set in like rigor mortis. In my mind, the door to Çalvin's room kept shutting sharply behind me as if forced by a fast wind.

Monica whispered to me that she had a fifth of Wild Turkey in her Rambler. I rose up and followed like a sleepwalker, leaving Lisa and Paul and Tommy sitting there. Outside in the wintry air I shivered in my thin dress. We sat on chilly vinyl car seats, me on one end, Camille on the other. Monica opened the bottle deftly, trying to prove she was practiced. Before us, our lighted school blazed like an alien spaceship that had just landed next to the expanse of football field.

I took several long swallows of fiery liquid.

Monica poked me with her elbow. "Come on, girl, what's bugging you? It's Christmas. Tommy looks go-o-o-d." She urged the bottle on me again.

I swallowed my agony and enough Wild Turkey to fuse my

nerves back together. The slow burn rounded off the razor-edge of suffering. Camille took the bottle and shoved it under the front seat. The three of us climbed out and bent, shivering and coatless, into the fury of white.

The fiery pain that seared me comes only once in one's life: it is that first scorch of real grief. It is like losing a limb; surprise and horror join forces at the junction of what should be the impossible. At that moment I would have traded my sight to erase what I had seen in Calvin's room.

When Camille and Monica got up to dance with their dates, I informed Tommy flatly that we had to leave. No explanation. He seemed only mildly surprised. As I gathered my coat and purse, I saw him pause and say something to Paul. When we walked out, Camille and Monica cast knowing glances at me over their dates' shoulders.

In the car, when I put the key in the ignition, I burst into tears and cried for several minutes into the collar of my maxi coat, without explanation. I lowered my head onto the steering wheel while Tommy sat dutifully by.

Finally he said, "Is there anything I can do, Marsha?"

"No," I sobbed.

"It was probably hard for you to see Phil Willis there with someone else."

Phil! I hadn't even noticed.

"I know," said Tommy, "it's always hard to be with the wrong person." Consumed with my grief, I took this as an apology, Tommy's acknowledgment of his failure.

"I'm not ready to go home yet," I told him. I eased the car onto the highway, away from town, and turned directly into the snow. I had no destination, only found satisfaction in the motion of the car. We ended up driving eight miles in the wrong direction, to the edge of Lake Erie, where we sat in my father's car, listening to CKLW from Detroit and staring out at the black frozen space ahead.

As for what happened next, I can't make any excuses for Tommy, except to say that perhaps he was just plain curious about himself and desperate to have an answer.

And as for me, I had grown sleepy from the Wild Turkey and my own grief, and when I closed my eyes I could almost imagine it was Calvin, gathering me against him, then brushing his lips against mine, pressing against my chest, then bearing down on me, lifting my dress, tugging at my orange fishnets.

"Do you really want to do this?" I asked the boy hovering over me, my eyes still tightly closed against the black void. There was no answer, just a purposeful sigh into the hollows of my right ear.

That was all the encouragement I needed to move over the edge. How simple it was to plunge downward when the bottom was no longer in sight! All that foolish, dutiful teetering I had done, adding to the ever-spiraling tension between me and Calvin—the tortured refusals, the last-minute "I can'ts" whispered breathlessly through our tangled bodies—now gone flat as a bicycle tire. What did it matter? The next thing I knew, strong hands were extended and someone waited below to catch me. Warmth melted my frozen body, and I fell into forgetfulness, floating gently alongside the two joined bodies in the front seat of my father's car. I dropped off to sleep then, and upon opening my eyes later I was surprised, even shocked, to find myself crushed against Tommy Pendleton inside the cold damp car. The side windows had steamed over, the windshield wore a thick coat of snow. Tommy was sitting up straight again, staring out where the lake should have been. He was wearing his black-framed glasses. With one hand, he reached out and gently caressed my hair as if I were a small animal he had just rescued.

After that night, Tommy Pendleton and I still didn't speak much at school. Sometimes in class I'd catch myself looking at the back of his head, trying to connect it with an old longing that never surfaced. As for Calvin, I kept taking him back, a sucker for his inexhaustible excuses, so we were together off and on for the next year or so. He finally admitted he was engaged to a tall black girl named Charmaine from New Jersey. By the time we actually broke things off, it seemed easy. I was already packed for college, a new life ahead.

Over the years I have often compared myself to that anonymous girl, the one in Calvin's bed that night: her sweat-glistening face, her swollen mouth, her big brown legs unwinding themselves from Calvin's back, her breasts rising and falling obscenely, her eyes like flames.

Tommy and I performed nothing like that in the front seat of my father's car. It was something much simpler, much less eventful, and, under the circumstances, quite forgivable. So much so that I maintained I was a virgin until my freshman year of college when I met Nicholas Rush from Chapel Hill, North Carolina.

Now, as I headed back down the green slope toward where Tommy's casket was being lowered into the ground, I was startled to hear my own name. "Marsha! Marsha Hendrickson!" A tall brown woman in dark red, with a black hat, moved from the group of mourners toward me. "Is it really you, Marsha?"

"Mrs. Pendleton!" She saw my tears and approved of them. This was that same woman who had coaxed Tommy and me closer together in her living room some twenty years before, to record a lie that would give her comfort later on.

"Oh, I'm so glad you could come!" she said. "This means ever so much to me. You remember Tommy's brother Joseph? This is his wife Margaret." They were a handsome couple who studied me solemnly. I'd forgotten how much alike Joseph and Tommy looked; it was like seeing double. "This is Marsha Hendrickson, Tommy's high school girlfriend." I let the exaggeration pass.

Joseph and Margaret nodded with mild interest. Mrs. Pendleton clutched my arm. "Betty said you'd be here. She's already back at Tommy's now getting things ready for the potluck. You *will* join us, won't you?"

Before I could respond, she went on, "Praise the Lord, he didn't have to suffer long. The pneumonia came on so quick. He lost his hearing, then his eyesight. In the end, he couldn't remember even simple things. But he wasn't one to complain, not my Tommy. Always kept things to himself."

"That was Tommy," I agreed.

"Yes, Lord love him," she said. She turned to Joseph. "Tommy and Marsha shared an apartment for a while."

She let the innuendo sink in. Then she pulled me against her hip, her hand gripping mine. That was when I knew she knew, that the word "AIDS" would never pass her lips, that she was still trying to make things right. As if we were all off to a party, and not a tear on her face.

"I'm afraid I have to get going," I said. "I have to see students at four." It was a lie, but one that just as carefully matched the conviction of her own sweet deceit.

"Isn't that too bad?" She seemed genuinely disappointed. "It would be so nice . . . so nice to talk again . . ."

Suddenly I was sixteen years old, sitting impatiently on the Pendletons' sofa, thoughts of Calvin having reduced everyone around me to the dispensable. Mrs. Pendleton was removing the corsage from the box, eager to pin me down like a butterfly in someone's collection.

"Oh, please come," she was now insisting, then caught herself. "I'm sorry." She squeezed my waist briefly, eyes lowered. "I'm so sorry it all turned out this way."

I couldn't tell if she was apologizing or blaming me, but in that moment she had come as close as she probably ever would to admitting the truth.

"You take good care, Marsha. It was so nice of you to make it today." She stepped away then, awkwardly, the heels of her dark red pumps catching in the thick green lawn. She clutched Joseph's arm for support. Together they paused at the edge of Tommy's grave and stared down into it. Her face was resigned, and if I hadn't known better I would have thought she was a stranger hesitating out of curiosity, not a mother whose heart was wrung with grief. I wondered then how many times, over the years, she'd studied those photos of Tommy and me, maybe even had one framed for the mantel where it sat like an accomplishment, giving silent testimony. It may have given her much comfort, which was all she was really asking of me now. I turned and walked away. It seemed the only right thing left to do.

OFF-SEASON TRAVEL

A few weeks after Ellen won the contest that had something to do with peanut butter, the supermarket arranged to fly her and Glenn to the small resort town of Puerto Cobre, on the west coast of Mexico across from La Paz. Even as they bounced along in the dilapidated taxi on the dirt road from the airport into town, Ellen thought how impossible it seemed that they'd actually disentangled themselves from the multiple complications that shaped their collective life in San Francisco: the children, the fixer-upper house, the asthmatic dog, the stack of bills, the unfolded laundry, the undefrosted refrigerator, Glenn's job, her job, the firecracker-like gunshots at night from the projects over the hill, the surreptitious drug-dealing of hooded silhouettes on their corner, and their own mutual complaints swirling together and lost in the fog of what could never be fixed. Long ago, specifics were forgotten. All the two of them could remember was that at one time there had been something good, and that what was left was very, very wrong.

In the taxi Ellen was thinking how Glenn, so familiar he'd gone strange, seemed no longer to belong to her. She watched him stare out the window at the brown, barefoot children playing outside their tarpaper shacks alongside the road fifteen hundred miles south of San Francisco. He was murmuring, "They're so poor," while Ellen considered how she felt nothing, nothing at all.

The supermarket paid for all ground transportation and put

them up at La Gran Duchesa, a small, elegant hotel with a narrow stretch of private beach. The imported white sand was dotted with palm-frond cabañas. Inside the flagstone courtyard was an oblong swimming pool, complete with a full-service bar and submerged stools. A bartender in a red tuxedo jacket was briskly polishing glasses to the rhythm of piped-in Muzak. He barely glanced up as Ellen and Glenn made their way up the outside stairs to the third floor. Their room was small, with two double beds separated by a nightstand, but beyond the sliding glass door to the balcony was a wide view of the ocean.

While Glenn showered, Ellen pushed the door open and stepped out onto the balcony into the warm evening air. She wore cut-offs and her oldest son's Little League T-shirt, and carried a bottle of beer in her hand. At home she never drank, but now she took a long swig of beer and considered how, at forty, she still had time to try out a different sort of life.

That was when she noticed a woman to the right at the wrought-iron railing, her back to Ellen, studying the fiery halo of sinking sun that scorched the surface of the ocean. Ellen thought she should announce herself. "It's beautiful, isn't it?" The woman turned around, startled. "The sunset." Ellen gestured toward it.

The woman was tall, striking, and black. She wore a foundation a couple of shades too light so that her skin bore an eerie pallor. Her eyebrows had been plucked until there was only a thin arched line above each eye. Her full mouth was lipsticked pale orange, a color Ellen wouldn't have dared to wear at the risk of looking jaundiced. But on the woman it looked elegant. She wore white pedal pushers and orange sandals. Ellen couldn't help noting with a small pang of envy the long, elegant brown hands, neatly manicured, resting lightly, one on each slim hip.

"Looks like we're neighbors. We just got here."

The woman stared at her, like someone expecting an apology. After a moment she said, "I didn't realize they'd put anyone right next door. After all, it's off-season. The hotel's practically empty." She paused. "I'm Marjorie Pierce."

"Ellen Fitzgerald." Ellen held out her hand and Marjorie leaned forward perfunctorily to accept it. Her fingers were cool, her palm warm. She pulled away as soon as they'd clasped hands.

"Well then . . ." She straightened herself up, raising one slender hand to wave away a small insect. "I better go get dressed."

"Marjorie?" It was a man's voice, half-plaintive, half-annoyed, coming from the open door of her room. A white flash of curtain stirred in the breeze. "Marjorie?" There was a sense of urgency in his tone. "Where the hell . . .?"

He stepped onto the balcony, a tall brown man dressed in one of those awful flowered shirt-and-short sets American tourists wear when they travel to warm climates. When he saw Ellen, he looked as if he thought maybe she'd scaled the side of the hotel on a rope. "Oh, *buenos días,* or is it *noches* already?"

Marjorie introduced them. "Lafayette, this is Ellen. Ellen, my husband Lafayette."

They shook hands. His hand was huge and warm. He peered beyond her to the yellow rectangle of her open door. "We didn't expect neighbors," he said. "You here alone?"

"No, my husband's inside." The shower had stopped. She could hear Glenn moving around inside the room. "Glenn?"

The sunset behind Marjorie and Lafayette lit up their bodies like burning effigies. From behind the hotel the faraway evening sounds of the town, faint traffic and chatter, wafted up.

Glenn padded out on the balcony in bare feet and shorts. He was a tall man, instantly dwarfed by Lafayette. Ellen introduced him. More handshaking between Glenn and Lafayette.

Comments on the sunset, the warm night, the fragrant air.

Marjorie tried again to excuse herself.

"Hold on there!" Lafayette plunked one heavy arm down on her shoulders. His eyes were slightly slanted, his eyebrows thick, his forehead broad. He was handsome in a comical sort of way.

"We're having dinner at the El Toro. Why don't y'all join us?"

Ellen looked at Marjorie. She stood slightly behind Lafayette, her neck caught in the hook of his arm. Her orange mouth twisted, then tightened.

"Oh, I don't think so," Ellen was saying at the same time Glenn was accepting.

"Sure, sure, it'll take us a few minutes to get cleaned up . . ." Glenn looked smugly over at Ellen.

Lafayette's big face lit up like a jack-o'-lantern. He released Marjorie and clapped his hands together.

"Okay then! Half an hour? Downstairs in the lobby?"

Marjorie, without a word, pushed past him and went back inside. Ellen had the grim sense she wasn't interested in having dinner with a strange white couple.

"See you soon," grinned Lafayette, backing toward the door. "Glen and Ellen, right?" He clicked his fingers as if fixing their names in his mind.

"Like the wine," said Glenn. It was one of his favorite jokes. Ellen had heard it a hundred times, exactly ninety-nine more than she cared to.

"Hey, now, *there* you go!" said Lafayette, catching on. He jabbed his finger at Glenn. "That's funny, man. Very funny." And he kept the grin on his face as he backed through the door to his room.

Glenn whistled as he lathered his face. Ellen spoke from the shower. With water coursing over her, she generally found it easier to say what was on her mind. "I think it's weird to go off and eat dinner with total strangers."

The whistling stopped. "What the hell are you talking about?" Ellen knew from the tightness in his voice that he'd pulled one cheek taut to accommodate the razor. "They're nice people." He said this enthusiastically, in the hopeful voice he used to disguise disappointment.

"*Nice?* How can you tell?"

Glenn poked his head up against the shower curtain. Half of his jaw was coated with white shaving foam. "I think it's important to find opportunities to mix with people of other races."

Ellen opened the shower curtain. "Are you kidding? That's how you think of them? *People of other races?*"

"You know what I mean," he said. "We don't have any black friends and now's a chance to mingle. It's a good opportunity."

"Oh God, Glenn."

He turned around and picked up his razor. "Now you're going to tell me I'm a racist. Well, I think when people make an effort, you need to respond."

"I only wish you'd asked me if *I* wanted to go."

"What do you want me to do, go over there and tell them we're not coming?" He used his accusing voice, the "it's all your fault" voice.

"Yes, actually, I do." The shower water rained down on her. Ellen felt the familiar tightening of contrariness inside her, her final defense against anger.

Glenn shook his razor at her. "Why the fuck do you do this? We're on *vacation,* for Christ's sake."

"Not for *Christ's* sake." Ellen plunged her face into the powerful stream of water. "We won a supermarket contest because after I get off work I spend half my life at the supermarket. That's why we're here, Glenn."

Glenn's voice vibrated through the shower curtain. "You really expect me to go say we're not meeting them for dinner?"

"You mean these nice *black* people, don't you?" Ellen said. "You know we're not doing them any favors, don't you? You accepted. Now you can un-accept."

"You're out of your mind. They'll think we're . . ."

Ellen popped her head through the curtain again. "If you'd paid any attention, you'd realize that the wife, what's her name, Marjorie, didn't want to go out with us either."

Glenn was trimming carefully around his mustache. "Ellen, shut up. Can't we just go out and have a good time for once?"

They never fought with conviction anymore. They lacked the energy for it. As usual, Ellen thought, Glenn had missed her point and continued on, confident in his.

The El Toro was a big pink mission-style stucco five blocks down from the hotel. Glenn, dressed in a white shirt and black linen pants, fell into step with Lafayette. He and Ellen had not spoken the whole time they were getting ready. Ellen, in her loose cotton dress, watched his back with a mixture of annoyance and lost affection. The familiar hunch of his shoulders. The awkward launch of one slightly bowed leg stepping in front of the other. These things had once inspired tenderness. Now they conjured up, at best, indifference and, at worst, irritation. Over the last few years her heart had hardened and shrunk into a tight kernel of ill will. Ellen no longer loved Glenn. He knew it too, but they hadn't spoken about it. Now he was pointing toward the sea and Lafayette nodded furiously. Ellen's eyes followed the direction of Glenn's finger. In the twilight a surfer was cresting a wave.

Lafayette's voice drifted back to her. "I'll take you out there tomorrow, buddy. We can rent boards."

Ellen turned to Marjorie, who had been silent. "Is your husband having a midlife crisis too?" She meant it as a joke, an offhand way of connecting with Marjorie and trying to stave off her own rising despair.

But Marjorie kept her head averted, showing no sign of having heard. Ellen thought how beautiful Marjorie looked in her red linen shift and black T-strap sandals. Beside her, she felt matronly and clumsy, as if the extra ten pounds she carried had just announced themselves in some audible way.

Ellen fought the urge to turn around and head back to the hotel when Marjorie said, with precise enunciation, "What do you mean, a *midlife crisis?*"

Ellen tried to capture levity in her straining voice. "They're talking about surfing tomorrow. Two grown men. Isn't that *crazy?*"

Marjorie seemed not to comprehend. They were now passing three cabbies lounging around a taxi stop. Marjorie ignored the "*Ssssst, morena!*" from the shortest of the group, a man with his shirt unbuttoned and a gold cross on his chest, who had fixed his liquid-eyes on her legs. "Surfing?" she said vaguely, and looked out at the dark water without further comment.

They were given a table on the patio, just a few feet from where the band was setting up. Ellen listened to the rhythm of the incoming tide wash over Glenn's and Lafayette's voices, smoothing them out until they were indistinguishable from each other. In San Francisco it was usually much too cold to ever really enjoy the beach. Only crazy people went into the water there, and then not for long. Now Ellen had a sudden desire to abandon her dress and go fling herself into the water. It had been a long time since she'd been swimming and the thought of gliding through water appealed to her.

"Nice night for a swim," she murmured to Marjorie, who was busy studying the pink, portfolio-sized menu.

"I never learned to. I've always been afraid of water."

"We're in the minority in our neighborhood," Glenn was saying congenially, as if testing this fact out for Lafayette's approval. "Mostly Mexican and Asian, I'd say. A few blacks."

"Yeah, well, tell me about being in the minority," Lafayette said. "We're over in the Oakland Hills. We lived in San Francisco when we were first married, but the weather didn't suit us. Don't you know about the radio towers on the top of Twin Peaks, the ones that send out subliminal messages that say, 'Black people, move to Oakland'?"

Glenn looked startled. Lafayette burst out laughing. "It's a joke, man, though not far from the truth. For a major city, San Francisco's got a tiny black population, you know." The waiter interrupted for their orders, and Lafayette ordered two bottles of wine. "This your first time here?" he asked after everyone's wine glass had been filled.

Glenn was eager to tell exactly how their trip had come about. He had told their neighbors and relatives, and even now, as the words spilled from his mouth, his syntax never varied. It was as if he were reciting a speech. Ellen couldn't get over how small he looked across from Lafayette. Glenn, who at times had loomed larger than life, whose presence had taken up all the space in her life, now seemed to all but disappear in the candlelight, and if she squinted her eyes ever so slightly she could cause everything about him except for the white shirt to fade into shadow.

"We came here years ago for our honeymoon," Lafayette said. "Just after I got out of med school."

Glenn leaped on this. "Med school," he said. "So you practice medicine." He was obviously impressed. And pleased. A black doctor. Ellen could read his mind. She downed her glass of wine and poured herself a second. The wine went right to her head, bringing up a roar of unrecognizable voices, all clamoring to be heard.

"A cardiologist." Lafayette grinned and reached out to squeeze one of Marjorie's hands. "I take care of other people's hearts and she takes care of mine."

It was obvious, from the weary expression on Marjorie's face, that this was an old joke. "No I don't," she said flatly. "You're quite capable of caring for your own heart."

Touché! the voices in Ellen's head cried in unison. The woman has got some spark! Before she realized it, she was giggling aloud. Marjorie glanced up sharply. Ellen imagined what Marjorie was thinking: giddy white woman, no common sense. She recovered herself just as Glenn kicked her under the table. He quickly launched into one of his favorite stories about a client of his who was suing a drugstore over a folding lawn chair that unfolded and fell on her head. He had moved to rescue mode, diverting the attention from Ellen.

"Ellen doesn't usually drink so much," he remarked as Lafayette poured her a third glass. He had shifted into paternal mode, the one which guided him to apologize for her behavior.

"Yes, I do," Ellen lied and smiled broadly. She raised her glass and perversely proposed a toast. "To four days of rest and relaxation, to travel." She looked deliberately at Marjorie. "To new friends." It was the voices in her head talking. Strained, self-conscious. Ellen had never said anything so foolish in her life. She was sure Marjorie winced.

Everyone obediently raised a glass, then self-consciously clinked rims and stems together in the center of the table over a bowl of pink flowers floating in water.

Ellen leaned across to Marjorie. Maybe the woman was shy. "Do you two have children?"

There was a quick flicker in Marjorie's dark eyes. "No." She shook her head. "You?"

Ellen held up three fingers. "Three. Three boys. Bad, terrible boys. Three, six, and ten." She clicked them off on her fingers. "I haven't had a vacation since the little one was born. Between working and raising three boys . . ." Ellen stopped. She realized she was "going on," as Glenn would say.

Marjorie's eyes rested on her unwaveringly from across the table. In the candlelight Marjorie's skin glowed like bronze. "Boys can be a handful," she said carefully.

"Mine are monsters. They keep me in a constant state of uproar. I needed this break, let me tell you. Just the other day they had me so frazzled I wore two different colored shoes to work. I didn't even notice until one of the secretaries pointed it out in the afternoon."

Marjorie never changed expression. Ellen was sorry she'd made the effort. It's not shyness, she decided. Probably if I were black, I wouldn't want to feel obligated to sit and entertain some white woman.

Marjorie readjusted herself in her seat, then unexpectedly she leaned forward. "I can beat that, girl," she said. She spoke under the voices of the two men. "Last week I mailed our bills in a public trash can."

"You what?"

There was the merest hint of a smile on Marjorie's mouth. Lafayette glanced over at her. Marjorie, unaware, went on. "That's right, girlfriend. Walked right past the mailbox up to a public trash can and tossed my letters in. Bills mostly, if you can believe that. They just kind of floated around down at the bottom in a sea of Coca-Cola."

Lafayette laid a heavy hand on Marjorie's arm. "You don't need to be telling everyone about that."

Marjorie ignored him. "I had to reach down inside that can,

just like a bag lady, and fish out my stuff." Her mouth twisted ever so slightly. Ellen couldn't tell if she was smiling or getting ready to cry.

Lafayette frowned, removed his hand, and turned back to Glenn. He went back to explaining the difference between good and bad cholesterol.

Marjorie continued. "Sometimes," she said, her voice barely audible, "I think I'm losing my mind."

She pierced a prawn with the tines of her fork. And then, as if she had been asked, she leaned over and offered Ellen a taste of the broiled scampi. Very delicately, her bracelet jangling on her thin wrist, she lifted her fork to Ellen's lips and deposited one large prawn in her mouth. "They make outrageous garlic sauce," she said. "You'll love it."

Lafayette had launched into a repertoire of uneasy racial jokes. Ellen heard him say, "And then the rabbi said to the black guy . . ." He finished up one with the punch line "But the doctor told me I was impo'tant!"

She thought Glenn laughed too hard. He told a "There was a black guy and an Italian guy" joke, which came out badly for the Italian guy (though if told to an Italian, the black guy got the raw deal), and then launched into his "special pig" joke which could be adapted from the old black man to the "redneck farmer" version. Lafayette tipped way back in his chair and hooted.

Marjorie and Ellen managed to insert small bits of polite talk into the conversation. Marjorie was a registered nurse. She worked in pediatrics, but had taken a leave of absence from the clinic. She didn't say why. Ellen managed to find out she was originally from North Carolina, and that she and Lafayette had bought their house in Oakland almost ten years before.

Later, when the band, a group of four young men, struck up

a Spanish rendition of "Feelings," Lafayette dragged Marjorie up from the table to dance, and Glenn followed suit with Ellen.

For the next song, a fast salsa number, Ellen danced with Lafayette. She stepped all over his toes while he chuckled and skillfully maneuvered himself around and beside her. Marjorie danced distractedly by herself, with Glenn next to her rocking back and forth on his heels and clicking his fingers. Ellen thought how much of what Marjorie did seemed like a duty. The couples traded back and forth for several more numbers. Ellen felt embarrassed by Glenn, his awkward, jerky motions and the earnest working of his mouth in concentration. Then she felt ashamed of herself for her lack of charity. She saw herself and Glenn as she was sure Marjorie saw them: strangers straining too hard toward friendship.

When the wine wore off, Ellen pleaded weariness. She was surprised when Marjorie suggested that the two of them walk back to the hotel so the men could stay longer.

"Absolutely not!" protested Lafayette, though Ellen could tell Glenn thought it was an excellent idea.

Glenn asked for the bill, and it turned out Lafayette had already slipped the waiter his credit card. Glenn began objecting—Ellen thought, ah, methinks he protests too much!—and yanked out his own wallet, displaying an array of credit cards, most of which should have been buried in their back yard and put out of their misery.

"Put your money away, man," said Lafayette, "this is *my* treat. You can get it next time."

Ellen thought she understood what was happening, as she and Marjorie picked their way silently, even gratefully, over the darkened sidewalks—that Glenn and Lafayette, just a few feet behind, were taking odd solace in each other's anonymity. In the darkness she was filled with longing, but it had nothing to do with Glenn. Ellen knew she was mostly at fault with Glenn, that what she'd known for a long time he was now only beginning to realize. Cowards that they were, neither of them had the guts to bring it up. What Ellen couldn't figure out was why Marjorie didn't love Lafayette and which one of them, Marjorie or Lafayette, was at fault.

Before she fell asleep that night, she rolled over in the dark, confused by and drawn to the heat of Glenn's body. She began to kiss his chest, pretending he was a stranger, imagining a different face, maybe even Lafayette, dancing inches from her. Glenn exhaled sharply into the air, then pushed himself suddenly inside her. Afterwards, Ellen felt ashamed of herself. Glenn held on to her tightly and whispered, "I told you all we needed was some time away." Ellen closed her eyes and imagined she had dived into the ocean and was riding the crest of a wave just before it crashed and spilled her onto sand with the consistency of angel hair. She pushed away from Glenn and turned over on her side. She lay there for a long time pretending to be asleep. She knew from the way Glenn shifted around behind her that he knew it too.

The next morning, just as Ellen was rousting herself out of bed, Lafayette knocked on the door to invite Glenn to play golf, something Glenn had never done in his life, but which he eagerly agreed to without consulting her. Apparently the surfing idea had been abandoned. Ellen sagged back against the pillows and realized she was paying for last night's wine. Glenn brought her two aspirin and a glass of water before he left. She rested another half hour or so, with the drapes drawn, then got up and went downstairs, forcing herself to eat some of the continental breakfast offered in the hotel lounge. The lounge was empty, except for a small Mexican woman in white who was reading a magazine and sipping coffee.

A few minutes later, Marjorie appeared. She was wearing white shorts and a red halter top. She looked rested. Ellen felt self-conscious about the whiteness of her own legs compared to Marjorie's smooth brown calves. She tucked her legs under her, tried to make herself seem smaller.

"Good morning," said Marjorie coolly. "I see Lafayette talked Glenn into golf." She studied the tray of breakfast rolls a moment, examined a piece of fruit which she rejected, then poured herself half a cup of coffee.

"Glenn's thrilled. I woke up with a hangover."

"They're kind of two peas in a pod," Marjorie observed. "I don't play golf."

Ellen had finished her second pastry and stood up. "I think I'm going down to the beach to get some sun," she said, by way of invitation. "What are you planning to do?"

"I have a massage appointment," said Marjorie. Before Ellen could ask her more about this, she had turned, coffee cup in hand, and headed back upstairs. Ellen watched her go, started to call out, then thought better of it.

Ellen strolled out on the empty beach and took a short swim. The water was warm. It was like taking a bath. She found herself staring occasionally up at the hotel for some sign of Marjorie on the balcony. No one else was on the beach. She tried pretending she missed Glenn, but she didn't. She floated on her back in the water and let the sunlight burn through her eyelids. She imagined herself being carried out to sea. She imagined washing up on shore on the other side of the world, dressed only in her swimsuit, without wallet or money, and no way to prove who she was.

On her way back to the room, she stopped at the desk and asked if there had been any phone calls. Nothing. She asked about going into town and the desk clerk told her to walk out front when she was ready and take a taxi.

Aside from the open-air market, downtown Puerto Cobre was mostly made up of stores with overpriced souvenirs. She stopped in front of a window displaying an orchestra of stuffed frogs dressed to look like mariachis. She bought postcards for the boys, though she'd see them before the postcards got to them, and she bought her mother-in-law a shawl that was exactly like something she could buy at home in the Mission District. Then she strolled out along the seawall and watched a group of teenage boys and girls flirt and tease one another.

The heat was overpowering. This time of year in San Francisco the fog was clearing late, if at all, and Ellen imagined the general dreariness of gray skies. She bought an *horchata* from a street vendor and drank it slowly, savoring the sweetness. Then she climbed in a taxi and headed back to the hotel. It was still early.

Glenn wasn't back yet, and the air in their closed-up room was suffocating. The maid had come and straightened, and left a card on the pillow which said, "Your room was cleaned by Rosa." Ellen opened the sliding glass door to let in the air, found a *People* magazine, and went down into the courtyard of the hotel. She longed for a breeze, but the air around her was still. The wind chimes overhead hung silent. An American couple sat waist deep in water at the pool bar, laughing and drinking, and getting drunker by the minute. Ellen guessed they were in their sixties. The woman was dressed in an awful, ruffly, skirted pink one-piece, her fat white thighs floating in the water. The man wore turquoise swimming trunks that came up to his armpits, and wrap-around sunglasses. Ellen heard the man say to the bartender in badly accented Spanish, "*Una otra bebida par la mujer!*" and then he yelled over to Ellen, "How do you say 'bride' in Spanish?" Ellen shrugged. Newlyweds.

She tried to imagine what it would be like to get married at their age. Twelve years she had been married to Glenn, plus the three years that they lived together while he finished law school. Her mother had warned her. "If you live together first, chances are it won't work out." Ellen had laughed, called her provincial, myopic, old-fashioned. Last year her mother died very quickly of cancer. She had been married exactly fifty-three years, something which she saw as a triumph.

The woman in the pink bathing suit began to sing "Well, I'm always true to you darlin' in my fashion . . ." The man leaned over and kissed her on the forehead. The top of his bald head was freckled from the sun. They both looked as if the reddened skin on their shoulders were made of leather.

Feeling weak from the sun, Ellen got up and went back upstairs. She was halfway curious to see if Glenn had returned, knowing he wouldn't have, and he hadn't. She rinsed out her bathing suit in the bathroom sink and hung it on the balcony railing to dry. The sliding glass door to Marjorie's room was closed, the curtain drawn.

Ellen wandered down the hall. It was dead silent. She paused in front of Marjorie's door and listened. She wondered if Marjorie were in there and if she would mind if Ellen knocked. Ellen raised her hand and tapped lightly on the door with three fingers. She waited. The hallway carpet smelled faintly of insecticide. She tapped again.

Just as she was about to give up and turn away, the door was cracked open just a couple of inches. Ellen could make out only the tips of Marjorie's fingers, and a crescent of light from one of her eyes.

"Yes?" she said coldly, as if they were strangers.

"Oh, sorry, did I wake you?"

"Do you need something?"

"Just wondered if you'd heard from Glenn and Lafayette."

"No, and I don't expect to."

"They've been gone a long time. How long does golf take?"

Marjorie shrugged.

Ellen couldn't make herself leave. "How was your massage?" she persisted. "I was thinking of getting one myself." This was a lie. Ellen disliked massages.

Marjorie widened the door slightly. She was wearing a robe that she held together with one hand. Ellen could see the white lace of a brassiere through her fingers. "Massage is relaxing," said Marjorie. Ellen couldn't decide whether Marjorie was making fun of her or not.

"Did you go to a man or a woman?"

"It's a woman, but she leaves at noon," Marjorie said. "You have to check with the desk clerk for her schedule." For a moment Ellen thought she was going to shut the door. Instead, she said, "Come on in," and stepped back to let Ellen by.

The room was dark and claustrophobic, the curtains pulled shut. There was a stale, tight odor Ellen associated with sleep. A man's wet swimsuit dried over the bathroom doorknob. There were two open suitcases overflowing with clothes. Right off the bat, Ellen noticed the twin beds, like out of a fifties movie. Both had been slept in. Otherwise, the room was like Ellen and Glenn's room, just turned around.

"Lafayette thrashes," Marjorie remarked, though Ellen hadn't asked. Her robe fell open partially and Ellen saw the flatness of her brown stomach. Marjorie's hair stood stiffly off her head.

The twin bed nearest the door was rumpled.

"What time is it?" Marjorie yawned.

"Three. Four. It's really hot outside. I'm bored to death. I guess I don't know what to do if there aren't kids jumping all over me."

Marjorie sat on the edge of the unmade bed and scratched her scalp.

"Look," Ellen said, "Maybe I should go . . ."

Marjorie looked up. In the semidarkness the blue-white globes of her eyes stood out against her dark face. "It's up to you."

But Ellen didn't go. Instead she took a chance. "You want to go down in the courtyard and sit in the pool and have a drink? They have a bar right in the pool. I never drink at home, but you're supposed to drink on vacation." She meant this as a joke, but Marjorie didn't respond. She looked at Ellen as if expecting her to make the decision for her. "Of course if you don't want to . . ."

"Okay," said Marjorie. She got up and went into the bathroom to shower. Ellen took a seat in the vinyl chair in the corner. It took Marjorie almost half an hour to get ready. Ellen stared at the chaos of the darkened room and thought about what it might be that makes people fall out of love with each other.

They waded waist-deep to the bar and sat on the submerged stools.

"This is nice," said Marjorie. She looked down at her legs floating weightlessly. "I don't usually like the water."

Ellen smiled. She felt she had accomplished something, that Marjorie was beginning to trust her. "These places always seem so artificial to me," she remarked.

"How do you mean?"

"You know, fake sand, a pool, when you could swim in the ocean . . ."

Marjorie shrugged. "I like it. It's not meant to be like real life. That's the whole point."

Ellen's piña colada was too sweet, almost syrupy, but she sipped at it anyway.

Marjorie surveyed the courtyard with its large pots of colorful flowers. "I'm leaving Lafayette," she said matter-of-factly and toyed with the umbrella in her drink.

Ellen wondered if she'd heard right.

"We don't even live together anymore as it is. I've been staying with a girlfriend in East Oakland. And I've just rented an apartment down by the lake. When we get back, I'm moving there."

Ellen curled her toes over the rungs of the underwater bar stool. "I don't understand."

"Lafayette begged me to take this trip with him. I told him there was no point, but you can see how Lafayette doesn't take no for an answer. It's what makes him a good doctor, I guess. That drive he's got. The man never gives up. Nothing's ever finished. Not even us." She took a sudden interest in the gold cross she wore on a chain around her neck.

Marjorie was perfect, thought Ellen, from her earrings to her nails to her long legs shimmering in the water. "You both seem like such nice people." As soon as the words were out of her mouth, she knew she'd said something foolish.

"Oh, we are. You know, responsible, respectable, nice people. Lots of friends. Church-going. Very nice. No one nicer than Marjorie and Lafayette." There was an edge to her voice.

"You can't work things out?"

Marjorie shook her head. "Out of the question."

"You're sure?"

Marjorie trailed one of her manicured hands through the water. Without looking up she said, "Three months ago our son died. It was a Saturday. I was at home painting the trim of our new sunroom."

Ellen didn't say anything. She looked up at the brilliant blue sky and tried to imagine infinity. She couldn't make sense of what Marjorie was saying. She hadn't even known Marjorie had a son.

Marjorie began to recite. "It was an accident. You know how accidents are. Nobody's fault. Lafayette took Michael—that was our son's name, named for my father—ten years old—for a bicycle trip. An overnighter. Up to the Napa Valley. You know, sleeping bags, the whole bit. They were crossing the highway. I don't even know where exactly. Lafayette said the road was clear. No cars. Michael was right behind on a new mountain bike we'd just bought him. There was a rise to the right. A car was coming fast, but Lafayette didn't see it. Lafayette got to the other side." She paused. "Michael didn't."

Marjorie ordered another drink. "I hate to drink," she said. "I work out too much to handle alcohol."

"When?" Ellen asked softly. "When did you say your son died?"

"Three months ago. Three months ago yesterday actually. He's buried in that cemetery in Piedmont. But you didn't ask me that, did you?"

"How terrible," said Ellen. Her mind jumped to her own sons, fifteen hundred miles away. "Lafayette must feel terrible."

"Lafayette feel terrible? Jolly old good-time, good-natured Lafayette?" Marjorie laughed. "Yeah, he's heartbroken, but you'd never know it, girl. No, he's too busy being the big strong black man, just like he wanted our son to be. Tough. Better than everyone else. Faster, smarter, sharper, tougher. Better than the white boys is what Lafayette always said you had to be."

Tears appeared from under Marjorie's sunglasses and ran down her cheeks. The bartender looked away. Ellen wanted to reach over and touch Marjorie's hand, but she didn't.

"The thing is," said Marjorie, "I can't stand to look at him. I can't tell you just how much I can't stand to look at him."

Ellen ordered them each another piña colada. She took several long sips. The combination of the alcohol and the sun made her feel fuzzy, forgetful, almost relieved. Ellen imagined losing her boys. She imagined losing Glenn. In the crossfire from the gun battles in their neighborhood, to a falling tree, to a reckless car, to one of those rare lightning bolts that could mean the demise of an entire family. It was a terrible thought and Ellen knew it, but she had run it sometimes like a dare through her mind. And now here was Marjorie, a lightning rod for Ellen's own fears. It had actually happened. The worst had actually happened.

Ellen said to Marjorie. "What a terrible loss for you."

"You have no idea," said Marjorie and she took a long sip through her straw.

"No," said Ellen. "You're right, I don't." Her legs were suddenly chilled in the water. "Is there anything I can do?"

Marjorie turned and looked at Ellen as if she were a crazy woman. "Anything you can do? Don't you think if there was, I'd ask?"

Glenn was exhausted and sunburned when he returned at seven from scuba diving. Ellen had fallen asleep on their bed and awakened to the sound of the key turning in the lock.

"Scuba diving?" she said drowsily, wondering if she'd somehow gotten the day wrong. "Scuba diving?"

Glenn scratched his head sheepishly. "Golf didn't exactly work out." He explained that he and Lafayette had decided instead to rent equipment from someone named Hector who took them out in a leaky boat. "Lafayette's a maniac," he told her proudly, as if this signaled some accomplishment of his own. "The guy is fearless, utterly fearless. Doesn't let anything stop him."

"And you?" Ellen said. "You've never scuba-dived in your life, so tell me who's the maniac?"

"It was incredible, Ellen. You should see the stuff that's down there."

"I think it was a very dangerous thing you two did."

"The man's a barracuda," said Glenn. "You know where he grew up?" He paused for emphasis. "South side of Chicago. You know, poor. Serious poor. Typical story. No dad. Just a grandmother. He told me it was sheer stubbornness that got him to college and into med school. I believe it. The man is a barracuda."

"I thought you had to have a license or something for scuba diving."

"This is *Mexico*," said Glenn. "I wish I'd had the boys with me."

Ellen's mouth felt dry and thick. "I hope you don't really mean you wished you'd had the boys with you. It's bad enough you'd risk your own neck."

Glenn peeled his clothes off. His skin had a sheen, as if it were still coated with water. "What did *you* do, sleep the day away?" He meant this as a joke, but Ellen sensed he might have also considered it a possibility.

"No. I sat in the pool bar and got drunk with Marjorie."

She flung herself back on the bed and let the ceiling whirl. Four piña coladas and a bowl of pretzels for dinner. Ellen was in love with Marjorie, the mystery of Marjorie, all the pain inside her. That Marjorie had made her her secret sharer, something that Glenn had no idea about, gave Ellen a sense of sudden purpose.

"Marjorie's some woman," Glenn said, standing naked before Ellen. "Lafayette's a lucky man. He's so in love with her. Just like me with you." He bent down and rubbed his face against hers. Ellen pulled away from the sandpaper roughness of his cheek. He kept on. "You were so sweet last night!"

Ellen sat up and pulled even farther away. "They're getting divorced," she said fiercely.

Glenn laughed. "Yeah, right." He poked her playfully in the crotch.

"I'm serious. They're getting divorced. Marjorie told me this afternoon."

Glenn didn't buy it. "Nah, she's just pissed we went off today."

"I don't think so," Ellen said. "I think that's Lafayette's version." She wanted to hurt Glenn. "You know he's just using you to avoid being around Marjorie. You're a distraction."

She was saving the best for last.

"JE-sus," said Glenn. "Am I in the right room?" He looked around with an exaggerated gesture.

Ellen pulled on her cutoffs and the Little League T-shirt. "I want to do something interesting tomorrow, Glenn. I want to rent a car and go see some sights. We only have a couple days here and I'm bored out of my mind."

Glenn looked uncomfortable. "Well, maybe in the afternoon. I promised Lafayette I'd do this fishing thing with him tomorrow."

"Fishing thing?"

"Yeah, fishing thing. You know, a couple of hours out in a

boat. I'll be back before you know it."

"But you hate boats. You get seasick."

"Lafayette does too. But he's got these patches . . ."

Ellen managed to stand up. "I don't fucking believe you!" she said and went into the bathroom and started the shower full blast. "You don't know the first thing about your friend Lafayette!"

When she came out, Glenn was gone. She went downstairs and ate a bowl of lousy American soup by herself in the empty hotel snack bar. Disgusted, she went out for a walk on the beach to clear her head. The sun was setting. She left the pristine strip of white sand and wandered down a beach littered with beer bottles and scraps of paper. Several Mexican families were grouped along the sand staring out at the glowing horizon. A woman with a baby squatted by the edge of the water. As Ellen passed, the woman smiled up at her. Ellen smiled back, enjoying the thought that what had just passed between them, two strangers in a lightning-quick exchange, went deeper. She considered then how easy it would be to keep walking, never looking back until La Gran Duchesa was a speck in the background. She wondered where she might spend the night and what Glenn would do if she didn't return. She tried to imagine what he would tell the children when he returned home without her.

On her way back, the wet sand cooled the soles of her feet. A half dozen young men sat on a rock in the shallows drinking beer. One of them waved and Ellen waved back. She could hear Glenn telling her she was too careless, but she was beyond caring. La Gran Duchesa loomed ahead, turned a rosy pink in the sun's last light. Ellen ducked under the rope that separated the two beaches. She considered her return a defeat. She glanced up toward the shared balcony. It was empty. Her own door appeared to be shut, but the door to Marjorie and Lafayette's room was wide open. From where she stood, Ellen could see the sail of white drapes luffing in the breeze. She stopped and listened. Drifting downward was the muted sound of crying. Immediately she thought of Marjorie, so tightly contained, finally giving in to grief. Then she got a pang thinking it might be Glenn, but she was sure it wasn't. A moment later she caught sight of Marjorie exiting the hotel and briskly retreating down the beach. The thin, disturbing sobs continued from above. Ellen tried to imagine the person who could make such sounds; she was both fascinated and saddened.

Lafayette and Glenn left mid-morning. They'd invited her, but she'd said no. It was just as well, Ellen thought, she would go to the beach and read. She had no idea what kind of fishing they could do at that time of day, but she put on a cheerful front as the two of them trooped off together toward Lafayette's rental car, Glenn with his long pale legs in a pair of shorts and Lafayette sauntering in his flowered shirt and shorts.

Ellen stopped by the desk and picked up a beach chair. She spent the next few hours on the sand, with a book she'd brought along. The sun burned into her flesh, and she imagined all the dangers away as she watched her thighs darken. Mexican peddlers appeared now and then on the opposite side of the rope and called out to sell their wares. This time of year there weren't many, but occasionally she was interrupted by an insistent "Psst, señorita!" and someone holding up a scarf, a shawl, a dress, a hat and motioning for her to come take a closer look. She shook her head no, then discovered that any acknowledgment was interpreted as encouragement. She turned her chair and pretended not to hear them.

An older Mexican man in a white shirt and loose dark pants

came along the beach sweeping the sand smooth with a broom. He passed close by, and Ellen observed him peripherally, but he never looked her way. Besides her, there was only a middle-aged gay couple in matching blue briefs, each with a pair of blue eyecups, spread-eagled on mats. Shortly after, the elderly newlyweds she had seen the day before in the pool spread out an oversized Mickey Mouse towel and played cards. They got redder and redder in the sun.

So this is vacation? Ellen thought. To hell with vacation. Vacations are for people who have good lives they can return to. She closed her book and gave in to the dizzying heat.

It was mid-afternoon when Ellen woke up, hungry and dazed. The sand was too hot to walk on. She slipped on her sandals, wrapped a towel around her waist, and went inside to order a sandwich and a soda from the hotel snack bar. As she passed through the lounge area, she caught sight of Marjorie sitting by the window overlooking the pool bar. She was holding an ashtray in one hand and smoking a cigarette.

Ellen started to walk the other way, but Marjorie glanced up calmly. "Hey." She blew out a stream of smoke.

Ellen tightened her towel around her self-consciously. Now that she was inside, she became aware that her oiled skin was not browning, but reddening. She made a joke about how vacations encouraged unhealthy lifestyles: drinking, smoking, tanning. "I'm out working on a case of skin cancer. Want to come out and sit in the shade with me? We could grab a cabaña."

Marjorie stubbed out the cigarette. Her expression was blank. "Okay," she said. She seemed relieved, as if she were being rescued. "I have to get my suit."

A few minutes later Marjorie joined Ellen in the cabaña. She was wearing a black two-piece bathing suit and a pair of sunglasses. She tied a red scarf over her hair and draped a white towel over her legs. Neither of the two women spoke. Though she had hoped Marjorie would talk, Ellen said nothing. Instead, she read her book and Marjorie slept. Or at least Ellen thought she slept. It was hard to tell whether her eyes were closed behind the dark glasses. Her body remained perfectly still.

At last, when Ellen reached for a bottle of water, Marjorie said, "I could lie here forever. This is almost as good as massage."

Ellen took a long swallow of water. The sun blazed against her exposed feet in the sand. "I have no desire to go back to San Francisco," she remarked. She wanted Marjorie to ask why, to recognize their common bond.

What Marjorie said was "You have good reason to go back. Your children are there." She was reminding Ellen of the gulf between them.

Ellen carved a little hole in the sand with her big toe. She watched it fill itself, grain by grain, in a miniature avalanche. "If I didn't have them, I wouldn't go back."

"But you do," Marjorie said. "You're blessed."

"I don't believe in God," said Ellen. "Not the way you do."

"I don't believe anymore," said Marjorie from behind the dark glasses. "It's easy to believe in God when you have everything you want." She placed one hand on her forehead, as if checking her temperature. "Lafayette says what happened is God's will. I say any God who would want my son to be dead isn't the God I want to worship."

She said nothing else after that, but lay absolutely still. Ellen studied her periodically from over the top of her book: the narrow waist, the slight pucker of her navel, the muscled brown legs, and the gold cross glinting on the chain between her breasts. She felt a deep protectiveness toward Marjorie, infused with a longing and envy that extended beyond the boundaries of the roped-off beach.

When Glenn returned, Ellen resigned herself to temporary forgiveness and agreed to wander with him through the streets. They bought tacos at a small stand several blocks away and sat on the brown sand of the Mexican side of the beach. Glenn chatted about inconsequential things: his plan for cementing over the garage floor, which flooded during the rainy season; his thought that he would circulate a neighborhood petition to get rid of the bus shelter on the corner where kids dealt drugs. Because she thought it was deceptive of her to talk about their life together, Ellen changed the subject and ended up telling him about Marjorie and Lafayette's son.

It came as no surprise that Glenn knew nothing about it. He was silent for some time afterwards, staring out over the water, holding his half-eaten taco as if it were something he'd just found on the beach.

"Are you sure?"

"That's what Marjorie told me."

Glenn looked as if Ellen had somehow betrayed him. "He never mentioned it."

"He probably won't."

"I don't get it. He said nothing!"

"He's putting on an act."

"Jesus," said Glenn. "Marjorie really told you this?"

Ellen almost felt sorry for him.

"Yes."

"I didn't realize you and Marjorie covered so much territory."

She could tell by his expression that his mind was working quickly, running over the events of the last two days, trying to put the pieces into place.

"We haven't really," Ellen tried to explain. "Marjorie keeps a lot to herself."

"And you?" asked Glenn, turning to her sharply. "What do you keep to yourself?"

"Oh, Glenn . . ." She scrunched her napkin into a tight ball in her fist.

"I'm going to go call the boys."

"You don't need to . . ."

Glenn got up and began walking swiftly back toward the hotel. He never looked behind. Ellen followed, but didn't catch up. When she got back to the room, Glenn was already on the phone.

Ellen went out on the balcony. She stood against the railing and looked out at the ocean, now dark and turbulent. She could hear Glenn's voice, full of fake cheer. "Hey, *amigo,* this is your old *padre* calling you from Mexico!" From the tone of his voice she knew he was talking to their oldest, Mark. He was telling him about the scuba trip, the fish, the plants, the coral. "Let me speak to John for a minute . . . Well, get him and tell him to hurry . . . Hey, Ben . . ." His voice rose. Ellen imagined Little Ben at the other end with his funny, crooked smile. "I went fishing, Ben, and scuba diving . . . your mom's fine, want to talk to her?" At the reference to herself, she stood poised to go back inside. But Glenn rattled on, excited. He talked on, faster and faster, as if time were getting away from him. "We'll be home day after tomorrow. You boys behaving? Let me speak to Grandma . . . Hi, Mom . . . yeah, yeah, I know I said that, but I thought we should just check in . . . they haven't burned the house down? . . . oh, she's fine . . . we're having a blast. Couldn't be more beautiful."

What? thought Ellen. This place isn't beautiful, it's hideous. There's not one pretty thing here, except the sunsets. There was a chill to the air. She wrapped her arms around herself and stood shivering against the railing. In a moment she would have her turn with the boys. But for now she was content to stand at a distance and simply imagine their voices.

It didn't bother Ellen one bit that Glenn and Lafayette set off to rent horses the next day. She had made it clear, hadn't she, that she preferred to be left alone? Yet as soon as Glenn was gone, she had regrets for the way she was going about all this. Marjorie had left for her masseuse and then was scheduled over at another hotel to have her nails manicured. Ellen learned this from Lafayette, who let it be known that he had arranged in advance for all sorts of appointments for Marjorie and that so far she'd had her hair done and her legs waxed. "I promised her the works!" he said cheerfully. He winked at Glenn. "You know how women are, they love to be pampered." For the first time Ellen noticed the thick gold band with a row of diamonds on Lafayette's ring finger. It was an ugly ring, expensive and gaudy.

"Not all women like to be pampered," she said.

Glenn shot her a warning look, but she pretended not to see and gathered up a string bag with her suit and towel, and fastened her money belt around her waist under her T-shirt.

Outside the hotel she caught a cab into the center of town again and bought serapes for the boys. She bought more postcards and sat in a cafe and addressed them to a long list of people, some of whom she only vaguely knew. "What heaven!

Puerto Cobre sunsets are the most beautiful in the world," she wrote. It took her over two hours to finish all the postcards. Then she went for stamps and mailed them. Duty accomplished. She'd told everyone what they would want to hear. Then she counted her traveler's checks, wondering how far they would get her.

She imagined herself traveling around the world. She would write to the boys every day. She thought of Ben's small hard body in her arms and his sour baby breath on her face. Ellen began to cry. She left the cafe and walked along the seawall. She wept loudly, knowing that it was safe because she was anonymous, and because no one would really care about an unhappy *gringa*.

"Our last night!" said Glenn, with intended irony, when they'd both gotten back to the room. He was making an effort to keep things light. "Are we speaking? You want to go out to dinner, or are we still mad?"

Ellen started to say "Mad?" but didn't. Instead she said, "No Lafayette?" as a joke, to ease the tension.

"No Lafayette," he said. There was a rueful edge to his voice. "We're stuck with each other tonight." He added with hope, "Lafayette and I've got plans to get together back home. Know what he wants to learn to do? Hang gliding. Over there south of the Cliff House. Is this guy a nut, or what?"

"He's a nut all right," Ellen said. "A real nut with a death wish." She added, "Dinner sounds fine, your choice," because she didn't have the courage to disappoint him. She felt almost friendly toward him, but that was only because she knew that soon she would have to tell him. "I'm going down on the beach for an hour or so, before all the sun is gone."

"Take your sun protection," Glenn warned. "You're starting

to burn." He reached out and caught her in his arms. "Ellen, do you even love me anymore?"

She stared into the face she knew so well it struck her as comical. His anxiety pulled on her like a weight. "Of course I do," she lied, wresting herself free. "Don't be silly."

"I tried to give you time to miss me over the last couple days . . ." He slowly released her. There was no anger when he turned away, only a tired sadness. "I think I'll call the boys while you're gone," he said. "Make sure they're okay."

"They're okay." Ellen started out the door. She paused and said with emphasis, "They're *okay,* Glenn." She felt bad for them both. "Tell the boys I love them. Tell them I've got presents. Tell them I'll see them very soon."

It was sunset. The sky was lit up as if it were on fire. Along the horizon the light was so blinding Ellen was forced to avert her eyes and focus on the dark waves lapping at the edge of the beach. Tomorrow they would go home. Tomorrow she would tell Glenn.

She found a spot on the sand and sat down. Instantly her chest expanded and she filled her lungs with air. She stretched her arms up over her head and let the last warm rays of sun play over her face. When she turned to lie down, she caught sight of a figure running down the beach toward her. She made out pink shorts and the flash of white T-shirt. As the figure got closer, Ellen recognized Marjorie, barefoot, pounding along the shore. She was coming fast and hard, her arms pumping at her sides.

Ellen put on her sunglasses to block out the glare of the setting sun and watched as Marjorie picked up speed. She was pounding harder and harder on the packed sand. Her head was thrown back, she was gulping in air. Ellen had no idea Marjorie was a runner. But then she thought how little she really knew about Marjorie at all. As she got closer, Ellen could hear the faint smack, smack of her bare feet striking the wet sand. She ran past Ellen, never noticing her. Ellen had a sudden urge to leap up and try to follow. There was an intensity in Marjorie's stride that dissuaded her. Without warning, Marjorie made a ninety-degree turn and plunged headlong into the surf. She completely disappeared. For a moment Ellen thought she was witnessing a suicide. Marjorie, who had made such a point of telling her she couldn't swim. But Ellen found herself rooted to the spot, unable to make a move to stop her. Her eyes focused on the spot in the water where Marjorie had disappeared, now streaked by orange light. Ellen had a vague thought that if she had to go for help she needed to know exactly where it was Marjorie had gone in. The waves rolled in and curled onto the beach. Ellen sat transfixed.

A moment later Marjorie resurfaced, and Ellen saw her dark arms pulling water and the flash of pink shorts above the waves. Now she swam as hard as she had run, her arms punching at the water. White foam followed in her wake. Her body bobbed up and down on the waves. Behind her, a large wave broke and rolled in. Marjorie came with it. She landed on the beach, coughing, her legs spread out behind her. When she stood, her hair hung ruined, dripping wet and sparkling with sand. She let the water run off her legs and onto the sand. She was out of breath, and her chest heaved. She placed her hands on her hips and sucked in air.

Ellen got up and moved cautiously toward her, beach towel in hand. When Marjorie saw her, she turned her head fast and looked back out over the ocean, her chest still heaving.

"Take the towel," said Ellen.

"I want to stay wet," Marjorie said. Droplets of water glistened on her eyelashes. Without makeup, she was beautiful, young. Three Mexican boys in blue jeans stood on the other side of the rope, idly watching the water. Marjorie observed them. "You know, this place makes me really sick. They aren't even allowed on the hotel beach."

Ellen didn't say anything.

"I guess it's the same the world over," Marjorie remarked matter-of-factly. "Black and brown people are usually on the other side of the fence."

"I thought you said you don't swim," Ellen said.

"I don't, I almost drowned out there." She cleared her throat several times.

"That was stupid," Ellen said, but Marjorie didn't answer.

Ellen turned and walked toward the hotel. She glanced back twice. Marjorie stood motionless in the same spot, her back to Ellen. Dwarfed by the ocean and backlit by the lowering sun, hers was a childlike silhouette. A breeze came over the water. Ellen thought about how she would explain it all to Glenn. She'd try first getting an apartment. Just during the weekdays. She'd come back on the weekends, help out, take the boys places. She'd still be involved, she'd still be a mother, but she wouldn't be a wife. And during the week she'd work longer hours. She might even exchange numbers with Marjorie. They'd get together and have coffee in the afternoons. Or lunch. They'd get massages, have their nails done together. Ellen would buy better clothes.

She passed through the courtyard. The pool was empty. She took the stairs fast and easily. The door to their room was partially open. On her approach, she heard the sound of voices. Then falsetto male laughter, followed by a deep voice. Ellen paused just outside the door and peeked in. Glenn and Lafayette were sitting, one on either side of the double bed by the window, drinking beer. Glenn was in his boxer shorts and Lafayette had on the ridiculous flowered shirt and shorts. Glenn said something Ellen couldn't quite catch and Lafayette threw his head back and howled too hard, like a wolf. Then Glenn burst out laughing and rolled back on the bed, clutching the beer bottle to his chest. They were playing at being great big ignorant boys getting away with something.

Ellen backed away a couple of inches so they wouldn't see her. She stood shivering in the hallway and listened to her husband laugh in a voice that could have been Lafayette's. Then she realized it was Lafayette's voice, full of exaggerated heartiness. Why was it, she thought, she was no longer able to distinguish the joyful sounds her own husband was capable of?

A COLD WINTER LIGHT

The winter Olivia turned sixteen she discovered her father had taken up with a black woman, someone unknown to her, but someone possibly connected with her father's old high school counseling job in Elyria, eight miles north by the edge of Lake Erie.

Olivia came across the snapshot stuffed in the back of a dark drawer of her father's basement work table. It lay imprisoned under a screwdriver and a crushed nail box half full of old rubber bands. Olivia had been deliberately snooping again, as was her habit of late. She considered it her duty to periodically patrol the cabinets and closets and drawers of her house. On the days she got home from school before everyone else, she held unopened mail up to the light. It seemed to be the only way she found things out in this house, now that her parents no longer spoke to each other.

The snapshot, a Polaroid, was stuck to the bottom of the work table drawer. Olivia carefully pried it out with the tips of her fingernails and held it up to the rectangle of winter sunlight framed by the high basement windows: a tall, dark black woman stared back coyly, the way subjects do when the photographer knows them intimately. Along the bent edges of the snapshot, spots of color and paper were missing. But the woman herself was intact.

Olivia stared hard. The woman was beautiful. She was what her father's mother would call "*too* black" in that half-deprecating, half-sympathetic way some light-skinned people had, even though her own husband, Olivia's grandfather, was the color of black walnut shells.

The woman wore a medium-sized natural; her features were broad, perfect, her eyes shaped like almonds. She was long and leggy, about the same age as Olivia's mother. She wore a short red leather skirt that hugged her hips and a see-through black blouse with lace on the wide collar. From her earlobes dangled large silver hoops that reflected light from a source Olivia couldn't see. The woman had posed herself familiarly in the doorway of a kitchen Olivia didn't recognize. The bottom right-hand corner of the photo was feathered by the decorated lower branches of someone else's Christmas tree.

Down to the last detail, this woman was the exact opposite of Olivia's small, white, red-haired mother.

Olivia turned the photo over. On the back in lazy, loopy handwriting was written: "Merry Christmas to my Chocolate Santa. Love, Wilma."

Olivia suddenly understood what she'd suspected all along. Christmas Eve, two months earlier, she and her mother and Pam and the boys lounged around the living room idly stuffing themselves on tangerines and nuts and chocolate while the open boxes of Christmas tree ornaments sat untouched. A space had been cleared over by the picture window for the Christmas tree. Hours before, Olivia's father had slammed off in a huff to search for one, irritated that her mother had waited until the last minute. No one else had wanted to ride along with him, preferring the warmth of the house to the freezing night. The red and green metal tree stand stood empty under the mantel.

Waiting for him, they'd all pretended not to, as Olivia's mother played a Nat King Cole recording of "Winter Wonderland" over and over, and flipped through magazines. Around ten or so she brought out eggnog from the fridge. She seemed about to burst from some unnamed emotion, and turned giggly and reckless, mischievously pouring a shot of rum in everyone's eggnog glasses. She could be capricious, a bad child, when Olivia's father wasn't around. In his absence, she often resorted to small, harmless indulgences, treating her children as if they were all just friends.

Then, much to Olivia's annoyance, her younger sister Pam had started acting drunk and talking crazy. Leave it to Pam to spoil things! Olivia's mother sighed and put the rum away and told Pam she'd better straighten up fast before her father returned.

The hour had grown late. The fire in the fireplace burned down to embers, and a chill spread inward from the walls. Olivia glanced at the ticking clock with growing agitation. Her mother fell asleep curled up on the sofa and the boys sprawled in the middle of the floor and played with their Lego set. Pam slipped off to the kitchen and whispered to someone on the phone behind the closed door.

Chilled, Olivia pulled on her robe and sat in the overstuffed chair, staring out the broad picture window at the snow falling, cold and white. She pretended to be watching her brothers, but she was waiting. Each time a car passed on the snowy road, she felt herself stiffen. When at last the headlights of the red station wagon turned into their driveway, Olivia leaned over and poked her mother awake. Just in time, too. Her father crossed the threshold, irritable and flustered, dragging in a short-needled, scrawny tree. "Well," he said, "what do you expect when we wait until Christmas Eve? All the lots were empty and I wasn't about to go tromping off through the woods at one of those cut-your-own places." He fussed on and on and stamped his snowy boots in the front hallway. Then he argued with the boys about the mess of Legos on the floor while the tree lay on its side, forgotten.

That was when Olivia first noticed that her father had skipped several shaves and his hair was lengthening into a natural. It had been a while since she'd looked directly at him, but while he and the boys screwed the tree upright into the stand she sat in the overstuffed chair, warm inside her robe, studying his gestures and expressions, and drawing her own conclusions.

Olivia considered stealing the snapshot, but then decided against it. She pushed the picture to the back of the drawer and placed the screwdriver on top. She kept thinking of the woman's wide, pouty smile, intended (and this was the unthinkable part!) for Olivia's father.

Bastard, Olivia thought. She thought of her mother upstairs in the den, obliviously glued to the Merv Griffin show and waiting for the children to get home from school. It was like a quadruple deception somehow: her father's infidelity, the woman's beauty, the woman's blackness, and now, Olivia's discovery.

Olivia stood a moment longer under the bare beams, her sock feet soaking up the cold from the cement floor. Her father had promised last year to finish off the basement and turn it into a family room, but he'd gotten busy with his new job at the college and never found time. The room remained rough and approximate, the ceiling pipes exposed.

Olivia turned and walked back up the basement steps to the kitchen, closed the door softly behind her, and took the wide-mouthed jar of cold water out of the refrigerator. She poured a drink. Outside the kitchen window the yard lay blanketed in snow, and the pond beyond was frozen solid. Grim February, what Olivia's mother jokingly called "the longest short month."

The front door banged shut, and Olivia knew Pam had finally dragged herself in from school, a good hour late. Pam was only thirteen, but she tried to act grown, wearing her skirts so short there wasn't much left to the imagination. Now she was going with a twenty-year-old hoodlum named Reggie who wore a dew rag and washed dishes for a living over at the college cafeteria. Reggie drove a beat-up Ford around town and called Pam "sweet thang."

Imagine, in the eighth grade, with a grown-up boyfriend! Old fast yellow Pam, calling herself slick, walking downtown and swinging her hips with her big chest poked out.

Sometimes, at night when everyone was asleep, Pam would go out. Last summer Olivia had caught her at it. She awakened to muffled clunks and bangs in the next room, Pam's room. There were voices whispering. She sat up in bed and looked out the window. Once her eyes adjusted, she made out two silhouettes of neighborhood boys over by the pond. A moment later the soft swift shadow of Pam in her bathrobe and bare feet made its way across the grass in the moonlight. Olivia watched Pam and one of the boys disappear across the field and past the line of trees that marked the edge of their property. The second boy paced along the edge of the pond, staring into the dark water.

Olivia crept quietly out of her room to Pam's. The high aluminum-framed window had been pulled to one side. She had a clear view of the pond straight ahead. She knelt on Pam's bed and leaned her elbows on the windowsill. The air smelled of moist, freshly cut grass. Olivia thought of closing the window and locking Pam out, but she didn't have the courage to hurt her mother. Instead, she did nothing, just watched with a mixture of envy and disgust. Sometime later Pam traipsed back across the damp lawn, her hair askew. She wore a smug, elfish grin. Olivia ducked down and scurried back to her own room. She heard Pam's feet scrape heavily over the windowsill, then the thunk! of her body hitting the bed. A few moments later a car engine revved from the road.

The next morning Olivia eyed Pam hard until Pam put her hand on her hip and said, "What are *you* looking at?"

Olivia hissed, "You better not get pregnant, girl," and Pam rolled her eyes.

"I'm *serious!*" Olivia warned.

Pam snaked her neck several times and glared. "You don't even know what you're talking about, Miss Whitegirl."

Now, Pam strolled into the kitchen with the one book she'd bothered to carry home from school. She was lighter than Olivia, with skin the color of shredded wheat, but her features were broader and her hair was naturally nappier though, like Olivia, she had a perm and wore her hair in a shoulder-length page-boy. She clunked across the floor in her black snow boots.

"Anybody call for me?" she asked in her deep raspy voice.

"I don't know, stupid, I just got here myself." Olivia sipped her water. She considered telling Pam about the snapshot, just to shock her into getting all big-eyed. But the timing was wrong.

Pam leaned back against the kitchen counter. "Reggie said he saw you today."

"Big deal," said Olivia. "I wouldn't know him if I saw him." She walked out of the kitchen.

"That you, Olivia?" her mother called out from the den.

Olivia poked her head in. The drapes were drawn and the room was dark and overcrowded. Over in the corner her mother's sewing machine was set up with a long piece of brown wool fabric spread out under the needle. Olivia's mother made almost all of the girls' clothes. She saw to it they were two of the best-dressed girls at school. New clothes every week when she could. She spent a lot of time poring through catalogs and choosing patterns and calling the girls into the den to be measured.

"Have a seat." Olivia's mother patted the empty space on the sofa next to her. She'd pulled her bathrobe on over her nurse's uniform and propped up her small white feet on the coffee table.

"You sub at the hospital today?" Olivia asked. She sat gingerly on the edge of the sofa.

"Just this morning. Pam home yet?"

Olivia nodded. The den struck her as depressing. Her mother spent too much time there. Beyond the heavy drapes spread the cloudless blue sky, and in the over-bright, frozen air the winter sun sparkled on the snow banked along the sidewalks.

"Can you pick up the boys from Boy Scouts at five? Gina and Jerry are coming by tonight for ribs and I've got to make potato salad."

"I thought Daddy picked up the boys on Wednesdays."

Olivia's mother never took her eyes from the TV screen. "Well, he can't tonight," she said sharply.

Olivia pulled herself up off the sofa. She towered over her mother. "Is he going to be here when Gina and Jerry come?"

Her mother shrugged. "I don't know and I really don't care. You know how he is." She reached up and ran one small white hand over Olivia's brown arm. "You look so pretty today. I'm glad the new skirt fit."

"I don't understand why Daddy can't pick up the boys." It was the closest Olivia had gotten to outright accusing her father of what she now knew to be true.

Her mother sighed. "Don't pay any attention to your father these days. What matters to me now is you and the other kids."

Gina and Jerry Woods were Olivia's parents' longtime best friends. They lived on the other side of town by the golf course with their six teenage children. Gina wasn't American, she was actually from some war-torn Eastern European country, and she had an unpronounceable name, so everyone just called her Gina. She was heavyset, blonde, and pale, and spoke rapidly in a heavy accent, a mixture of black and Eastern Europe. She did hair for a living. Jerry was quiet, a mail carrier with light skin the color of wheat and eyes with a greenish cast. All the Woods kids had the same wheat-colored skin and green eyes and sandy hair. They were notoriously wild kids, rowdy and undisciplined, and the boys were as handsome as the devil himself. You could spot a Woods boy a mile away. It irritated Olivia when people mixed her up with them and asked her if she was a Woods.

Gina and Olivia's mother were drinking beers together in the kitchen while Gina stuffed herself on barbecue. "Earl don't know what he's missin'," she said of Olivia's father.

Olivia's mother shrugged and said, "Maybe he does."

Over ribs and potato salad Olivia listened to her mother and Gina Woods talk, as they had for years. Their words were familiar, even predictable, but the meanings shifted with kaleidoscopic quickness into new patterns Olivia could now comprehend. She knew that by listening, without appearing to, she would find out the things no one told her directly. Jerry Woods and Olivia's brothers were huddled on the sofa in the den watching the game on TV, and Pam was in her bedroom, tying up the phone. The two women seemed to have forgotten that Olivia was even in the same room.

Olivia's mother's voice was tired, uncertain. "I don't know what I'm going to do with Pam. She acts just like her father. Doesn't tell me a thing." And Gina, through a mouthful of barbecue, spat back advice and gestured emphatically. "Don't let her throw you off balance. I've got *two* of 'em at home don't act right. Just last week I caught Rita and Lizzie smoking, and then turns out they been cutting school together. Jerry don't know. He'd kill 'em."

Olivia picked a piece of white bread apart and rolled the sections into little hard balls between her thumb and index finger. Her mother let out a sigh of sympathy. "It's hard nowadays," she said. "I try to give both my girls a certain amount of freedom. I don't want them to feel . . . you know, any more different than they already do."

Gina licked barbecue from her fingers. "Thaz why I let my girls do like they want. I can't keep 'em under lock and key. I hear the talk. But you got to go easy with mixed kids. They got it rough."

Olivia pushed herself forcefully away from the table. "Excuse me," she said stiffly, "I have homework."

Her mother and Gina smiled up at her in unison. Their faces were bright and approving. "You're a good girl," said Gina, patting Olivia's behind. "And getting so grown-up too!"

Olivia was halfway down the hall when she heard her mother say with conviction, "Olivia's my dependable one. I don't know what I'd do without her."

By Saturday another big snowstorm was predicted, and Olivia's mother left early with Pam for Fisher-Fazio to stock up on groceries. The boys played whiffle ball in the cold basement with their jackets and gloves on. Olivia could hear the smack-smack of the bat hitting the plastic ball. She turned on the vacuum in the living room and cranked up Aretha Franklin as high as she could on the stereo console. "Ain't no way / for me to lo-o-ove you-ou / if you won't-a let me . . ." Sister Caroline's background vocals soared on top at ear-splitting levels. Olivia sang along, squatting down to get under the sofa with the vacuum wand.

Out of the corner of her eye, she caught a movement in the doorway. She glanced over to see her father opening the front hall closet door. He pulled on his heavy winter coat and pressed onto his rising natural the Russian hat with ear flaps that so embarrassed her. At Christmas she had given him a black beret and he rejected it, saying he'd look like a Black Nationalist. He had treated the hat as an insult from her, uncomfortable with the implications.

"They wear berets in *France,*" Olivia had said sarcastically, and her father snapped back, "I'm not French." What she felt like saying now was "And you aren't Russian either," but she didn't.

Her father gestured impatiently for her to turn down the music. She pretended at first not to understand, then shut off the vacuum and stood up stiffly, arms folded across her chest. "What?" she mouthed.

"You're going to blow my damn speakers!" He'd taken to referring to their collective family belongings in the first-person possessive: my sofa, my refrigerator, my car.

Olivia leaned over and lowered the volume to a whisper.

"Where's your mother?"

"Grocery."

Olivia stabbed at the living room carpet with the long wand of the vacuum.

"I have a committee meeting this afternoon. I'll be home late."

"On a Saturday, Daddy?" She had the snapshot on her side. She could afford to be impulsive.

"I have no idea what you mean." He took up his briefcase in one hand and an umbrella in the other.

"When will you be home?" Olivia pushed, hand on her hip.

He frowned. "Did she take your car or mine?"

"I thought it was her car too."

"Don't be smart-assed, girl, and you know what I mean." He cleared his throat several times. "I'm asking you in a nice way, am I stuck with the Corvair?"

"No, she took the Corvair. She wouldn't think of taking *your* precious station wagon."

Olivia's father pulled open the front door. A blast of cold wind gusted through. He paused. "By the way, I read in the paper that your boyfriend what's-his-name Michael Blakely got a speeding ticket. I don't want you driving around with him anymore."

Olivia laughed. "If you paid attention to what goes on around here, you'd know that Michael and I broke up over two months ago."

Her father slammed out the door. Through the picture window she watched him scuttle like a beetle down the icy driveway to the station wagon. Big white flakes floated down and settled on the shoulders of his heavy dark coat and on the crown of his Russian hat.

Olivia held up the vacuum wand and shook it at his receding back, as though marking him with a curse. He climbed into the station wagon and sat behind the frosty windshield, warming the engine. "You know how I hate your lyin' ass," she yelled after him. "It's a little late to try to get black on us now!" She switched the vacuum back on, and cranked the stereo volume up so loud the walls vibrated. "This is the house that Jack built, y'all!" Olivia sang. "Remember this house. This is the land that he worked by hand / This is the dream of an upright man . . ."

All that Olivia told Tonya when she drove over through the thickening snow in the Corvair was that they were going for a drive. Tonya's mother was perturbed about the weather. "I'd like to know where you two are off to, just in case," she said in her polite white way. "The roads could get really bad."

Olivia smiled broadly. "I'm running an errand for my mother at the mall."

"Just the two of you?" Tonya's mother had never come right out and said it, but Olivia knew she was growing more and more worried about "certain influences."

Tonya got busy with her mittens and boots.

"Just the two of us," Olivia confirmed.

"This doesn't involve boys?"

Olivia knew exactly what kind of boys Tonya's mother meant. Black boys. She felt irritation rising in her chest. Her friendship with Tonya had been so much simpler when they were younger. Now sometimes Olivia wondered why she bothered with it at all.

"No boys," said Tonya. "I told you, Olivia and I are going alone!"

"When can I expect you home?"

"How about six?" said Olivia. She had learned that by phrasing her responses as questions she got a lot further with Tonya's mother.

Tonya's mother was not pleased. "Tonya will miss dinner." Olivia knew dinner was not the issue at all.

"Tonya can eat at my house."

"Well-l-l . . ." Tonya's mother couldn't look Olivia straight in the face anymore.

"My mom's making spaghetti, Tonya's favorite."

"I wish you'd asked in advance."

This was how it always was with Tonya's mother—Olivia negotiating and reassuring, Tonya remaining silent and depressed.

"We'll call you from my house, okay?" said Olivia brightly.

Tonya's mother looked at Tonya. "Seven o'clock," she said sharply. "I want a call from you by seven o'clock."

Inside the Corvair, Tonya let out several groans. "I *really* want to run away. I can't stand it anymore." She said this at least three times a week. "Let me come live with you, Olivia."

"Why? You think I have it any easier?"

Tonya smiled ruefully. "At least your father's gone all the time. My mother is *always* there."

Olivia started up the clanking car heater.

"Quick, get out of here before she changes her mind." Tonya sank low into her seat. "She's in there thinking up some excuse to call me back in."

There was a slight movement of the curtain at the living room window.

"Your mother's changed" was all Olivia said bitterly as she backed the Corvair down the drive.

Snow fell steadily in big, wet flakes. The houses and bushes looked like pieces of furniture covered in protective white sheets. Olivia made a left at the corner and drove slowly over sludge and ice to the edge of the college campus. She peered out the fogged-up window. "Look and see if my dad's station wagon is in that parking lot over there."

Both girls craned their necks. The lot was empty.

"I knew he was lying," Olivia muttered to herself.

"What are you talking about?"

"You'll see." Olivia stopped at the red light marking the main intersection downtown. She turned on the radio and sang along to "Ooh, Ooh, Child" by the Five Stairsteps. She felt bored by Tonya, irritated with her presence. She was sorry now she'd brought her along, but she had, and now she was stuck.

Turning onto Route 58, they found themselves on the tail of a large truck. The snow was so thick now that all they could make out were red taillights and an occasional glimpse of revolving rubber tires spitting snow. Oncoming traffic was dense and slow, a succession of blurred headlights on the two-lane highway.

"Maybe we shouldn't go," said Tonya, nervously wiping at the windshield with a mittened hand.

Olivia boosted the volume on the car radio. When she didn't know the words to songs, she substituted nonsense syllables. It didn't really matter, you could sing whatever you wanted, it was all the same.

"What are we doing, Olivia?"

Olivia clicked her fingers and hummed. The song ended. "What are we doing? Looking for my father, that's what we're doing." She dug down in her coat pocket and pulled out the snapshot of the black woman. She handed it to Tonya, without explanation.

Tonya held the snapshot in her mittened hands and stared. "I don't get it." Recognition slowly dawned. "Your father? Does your mother know?" Olivia could see that Tonya was intrigued.

Olivia shrugged. "My mother needs to dump his ass. She sacrificed everything to marry him and now look at how he's acting." She said it as if the events signaled some fault of Tonya's.

Tonya was poring over the snapshot carefully. "She sure is pretty. God, what I'd give to have skin like that. I get so white in the winter."

Olivia snatched the snapshot back and stuffed it in her coat pocket. "She's not that pretty. My father's rebelling, that's all," she said sarcastically. "My father's decided to try being black after years of being an Uncle Tom."

"Why do you hate him so much?" asked Tonya.

"You don't know him." Olivia felt the car tires spin briefly on a slick patch in the road. "You don't have a clue."

Tonya asked Olivia to stop at Lawson's. She returned with bubble gum, a sack of chives and sour cream chips, two blisteringly cold red cream sodas, and two sticks of beef jerky.

"Why do you wanna buy that old nasty stuff?" remarked

Olivia grouchily, but she ate anyway, sitting there in the Lawson's lot, staring out at the bleak intersection and watching the snow pile up on the sidewalks, the bushes, even the telephone wires overhead.

A low-slung black Olds pulled into the lot and honked. One of the windows was covered over with a piece of tattered plastic attached by long strips of masking tape. There were three boys inside, two up front, one in back. The driver pulled up next to the Corvair and motioned for Olivia to roll down her window.

"Say, mama," he called cheerfully, leaning out of the car so that his thick hair caught the falling white snow like a net. "I couldn't help noticing you and your friend over here by yourselves."

"I'm not your mama," Olivia responded, but she kept her window down just the same.

"And just where might you two lovely young ladies be going on a cold, wintry afternoon like this?" the boy asked. He was brown-skinned with wide eyes and long lashes. Pam's type, thought Olivia. Fast. Nothing but trouble.

"We're visiting a friend," she said, keeping her jaw tight. She felt the pressure of his eyes. Let him look all he wants, she thought.

"We'd sure like to hook up with you two and your *friend*," said the boy. "I'm Freddie and this here's my partner Bobby and that's my play cousin Louis. Where y'all from?"

Tonya was trying to peer past Olivia. "The driver's so cute," she squealed. Olivia silenced her with a look.

"I'm Rhonda, and this is my friend Regina," said Olivia. "We're stewardesses from Cleveland."

"Stewardesses!" the boy guffawed. "Stewardesses! You two?" He consulted with the two passengers in the Olds and turned back to Olivia. "Where y'all from in Cleveland?" he asked, amused.

"East 98th," Olivia said coolly. It was the first thing that came to mind.

"Both y'all?" Freddie began to laugh. He gestured toward Tonya. "Her too? You're pulling my leg. I know *she* ain't from there."

Olivia poked out her lip and raised her eyebrows. "She's my cousin," she said meaningfully.

"I don't mean no disrespect," Freddie chuckled, "but I'd like to catch *her* down on East 98th." He turned back to his companions and said something. The sound of laughter spilled from their open window. He looked back over at Olivia. "Y'all like to skate? We're going to the roller rink."

Olivia let out a world-weary sigh. "I told you, we're on our way to our friend's house."

She rolled up her window and started the engine. The boy tooted his horn in a fast staccato, but Olivia concentrated on shifting the Corvair in reverse.

"Why can't we go to the skating rink?" asked Tonya. "Just for a half hour. Come on, they were *cute*."

Olivia resisted the urge to slap her. "You sound just like Pam," she said. "Besides, your mother would kill me."

"My mother's not here. Why do you always have to be such a goody-goody, Olivia?"

"Why do you want to go off with some hoodlums?" said Olivia. "That driver was a white-girl lover, couldn't you tell? He figured you'd be easy. Don't you know anything, girl? I was just saving you a lot of trouble."

"I really hate it when you play me off," Tonya sulked.

"I *said* you were my cousin." Olivia's patience had worn thin.

"You played me off," Tonya insisted. "Why don't you make up your mind whether you're my best friend or not?"

Olivia clicked on the wipers to clear the windshield. She kept her voice steady, purposeful. "I can't get you in with black kids, Tonya. I have my own troubles. You're on your own."

They both fell silent as Olivia made a right turn toward the lake and the north end of town where the high school was. She didn't care that she'd hurt Tonya, her words had come as a relief. She was worn out trying to keep people around her happy.

They sat in the empty high school parking lot and watched the snow fall. Every few minutes Olivia started up the engine and ran the heater. Snow covered the hood of the Corvair.

"This school looks like a prison," remarked Tonya.

"This is where my father used to work."

Olivia's father had counseled dropouts and taught driver's ed in the red brick building for almost fifteen years before he was hired last year to teach sociology at the college. He had been asked as a response to increasing pressure from black students who demanded more black faculty. Olivia had been present at several of the student demonstrations. She remembered the night her father had gotten the phone call.

"They never wanted me before," he told Olivia's mother bitterly. "Suddenly I'm in high demand when it's convenient for them."

"It's only right," she said. "You deserve this."

"They don't believe that. I'm just a quick fix. And these young black students . . ." He'd paused. "They think I can work miracles."

"Maybe you can," Olivia's mother had said. Because, Olivia thought bitterly, it would take a miracle.

It was only weeks later that D.T., one of the campus radicals, stood in the band shell of the square and announced through a bullhorn to a crowd of college and high school students that

Olivia's father was "an Uncle Tom, the white administration's puppet, married to the oppressor, hired to appease, and an enemy to the struggle." Olivia had been standing right there, after school, on the edges of the swelling crowd with three black schoolmates, and she'd heard it with her own ears, the truth that she had never dared put into words. She found herself caught up in the words themselves, felt the crowd's anger and frustration, and found resonating deep within her the chant that grew with the crowd's increasing enthusiasm, "Power to the people!" She never mentioned it to her mother, but when she looked at her father from then on, she felt wave after wave of pity and contempt.

Inside the idling Corvair, Tonya began to complain. "I'm so sick of cold and snow. When I go to college, I'm going to move some place warm. I want to have a tan and feel warm all the time."

"I like the snow," said Olivia, feeling ornery, "even if it is white."

She was considering the one lone car parked in a far corner of the lot. It was a blue Buick LeSabre with a solid layer of snow on the hood and roof. Ice covered the windows.

"How long do we have to sit here?" Tonya asked.

"You didn't have to come," Olivia reminded her. She put the car in gear and, as a concession, slowly circled the lot. She drove past the LeSabre. There were no tire tracks anywhere near it, just a smooth layer of snow.

"What are we doing here?" Tonya asked.

Olivia didn't answer.

"Let's go to the mall. I never get out of the house."

"Just cool your jets," said Olivia in her mother's voice.

Tonya slumped in the seat and pulled her coat more closely around her.

"Okay, Miss Impatient, we'll go to the mall."

Olivia turned the Corvair in the direction of the street. Out of the corner of her eye she saw the flash of headlights. Through the falling snow a car approached, turning slowly into the wide white parking lot from the other side. The shape of the front of the car registered as vaguely familiar, though Olivia's thoughts didn't acknowledge this. The car plowed through the curtain of white, a slow, heavy creature, headlights glowing, windshield wipers slapping against the glass. And then, without warning, Olivia was seized by recognition.

"Oh, my God!" she exclaimed. "Oh, my God!" She hadn't really believed, had she? She hadn't bargained for the sudden wave of panic that swept over her. She slammed on the brakes and ducked her head below the windshield. Her right foot trembled on the brake.

Tonya was a second behind her, sliding out of the seat onto the floor. "Did he see us?" she whispered from under the dashboard.

"Shshshsh!" Olivia raised her head slowly. She heard the rumble of the other engine beside them, and the smack of wheels on wet snow.

"Oh, my God, he's seen us."

"What should we do?" asked Tonya, still crouched on the floor. She was furiously twisting the ends of her scarf.

Olivia gave a backwards glance, but the rear window was a blur of white. She cracked her window and peered over the top into the frosty air. The red station wagon had pulled up next to the blue LeSabre, where it sat, exhaust smoking in the air. Now the passenger door was opening. Out of the car stepped a tall dark-skinned woman in a long navy-blue maxi coat and black boots. She was drawing up the hood of the coat over her head with red-gloved hands. She leaned down into the car, and at that moment Olivia felt every muscle in her body constrict. Then the driver got out. He came around to the passenger side, and the two figures stood there in the snow, apart and talking. Gone was the mystery of the woman in a red leather skirt posed in the kitchen doorway. The very ordinariness of the two figures, man and woman, struck Olivia with a note of sadness. They were trapped like figures in a paperweight, snow whirling around and containing them.

Tonya dragged herself halfway up to the passenger seat. "Are you going to talk to him?"

"Hell no, I'm not going to talk to him!" said Olivia fiercely. She watched her father lean forward and plant a kiss on the side of the woman's face. She realized then that he was wearing, not the Russian hat he'd left the house with that morning, but the black beret she'd given him on Christmas. Flat like a saucer, it caught the snow, turning the top of his head white.

Olivia's foot slipped off the clutch. The car jerked forward, then died.

The woman turned ever so briefly in their direction, but her face was hidden by the wide hood of her coat. She looked back at Olivia's father for a moment before walking quickly toward the LeSabre, her shoulders drawn up in the cold. Olivia's father, head down, trudged back around to the driver's side of the station wagon and climbed inside. Olivia heard the dull thud of his car door closing.

"Here he comes," warned Tonya, her face stricken.

Olivia turned the key several times in the ignition and pressed the accelerator. The engine wouldn't turn over. She began to curse, her exhalations making soft, smoky circles in the air.

The red station wagon backed up slowly, exhaust curling up over it like smoke from a chimney. It turned and crossed the lot. The LeSabre's headlights flashed several times. The station wagon honked twice. Now headlights flooded Olivia's rear mirror. The station wagon was behind them, then swerving, and now the red hood of the car was abreast. It slid past, slowly, and made a sharp turn back into the snowy street.

"He looked right at you," said Tonya. "I saw him."

Olivia rammed the accelerator again with her foot. The engine roared, and the car lurched forward.

Now the LeSabre was alongside. Tonya twisted around in her seat. "Can you see her?" she asked.

"Shut up" was all Olivia could say. The LeSabre passed and turned in the same direction the station wagon had.

Olivia braked softly on the ice, felt the slight skid of tires, and then because the LeSabre had turned right, made a left. She roared up to the stoplight and made another fast left.

"That light was red!"

"I don't care." Olivia sped up and shot over the icy railroad tracks that separated one side of town from the other.

"Slow down!" said Tonya.

The Corvair's wheels spun on a hidden patch of icy railroad tie, the back end of the car swung unexpectedly halfway around to where the front had been, and Olivia found herself completely turned around on the snowy road staring into oncoming headlights from the other side of the tracks.

"You're going to kill us!" Tonya slapped the dashboard with her mittened hand. "Olivia, stop it!"

Olivia backed up against the curb and turned the steering wheel. Two cars swerved around them with a blare of horns. Between the falling snow and the tears she couldn't be sure which way the road went, but she made no apologies to Tonya, just buried her chin in her coat collar and counted in her mind the number of times the sticky wipers clicked across the windshield.

Tonya ate at Olivia's. She phoned her mother to weasel permission to spend the night, citing bad weather and snowy roads as good reason. Olivia, the only one still at the dinner table, heard the painful struggle on Tonya's end. No, she didn't need to come back home and pick up her nightgown, she could wear one of Olivia's. Her voice was feeble and discouraged. Yes, Olivia's mother was home, and no, there wouldn't be boys there. Finally, Olivia's mother intervened.

Olivia busied herself with twirling strands of overcooked spaghetti onto her fork with the help of a soup spoon.

"Hi, it's Lois," her mother said reassuringly into the phone. "How are you, Sue? Can you believe this weather? I didn't think the girls should try to go back out in it."

Olivia chewed, and concentrated on her mother's negotiations. She wished Tonya would go home.

When Olivia's mother hung up, she winked and said triumphantly to Tonya, "It's all set."

"I hate my mother," said Tonya.

Olivia's mother squeezed herself back down at the table between the two girls. There was a weariness about her that made Olivia feel protective. "Your mother means well."

"But you don't track down Olivia every step she makes," Tonya said. In the harsh kitchen light her features seemed all squeezed together and pasty. "You let your kids have *freedom*."

Olivia's mother sighed. "I don't know if it's so much freedom . . ." She paused. "I guess I just try to take into consideration that my children are, well, half black, and these are difficult times." Dead silence followed.

Olivia thought how those were Gina's words coming out of

her mother's mouth. *Half black. Difficult times.* She hated her mother's small, thin mouth, so smugly set in the shape of those words. Olivia began to imagine the snow falling on them there in the kitchen, forcing its way through the roof and the ceiling and piling up on the table. She saw her mother and Tonya, two strangers suddenly lit up in the cold winter light. Slowly they disappeared into the whiteness, indistinguishable from all the other white people she knew.

"If my children were white," Olivia's mother went on matter-of-factly in this new voice of betrayal, "I would probably be inclined to be more like your mother—stricter . . ." She glanced over at Olivia. "I believe in speaking frankly about these things. It's so much better when things are out in the open, don't you agree, honey?"

The front door opened, then slammed shut. Heavy footsteps announced Olivia's father's return. Olivia heard him bang the hall closet door and bark something at the boys.

Olivia's mother sighed. "Oh, well, just when we were having a *real* conversation." She got up with her plate in hand.

Footsteps thudded toward them in the hallway. A moment later Olivia's father filled up the frame of the kitchen doorway. He was only a medium-sized man, unremarkable in most respects, but he suddenly seemed bigger. His hair, Olivia noticed, was mashed flat on his head from the beret.

"What's for dinner?" he asked without looking at any of them. He took the lid off a pot on the stove and stared down inside.

"I didn't realize you'd be home for dinner," said Olivia's mother. "It's all gone."

His expression tightened, but he made no comment. Instead, he went to the refrigerator and caused a big commotion going through its contents.

While he searched, Olivia's mother brushed past him on her way out of the kitchen. Olivia heard the den door close and, a moment later, the muted sounds of canned television laughter.

Without looking at the girls, Olivia's father began to speak. His face was as blank and remote as the empty parking lot earlier. "I'm going to need to use the Corvair tomorrow morning." He cleared his throat and leveled the words in a careful monotone just above Olivia's head. "So don't plan anything. I'm taking your grandmother to church."

He seemed to notice Tonya for the first time. "Well, hello there, Tonya. How are you?" Without waiting for her answer, he turned and walked out of the room.

Olivia let herself collapse back in her chair. "God, I hate him," she muttered. She slouched lower, kicking her legs out. "And I can't believe what my mother just said to you. I can't believe either of them anymore."

Tonya sat wordlessly. She poked indifferently at the food on her plate.

Olivia straightened herself. "Hey, you want my family so bad? You want my mother? You can have her. But, remember, then you get *him* too." She stood up and pushed her chair in hard under the table. "You can have them both!"

She strode down the hall to the coat closet where she found her winter coat and boots. The Corvair keys jingled in her pocket. The snapshot was still stuffed deep inside her coat pocket. She fished around and pulled it out. On a whim she held it up, exposed, where anyone could walk in and see her with it. Excitement surged through her as she waited to see who might happen in. Pam? Her father? The boys? Her mother? She could imagine the expressions of shock on their faces.

It was Tonya, though, who appeared in the doorway. Her cheeks were streaked with red. "Your father went down to the basement," she whispered. "He looked mad." Then she saw the snapshot. "What are you doing, Olivia?"

Olivia smiled and gently waved the snapshot to the empty living room.

"I think I should go home," said Tonya. "I better call my mother."

"Do what you want." Olivia walked around Tonya and headed back into the kitchen. A cold draft blew up from the basement through the open door. Below, she could hear her father pacing and the sound of his radio being tuned. A few seconds of station-searching, then the radio was snapped off. It got very still. Olivia inched herself to the top of the basement stairs. A pool of yellow light marked the center of the basement where her father's work table stood. She was certain he was going through the drawers.

Behind her, Tonya waited pale and uncertain in the kitchen door.

"Watch this," Olivia said, holding up the snapshot by just a corner, between her thumb and forefinger. The black woman twisted back and forth in her fingers. A flash of red leather skirt, the sparkle of silver earrings. It was as if she had come alive.

"Dare me?" said Olivia. She didn't wait for the answer.

She released the snapshot. It hovered for a moment, caught on a current of air, and then the black woman began her looping descent. Slowly, slowly, she fell over the basement stairs, graceful as a falling leaf. Olivia looked down. The picture had landed face up on the bottom step.

With great calm, Olivia carefully closed the basement door, taking comfort in the soft click of the latch.

Her mind leaped forward to the tremendous changes that lay ahead. They began with her descent into the wintry night, leaving Tonya in her place. From now on, regardless of the lateness of the hour, the changing months, the shift of seasons, the occasions that would mark her growing up, she, Olivia, would come and go in the Corvair as she pleased, unhurried and unquestioned. Now it was just a matter of saying, "Excuse me," as she slipped past Tonya and down the hallway to the coat closet. She pretended she didn't hear her mother's voice calling from the den, "That you, Olivia?"

THE NATURE OF LONGING

When Cousin Pearl was young she was the most beautiful of the Farrell girls, or so everyone said. I hoped to be just like her when I grew up, but folks cautioned me how a boy shouldn't want such things.

Cousin Pearl sewed for white women. Sometimes, when Mother and I visited the house, Pearl let me sit among those perfumed and powdered ladies, testing the very boundaries of my small boy's desires as I devoured with my eyes and mind the lay of silk, the up- or downsweep of a poignant line, the fluid contours of the female body, so unlike my own poor boy's shape, celebrated in the tease of texture and color. I began to suspect quickly the impossibility of my desires, distilled in Pearl, but denied to me as a man.

Everyone knew about Miss Pearl's abilities as a seamstress. By the time I knew Pearl she was famous in our county. Well-to-do women rustled up to her doorstep in their long skirts with requests for custom-made clothing. "Our Pearl," they cooed over her proprietarily, sipping tea in Grandmother Blanche's parlor.

That was around 1909, the year the National Association for the Advancement of Colored People was founded. How things change! Why, just this last year our Mr. Edward Brooke in Massachusetts became the first black U.S. senator in eighty-five years. (They do say "black" now. Everybody does.) And our poor Mr. Adam Clayton Powell enmeshed in some tedious scandal that makes me cringe just thinking about it. Thank goodness Pearl isn't alive to see all the trouble.

Pearl, for whom the world was a petal-perfect flower! My beautiful Pearl. Exquisite she was, like a fragile beach shell. Her father's Irish blood had bleached her skin to beige. A Mohawk ancestor can lay claim to the indigo blue in her irises. How I loved that haughty twist of her head when she concentrated, and the confidence with which she pulled against her enviable frame the yards of uncut crepe and messaline, measuring and honing, articulating the endless possibilities of form.

Sometimes she'd use me as a mannikin. "Now hold this over your shoulder. Let me see, no a little more here." My skin fairly jumped at the soft brush of her fingertips working to protect me from the stick of the pins she inserted with lightning speed.

Those white women, young and old, may have loved her, but I adored her. Pearl. Pearl at the piano on hot summer evenings, playing Strauss waltzes, Chopin preludes, Debussy. Pearl with her what-they-used-to-call "good hair" twisted back from her face in a braid or a bun, little ringlets spilling onto her smooth forehead.

She and Grandmother Blanche and Minnie and Inez all lived in the old Victorian house on Pine Street I now inhabit and maintain with the same fastidiousness they once did: the rosy twilight parlor, the cool, darkened pantry where I once sneaked jam, the English garden still full of misty spires and lacy foliage where sometimes, as a boy, I lay on my back among the foxgloves and columbine, concealed and ecstatic.

In the evenings now, when I have repaired to the living room, I close my eyes and conjure up the melodies of Pearl's crepuscular serenades drifting over the decades like ground fog.

Minnie, mostly silent, sits in the parlor sewing by hand, dreaming of unspoken things. Grandmother Blanche and her niece Inez, corsets loosened, rest in their chaises on the screened-in porch, murmuring. Outside, the summer breeze stirs, never violating the stillness within.

There were moments when the music stopped being music and became an intimate outpouring of Pearl's soul. None of us dared even to tremble.

Pearl went to finishing school and then to college. For several years after, she taught part-time in a nearby academy for young "colored" women, but it closed, and after that, there were no such jobs for "colored" women. She had always wanted to be a poet, but instead turned to sewing, richly textured materials, satins, silks, and lace.

"Always be nice," Grandmother Blanche inculcated. "A real lady never shows her true feelings."

How obedient was my dear Pearl. So obedient that she gave up what she loved best and came home to spend her entire life in this very house.

Shortly before I was born, Cousin Pearl took up with a light-skinned man named Trevor something. How long this went on I can judge only by the letters they exchanged, almost six months' worth. But Trevor was only a porter on a train that ran North to South, and soon his tales of travel bored Pearl, who strove for real experiences (experiences of the soul, as she put it). She needed an educated man, everyone could see that, someone who understood her finely tuned sensibilities. "Pearl's so high-strung," they used to say, "so nervous." Pearl kept Trevor's letters in her gilded memory box, letters that Minnie sneaked and read on the sly. She divulged their contents years later just before she died. Those letters, Minnie wept to my mother, were so unworthy of Pearl, oh that poor, poor Pearl! They were so *physical,* Minnie whispered, her voice raw with emotion, so *low.*

I was almost fifty before I got my hands on those letters; Minnie had not destroyed them after all but stored them among her own things, even relished them, after Pearl died. I came across them when I packed up the last of Pearl's things for safekeeping.

Even now, sitting on Pearl's love seat, which I reupholstered last year in red velvet, I read those rough-hewn words with unexplainable pangs of jealousy and the slightest churning of my own fleetingly satisfied desires. Trevor's letters were the outpourings of a man's deepest passions. I have often found myself yearning for Pearl's poor Trevor, now dead in his grave, whose explicit tendernesses dedicated themselves so genuinely to Pearl. For I myself have certainly never known such love; *a real lady never shows her true feelings.*

And so it was one afternoon in the garden, where Pearl's old-fashioned roses still climb untamed around the arbor and over the walls, that Pearl did what she believed to be right and extended her hand in farewell to Trevor. They parted as friends. There were no more proper colored men around.

Minnie and Inez were much plainer and simpler than Pearl, and a little older, and they jokingly referred to themselves as unclaimed treasures, even when they were well into their eighties and white-haired. Frail women with the foreshortened vision of those who have not been out in the world. Women whose limited knowledge of men kept them sequestered in their own tight company. Women whose tomorrows promised little more than repetitions of yesterday.

They were the warning I didn't heed. Though it roared through my blood, so did the generations. We are, I have discovered through these bitter years, stitched together with the same constrained stuff, but different only in this way: a man alone has so much more to hide beyond drawn blinds, for companionship comes more naturally to women. My own fraternity has been limited mostly to books. I am of the generation that keeps its own secrets and its own shames.

I am, after all, the town librarian here. Such a man may live alone, keep a maid, cook for himself, and no one raises an eyebrow except in greeting.

Over the years nephews have come and gone, unobtrusively, innocently, quickly; my own light complexion has made mention of blood ties conceivable. These boys were the troubled sons of women who could never love them enough. Two hours out of New York City, these boys walked the cobblestones of my garden paths, shimmering and muscular in my dressing gown, their necks white in the sunlight. They were quick for my hospitality, just as quick for my generosities, and even quicker with good-bye. That was when I was much younger, when the full torture of my desire moved me to haunt the very same train station where Pearl met her porter. I often roamed that platform unobserved, bird-watching binoculars around my neck, discreet to the point of extinction.

Or so I thought, until today. But I will never visit that platform again. A good citizen I have always been in a town that tolerates nothing else. I am, after all, the keeper of books, in the stone library built in 1805, fifty years from the day my paternal grandfather found himself a free man above the Mason-Dixon line. My father's people were slaves. My mother's people on Pearl's side had always been free. My father never learned to read, but Pearl and my mother saw to it that I had books as a child.

And I, in reciprocation, see to it that the town's children and grandchildren are nourished by the books I carefully stamp and date for them. Winter, summer, fall, and spring, scores of them climb the stone steps and push open the heavy doors to browse my shelves. Nine to five, Mondays through Fridays, Saturdays noon to four. I have come to know them all by what they read. They bring hearty literary appetites it is my duty to satisfy. I direct the young ones to the Young Adult section and introduce them to such literary children as Gritli's and the Peppers and the young March women. "Thank you, Mr. Farrell," they chorus, using the surname I inherited with the house. Their faces are fresh as new paper. They clutch my worn books in their hands. I roam the aisles, among my bound companions, occasionally sampling aloud the familiarity of a paragraph, something to recommend to a young friend. My own joy builds under the tight cork of expectation as I observe the freshness of their imaginations, the certainty of their trust. I have tended the minds of our town as carefully as I tend my garden.

Which is why the unthinkable occurrence of today has brought me up short, like a fist to my stomach. Quite by accident this afternoon, I came across the scribbling on the wall in the 800 section. The dreaded words I'd hoped never to see, etched in an almost illiterate hand, flashed at me next to the second shelf. White chalk on the green wall. The last rays of afternoon sun tinged them ever so slightly with pink. I never doubted for a moment that they were intended for me. I glanced around for my accuser, quickly combing my mind for the names of those who had come and gone today. I swatted at the green wall with my open palm, oblivious to the sting. I furiously erased. The filthy words clung to my fingers, their fetid odor filling my nostrils. I went directly to the washbasin and soaped my hands over and over until the white dust dissolved and I could catch my breath. When I returned to the desk, two women and a small boy awaited me with expectation and a stack of books an arm long. I broke with policy and allowed them all, adding an extra week besides.

"Thank you so much, Mr. Farrell," the two women said, the one prodding the little boy to do the same. I watched them leave before I went over and locked the door behind them.

Now I am alone. I begin to stack stray books on the reshelving cart for my assistant. I check the wall once again just to be sure. It appears clean, like new, but the memory has left me weak with agony. Back at my desk I open a drawer and pull out one of Pearl's old hand mirrors. In it, peering back at me, is my light brown face, the small pouches of flesh forming under my eyes, the thinning hair, the full, wasted mouth. The words fill my throat with phlegm. I speak them slowly, for the first time in my life, to that passive, old man's face searching mine for answers, in the hushed boundaries of the closed library, when the rest of the world is safely on its way home to the supper table.

It is true, I think, *I'm nothing but an old black faggot.* Except that my accuser spelled it *fagut.* And I consider the poignancy of such ignorance and wonder if it might not have aroused a certain perverse amusement in old Pearl herself.

Mirror away, I collect my briefcase and pull on my sweater. Outside, the air is warm, the streets benign. My organs are gripped by agitation. I choose the shortcut to the deli, where I pick up a little creamed herring and a loaf of bread for dinner. The ugly incident replays itself in my mind. I keep hoping it isn't the boy I gave *Oliver Twist* to earlier. And then I hope desperately it isn't any of them.

All the way home I am on guard, expecting the words to ambush me again. Where are they? I wonder. Are they lurking behind each row of neatly trimmed hedges, or a passerby's spectacles, or in the window of that house?

The security of all the years I have lived here, respected and considered, now teeters like a pane of glass on the edge of a cliff. What will tomorrow bring? And what, after all, is my defense?

My German woman Hannah, who lives downstairs and keeps house for me, is off tonight. Every Wednesday she goes two towns over to visit her sister. Normally I relish the time alone, but tonight I feel an urgent need for the comfortable routines associated with Hannah's presence in the house. To hear her greet me with "Gut even'ning, Mr. Farrell" and offer me a taste of whatever she is preparing for us both. To give things the shape of habit. Though we seldom eat together, at my request she has joined me occasionally on the porch for a light supper. Tonight would surely have been one of those nights. We would have sat together, Hannah and I. She is a genteel, quiet creature, one who understands my need for solitude, who has never questioned the things she does not understand.

She is priceless, in sharp contrast to the servant Grandmother Blanche kept here in the old days. Willie, the young, fast dark-skinned black girl who used to sneak me cookies and twist up her face to make me laugh. I quicken my pace, briefcase heavy in my hand. Even Willie, I think, would be a welcome sight tonight.

Cousin Pearl called her Wily Willie. Willie had worked for my grandmother for years, and was probably forty when I first knew her, but she looked and dressed like a child. She giggled through household tasks, swiped butter from the pantry, and hid my grandmother's little trinkets in her room until she was caught and slapped. There would be tears all around, a firm reprimand from my grandmother, and all would be forgiven, the two embracing in mutual adoration.

Cousin Pearl considered Willie "uppity" and ill-mannered.

She went so far as to blame Willie's complexion. To be born so black is a terrible burden, she told me once. Darker races lack breeding. They simply can't help themselves. But Willie worshipped Pearl. It was Pearl to whom Willie came for counsel when she crept into the house at dawn after a weekend in a Harlem dance club, where she'd picked up a man and a swollen eye. Pearl briskly set about preparing Willie an ice pack and ordering her to rest all day in the overstuffed chair next to the fan in the parlor. Minnie and Inez discreetly looked the other way as they poured their own breakfast tea and commented on the weather (which was going to be unquestionably hot, but always made a good topic). "Willie fell down the basement steps," they told me soberly when I asked. "You mustn't go down in the basement. It's no place for a boy."

As I turn up my walk, I have an unexpected pang for Willie. I miss her, and for a moment I imagine her small figure in the garden, like a haunting. The day lilies have done surprisingly well this year, peach and tangerine blooms bursting from their beds holding the last glow of twilight. This time of day the light plays tricks.

By the porch I pause to check the mailbox, just as Pearl always did. I pull out a handful of routine bills, bank notices, and an advertisement. In their midst is, however, one light blue card-sized envelope addressed to me in a mysterious hand, with no return address. My heart quickens. The words from the wall are in my throat again. I imagine them written across the blue stationery, and then across the hedge dividing my property from the next. My neighbor's wife is filling the bird feeder suspended from a low branch of their flowering plum. Her back is to me. I set down my deli sack and briefcase and raise one hand in greeting. How badly I want her to turn around right now and wave back, to call out, "How are you this evening, Mr. Farrell, don't you wish it would rain?" But her back remains to me, intent as she is on filling the feeder.

My hands shake. I break the seal on the envelope with my finger. It is a personal letter, written in dark ink on thin blue paper in lovely scalloped penmanship.

It reads:

> Dear Mr. Farrell, This is regarding the note you sent me some time ago in response to an advertisement I ran last winter for a pen pal. I am sorry to have delayed so long, but I was ill and am just now recovered. I, too, am a book lover. I live just outside New York City in Piermont, and am a retired schoolteacher. You mentioned that you are a librarian. If you haven't already selected a pen pal, perhaps you would like to exchange some correspondence with me, as I suspect we have much in common. At your suggestion, I am currently re-reading all of Trollope. I agree that "there are worse things than a lie . . . it may be well to choose one sin in order that another may be shunned." Sincerely yours, William Tunning

I reread the letter twice, repeating the words aloud. Then I carefully fold the blue stationery and replace it inside the envelope. My note! I'd forgotten all about it, sent months ago during that long, dark crawl through February when the snow seemed to never want to stop. But now, with the scales tipped in favor of anonymous cruelty, an unknown friend has restored the balance.

A faint pulse of excitement stirs inside me. Trollope, I think, with small delight, another old queen who likes to read. And as I gather up my things and mount the front steps, I begin to consider exactly how I might open my letter to this Mr. William

Tunning and what all I will convey to him. My breath stops. I pause to catch it. Words!

My neighbor's wife has gone back inside. Briefly I look out over their empty yard where an occasional firefly flickers gold. My house is silent. It is only of late that I no longer think of it as Pearl's house. The night is warm. I pour a glass of red zinfandel from a corked bottle and take my meal to the front porch where I watch the shadows deepen. I wait for someone to walk by, someone who will see me sitting here, and who will call out.

This is the same porch on which my Grandmother Blanche sat on similar summer evenings next to a kerosene lantern, reading bowdlerized Shakespeare with an eyeglass held stiffly in one hand. Her favorite play was *Othello,* but I am confident her version bore no reference to "the beast with two backs." I often sat next to her, waiting patiently for Pearl to emerge from her room where she took a "ten-minute lie-down" before the evening meal.

How I loved the women of this house! How I looked forward to their familiar routines and shared in their simple pleasures. And how courageously they suppressed the unwitting desires that beat on soft wings at the backs of their hearts. They satisfied themselves with mouse-sized portions of well-cooked food on the Haviland china I still keep carefully laid out behind glass (it comes out only on those rare occasions I have a visitor). They took their pleasure in reading nightly to one another from the Bible, and maintained a decorum in their lives that allowed for no disruptions of routine, no nasty intrusions by those who might not understand.

A manless world, forged by their feminine imaginations, inward bound by the peculiar laws of that time.

I learned early not to inquire about Mr. Farrell, Pearl's father, who had long ago deserted the family after periods of unemployment. Grandmother Blanche kept tucked away inside her bureau drawer an old daguerreotype of him, which she impulsively thrust at me one day. I looked only briefly before she caught it up in her hand and buried it once again beneath her cotton underthings.

He was handsome, brown-skinned, wore sideburns and a confident smile. From my grandmother's few references to him, I learned he'd gone to Alaska to fish, where his party was either set upon by wolves or froze to death. But Pearl and Minnie and Inez pieced together, sotto voce, a scandalous portrait of the young dancer from New Orleans who lured him to the flashy nightlife of that southern port.

Pearl wrote numerous poems about Mr. Farrell. She kept her little couplets in a lacquered box which she gave me shortly before she died. The poems were shockingly candid, often written from the point of view of the dancer. As a young boy, I had so learned to treasure words, and my innocent Pearl tested hers aloud on me in a throbbing voice, assuming, I suppose, I was too young to understand. But unbeknownst to me and thanks to Pearl, I became in those secret moments the wicked dancer in red, bangled and sequined, swirling through shadow and smoke in pulsing rhythms for strangers below the edge of a stage, just out of reach of the hands reaching for me, stroking the air beside me, and always, always, and infinitely desiring.

Shortly after my mother and I arrived for our Sunday visits, Pearl summoned me upstairs. Her bedroom was my sanctuary. She'd remove my shoes, then hoist me up on the middle of her four-poster bed, covered by the hand-stitched silver quilt intended for her trousseau. I lay back, feigning weariness, but it was only an excuse to scrutinize the framed Degas print overhead. It was a study of dancers, young girls bent over to lace their ballet slippers, their net skirts standing off from their buttocks as vain as peacock feathers. If I looked closely enough, I could make out their hard, taut naked bodies beneath. I knew better than to ask about the painting, fearful she might put it away. I dreamed of myself among the dancers, absorbing and being absorbed, until we were one long feminine body, swirling under the canopy of Pearl's silver quilt.

Sometimes Pearl sewed and we listened to arias from her favorite Italian operas. Passion, love, jealousy, murder, revenge: Lucia's mad scene, Adelina Patti singing "Casta diva." Pearl sang along in undecipherable syllables that elicited dangerous visions of rapture, and lifted the veils of gloom from my young soul.

Occasionally she explained the stories to me with euphemistic precision full of "berefts" and "forsakens" and "unrequiteds." She hinted at unmentionable explosions of emotion under a harmless surface of pageantry and music. I lay contentedly on her bed, shoes off, toes free, staring at the dancers overhead, running bits of Pearl's filmy leftover material between my fingers. Pearl's voice wove itself in and out of my thoughts.

Now the air has thickened with the scent of jasmine crawling over the porch trellis. It is a heady fragrance, one which makes me light-headed, almost fearful. There is a movement in the neighbors' yard, a young girl walking down the drive to the street. I believe she is visiting the family, though we have not been formally introduced. She wears a light-colored dress that shines in the darkness above the hedge. I stand up in hopes that she will notice me, but she is looking toward the corner where a car has eased to a stop. The girl stands at the edge of the drive and stares. It is a young man in the car, and he peers out the open window. A woman's voice calls from out of the darkness, "Elaine!" Or is it "Ellen"? I am suddenly saddened that I don't know who the girl is. She turns quickly, furtively. She says something to the boy that I can't catch. The boy says something back. He drives halfway down the street and waits while she hurries back to the house. I hear a screen door squeak open, then slam. The street is quiet. The boy has turned his motor off. I wait, but the girl does not return. The boy finally drives off. I find my wine glass is empty and so go inside to fill it.

I am haunted by the silence of my own house and the loneliness welling up inside. Today's episode is a fearful presence, a ghost pursuing me, shaking its wispy finger at me, warning that books will never be enough. Not so, I murmur as the crickets stir outside. I feel the weight of the day pressing down on me. Panic builds to dizziness. I inhale and lean against the kitchen counter. Not so, I repeat.

Pearl was in her fifties when she began to have fainting spells, especially in the summer. Minnie and Inez would administer smelling salts and bring her to, whereupon her eyelids fluttered and her expression turned morose. She would accept a little cordial, which the women called medicine, and sit quietly, fanning herself and staring steadfastly into the yard. Sometimes she would turn to her piano and play. Everyone would remark with relief how good it was to "have our Pearl back."

When Grandmother Blanche died at ninety-five, it was just Pearl and Minnie and Inez living alone in the house with Willie. They quickly closed the gap my grandmother had left, tending to the house and garden with characteristic resignation. Mother and I continued to visit on alternate Sundays for what Cousin Pearl referred to as "supper." My mother saw it as her duty. "They're all alone," she explained to my father. He couldn't have been dragged here by wild horses. He died never having set foot in Pearl's house.

I recall that one Sunday evening we arrived for a late supper at the house. I was eight or nine, dressed in a white linen suit and straw hat I had begged Mother for. The women fussed over me tremendously. "Isn't he precious?" And Pearl filled my pockets with hard candy root-beer barrels. My mother herself wore a filmy, flowery summer dress and a matching hat. My mouth full of sweets, I observed the outline of her loose, warm limbs through that dress, catching the scent of perfume that rose off her biscuit-colored skin.

Pearl insisted this evening I was to sit at the table next to her, and not eat with Willie in the kitchen. "He needs to learn proper table manners," she explained as she sat me down beside her.

Minnie said grace and carved a plump, parsley-covered chicken. Inez passed around homemade apricot jelly and stuffing. We ate from the good china carefully arranged on my grandmother's monogrammed linen tablecloth.

Pearl spoke longingly of Paris, as she often did, but this was the first time I understood she had traveled there for three weeks with a white family whose children she once baby-sat. Though the trip had taken place years before, she talked as if it had been yesterday. The subject of Pearl's travels disturbed the others. "Shshsh!" said Minnie. "You'll give *ideas*," and she nodded in my direction.

Pearl sighed. "*Bon appetit, ma famille!*" she said and began to eat. When my plate was filled, I remarked, "*Merci beaucoup!*" for Pearl's benefit and everyone laughed. "Listen to him!" cried Mother. "Listen to how he talks!" She grinned down at me. But Pearl reached over and touched my hand gently. "You, my dear, are a most elegant little boy, and you mustn't let others tell you otherwise."

After dinner we clamored for Pearl to play the piano. Willie was in the kitchen scrubbing dishes. Minnie and Inez and my mother and I sandwiched ourselves together on the love seat. We waited for Pearl to strike her first chord.

In the twilight Pearl could have been twenty. Her noble face glowed from the falling shadows. I watched in fascination as her fingers strode over the ivory keys, then trickled lightly downward, her head in soft sway at the end of that long, smooth neck. Pearl played for an hour: Chopin waltzes, Bach preludes, a little Schumann.

"Oh, do play on," said Minnie, as she always did. She used the time to doze softly and think. We all urged Pearl on, and as the evening came, a soft sort of languor overcame us, a sense of overwhelming peace and contentment. My mother pressed my hand, grateful for what she perceived as my patience.

Pearl announced each piece she played. She moved to a transcription of the Flower Duet from *Madame Butterfly.* It was pleasant and light, and I found myself matching the beat with a happy rhythm in my own head. Then she paused and the house fell silent. Mother squeezed me to her. Pearl's hands were poised over the keys. She stared straight ahead at the gathering gray. Then, without warning, she began a disturbing piece in a minor key. To this day I don't know what it was, but suspect it may have been Tchaikovsky, or something equally inflammatory, the vibrations of which penetrated the deepest recesses of my soul and drew out passion like a sickness. I saw Pearl's face grow more and more darkly animated, her eyes taking on a hellish brightness. Her fingers flew over the keys, her breath came in gasps. I felt a wild explosion of expectation. Then Pearl stopped. Her hands crashed down on the keys in a violent, rebellious discord. A shudder ran through her slender body. With ferocity, she struck randomly at the keys again and again until the music became a jangle of frayed nerves and anger. To everyone's horror, she swept the music onto the floor. The women all leaped toward her.

Pearl reared up, tall and formidable, clutching at her throat with her hands. I don't know if that gesture was meant to stifle or wrench forth the silent scream that seemed to grow from deep within, emerging ever so slowly, but with fluidity, from that small, delicate throat. It was a noise I will never forget, like the sound of water trying to escape the tiny aperture of a broken pipe. She staggered as Minnie and my mother caught her on either side. Mother plucked up Pearl's fan from the piano bench and waved it at Pearl's constricted face.

"I—I," began Pearl.

"Not in front of the boy," hissed Minnie. "Oh, thank God Mother isn't alive."

"I can't take any more!" cried Pearl before she wilted against the piano. At least I believe that is what she said.

Minnie waved salts under her nose, Mother knelt helplessly at Cousin Pearl's side, and Inez wrung her hands. A trio of mercy and despair. But Pearl hadn't fainted, she was crying. I had never seen a grown-up cry, and I remember even now the weight of my astonishment. Minnie quickly escorted me to the back of the house, where she advised me to sit quietly. I didn't move, but sat obediently, measuring the soft quickening in the very center of my heart against the murmurs from the front rooms. I paged through Pearl's postcard album, studying castles and cathedrals and colorfully dressed white people dotting green hillsides, places I have since visited many times over, going beyond where Pearl ever went. But then it was not the pictures I was thinking of. My boyish eye moved feverishly beyond. At its sharpest point of vision, it witnessed over and over the spectacle of Pearl's wanting to give in to the floor below.

While Pearl rested, Minnie drew me to her and proclaimed in a firm voice, "You needn't worry, my little lamb. She only had a little spell. Your Cousin Pearl is just fine now."

At that moment a faint connection worked itself between Pearl and me like an insistent cat: recognition began uncurling from its sleep. In the years that followed and never separated us, understanding grew. I visited and wrote her faithfully. We spent hours in each other's company without a word. Since her death, it is Pearl's posthumous consent I have counted on. It is that which forms my company. She protects me even now from the dark lies of others as I glide easily through these unchanged rooms, stacked on top of one another, the walled mazes of her celibate will offering up the startling evidence of our very likeness. It is from her own desires that I must draw my courage.

In the fading twilight of my curtained living room I remove my clothes, abandoning the constraint of stiff seam and tyrannical stitch. Pants folded, shirt off, I go to the hall closet and pull from the hanger my silk dressing gown, pure fluidity, the one Pearl made for herself and wore, oh, those many evenings in her room while she sewed.

I pour a second glass of wine, urgency summoning me as Pearl once did. What appears to be the ease of my next decision is exigency in disguise. At my secretary, I pry open several boxes of stationery, choose the plain, and select two pens in case one runs dry. I arrange them on the butterfly table beside the love seat. I lean over and turn on the Venetian lamp, pausing to observe both pens and paper in the expectant way one might consider a silent phone. Words! My greatest fear is just how wrong they can be.

The pens, the paper, the rising imperative of my own longing fill me with agitation. I roam along the edge of the wall of books, counting off the book spines with the tips of my fingers until I find what I am looking for. There, among the hardbound Trollopes, is a well-worn volume of *Barchester Towers,* left unfinished from last winter, page marked by a thin scrap of red velvet. It is here, I tell myself, I will make my start. It is here I must take my comfort. There is no trick to warding off tomorrow. For the moment Trollope is my sin. Mr. William Tunning is another.

COLOR STRUCK

They'd always gathered at Mother's for Thanksgiving. That was before Daddy died and the house on East 23rd was sold to a Chinese man, Lee Wong. Think of it! Ten of those Wongs crammed into the old stucco house that used to feel crowded with just five: Mother, Daddy, Caldonia, Vesta, and Clayton. It made Caldonia shake her head in disbelief. At the phone company she worked with several Chinese women who could barely get their mouths around English words. The words, when they spoke them, stuck like peanut butter in their throats.

Caldonia's latest obstetrician was Chinese, or was it Japanese? She never could keep it straight. A Chinese girl at work had recently corrected her and said, "I'm Filipina." Then she reached out and laid her narrow hand on Caldonia's rounded stomach, so unexpectedly that Caldonia felt she'd been intruded on. The girl, seeing her surprise, smiled and said, "For luck. For me. I want a baby too." Caldonia was troubled by the warmth of the girl's hand long after it had been withdrawn.

Up until a month ago, Caldonia's Chinese or Japanese or whatever-she-was obstetrician had been seeing her once a week for the last month of pregnancy. The doctor was a small, friendly woman with bright eyes who dressed in elegant suits, as if she were running off to business meetings instead of squatting on a chair to peer up between her patients' legs. She spoke proper English without any accent. "Everything looks good," she told Caldonia. "Everything looks just as it should."

This was Caldonia's third child, the conception so unexpected that at first she had not told Fred about the pregnancy. She waited over a week. Not that she would have ever considered not having the child, but she needed time alone to absorb the fact that, even with Iris and Nadia both in school, she was going to be the mother of a baby again, faced with diapers and sleepless nights.

Now, as she busied herself in the kitchen, she longed for the past Thanksgivings at the East 23rd Street house, when Mother had festooned the doorways with crepe paper and Daddy, in his matching slacks and sweater, carried out the holiday routine of washing and polishing every inch of his two black Cadillacs. Standing in that immaculate driveway, chamois in hand, he always greeted and chided them all as they arrived, his children, then his grandchildren, encouraging everyone to pause and admire the shine of fenders and hoods, and listen to him brag for the hundredth time, "Look at that, a hundred thousand miles and not a scratch, not a bump . . ."

Thanksgivings with Mother and Daddy had always been so perfect. There was plenty of room and more than enough food for anyone who happened along: neighbors, friends, extra relatives, dropping in for some of Mother's famous sweet potato pie. "Oh, and while you're at it, honey, try a little taste of turkey and a bit of oyster dressing, and just go on ahead and get you some of my bread pudding too."

But the last year had brought many changes. Daddy was dead and Mother had squeezed herself and her possessions into one of the cement-block Harriet Tubman Senior high rises in West Oakland. Her cramped fourth-floor apartment with its tiny kitchenette overlooking the freeway no longer accommodated the swell of family. She now boiled tea water on a two-burner stove and heated up frozen dinners in a microwave.

And Mother, gone stoop-shouldered and irritable, complained that the grandchildren made her nervous when they came to visit. She reproached them for being too loud in the elevators, always threatening to pull on the emergency buzzer, and she worried they'd tear up her furniture, so she'd covered everything in plastic, including runners along the beige pile carpet. She spoke more sharply to Caldonia, Vesta, and Clayton, her three grown children, as if they were still children themselves, wearing on her last good nerve.

Everyone agreed Mother wasn't herself these days, dependent on a cane after her hip operation in the spring, forgetful, eyes blurring from encroaching cataracts, balance uncertain. As Vesta took to saying, "Mother's just an old crab. I can't stand to listen to her."

What Mother announced to Caldonia about Thanksgiving this year was "I've retired from cooking and now it's somebody else's turn."

What she meant was "It's up to you, Caldonia. Clayton and Vesta are useless."

So Caldonia and Fred won by default, even though Caldonia was just a month past giving birth and still feeling sore and irritable. This child had come cesarian, a fact that dulled Caldonia's sense of accomplishment. It seemed the child had not really come out of her own body. Now here she was, barely recuperated, roasting the turkey and browning homemade bread crumbs, all because she knew better than to count on Vesta and Clayton.

"Y'all gonna have to pitch in, I'm not the Lone Ranger, you know," she told them by phone, with special emphasis in her voice just to make the point. She wondered if God was growing weary with her impatience. After all, He'd seen to it that Caldonia and Fred were blessed with so much.

That's how friends and family saw it too. She and Fred seemed to make good choices, beginning with each other. Fred was always getting promotions and raises on the police force. Caldonia had just made supervisor down at the phone company. They paid their bills on time, they attended church, and they'd saved enough money to put Nadia and Iris in a private Christian school.

Their good fortune wasn't lost on Vesta. "Y'all got all my luck," she was fond of saying. "I can't seem to win for losing."

But luck always has a limit. It started with the cesarian birth of this third child. Caldonia suspected Fred was a little disappointed the baby wouldn't be a boy, though he'd never say such a thing.

In her hospital bed, breathing hard and pushing, she recalled the Filipina woman's hand touching her. At the time, she had felt too startled to be annoyed, and then she realized the woman meant no harm. But it felt like a curse. And her labor was long and hard.

When the pains got worse, the doctor ordered a cesarian. It was a disappointment, but after a short sleep and the drowsy aftermath Caldonia found herself coming to in the bright light of her own excitement. She made out the shape and length of a perfect form—eyes, ears, fingers, and toes all there and accounted for. She cried out in happiness, a miracle even the third time, grasping the wrinkled little thing in her arms. But later, after her mind cleared, Caldonia got a good look. She began to suspect a blunder, a genetic contretemps. During her sleep something had happened. The child, made up of parts of her and Fred, did not seem to belong to either of them, and she wasn't sure where to lay the blame: on God (whom she fiercely loved) or Nature (whom she tried to respect) or the very chromosomes in the cells of her own body which had bleached the child the color of milk, tinted her eyes pink, stained the thin spread of hair an off-shade of lemon.

If Fred hadn't reassured her that the baby emerged from her body, she would have been certain there was a hospital mix-up and some white couple was going home with her child. Later she recalled an article she had seen once years before in *National Enquirer:* White Couple Gives Birth to Black Baby. The article went on to say that the woman, unbeknown to her, carried black genes. The husband accused his wife of infidelity and divorced her immediately. Caldonia thought about the situation in reverse: Black Woman Gives Birth to White Baby. But it wouldn't work because a black woman's baby, no matter how light, would always be black.

Fred had to remind her that this was a gift from God, and that whatever God had in His plan they must accept with humility. Caldonia cried bitterly anyway. "It's our child," he kept telling her. "What is wrong with you?" But Caldonia prayed secretly and fervently that the child would darken.

From upstairs there came a soft cry. Caldonia set down the wooden spoon she'd been stirring the cranberry sauce with and turned down the flame under the pot. She was quicker to attend to the needs of this child than she'd been with Iris and Nadia. By the time she'd gotten upstairs and was peering into the crib, the baby was sleeping soundly again in her nest of quilts. Caldonia had taken to dressing her in blue; pink was so unflattering, causing her features to all but disappear in that little white face.

Often, while the baby slept, she sat close by and watched her. She wanted to understand exactly who this child was. She couldn't help comparing the luscious dark silk of her two older daughters' baby skins, how warm they were to the touch. This child seemed cold and foreign, a baby from some northern clime—Scandinavia, perhaps, a place inhabited by people with white skins and canary yellow hair, with eyes like frost. And yet Nature had played a trick, for the baby's small lips were full, her cheekbones high, and her nose broad like Fred's. And her hair, which was plentiful, was a thick cap of tight nappy curls. Daily, Caldonia checked the little crescents just below the child's tiny fingernails, but she found no indication that the skin there intended to darken.

Caldonia lingered by the sleeping baby, reassured by her soft breathing. From a certain angle, with the blinds drawn, the child might almost be considered pretty. There was a loud knock, followed by several more, at the front door. Caldonia pulled herself away from the child and hurried down the stairs, fastening her apron strings as she went. It was baby sister Vesta, the first to arrive. And barely noon, but since Vesta's tenth or so separation from Harold Sr. she was in the habit of showing up places early.

"You're going to take all the skin off your knuckles pounding on my door like that," Caldonia scolded. Vesta was holding a large green salad in a wooden bowl, covered with Saran Wrap. Behind her, Rosie and Li'l Harold were still piling out of their dented and badly rusted red Toyota with the bad starter and moody brakes and the cockeyed windshield wipers. As usual, they were already fussing with each other.

Caldonia stepped back and let Vesta pass, bearing the salad bowl, which reminded her of a miniature terrarium.

"Now, why'd you go and dress the salad like that?" Caldonia was annoyed. "Dinner's not until two."

Vesta was unfazed. She was already peeping into the living room to inspect the new sectional furniture Caldonia and Fred had ordered from a catalog. "Oooooh, this musta costed y'all a fortune!" she exclaimed. "Mmmmmm, and light colored too.

I'd never dare have something light colored with Rosie and L'il Harold around."

Vesta had never been considered pretty (certainly not the way Caldonia was—high school homecoming queen and so on!), what with her lumpy potato shape, funny lopsided smile, and eyes set too close together like a moth's. She was the lightest of Mother's children, honey butterscotch, but her complexion was uneven in places, scarred dark by childhood acne. And Vesta had never learned to dress. "*Really,* Vesta!" Caldonia would exclaim as Vesta arrived in skin-tight pants displaying all her bulges, teetering along in shoes so high she'd break her neck if she fell off. Today she was wearing yellow and black striped tights two sizes too small and an oversized yellow turtleneck with black pockets. Caldonia thought her sister looked like a misshapen bumblebee. And those red shoes, like Minnie Mouse! She had never seen anything so ugly and cheap-looking.

Rosie and Li'l Harold burst through the door and flung themselves on her. These wild children were the opposite of Iris and Nadia—careful, precise children who rarely made messes, and whom Vesta had referred to disparagingly one infamous Christmas as "those little prisses." It took two whole weeks for Caldonia to get over that slight.

"Where's the baby?" cried Rosie, and Harold echoed "Where's the baby?" They'd come clutching armloads of complicated toys with small and multiple loose parts that would soon be scattered. They continued to press themselves against Caldonia with wet kisses and sticky hands.

"Yes, where *is* the baby?" Vesta wanted to know, bending over to see if the plastic flowers in the vase were real.

"She's 'sleep, upstairs," said Caldonia gently.

"Y'all named her yet? Mother's fit to be tied about that poor child."

Caldonia made her voice firm. "*No*, we haven't decided on a name yet."

Vesta clucked her tongue like an old woman. "Scandalous," she said cheerfully. "You can't have a no-name child."

Before Caldonia could snap back, Vesta went on, eyeing Caldonia's new beige curtains at the window, "I can't wait to have me my own place. I'll tell you, girl, Clayton is driving me nuts. He's so damn picky, picky this, picky that. He blew up at the kids the other morning, I mean really lost it, because he said they'd eaten all his cold cereal. Can you believe that? Yelling at my kids. Over cold cereal!"

"Brother's doing you a favor," Caldonia reminded her. "What you need to do is get things straight with Harold."

Vesta blew big air from her mouth. "That man works my final nerve!" She turned so quickly on her red shoes that her heel left a scuff mark across Caldonia's polished hardwood floor.

"Harold *is* your husband . . ." said Caldonia.

Rosie and L'il Harold started on a mess in the hallway.

Caldonia jumped in. "You kids set your toys over there and then you can go swing out back. Take turns. No fussing. I don't want to have to come out there."

When she turned around, Vesta was poking her face into the oven for a peek at the turkey. "This thing's big as a elephant!" she exclaimed, swallowed up in steam.

"Girl, get outa my oven. You're gonna make it cook uneven."

"I could baste it."

"It's self-basting," sighed Caldonia. "Close the door."

"Where *is* everybody?" Vesta asked.

"Fred's in the family room watching the game, but don't bother him, and the girls are down the street."

Vesta was wearing that awful wig again, the straight hair page-boy three shades too light for her complexion. It reminded

Caldonia of one of the old Supremes. So what if Vesta's real hair was thinning, it was all that worry over Harold. If she'd just ditch him once and for all, her hair would thicken, her skin would clear, and her whole life would improve. She'd lose some weight, could afford decent clothes, and she'd get another man if that's what she wanted.

Caldonia didn't believe in divorce, but in this case she thought it was high time Vesta and Harold Sr. split up for good. How those two had managed to last all these years was a mystery! Everybody'd warned her from the start, that very first day Vesta dragged Harold home from high school. They'd succeeded in putting a stop to their eternal fussing long enough to produce two unruly children, but otherwise it was always hurricane weather at Vesta's.

Daddy'd had a fit. He had forbidden her to marry Harold, told her the boy was all flash and foolishness, barely one step up from a hoodlum. But Vesta was so hardheaded and downright silly (Caldonia frequently thought, a little simpleminded, if you wanted to know the truth), she just thumbed her nose at Daddy and forged ahead with a huge wedding, marrying Harold in an expensive ceremony at the Methodist church Mother attended. Daddy ended up bankrolling the whole business, including the expensive lace dress with train, though everyone knew Vesta had about as much business wearing white as the devil himself.

So it was that Vesta had spent these last fourteen years paying the piper. Over and over she'd packed up the children and left Big Harold lock, stock, and barrel. This time it was Clayton who relented and let her move in with him in his two-bedroom apartment down on Lake Merritt. It was supposed to be temporary, just until Vesta made other arrangements, but now six months had passed and Clayton had confided to Caldonia his patience was wearing thin.

Foolish Clayton! It wasn't as if Caldonia hadn't cautioned

him. He was always getting suckered into things like this, and now he was whining to her. Said he was tired of coming home from the college where he taught accounting to find the living room floor littered with Rosie's black Barbie and her accessories, and the horse doll with the eyelashes and purple hair and all *her* accessories, and pieces of Little Harold's Lego set strewn around, and an oblivious Vesta curled up on the sofa with Clayton's plaid bathrobe over her legs watching *Jeopardy* and eating Cheez-Its out of a crumpled bag.

At first Caldonia tried to listen patiently, the way the Lord would want her to. But she finally had to tell Clayton straight out that he needed to "put the girl out." She spoke from experience. Just a year ago she and Fred had hosted Vesta and the kids, and now here they were having to spend good money replacing their sectional furniture that Rosie and L'il Harold had crayoned on.

Vesta leaned across the countertop to steal an olive from the cut-glass dish. "You know, Clayton's bringing a woman over today," she announced coyly.

Caldonia launched into making biscuits. "A woman? He didn't mention it to me."

"That's because he's afraid you won't approve." Vesta let that sink in. "Let's see, Jean or Jane. Shoot! I never can remember her name." Vesta headed over to the fridge for a diet soda. She found a can, popped the tab, and brushed a loose strand of wig hair from her face. "You ain't heard about her yet?"

Caldonia shook her head. "I can't keep up with Clayton's women. It's enough to keep up with three children."

"This one's *different,*" said Vesta knowingly. "And he's crazy about her too." She paused, watching for Caldonia's reaction. "Now I don't want to say something I shouldn't . . . Mother said don't upset you . . ."

"Then don't," said Caldonia and rinsed her fingers off at the sink. From the basement family room came a whoop and a shout from Fred.

"Well," Vesta went on, "I haven't seen him like this with anybody for a while. She spends the night four, five times a week."

"What? With you and the kids there?"

Vesta nodded and swiped another olive.

"She's pretty and polite. Mother thinks so too."

"Pretty and polite!" murmured Caldonia. "You and Mother."

Vesta seemed especially pleased with herself. "There's something you won't like about her, but I'll let you find out on your own." And she let out a ladylike belch and squished the diet soda can in her right fist.

To herself, Caldonia murmured, "Lord, Lord, Lord," and then, mercifully, the baby cried and she excused herself and went upstairs in search of her third child.

Clayton arrived shortly after one-thirty, sporting a new trim haircut and supporting Mother's stout crooked body against his skeletal frame. He reminded Caldonia of a marionette, arms and legs dangling off the sides of his body as if held on by wires. Nervous energy seemed to eat up any pounds that might have settled onto his frail frame.

Once Caldonia had asked Mother about Clayton's puniness and his high voice, worried that Clayton was being denied entry to manhood, but Mother cut her short and asked her what on earth had gotten into her? What could she possibly mean bringing up something like that, was she trying to say her baby brother was *gay?* Mother's eyes had hardened like marbles. No, that wasn't what Caldonia had meant at all, she'd only said he was "frail," but by then it was too late because Mother'd already interpreted, in the narrowest terms available, what Caldonia meant about Mother's favorite child. "He's a good son.

He finished college. He's done well for himself and he does well by me. Don't you talk about your brother that way."

Clayton kissed Caldonia on the cheek, and now he was kissing Vesta too. "Let's see, it's been an hour since I've seen *you,*" he teased.

"Ha ha ha," murmured Vesta, unaware her wig had slid an inch off her forehead and a portion of her mashed-down real hair was exposed. "You're still pissed off at the kids about that cold cereal, I know you."

Mother shot them both a look and said she needed to sit down right away, she wasn't feeling right. They found her a comfortable spot on the new sectional sofa in front of the living room television where she announced, "Now, I don't want to look at no football." Clayton crouched on the floor and began to search the channels. A quick perusal through the networks produced mostly oversized men tumbling around in helmets.

"How about a parade?" Clayton suggested.

"Don't want to see a parade either. Just find something pleasant for me to look at and turn down the sound."

Clayton settled on a PBS travelogue of pubs in Ireland and got Mother adjusted. Caldonia brought out glasses of juice for them both.

"Oh, goodness, you know I can't digest all that acid," said Mother.

Caldonia took the glass back to the sink and added water. There was just the slightest edge to her voice as she said, "Vesta, take this back out to Mother, please, and tell her it's good for her. Just a little cranberry juice and some mineral water."

Clayton hovered in the kitchen doorway, glass in hand. His eyes burst like raisins from his light-brown face.

"Jill call yet?" he asked in a voice meant to sound matter-of-fact, but which came out overeager and tinged with plaintiveness. He had a nervous habit of rocking on his heels, then rising onto his toes as if in preparation for ascension.

"No, nobody's called," said Caldonia primly, wiping her hands on a kitchen towel.

Vesta let out a shriek. "Ooooh, honey, and I called her Jane. Shoot, you know me, I'm just bad with names. Guess I been so nervous I'd call her Evelyn, I just don't call her by a name at all."

Clayton's complexion went gray for a moment. He leaned back hard onto his heels, suddenly grounded.

"Vesta, you are something else, bringing up Evelyn like that!" snapped Caldonia.

Evelyn had been Clayton's fiancée the year before. A beauty queen, Miss Black Something or Other, standing over six feet tall, with legs like a giraffe's, and eyes that had seen just a little too much of life for Caldonia's tastes. Evelyn Gilroy: the color of dark butterscotch, with flawless skin and a set of thick eyelashes that swept across her cheeks, blinking like a doll each time anyone asked her something. "I believe so," she'd say if something were true, or "I believe not," if it weren't. And she'd cold-shouldered Clayton's family, let them know they weren't really good enough.

But Clayton hadn't seen it coming, he never did. Evelyn kept him tied up in a knot so tight he wouldn't eat and he lost weight and took to having migraines. Like a fool he went ahead and spent all his money on the diamond ring he placed on her finger. He saw engagement, a lifetime of long, brown Evelyn, his forever; Evelyn saw only an expensive diamond. She had the gold melted down after the breakup and put the diamond in a pendant.

Caldonia had kept her mouth shut. "Six things the Lord hates . . . a false witness telling a pack of lies, and one who stirs up quarrels between brothers." She tried not to say anything bad about anybody.

Clayton looked at his watch. "Almost two o'clock. I better try calling Jill again."

"Turkey's about ready," said Caldonia. "And what did *you* bring for dinner, Mr. Clayton?"

Clayton's eyes shot over to Vesta. "Didn't Vesta bring my salad?"

Caldonia turned, hand on hip, eyebrows arched. "Well then, what did Miss Vesta bring?"

"Oh, shoot," Vesta moaned, without shame. "I thought the salad was from all of us. I mean, we live in one place, me and Clayton and the kids . . ."

"But there are four people living there," Caldonia pointed out, "and that means four big appetites."

"I'm sorry. I've got so much on my mind," sighed Vesta. "Harold called this morning wanting to know what me and the kids were doing today. He's wanting to come back . . ."

"I don't want to hear it," said Caldonia.

Fred was cheering again from the family room. Caldonia cast her eyes ceilingward. "Now watch, the baby'll start crying any second."

"I'll get her!" said Clayton. "You named her yet?"

As predicted, the thin high siren of Caldonia's newest addition scored the air. "Oh, shoot," said Caldonia. "I knew this would happen. Vesta, would you set the table, please?"

From the living room Mother's voice rasped out, "The baby's crying. Aren't we going to eat sometime today?"

Then the children surged through the back door, all four of them, Iris announcing that she and Nadia were back and that Rosie had yanked the barrettes from her braids, L'il Harold was spitting on ants, and what was Caldonia going to do about it?

Upstairs, Caldonia found relief from all of their demands, lifting the fussing child from the little crib. The blue watery eyes were squeezed into slits. The doctor had said sensitivity to light might lead to blindness. Keep her out of direct sunlight, protect her eyes and skin. He sounded like he was speaking of a household plant, to be tended in the dark. Caldonia held her until the cries turned to soft whimpers.

"There, there, sweetheart," she murmured. She carried the child down the back steps, avoiding the rest of the family, to where Fred sat on the edge of the family room sofa. She handed the baby to him. "There's my little girl," he said joyfully. His long-limbed dark body dwarfed the pale doll beside him. "There's my little sweetheart."

"Everyone's here," said Caldonia.

"Shoooooo, my little baby," he cooed into the child's ear and lay her against his thick, dark chest. "My little Angela, my little Monica, my little Bo-Peep."

Caldonia started out the door, then turned and paused a moment. She was trying to make sense out of Fred's long arms and the tiny wriggling shrimplike creature now being caressed, ever so gently, by his capable black hands.

I wonder, thought Caldonia, if I'll ever love her enough. It was an ugly secret thought, one that haunted her with all its awful possibilities.

Three o'clock, and Mother snored on the sofa. The turkey sat browned but untouched in its pan on top of the stove. The salad continued to wilt in the refrigerator.

The table, arrayed with Caldonia's wedding china, held an air of empty expectation. The kids were snacking on peanut butter and arguing over Chutes and Ladders on the dining room floor.

"I really think we should go ahead with dinner," Fred finally said, "meaning no offense to your lady friend, Clayton, but I don't want to hold things up any longer."

Caldonia saw her brother's face fall. "Maybe just a half hour more," she said sympathetically. "You sure she's got our number and the directions?"

Clayton nodded. He sat hunched on a hassock in the living room, clasping and unclasping his hands, looking himself like a scolded child. The phone rang. Both Vesta and Clayton practically leaped from their seats, but it was only a friend of Fred's from the police force.

The baby's tiny bright pink face nestled itself against Caldonia's bosom. She squeezed the nameless child to her. The funny little face called to mind a newborn kitten's. Caldonia knew the family was talking behind her back. Even Fred was running out of patience. She kept waiting for the name to announce itself, the way Iris's and Nadia's names had.

By four o'clock everyone was so bad-humored that Clayton finally gave in and agreed they should eat, but his voice was tight and hollow when he spoke. "Something must have happened to her," he said. "I really wanted us all to eat together."

Fred rounded up the kids. The girls danced their way to the table; the adults settled themselves around somewhat grimly. There was a scraping of chairs and the usual compliments about how good everything looked.

"I don't know *why* we had to wait so long," complained Mother. She surveyed the table with a critical eye. She focused in on Vesta, who was now holding the baby. "Oh, there's my sweet little grandbaby." She looked the child up and down. "When are they going to find you a name, hmmmmm? You've got to have a name. Such a shame, poor little thing!"

"I think my cousin's so pretty," said Rosie. "Pretty cousin!"

"My sister's going to be blonde!" Iris explained. "There's a girl at my school with really blonde hair." She added exploratorily, "The girl is white."

"Child needs a name," murmured Mother into her plate. "It's been a month now." She looked up hard at Fred. "I thought you were going to call her after your aunt."

"Iris, eat your food, Iris," said Fred warningly to his daughter. Mother maintained her sharp stare.

The doorbell rang. Almost a quarter to five. Clayton leaped up and disappeared into the hallway. Fred caught Caldonia's eye and winked as if to say everything was all right, she should ignore Mother, ignore them all. Caldonia could hear a woman's voice, hushed, then Clayton's, apologetic.

A moment later Clayton reentered the dining room with false cheer. "Hey, hey, hey!" he announced. "Everyone, can I have your attention? I'd like you all to meet someone. This is Jill."

At first Caldonia couldn't see much more than a pair of brown boots and a long black coat, but when the woman stepped from the shadows she was startled by the fine, straight hair the color of corn silk and skin the color of eggwhite.

Caldonia immediately looked at Mother for an explanation, but Mother was placidly spooning more oyster dressing into her mouth.

"You know Vesta and my mother," said Clayton, "and this is my sister Caldonia and her husband Fred."

"Hi, Jill," called Vesta cheerfully, then turned to Caldonia with a sly smile. She was enjoying this moment thoroughly. "Isn't she pretty? I *told* you she was so pretty," she observed for Jill's benefit.

Caldonia sat stunned. She felt betrayal, from Clayton, from Vesta, but most of all from Mother, who went right on eating. Vesta's ignorance could almost be excused; the girl was color struck, thought all white women were pretty, had been that way since she was a child. When she watched old black-and-white movies, she was always sighing over old pale-white, dead actresses.

Fred got up from the table and took Jill's coat. Clayton pulled out the empty chair at the end of the table for her, and Jill set about squeezing herself in between Nadia and Iris.

Still, Caldonia hadn't said a word.

"Let her see the baby!" cried Vesta. "Show Jill the baby!"

"Let her get settled first," Caldonia murmured. "She doesn't need to be bothered with the baby." She felt suddenly proprietary toward her child.

But Vesta was on a roll. "Ask Jill what she thinks about the baby."

Anger rose in Caldonia. "I don't need to ask Jill anything" was what came out of her mouth, and Mother's head shot up with the speed of a bullet.

Vesta didn't seem to care. "Now that I think about it," she grinned, "that could be Jill's baby."

Clayton was trying to change the subject, but Jill interrupted. Her voice, when she spoke, had the sharp bell-like sound of so many white women. "Clayton tells me you just had a baby. Congratulations."

"Thank you," said Caldonia, surprised by her own relief.

Vesta wouldn't let up. "Jill, look at this pretty child my sister has. She's got your coloring."

Clayton went to work fixing Jill a plate. "Turkey? Cranberry sauce? Gravy?" He went down the list with an eagerness that filled Caldonia with loathing. Jill murmured, "Clayton, not so much, you know I've already eaten."

Already eaten! Caldonia thought. Well, knock me over with

a feather. *Already eaten!* This, while everyone had waited so patiently, the kids getting fussier and hungrier. As if in sympathy, the baby on Caldonia's lap let out a long wail.

"Mama!" cried Iris and Nadia simultaneously. "The baby's crying." It felt like an accusation.

"Bring the poor little thing over to me," said Mother. "Let me hold her."

Caldonia snapped back, "Not now, she needs to be fed."

The baby began to howl full force. It was as if all the tension in the room had settled over her and drawn her little face up into tight red fury.

Jill asked Clayton to please sit down and not worry over her. Caldonia had a sudden, unexpected image of Jill emerging from her brother's bedroom and traipsing into the bathroom, dressed only in her panties and bra, in front of the children. Caldonia alternated between fury with Clayton and fury with the girl.

Fred turned to Caldonia. "Honey, want me to take the baby downstairs with me?"

"I'll keep her," said Caldonia. She got up from the table.

"Isn't she just the prettiest little thing?" Vesta prodded Jill. "I think she's so *cute*."

"She's sweet," Jill agreed, but she was staring hopelessly at the mounds of turkey and dressing Clayton had heaped on her plate.

"I told you the baby was cute, didn't I?" said Clayton, as if to leave no doubt as to what he might have said about the child. Then for Jill's benefit he launched into his version of how he'd been the one to get Caldonia to the hospital just in time.

"Don't be tellin' her that," said Mother, biting into a turkey wing. "Your sister was in labor for almost eighteen hours before that Chinese lady did something about it."

"MO-ther," warned Caldonia.

Jill tentatively reached out one pale hand and touched the baby's blanched skin. "I don't get to see newborns very often," she said.

"Let her hold the baby," insisted Vesta. Her eyes had gone round and bright. Without explanation, the baby stopped crying.

"Jill's eating," said Caldonia, pulling the baby back against her body. "The baby's too fussy."

"No, it's okay," said Jill. She was working hard at being polite.

Now Clayton was urging. "Come on, Caldonia, let Jill hold the baby."

Caldonia could see she had no choice without offending everyone. She leaned down and handed the baby to Jill. Jill gathered the child against her and rocked gently from side to side. "Mmmmm, she's so little."

Caldonia arranged the loose-knit blanket under the baby's body.

"Look at Jill holding the baby," commented Mother, her turkey leg held up in one hand. "Isn't that something?"

"The baby could be hers," said Vesta.

Caldonia caught Fred's eye and she saw a warning there.

"They sure look a lot alike," Mother went on, hope in her voice. She leaned across the table and studied first the baby's face, then Jill's. "They got that same pretty complexion, don't you think so, Clayton? What do you think, Jill? Is that a pretty baby to you?"

Jill was trying to be polite for them all. "What's her name?" she asked. A moment of silence followed.

"She doesn't have one," Mother said bitterly. "It's been a month now and Caldonia can't decide what to call her."

The heat rose in Caldonia's face. She snapped back, "The baby's albino," as if that answered anything. She meant the word to sound bold, even cruel, despite the fact the Lord would be shaking His head at her.

Clayton jumped in. "What Sis means is that she's not sure if the baby's eyes will have sensitivity to light . . ."

"That's not what I meant at all," Caldonia said matter-of-factly. "I mean what I said, I'm upset my baby is white."

It was the first time she'd actually said it. Not to Fred, not even to herself. But now it seemed necessary. And truthful.

The room grew very still. Fred cleared his throat. Mother murmured, "Hmmmmm mmmmmm!" disapprovingly under her breath. The children eyeballed one another with keen interest. But Jill didn't seem to mind. She looked straight back in Caldonia's face. "Isn't the albino trait inherited?" she asked.

Caldonia nodded. "It's from Fred's side."

"I still think she's pretty," defended Vesta. "Maybe she'll grow up and look like Jill."

"Being albino," said Caldonia, "is different from being . . ." She paused. She saw no point in offending Jill further. "A blonde nappy head just isn't pretty," Caldonia heard herself saying. "That's called funny looking."

Everyone laughed uneasily except Mother, who pursed her lips and murmured, "Y'all some wrong folks!"

Caldonia bent down and retrieved the baby from Jill. "I'm afraid she'll spit up all over you," she said with false concern.

"Maybe everybody'll think the baby's mulatto," said Vesta, her mouth full of stuffing. "That's what they call a white and black mix. You know, like you and Clayton." She used her fork to gesture toward Jill, as if joining her with Clayton in midair.

"Clayton and Jill are not mulatto," Caldonia said stonily. She felt her anger giving her direction. "Clayton is black and

Jill is white. Mulatto would be what they'd have if they had a child, Vesta. It's not the same thing."

"Hold on there, don't rush us now," said Clayton, but he said it only for Jill's sake. His smile had broadened, his eyes brightened. Caldonia could see he rather liked the idea of having a child with Jill. And she could see by Jill's tense but civil expression that this would never happen.

"I don't mean nothin'," said Vesta cheerfully. She grinned at Jill. "You know me, I'm just over here runnin' my mouth like I usually do. My best friend in grade school was white. 'Member her, Caldonia? Patty What's-her-face, that big old fat girl, pretty face though."

The baby began to fuss in Caldonia's arms. Quickly her bad humor escalated to rage and her face turned the color of Pepto-Bismol.

Caldonia excused herself.

"Feed the baby here," Clayton called after her.

But the truth was, Caldonia didn't want to nurse her baby near a stranger. She pulled shut the louvered doors that separated the kitchen and dining room. She sat down in one of the vinyl-backed kitchen chairs and arranged the baby's pink mouth at her brown breast.

The louvered doors opened ever so slightly and Fred squeezed through. If he was annoyed with Caldonia, he didn't show it. Instead, he bent down and kissed the nursing baby. "You know I love you," he whispered in her tiny shell-pink ear, "even if your mama's actin' crazy."

Caldonia had to smile in spite of herself. She hummed softly to the pink and yellow child. When Fred went out again, she caught a glimpse of Clayton's slender brown fingers caressing Jill's pale arm, and then the stiffening of that arm as Jill carefully and surreptitiously moved just out of reach. It was a simple gesture, designed not to embarrass Clayton in front of his family.

Caldonia looked down at her youngest daughter. She didn't know which was worse, going through life toward blindness or going through life white. In a way, it was kind of the same thing. How was her daughter going to feel, this little pale stalk in a dark field?

Iris and Nadia let themselves through the louvered door into the kitchen.

"Close the door!" Caldonia hissed.

"Mama, we love our sister," said Iris pointedly.

"Well, of course you do!" Caldonia hadn't meant to give the girls a wrong impression.

"We could put her in the sun," suggested Nadia helpfully. "She could get a tan and be like us."

The two girls ran their hands over the baby's little pink ones and cooed at her.

"She is like us," Caldonia corrected. "She *is* 'us.' "

"Excuse me . . ."

Caldonia's head shot up. The voice was clear and precise. It was Jill, first poking her head through the kitchen door and now standing in the doorway, small and white, not much taller than Nadia and Iris. Caldonia quickly covered her breast.

"I want to thank you for having me," Jill said softly. "And I'm sorry about all the inconvenience and the mix-up."

For a moment, before she was able to line up her thoughts, Caldonia actually thought the girl was apologizing for the absence of the baby's color. "The mix-up?" she said vaguely. She reached for the right words. "Clayton's friends are always welcome," she said. "Come back any time."

"I will." The girl smiled, and Caldonia knew they both were thinking how this would not happen. "Thank you," said the girl, relieved and forgiven, as if Caldonia had it in her power to do that.

That night, when the dishes had been washed and the kitchen swept, and the children put to bed, Caldonia asked Fred tentatively, "I've been thinking, do you think it would be foolish to name the baby Ebony?"

Fred burst out laughing. "Girl, what are you talking about?"

"I want to give my child a *real* name," said Caldonia.

"That's real all right," he chuckled. "What is wrong with you, Caldonia? You can't *make* her black, you know. Naming her Ebony would be as bad as naming a dark child Pearl, or Magnolia. We should call her Angela, after my grandmother."

"I just want her to know . . ." Caldonia began. "I just want her to feel . . ."

Fred looked at her long and hard. "She *is,* Caldonia" was all he said before he went upstairs and turned on the news.

Caldonia stood next to the sink under the framed "God Bless This Mess" sampler Mother had made for her last Christmas. God, she thought wistfully, in His infinite wisdom has given me this child without a name. She wasn't blaming God; she wasn't blaming anyone but herself for the pinch in her heart that prevented her from running right upstairs and calling the child by her rightful name.

WHAT JASMINE WOULD THINK

It was months before King was assassinated. It was the fall after the Detroit riots. Jasmine Bonner cornered me in the corridor at school. She came straight to the point. "You have study hall with Lamar Holiday, right?"

Lamar, Lamar, of course Lamar. Tree-tall, dark chocolate, with a three-inch natural and a wide, sloppy grin that could change your life. He wore black and green Ban-Lon shirts and a small gold medallion of Africa around his neck. He sat two chairs over from me and took copious notes from his civics book in small, curved handwriting.

"Everyone knows Lamar and I are 'talking,' but I think he's creepin' on me."

It felt like an accusation. "Lamar?" I was breathless, all legs and arms and curly unkempt hair.

Jasmine glanced behind herself briefly. "Yeah, with this little half-and-half Oreo, Jeanie somebody. She's been trying to beat my time. All I'm asking you to do is keep your eyes open. Let me know what they do in study hall. You know, anything *suspicious*."

I nodded vigorously. Talking to Jasmine in the hallway of our school was a promotion of sorts. Students passing by took notice, and I stood straighter.

"Cool," said Jasmine, closing the deal, and she smiled.

After that, I went on red alert. Lamar didn't know it, but

we were now connected. Jeanie Lyons, the girl in question, sat by the window. She was high-yellow, with curly sandy hair and sea-blue eyes, but a flat, broad nose that gave her away. Not that she was trying to pass; everyone knew her father, our postman, black as the ace of spades.

I watched. Lamar didn't even pass her en route to the back table next to me where he and his friends congregated. And Jeanie, too sallow and freckled to be pretty, sat engrossed in *Valley of the Dolls,* and licking her long slender thumb carefully before each turn of the page.

Then, early one Saturday morning, on my way to a piano lesson, I spotted Lamar's white '63 Chevy convertible whistling down Route 10. No question that it was Jeanie crunched against him shamelessly, her sandy curls pasted by the wind against his dark chin.

I ran myself into a sweat getting home, where I dug in my schoolbag for Jasmine's phone number. My heart was in my throat when I dialed.

Jasmine's mother answered, sharply. "Who's calling, please?"

"Tish . . . Tish from French class."

"Tish?" Pause. "Just a moment."

The receiver clanked against something Formica-hard.

Time inched along. Nervously I chewed my thumbnail. Finally Jasmine picked up the receiver and spoke while crunching potato chips. "Uh-huh?" Her voice sprawled long and lanky on the other end. I pictured her spread out on a sofa inside her house on the other side of Main Street, large silver hoops dangling from under her halo of hair. Jasmine was one of the first girls at school to wear an afro and risk suspension.

"It's me, Tish." Conspiratorial. Hard as nails.

"Mmmmmmmmm."

I threw out the bait. "I saw Lamar today."

"Ummmm-huh? Where?"

A woman's voice snapped in the background, and Jasmine said, "All right, all right." Into the phone she whispered, "I'm on punishment, talk fast."

This forced me to the point. Did she remember what she'd asked? Mmmmmmm-hmmmmm. Well, I'd seen Lamar's car. Oh, yeah? Yeah, and Jeanie Lyons was in it. What did I mean in it? *In* it. You know, close to Lamar. How close? Close. Just close or very close? Very close. It got so quiet on the other end you could have heard a rat pee on cotton.

At last Jasmine said, "I knew his black ass was up to no good," and hung up.

That was it? I turned around and dialed my best friend Angela. Rarely did I have anything newsworthy to say; mostly it was Angela pasting together the meager details of her overlapping romances with the squarest boys in our freshman class. I acted casual, introducing Jasmine's name with the smoothest inflection. I repeated the whole conversation, word for word, without one interruption from Angela. A long silence followed on the other end.

"I didn't realize," she said cooly, "that you were currently friends with Jasmine Bonner. I know for a fact that she's two-faced and uses people."

"Maybe *some* people," I shot back.

"Sounds to me," said Angela sullenly, "like Jasmine isn't interested in you at all, she just wants information on Lamar. Besides, she doesn't like white girls, you better be careful."

"What do you mean, 'careful'?" I kept my cool.

"You'll find out," retorted Angela in that knowing way she had when she didn't know anything at all. "You don't understand you and Jasmine can never be *real* friends."

In our town, Angela and I both trod a thin line. Angela lived on the right side of town to be friends with Jasmine, but she still straightened her hair and worried about it napping up in the rain, and secretly thought the Revolution was just mumbo jumbo. Her mother wouldn't allow her to go dancing at the Boot Center where all the other black kids went. In all fairness to Angela, she'd been stuck with me as a best friend since grade school, old goody two-shoes Angela, who could least afford it.

Contrary to Angela's prediction (and much to her annoyance), Jasmine passed me a note, folded into a triangle, in French class the next day. "Just wanted to say HIGH," she wrote. Tuesday, another note followed. Jasmine Bonner had invited me to sleep over. As if it were the most natural thing in the world, Jasmine and me, matching the rhythms of our lives, as if she weren't two grades ahead, as if I were an equal. Jasmine of the rainbow fishnet hose and matching sweaters and pleated skirts, who sauntered the halls with queenly grace. She must have owned twenty pairs of pointed-toe shoes, purple, orange, lime, with fishing-line thin laces. Jasmine who with bold nonchalance popped a piece of Wrigley's Spearmint and calmly picked out her giant afro with a cheesecutter in the middle of French class while conjugating the present subjunctive of *etre*.

I couldn't stuff my pajamas into a paper bag fast enough. It was a cool autumn night. My mother dubiously drove me south across the tracks, down through the park on Spring Street, past Angela's ranch house. She asked me what I really knew about Jasmine's family. Were her parents responsible people? Did Jasmine have a boyfriend?

"Jasmine makes good grades," I said, as if that proved anything. "She's always on the honor roll."

"And what about Angela?" asked my mother. She seemed to imply I could only have one friend at a time. "I haven't seen her around the house much lately."

I didn't dare condemn cautious, fraidy-cat Angela, carefully mincing her words at our supper table, easing my father's troubled conscience by her very presence. Angela, the Good Negro, agreeable and self-effacing.

When we got to Jasmine's I jumped out of the car, but my mother didn't drive off right away. I saw her hesitate, taking in the unfamiliarity of this end of the street, peering into windows darkened by early twilight, as if searching for a clue as to where exactly I was going.

Just before Christmas, Jasmine and I stretched ourselves across her unmade mattress inside the Bonners' gray shingle house at the bottom of Washington Street. As usual, the house was a pungent medley of frying fatback and greens and her younger sister Camille's hot-combed hair. Overhead, fine Huey Newton, framed inside his wicker fan chair, observed us skeptically. Jasmine rolled over on her stomach and came up on her elbows. I was envious of her perfectly round buttocks, slim hips, and long dark legs.

She studied me carefully, plucking wrinkles in her top sheet with long, slender fingers.

"I think Lamar's messing around with this white girl, Tish." Her tone was sepulchral. My flesh crawled. "She lives out on Gore Orphanage Road—in a farmhouse in a cornfield. Cindy something—Pavelka."

"You mean the one who hangs around Wanda and them and acts black?"

Jasmine nodded. "Little no-nothing triflin' tramp. She's got legs like bowling pins, girl. And she's been with just about every brother in town. They say she had an abortion last year."

"Why do you go on with Lamar?" I asked.

Jasmine studied me almost pityingly. Her eyebrows arched with older-girl wisdom, and then it dawned on me what she would never admit: that she and Lamar were connected sexually in some mysterious way only hinted at in the Motown 45's I knew by heart. I loved those melodies, the innocent lyrics shaded lightly with innuendo. Pure poetry and simple rhythms inciting the ache of fantasy. Without a word, Jasmine handed me Miles Davis for the turntable. We both lay back on her bed and listened somberly until twilight fell. That's how I passed my winter that year, vicariously learning the sting of passion without trust, a ragged wound torn open by Miles's horn.

There were evenings we'd drive around town with a stop at Dairy Queen for ice cream, with Jasmine peering through sleet-filled twilights in search of Lamar's Chevy. "He said he'd be at work," she'd say, "and he better be." A quick trip past Fisher-Fazio's parking lot proved he was: the pristine Chevy sparkled there like a diamond on the frozen blacktop. Jasmine's face would relax.

And sometimes, as Jasmine fussed at Lamar on the phone, twisting the cord with her fingers, I'd patiently feign interest in magazines, trying to pretend I couldn't hear the soft inflections of her voice, or understand their implications.

Evenings she wasn't off with Lamar, we listened to Miles or Coltrane ("traditional," Jasmine called it—she got the albums from her older sister Bekka, a student at NYU) and sneaked drags off the Kool Longs she stashed in her earring box ("Blow it out the window!" she'd hiss, fanning at the air around my face).

Sometimes she'd read me Sonia Sanchez or Baraka. As twilight moved to darkness, neither of us made a move for the light switch. Instead, we sank into silhouettes of ourselves, dark and indistinguishable shapes, consumed by words. We'd talk about who really killed Malcolm, and the importance of black economic power for self-determination and why the terms "Negro" and "colored" were passé, until Mrs. Bonner hollered through the curtain that hung instead of a door that it was two in the morning and we better shut that damn music off and let reasonable people get some sleep.

After Jasmine dozed off, I would lie awake, made nervous by the touch of her foot against my calf, wondering what on earth she could have ever seen in me, and promising myself to never disappoint her.

One afternoon after school a bunch of us drove to a frozen Lake Erie in Jasmine's father's black Ninety-eight to smoke and talk smack and look for someone named Peppy from Lorain who never materialized. Every time I spoke up, two of the girls exchanged glances and snickered. One of them pointedly stated she was sick of looking at peckerwoods every which way she turned.

Jasmine relished controversy. She seemed amused. "You talkin' about Tish? You don't know Tish," she snapped. "I got cousins in New Orleans lighter than her. Least she's got some wave in her hair. She *could* pass, you know that?" She reached over the back seat and ran her hand through my curls as proof. "See what I mean? Look at her mouth. Now try to tell me those are typical white lips."

I felt proud then, as proud as if I'd been black as ink. In grade school, stuck-up white girls like Kimberly Hubbard and Marjorie Grosvenor had called my mouth "bacon fat." Now Jasmine praised it. A full mouth was beautiful, couldn't be pursed like Kimberly's and Marjorie's into thin lines of superiority.

I began to sense I was someone other than the person I'd always been told I was. Over and over, the girl Jasmine saw inside me was being revealed.

But it all started long before when I came to understand that our town was really two. In one of Angela's more generous moments she had assured me, as if to assure herself, that I was really meant to be black, and she'd stuck her arm through mine and marched staunchly through the football stadium bleachers with me in front of everyone. Later, behind those same bleachers, she and three other girls jokingly christened me an "Honorary Negro." They each touched me and spoke words over my head, and I responded with "I do," to unite us forever. We were earnest, treating my whiteness like some cosmic prank that could be easily corrected. Then there were wisecracks about a fly in the buttermilk, which left us doubled over laughing. But deep inside I believed, and when you believe, the world shapes itself accordingly. Like the baptized, I saw through the eyes of the reborn.

On our way back from the lake Jasmine remarked, "You know, I take a lot of flack for hanging out with you."

"Then why do you do it?" I asked.

"Because," she grinned, smacking my arm, "you're different."

So I told her about my Honorary Negrohood and she fell out laughing so hard I thought she'd rear-end the car in front.

My family didn't grasp the incongruity of my presence in their lives. Instead they seemed to be blaming me for being other than what they expected. Sometimes I stared back at their puzzled faces, as we were seated around the dinner table, and saw only winter-pale strangers wearing masks of disapproval. The way my mother would turn to me sometimes and say, "Letitia, what on earth are you trying to prove?" pained me so much that I prayed they'd admit a terrible mistake had been made and confess to me who I really was. I was coming apart like a seam at the other end of a loose thread. I studied myself in the mirror, turning sideways, backwards, then facing myself again, trying to discern who it was that stared back at me. Not a person who belonged to these strangers. Just a person who knew the Revolution was inevitable. *By any means possible.*

"I don't know what you think you're doing," said my father, furious with me for announcing at the dinner table one evening that all whites would be dead by the end of summer. "I suppose this is what you call being 'cool'?"

The word slipped off his tongue like a mistake, and I cringed, secretly glad Jasmine couldn't hear the ignorance in his precise two-syllable inflection.

Keeping my eyes on my plate, I quoted Don H. Lee: ". . . after detroit, newark, chicago &c., we had to hip cool-cool/super-cool/real cool that to be black is to be very-hot."

My father threw his hands up in disgust. "You see?" he said, appealing to my mother. "This is what happens when our liberal chickens come home to roost."

My mother shot me a baleful look. "I think it's Jasmine's influence," she said flatly. "I like Jasmine, but she's giving Tish wild ideas. We never heard this kind of talk when Angela was around."

My father muttered bitterly, "There hasn't been a white face in this house for over a year!"

Pain left me speechless. The countenances around me stared in silent accusation. What they couldn't know was that an unseen hand had reached inside and rearranged my whole genetic makeup, creating a freak of nature simply called Tish. Either side I chose I would lose myself. And living in the middle required becoming two people, split, like the baby Solomon threatened to cut in half. So I stared into my dinner plate until the Currier and Ives pattern of sleigh and horse melted into a swirl of icy blue and I was sucked into a storm of color so violent that I mistook it for redemption.

In June I, not Angela, was invited to Jasmine's seventeenth birthday party. My mother was dubious. Would adults be present? Would the lights be on? Would I leave a phone number?

It was a typical basement affair at Cintrilla Robinson's, with red and blue strobe lights blinking from the ceiling and a bowl of fruit juice punch spiked around eleven with Johnny Walker Red by some brothers from Lorain wearing three-quarter-length black leather coats and smelling of Old Spice. I slow-danced at least three times with Lamar's best friend Tyrone to seven scratchy minutes of the Dells' "Stay in My Corner." Tyrone sang into my ear in a precise, sweet falsetto and pressed me close against a hard place on his thigh.

He murmured approvingly, "Mmmm, you can keep a beat."

Jasmine and Lamar made out shamelessly in the corner by the record player. From time to time their two silhouettes, topped by halos of thick hair, seemed to merge into one. Someone teased: "Y'all need to take that stuff to the bedroom!"

Awkward, I walked outside into a warm, starry night, holding my paper cup of spiked punch. Cintrilla and some senior girls I recognized from school stood talking on the patio. Cautiously, I joined them under the paper lanterns.

Tyrone followed right behind, but kept his distance. I watched him from the corner of my eye, pacing in the shadows, his hands shoved into the pockets of his St. Joe's letter jacket. He kept looking at the sky as if he'd lost something, but neither of us said anything.

Cintrilla smiled at me with surprise. "Aren't you in my French class?"

I tried to look as grown-up as I could in my flowered culottes and lime green shell. My eyes were so deeply outlined in Jasmine's mascara they felt brown and ancient as the Nile. "Mmmmm hmmmmmm," I said.

"You come with Jasmine and Lamar tonight?" Ruby Mason

inquired in a friendly way. I nodded. It made an impression. The girls studied me with mild curiosity. When they asked questions, I found myself answering in a voice that could have been Jasmine's.

"Tyrone digs you," remarked Jasmine ever so coolly on the way back to her house. We rode in the back seat of her father's black Ninety-eight. She was trying to pull the collar of her blouse around her neck to hide the love bites.

I was so flattered I felt sick. "Yeah," I said, trying not to care.

"You know he's Lamar's ace boon coon. Lamar told Tyrone you're cool—for a white chick." She jabbed me with her elbow. I looked out the window at the small dark houses rolling by. "Lamar and I are back together for good this time," said Jasmine. "He gave me this opal ring." She thrust her left hand out to show me, and I saw a flash of milky white under the streetlight we'd just passed.

I understood then her sudden burst of generosity about Tyrone. Ring planted firmly on her finger, she gave me a conspiratorial wink. Tonight she could afford to share.

Call it guilt or mild yearning, the next day I made my way over to Angela's. She asked about the party in a deliberately offhand way. I described Tyrone. I made sure she understood this was a man with potential. For one thing, he was a senior, almost eighteen, and he attended *private* school. I described his hands moving over my back as we danced and the softness of his lips against my ear.

Angela dramatically threw her finger against her lips and hissed, "Shshshsh!" as if I had cursed in church. She rolled her eyes in the direction of her mother's bedroom.

"Your mother can't hear," I said, feeling myself rise tall above

Angela. I was becoming less and less grateful for the friendship she bestowed on me in stingy little segments.

"You're getting in with a rough crowd" was all Angela said. "Mama says Jasmine's fast."

What she really meant was that she hadn't been included, but I didn't see that then. Disgusted, I got up and left. Angela didn't bother to walk me to the end of her driveway as she always did. Outside, the heat worked its way up from the pavement and burned through the soles of my sandals. They were sandals Angela and I had found in the College Shoe Shoppe two years before. We'd each bought a pair, agreeing we wouldn't wear them without telling the other. Now mine were showing the effects of two summers' wear, and Angela had shoved hers to the back of the closet, forgotten.

Angela's house on East Jefferson was an easy mile and a half from mine. By making a right on Lincoln, I passed Mt. Zion Baptist and a horse farm, and then a number of square brick low-income units where children rode bicycles in the street and front yard clotheslines were always full of bed sheets.

Just beyond was Jasmine's block; the houses were even smaller and poorer. The narrow streets, like many of their residents, were named for U.S. presidents. On the sagging steps of a turquoise house, some older black girls from school hung out playing 45's on an old phonograph. The humidity was cut by the scratchy rhythm of one of the summer's hottest hits, "Express Yourself" by Charles Watts and the 103rd Street Rhythm Band. Maxine Watson, the homecoming queen, danced in denim cutoffs in the dirt yard. When she saw me, she raised one light brown hand in greeting, and I thrilled at the acknowledgment.

But it was short-lived as a bright-skinned girl named Chick snapped, "What'd you speak to *her* for?" Chick had sat sullenly across from me one semester in ninth-grade algebra class giving everyone the evil eye. If she didn't feel like answering the teacher's questions on a particular day, she'd stage-whisper, "Kiss my black ass, bitch," so that the whole class would snicker. Now Chick was expecting a baby by her college tutor. Evil old Chick who lived ruthlessly on a higher plane than the rest of us, above fear of reproach.

I crossed Main Street, which divided our town exactly in half. The air sweltered. On Professor Street I passed the statue of Horace Percival Huckleman, honored posthumously for leading a troop of black soldiers during the Civil War. My parents lived up on tree-lined Elm Street, our house nestled among all the other professors' families. The yards here were midwestern-ample and the old three-story homes sat back from the streets in comfortable superiority. The gray summer air was still, silent, oppressive. Here, people kept to themselves. No noisy barbecues, no lawn parties, no children running and shrieking through sprinklers.

Up ahead two shimmering figures made their way slowly toward me: Kimberly Hubbard and Marjorie Grosvenor, in culottes and poor-boy tees. They were my two mortal enemies on the other side of the dividing wall. In reality, they lived on my street, but I might as well have been invisible, living a parallel life, unnoticed.

Kimberly and Marjorie could walk by you as if you were a leaf on the sidewalk, flipping their long straight hair with a casual flick of the wrist. They had a secret language of gestures and words that I had never been able to master. It was a language of privilege and confidence, designed to exclude.

At the beginning of ninth grade they took it upon themselves to corner me briefly by my locker. "So, Tish," Marjorie said, her teeth a flash of white in her summer-brown face. "We were just wondering, are you still going to hang around with Angela Winters now that you're in high school?"

I didn't understand, and my ignorance tested their patience. Marjorie gave Kimberly a significant look. "Angela's nice," she explained to me, "but you need to think about what's best for you now. We think you ought to know, and this as a friendly warning, that a lot of people think you're spreading yourself too thin."

Now, passing me, Marjorie and Kimberly fused together into one girl. "Hello, Letitia," their shared voice said, forced. I felt no compulsion to answer. Instead, I squared my shoulders, taking my courage from Jasmine. I never glanced their way, never even gave the impression of having noticed them, blowing them from my mind as easily as if they were chalk dust.

Jasmine tried to get me hired at the College Restaurant where she worked, telling Bud Owens, the black owner, that I was sixteen. But when I showed up he shook his head and shooed me out, telling me I was a chance he couldn't afford to take. I waited outside, humiliated, until Jasmine went on break and we wandered over to the college art museum, finding relief in the cool interior.

We sauntered by Del Washington, the black security guard standing awkwardly over to one side, sweating inside his uniform. Del was in his late sixties; for years he had done odd jobs for families in my neighborhood, and adults and kids alike called him by his first name. Now I felt ashamed to know him.

Jasmine couldn't stand him and went on to prove it. "Don't you think it's weird," she asked me in a voluble tone, "that white people hire black people to guard white people's art that they copied from black people?"

She pulled me over to a small Picasso. "Now there's one white man made a whole career off of imitating Africans."

Del pretended not to hear Jasmine's words echoing off the cool walls. We strolled back past him into the next gallery. "Some people are so damn worried what white people think of them. You know, don't you, you can't be a healthy black person and please white folks at the same time. It's a sickness, it's what makes black people go crazy, and then white folks can't figure out why niggas act like fools."

Jasmine's shoulder brushed roughly against mine, her eyes focused into empty space ahead. "We've been trying to please y'all for a long time, but now enough is enough. You watch and see what happens in Hough and every other ghetto this summer when they burn again. The Revolution is here."

To our left, Del was turning a deep purple.

"I'm going to have to ask you to lower your voices," he said, "or leave the museum."

"I was about to leave anyway," snapped Jasmine and grabbed my hand. "Come on, girl, I'm about to choke in here."

Outside, she threw back her head and laughed aloud.

"What's wrong with Del?" I asked, torn. Del used to give me chewing gum when he was cutting the neighbors' lawn.

"He's a Tom, that's what's wrong. That man has kissed so much white ass I'm surprised his face is still black."

I felt sad then, for all of us—me, Jasmine, and Del.

"That's the difference between us," remarked Jasmine. "You're over there feelin' sorry for Del Washington. Well, he hates himself for being black. He's the most dangerous of all."

The summer dragged for me. Jasmine was busy with work and her college applications. She was applying for early admissions to Fisk, Howard, Morehouse, and Spelman. She laughed when Harvard wrote to her and asked her to apply. "Why do I want to be some place where they either flunk you out or bleach you out? I'm not going to be part of someone's nigga quota."

We were on Jasmine's front porch watching the rain and I was greasing her scalp. A streak of lightning startled us both. Thunder followed right behind. "The Temptations in A Mellow Mood" revolved on the turntable just inside the door.

A phone call had put Jasmine in a bitterly rotten mood. Someone had seen Lamar at Rocky's Roller Rink Monday night, and Cindy Pavelka had left in his car. The old wound was reopened. "Why can't white girls leave our men alone?" Jasmine fumed.

I yanked her head a little to the left and carefully separated the next section of hair with the teeth of the comb. I kept the parts even, creating little irrigation canals into which I smoothed fingertips of Royal Crown. Jasmine's scalp gleamed like hematite. I pulled the hair on either side of the part straight up into rows, like stalks of corn. Cradling her head in my lap, I used the comb rhythmically like a lullaby. Her shoulders rocked gently against my knee.

"Tish, I'll be honest, I've never loved a man the way I love Lamar, and he's breaking my damn heart!"

With her right hand she guided my comb to a spot I'd missed. Little white flakes of dandruff lodged in the teeth of the comb. "Come out with Chick and Benita and me tomorrow night." It was more a command than an invitation.

"Where?"

"The Boot Center," said Jasmine.

I felt mildly panicked. "You know I can't go."

"Oh, come on. Say you're spending the night."

I must have hit a soft spot in her scalp because her head

pulled a U-turn. The specks of amber in her eyes caught fire. "Watch it, I'm tender-headed."

"Well, don't mess up my lines." I tried to yank her head back into position, but she pulled away.

There was a long pause, marked only by the whirring of the fan from inside and the drumbeat of rain on the porch roof overhead. She reached her hand up to her scalp and felt where I'd left off. "You take too damn long." She stood up and paced. On one side of her head, where I'd been at work, her hair stood up in thick fist-shaped spikes. "I don't see why your parents think the Boot Center is so bad, except that it's full of *us,* a bunch of black boots. I bet if Kimberly and Marjorie were down there dancing to 'Turkey in the Straw' your parents wouldn't be scared to send you."

I ran my fingers down the greasy prongs of the comb.

"I'll try to come," I said, "but if my mother finds out . . ."

Jasmine bit her lower lip. "I'm telling you, if Cindy's there, I'm through with him!"

I felt the tension rise, along with the humidity and the smell of Jasmine's scalp oil on my fingers.

There was the unexpected sound of tires on gravel, and we both looked out to the road to see Lamar's Chevy pulling into the rain-soaked driveway. "Shoot!" said Jasmine. "Nigga knows he's in trouble." She grabbed the comb from me and began furiously to work her hair. "Tyrone's with him!"

My heart went heavy as lead as two figures splashed through the rain and up the steps. Jasmine kept her lips poked out sulkily when Lamar said, "How ya doin', baby?" I'd forgotten how tall Tyrone was, how good-looking. The combination terrified me.

"Mama and Daddy are down at their social club?" Lamar asked with a grin. "Thought we'd stop by."

Jasmine nodded. "I need to talk to you, Lamar. We can go

listen to records in the basement. Tish, grab that stack of 45's, would you, girl?"

She picked up the record player. Tyrone and Lamar both smelled of cologne. I followed them down the steps like a sleepwalker. Immediately "Ooooh, Baby, Baby" was on the turntable and Jasmine and Lamar were linked together, murmuring to each other. Obviously Lamar was denying whatever it was Jasmine accused him of. Convincing. Smooth. Jasmine was loosening up.

Tyrone reached for me and I felt myself melting against him, as he guided me slowly toward the furnace. The record finished and Lamar started it over again. I heard Jasmine say, "You're gonna wear that record thin as a dime," and I felt the vibrations of Tyrone's chuckle in his chest as he pulled me closer while Smokey moaned.

My first kiss happened there in Jasmine's basement with Tyrone, but the experience was disagreeable. The smelly old sewer pipe ran straight out of the floor at our feet, and so that moment was permanently framed in my memory by a rising, heavy, sour odor too awful to consider. But I was in love with Tyrone, my heart about ready to explode.

Later, after they'd left, Jasmine, who seemed to be in better spirits, asked me, "Tyrone say he'd call?"

I shook my head, still overwhelmed that just moments before a boy's mouth had been pressing against mine.

Jasmine sighed. "What's wrong with the Negro? You're my ace honky."

I hated her holding the other mirror to me like that. "Shut up," I said.

A shadow crossed Jasmine's face. "Maybe Tyrone thinks your father will shoot him through the phone."

"I keep telling you," I protested, "my parents don't care."

"Don't be so naive about your so-called liberal parents." Jasmine frowned.

"My parents marched in Selma," I said, uneasy.

"So, then why don't you ask Tyrone to come by and have dinner? Get to know your folks?"

She was mocking me so I didn't answer. I didn't know why.

"See what I mean?" said Jasmine smugly.

Anxiety marked my veins like medical ink. "You're wrong," I insisted.

"I'm more right than you realize. Your parents would lose their minds if they thought you'd gone cuckoo for cocoa puffs." She lit a Kool Long and French-inhaled so that the smoke looped back through her nostrils.

We went upstairs where she heated up the iron to press her uniform for work. Overhead, on hangers, the dashikis we'd sewn hung like half-people from the light fixture. Jasmine's was black and yellow and red; mine was blue and white and green.

She mumbled to the wall, as if enjoying a private joke, "I must be outa my mind making a dashiki for a white girl." She winked at me as steam rose from the iron. "I'll have it ready for tomorrow night. You're comin'."

Jasmine picked me up on her way home from work. She was still in her waitress uniform. My mother walked me out to the black Ninety-eight. She pointedly asked Jasmine if we were going out anywhere or if she could reach me at the Bonners'.

"We might go get Dairy Queen." Jasmine was sly!

"About what time would that be?" asked my mother.

Jasmine looked coyly at her watch. "Oh, maybe around ten."

My mother's eyes narrowed. "Jasmine," she said with maternal clairvoyance, "you know Letitia is barely fifteen years old."

"What are you trying to tell me?" asked Jasmine.

But my mother had turned abruptly and walked back toward the house.

At Jasmine's I changed into a short skirt and the dashiki. Now I was edgy as we drove past the Baptist church to pick up the others. I imagined coming face-to-face with my mother's car at every corner.

"Will you just relax?" said Jasmine. "I'm the one who should be nervous, what with Daddy being so fussy about his damn stupid car and all. One tiny scratch and I'm dead."

Mr. Bonner'd said if we weren't home by midnight he'd send the sheriff out after us.

"Your Ninety-eight ain't no Cinderella," Jasmine had muttered.

"Yeah, and you ain't meeting no Prince Charming neither," Mr. Bonner reminded her meaningfully. It was no secret he wasn't fond of Lamar, whom he called a "scalawag."

Jasmine was wearing blue jeans, her dashiki belted at the waist. On her long slender feet were slave sandals, the latest rage. I instantly regretted my short skirt, ashamed of my knobby knees. We split up a bunch of her metal bracelets, and crisscrossed our arms like gypsies.

Maxine and Jasmine made small talk up front. I envied their big afro silhouettes, blocking my view through the windshield. I was stuffed in back with Benita and sourpuss Chick. Benita commented sweetly on my hair. "You sure have some pretty curls. They natural?"

I thought how long I'd futilely envied the straight-arrow cuts of the white girls, every hair in place. Jasmine had picked out my hair, and now it bloomed around my head.

Chick scoffed from the corner by the window. "It just looks like some of that old flyaway shit to me."

As I leaned forward to check my eyeliner in the rearview mirror my leg accidentally brushed Chick's. She jumped back as if I had a disease. "Please keep your body parts to yourself," she said and crossed her eyes at me.

You could hear the Boot Center before you could see it. James Brown blared from speakers lodged in the open window frames upstairs. Shadows of dancers rose long against the walls.

"Ooooh, my song," said Chick and jumped out, full of baby, and headed up the stairs. "SAY IT LOUD!" she bellowed along with James Brown, "I'm black and I'm proud!"

Jasmine came up beside me and dug her fingernails into my arm. She hissed in my ear, "You better pray Lamar's at work tonight."

"Don't worry," I said, but I had serious doubts.

We tromped up the outside stairs, just as if we were a club. Girls accustomed to one another, who hung together. The music swelled from the packed dance floor. Across the room, through blinking lights, I recognized the black vice principal from our school, Mr. Foster, who'd been called down to chaperone after some fights between our town and Elyria. Everyone knew he Tommed. From what I'd seen, Mr. Foster faked it on both sides, playing "brother this" and "brother that" when it suited him.

The air was so close I immediately broke into a sweat. My head felt thick. Maxine yelled over at Jasmine, "See what happens when you get a bunch of niggas together?" She wiped drops of perspiration from her forehead with the back of her hand as proof.

Jasmine pulled me through the crowd like a needle dragging thread. We were headed toward Tyrone, standing alone in the corner. Jasmine thrust me at him in a way that made me suspect she had planned this all along. "Here's Tish," she said as if delivering a package.

James Brown over, Nancy Wilson began a lugubrious "You Better Face It, Girl, It's Over." The moody bass pulsed in my veins. "I didn't come here to hug the wall all night. Would you like to dance?" asked Tyrone, the perfect gentleman. He took my hand in his. My fingers went cold.

I looked around for Jasmine, but she was nowhere in sight. Tyrone drew me close. "You feel good," he said. I went sleepy inside. Out of relief, I rested my head on his shoulder. His arms tightened around me and I closed my eyes. "Follow me," he whispered in my ear. "Keep the beat." An anonymous hand in the dark yanked my hair down to the roots, checking to see if I was or wasn't, but I played it off, a mistake, a miscalculation. I felt the sharp pain at the back of my head eased by the hypnotic movements of Tyrone against me.

But the trouble began before I'd fully regained my senses. The record was still playing when Tyrone gently nudged me and pulled away. I misunderstood at first. Then I looked in the direction in which he was staring. Just as Jasmine had predicted, just as she had known, Lamar strolled into the Boot Center with a bigger-than-life Cindy Pavelka. He was wearing a black fishnet shirt, a cap, and the gold medallion map of Africa.

Lamar's car keys dangled from his hand. He was trying his best to merge with the dancers, but Cindy hung close. When his eyes caught Jasmine's, his face registered first shock, then mild sheepishness. They stared at each other, moving toward that inevitable moment they'd created together. Tyrone murmured, "Uh-oh, my boy's in deep trouble," and gripped my hand tightly, as if to console us both.

Heads turned from all directions. Lamar kept moving. He gave the fist to several of his cronies, a forced smile across his face. Cindy wore a defiant look, like someone who'd won something. And the shameful thing was she hadn't even bothered to comb her hair, as if she'd just climbed out of his back seat.

Tyrone left me for Lamar. They clasped hands, grabbed wrists, then stacked their fists in the air, desperate to seem casual.

I found my way to Jasmine's side. Her features had all moved together in a mask of horrendous rage. She had known, hadn't she, all along, that this was why we had come tonight? Maxine and Benita and Chick stood over to one side, observing. Jasmine walked slowly toward Cindy. "You stupid white bitch." Her voice rose over the music. Dancing couples slowly parted, as more and more people caught on to what was happening.

Cindy's smile was forced and impudent. She heaved a bored sigh and put her hand on her hip, challenging. But the heavy pulse in her throat gave her away. "Get out of my face, Jasmine," she said.

Chick and Maxine and Benita closed around her like a fence. A murmur of "Fight, fight" rumbled through the Boot Center.

"Jasmine . . ." Lamar reached out. He tried to stop her, but Jasmine shot him a bitter look and struck his hand away.

"Don't you touch me!" she said and advanced toward Cindy. "Are you out of your mind?" A little push and Cindy looked startled. "Don't you know Lamar belongs to me?"

I squeezed in between Maxine and Chick. Cindy glanced nervously at me, then shifted all her weight to one side. "Look, don't you touch me again," she shot back helplessly. "It's none of your business what I do." She was losing her nerve.

Then Jasmine burst into tears, accepting defeat. I couldn't stand it. Before I knew what I was doing, I had drawn up my fist and pulled my elbow back as if stringing an arrow in a bow. At the moment my fist touched Cindy, the needle scratched like a scream across the 45. The music stopped cold.

Cindy stumbled back a couple of steps, her mouth drawing downwards. She looked back in hatred. Next to me, Jasmine grabbed a fistful of Cindy's hair and cried out like a wounded creature, "Leave Lamar alone, you honky bitch, leave him alone."

I started for Cindy again and would have shoved her against the wall, except that someone took hold of my shoulder, yanking me backwards.

"Have you lost your mind, girl?" It was Chick, her eyes dark and startled in her yellow face. "How can you?" she asked me. "How can you do that? This ain't none of your business."

Someone shoved me hard from behind. I heard murmurs of contempt. Mr. Foster broke through the crowd yelling, "Break it up, break it up. Disperse. Let's go." People began pointing, accusing. In the confusion, I turned to see Jasmine disappearing out the back and down the fire-escape steps, her body bent in the shape of heartache. Lamar threw down his car keys in disgust, as if inviting anyone to drive off in his Chevy. Mr. Foster's eyes smoldered as they came to rest on me. "Hey, you!" he said, starting toward me. There was nothing left to do except push past Cindy, the only person blocking my way, and get down those stairs as fast as I could to the street below where I wasn't sure what to do next.

SUMMER IN DETROIT

"Where's the crazy ole white lady?"

Franklin was out of breath. The screen door to his grandmother's sunny yellow kitchen snapped shut with the ferocity of a firecracker. As a kid, he'd taken a number of switchings over that door. Grandma Freida, poised in fury, worn out from the kids running in and out all day, bang, bang, bang, tracking in the dust, the heat, the overripe scent of their heavy play, and hollering at the top of their lungs.

"You do that one more time . . ." Freida would warn, and the kids would plead ignorance: "But the door got away from me . . . ," "But I *held* it . . ." or, worse, "But I didn't mean to . . ." And then the sting of the flyswatter or the spatula, whatever Freida had handy, joining up with the backs of their dark legs. Freida's aim was impeccable.

It was pointless to protest; back talk earned only another swat. Freida had warned them all, over and over. Hadn't she lined them up and explained the spring mechanism of the screen door, pointing out exactly where to catch the metal with your hand so it would close like a whisper behind you? And hadn't they all nodded eagerly and agreed that they understood, that they'd be more careful? But hours later, worn out from chasing one another through the humid twilight alleys of Detroit, thinking only of making it home before nightfall, one of them would forget. Snap! Bang! The deed was done. Freida was all over them, raging about peace and quiet, calling them hooligans, swatting them all the way upstairs to the bathtub where she dumped in enough Ivory Snow to make your skin peel off, and then tossed them in, one by one, as if they'd been dirty socks.

Now Franklin stood huffing and perspiring from his run. He'd underestimated the warmness of this particular summer day, and he bent over to ease the knot in his chest. Then he stood up again and tore a paper towel from the rack above the sink and wiped the sweat from his head. He was running out of hair. He traced his ever-broadening scalp with the paper towel, then mopped the back of his neck.

"Shshshsh! You make too much noise!" For a moment, Franklin thought, it could have been Freida herself, her red hair streaming down around her shoulders. But it was Dawn, in a dark housedress and red espadrilles, her voice shot through with annoyance. She was standing in the darkened doorway of the room that used to be what Freida called the parlor, where she kept her sewing machine and a sofa and, as Franklin was growing up, a black and white television.

Now it was where they kept Freida, because it gave her easy access to the bathroom and there were no stairs to climb. Because times had changed and Freida was as fragile as the misty white heads of the dandelions that now ranged with a will through her back yard.

"Freida sleep?" he whispered to the dark shadow in the doorway.

"Yeah, if certain loud folks don't wake her up!" Dawn stepped out into the light of the hallway toward Franklin. "What are you doing here?"

"I came by to see my grandmother."

"Hmmmmm" was all Dawn had to say. She made a deliberately wide arc around Franklin to get to the refrigerator for a cold drink.

The sight of her stirred something in him. He couldn't resist, what with Dawn still so long and tall and pretty. He lunged playfully at her and tried for a kiss on her cheek.

"Don't start kissin on me." Dawn pushed him away. "God, you're just like a child. And your timing's lousy. I just got Freida to sleep and you come in here slamming the door. Some things never change."

She popped the tab on a soda. Franklin went to the sink and ran some cold water on his face. Then he looked out the window where the garden used to be. Silence reigned. Butterfly-wing silence, so quiet you could imagine the creatures' wings beating as they alighted on flower petals. At least that's what Freida had told Franklin so long ago, when they used to stroll in that once-flourishing garden, there in the old part of Detroit, where grasshoppers sizzled in the white heat of summer in the long, tall grass growing along her fence. And always, always, the butterflies fanning the air like so many orange, brown, and yellow angels. They vibrated over the brilliant flowers, touched down still trembling, then skipped lightly from cosmos to zinnias, the sun shimmering on their wings. As a child, Franklin feared the over-brilliant flowers might devour them. He had held his breath, believing the spell could be broken by the merest of exhalations. His heart swelled at the sight of swallowtails, the size of tiny birds, folded as delicately as origami, moving purposefully through the air like swimmers in water. And his grandmother's hand, tightening on his with promise, would lead him to the arbor where she would pluck him sweet, black scuppernong grapes the size of chestnuts.

"Mama said Freida was having a bad day."

"Every day's a bad day, far as I'm concerned. She's so weak now," said Dawn, sipping her cold drink and staring almost irritably at Franklin. "Bonnie and them hardly ever come by anymore, and your mother won't visit after dark."

Franklin's mother Jessie lived over in Ann Arbor and refused to drive into Detroit unless she absolutely had to. She made no bones about it. "Detroit's gone crazy," she said. "Folks'll kill you for breathing the wrong way." A friend of hers had been carjacked outside a food mart. Jessie wouldn't leave her car parked on the street and she locked her steering wheel with something that resembled a lethal weapon. She carried Mace in her purse and always wore running shoes for quick escapes. When Franklin suggested she was letting her fear get out of control, she silenced him with a look. "And don't you start talking black power to me again," she said bitterly. "I've watched us killin each other off for years, just finishin the job white folks started. People so crazy nowadays they wouldn't think twice about knocking off a sixty-eight-year-old black woman just minding her business."

It was futile to argue. Franklin had tried pointing out that statistically she ran more chance of being killed in an auto accident than shot by a drug dealer.

"You can talk statistics til you turn purple in the face," Jessie said, "but my point is, what if *I'm* the one?"

Franklin gave up.

"Freida has a lot of bad days," Dawn went on. "*And* she's talking all crazy again. She forgets what year it is, who I am . . . she still calls me 'Franklin's wife.' " She took another slow slip of soda.

"That must cut you to the quick," said Franklin.

Dawn didn't find it amusing. "I think it's the heat. It parboils her mind."

"Freida, Freida, Freida," murmured Franklin. "Sweet, sweet old Freida." He stretched his arms up over his head so that the black mesh tank top he wore followed upwards and exposed the tight stomach muscles he worked so hard to maintain. Another stretch and the top inched up to his broad chest.

Dawn gave his bared flesh a quick once-over. Not a flicker

of curiosity or interest, not even disapproval. She had a cool eye. "I see you're staying fit," she remarked wryly.

"Yeah, well," said Franklin, "not too bad for forty."

"Always wanting to rub it in, aren't you?" She filled a jelly glass with cold water and handed it to him.

"You look great for forty-se- . . ."

"Shsh! You don't need to say it." Dawn was laughing in spite of herself at her own vanity. "But you can't resist, can you?"

For a moment Franklin thought they might be friends, and he started to say something that would tie them together. But he caught the warning in Dawn's eyes, and he knew better. He turned to look out the window again.

He'd run the whole seven miles from his apartment, close to the junior high where he coached track and taught one class euphemistically called "Family Life." What it meant is that he, Franklin Breedlove, held forth to twelve-year-olds on the mysteries of human existence, trying to distill the complexities of passion and hormones into that weak solution known as testable fact, something you could quantify with *a, b,* and *c* answers and get a passing grade on.

He'd paired up girls and boys in his class and entrusted each "couple" with an egg, which was to be cared for as cautiously as if it were an infant. "Remember now," he said, "you can't just go dashing off without arranging for someone to watch your egg. And you can't forget it and leave it somewhere. You're responsible for keeping this egg intact until the end of the week. You can trade off caring for it, but as parents one of you has to be in charge at all times. Keep track in your notebooks how you divide your duties."

A smashed egg signaled failure. The kids took the assignment seriously. Some wrapped their eggs in cotton batting and carried them in slings around their necks. Some cradled the egg in their hands, moving cautiously from class to class as if they wore glass shoes. Each egg was carefully marked by Franklin so there could be no last-minute substitutions. When the week came to an end, he interviewed the egg couples one by one, helping them assess what was now being called "projected parenting skills."

"Hey, Breedlove, how can you teach us Family Life when you don't even have a family or a life?" wisecracked one kid named Rodney. A smart boy, growing up in the projects, where each day he was tempted by what everyone loosely called "the streets." He'd taken to hanging around a bad bunch, but so far showed up at school like clockwork. Franklin adored him, occasionally took him to see the Tigers and out for pizza.

"You trying to save me or what?" Rodney asked him once.

Franklin was so touched he came as close to tears as he had in years. "Naw, man," he said softly. "I can't save you. You have to save yourself."

Franklin had also resisted the urge to whack him. The kid didn't realize what he was saying, or maybe he did. He had Franklin figured out: a lonely man, without a family, and time on his hands to be worried about someone else's kid.

Now Franklin accepted another paper towel from Dawn and wiped his arms and legs. His shorts and the top he wore, even his own muscle and sinew, hung on him like weights, every inch soaked with perspiration. He badly wanted out of his clothes. But he knew, clothes or no clothes, his own skin would still be there to hug him like a tourniquet. There was no escaping. Not when he struggled so hard inside to free himself of all the years that had irrevocably changed him. But you can't untangle yourself so easily. Each choice chooses the next. Franklin kept moving faster, ducking and dodging, trusting that those thin cables holding up his life wouldn't finally snap and shackle him.

"I've got to go to the center," said Dawn. "I'm in charge of the music hour this afternoon. Can you stay and keep an ear out for Freida?"

Franklin leaned over and stuffed the crumpled paper towel into the waste can. Coming back up, he had an attack of vertigo and breathed in slowly to steady himself. "Sure," he said, though he hadn't planned to stay.

Dawn wasn't even mildly touched. She leaned against the counter, long-limbed and angular, studying him with her fawn-like eyes. Her knee-length cotton housedress had big white buttons all the way down the front. The sunlight through the window fell on her face harshly, made her look tired. Her brown skin took on a hard, metallic cast. After all these years, she was back to straightening her hair. It had grown out to almost shoulder length. She wore it pinned in a clip, a small wisp of ponytail at her neck.

"You know," said Dawn, "Freida's gonna die soon and it will be the end of an era."

Franklin bent down into a runner's stretch and felt tension shoot like electricity out the heel of his foot. "Don't be morbid," he said. He was breathing into his stretch. The toe of his fluorescent green and white running shoe was just in view. "That ole woman's got more life in her than you and me put together."

"Hey you just don't want to face the facts," said Dawn.

Franklin came up for air. The sweat broke out on his face in little drops. "Okay, okay, lighten up on me." He pulled himself up to his full height. His right hand hovered over the back of his head and then he stretched one long finger down through his thinning hair and scratched his scalp. "So I've been busy. Tell me what's going on."

"I just told you." Dawn moved around him and to the other side of the kitchen. "She's old and she's dying."

Franklin looked toward the darkened room where Freida now stayed full-time. He hesitated, could already smell the rankness of old age in the air. Dawn was right. He'd let too much time pass again. He knew he should come more often, but he just didn't, mostly because he couldn't stand the way Dawn judged him, always making her sly comments about what he was and wasn't doing. Or maybe it was Freida herself, prying and wanting to know about this and that, and was there a woman in his life.

He always imagined Freida to be partial to Dawn's side of things. He could picture the two of them shaking their heads over him still. "Out of sight, out of mind," he'd heard Dawn remark with such finality to Freida and Jessie one Thanksgiving, he knew without question that he had been the subject of that comment.

"Should I go in and say hi?"

Dawn shrugged. "Go on."

He wandered over the threshold. The drawn shades kept the room cool. As a little boy, Franklin had slept here in a four-poster bed wrestling against his younger sister Bonnie and his brothers for the covers, for space, for the right to stretch out his long body. There were all those times Freida kept them when Jessie and Franklin's father Eddie were just too tired, too busy, and too poor.

Old Freida and Grandpa Henry. An unlikely pair. Henry, dark and quiet, easy-natured, and soft on the grandkids; Freida, big and overbearing, an irrepressible talker, full of opinions on everything, her pale freckled face alive under her gardening hat, her strong arms hoeing peas and corn and collard greens, as if she'd always worked under a strong summer Michigan sun rather than dark German skies.

Franklin eased his way softly toward her, the rubber soles of his shoes making light sucking sounds on the floor. Poking out over the bed sheet was her shrunken face, the wisps of red hair gone white, the shriveled hands clutched at her sides. Her eyes were closed in sleep . . . or, thought Franklin with a start, in death.

"Freida," he murmured involuntarily.

The eyes flew open. Opaque blue, shimmering like water. All those years in the sun had wrinkled her badly. She had never darkened, just reddened slowly, her skin turning to the texture of tree bark.

She stared past him. Today she looked tiny and helpless.

"I didn't mean to wake you, Freida."

"You didn't" came the gravelly voice. "I was just fakin it." She paused. "Dawn was in here earlier singin like to burst my eardrums and I couldn't stand it, so I just closed up my eyes and pretended I was asleep. Or maybe she thought I was dead. I think that's what you all think, that I'm layin up here dead, and now you think you can help yourselves to my stuff. All those colored people out there burning everything down. Tryin to take my stuff."

Hers was a funny accent, part German mixed with English she'd learned primarily from rural black people in southern Ohio where they'd first lived when Henry brought her back with him.

"Naw, naw, come on now, Freida," said Franklin, settling himself on the edge of her bed. His huge frame dwarfed hers. He lifted one of her tiny gray hands into his and gently stroked it. "I was thinking of baking you a sweet potato pie, but it's too hot to turn on the oven."

"Boy, you ain't about to bake me no pie!" said Freida.

"That's right, it's too hot," Franklin repeated.

"Hell's hotter," murmured Freida. "But the flames don't touch the righteous."

Freida had never believed in God, though Grandpa Henry

had been a devout Baptist, going to church regularly on Sundays while Freida stayed home and baked heavy German dishes with gravy and sauces. This was Dawn's influence. Dawn with all her praying and singing: oh, the zeal of the recently converted! Franklin thought. She had told him once that finding Jesus was like growing a whole new skin. She described with a radiant light in her eye exactly how the smothering of the world had been pulled off her (those were her exact words) and she could breathe again, reborn into new flesh. How time had changed her, had changed them all. She had found an outlet for her grief, had finally put the past to rest. A crutch, Franklin told her. A drug to mask the pain.

"But you could too," she said. "Jesus will be a balm for your troubled soul. You can't keep going over the past in your mind. You have to move on with the spirit of Christ to guide you."

Franklin told her he didn't want to hear it.

"Dawn's upset with you," remarked Freida, with a sly lowering of her eyelids. "Just a no-good nigger."

Franklin was shocked, even though he should be used to it by now. Freida wasn't Freida anymore. They all tried to make light of it; after all, it was just words pouring out of her mouth, wasn't it, the endless babble of a senile old woman?

"Isn't Dawn *your* wife?" asked Freida, her face sinking into a shadow.

"She was," said Franklin, though legally it was still true. Even after ten years, he and Dawn hadn't bothered to finalize anything; why, he didn't know. Perhaps because he'd never really found another woman, and Dawn had found only Jesus.

"Tell me again who you are," said Freida, peering at him. Suspicion: she didn't trust herself to recognize. One minute she was lucid and full of memories, the next her thoughts scrambled, and the ordinary had gone foreign. She made it sound as if her memory lapse was his fault.

"I'm Franklin, Freida—Jessie's oldest boy."

"Well, you don't look like any boy to me," said Freida. Then, to herself, she muttered, "Black niggers burning down my house and garden."

Franklin swallowed hard. Jessie and Dawn claimed Freida didn't know any better, but he wasn't so sure the old witch wasn't taking advantage and getting back at everybody after all these years for the hardship of having been disinherited when she married Henry, and then being subjected to intense scrutiny by Henry's family, straddling for years the fine line between rejection and acceptance. "Henry's *white* wife," they used to call her. "Brought her back from Germany, couldn't find one of his own kind." Finally, after her fifth child with Henry, who was Franklin's mother Jessie, Freida became, well, just Freida, adored and honored, sharp-tongued and irascible. "I've graduated to matriarch," she jokingly told the family at her seventieth birthday party.

Franklin looked away from the old woman. He released her hand and shifted his weight. The bed exhaled slightly as he rose up. "Freida, I sure liked you a lot better when you weren't like this," he said.

"I don't know about all that," said Freida vaguely. "I don't know." She raised one hand. "You can still smell the smoke. I've been coughin all morning. Look out the window there, you can see them all, tearin up the streets like a bunch of wild animals. There've been sirens and police out there, and they say people have been shot. Dead people out there. Burnin down their own homes in this heat. Thank God Henry isn't alive."

Dawn appeared in the doorway, hand on her hip again. "Franklin, why'd you go and get her all worked up?" She let out a sigh of annoyance.

"Well, now, isn't that nice," said Freida, all smiles, as Dawn crossed the room and plumped her pillow. "Isn't that real nice of you."

"Yes it is, considering what a crab you are most of the time," Dawn countered cheerfully, moving the light blanket off of Freida. "Franklin, hand me that comb. I'm going to get her hair out of her face."

Franklin did as he was asked.

Dawn took a place next to Freida's head. She unpinned the hair and began slowly to comb. In the semidarkness she glowed like a soft brown light, the way she had when Franklin first married her, when he thought he was the luckiest man in the world.

"You're a saint," he said to Dawn.

"Don't you know it."

Franklin smiled in spite of himself. Even after everything, he still liked Dawn a lot. She was a good soul, generally speaking. And she took good care of Freida. She was family, more than she'd ever been a wife, Dawn was, as much or more of family than he, still hanging around his sister Bonnie's house three blocks over, playing whist and Scrabble, taking the nieces and nephews for the weekends, showing up at birthdays and Christmas with homemade casseroles.

Dawn carefully tugged the snags out of Freida's hair and pinned it back up on top of her head.

"How can you stand the way she talks?" Franklin asked.

Dawn shrugged. "You mean the 'N' word?"

Franklin suspected she was poking fun at him. "Yeah, you're damn right I mean the 'N' word. I can't believe it's coming out of her mouth."

"She doesn't mean it," Dawn said gently.

Freida perked up. "I'm not crazy, you know."

"See what I mean?" said Franklin. "She knows what she's saying . . ."

"She's remembering the riots," said Dawn softly. "What else? It gets hot and her memory gets confused and gets in a rut and she can't get out of it. She loses track of time, that's all. Last week she thought she was a girl in Germany again. Today she thinks it's the riots."

At that reference, Franklin felt the old pain ignite in him. "How can you stay here?" he asked. "You know, after everything."

Dawn looked up sharply. "This is my home."

Franklin got up and went back into the kitchen. He could hear Freida talking to herself. It was more of the same; she was trespassing on dangerous territory. Dawn's voice was consoling. Franklin banged his fist on the kitchen counter and looked out the window at the ragtag garden. Where flowers had once bloomed, weeds reigned. The old arbor had fallen apart; the crumbling fence looked like another weed itself. He had a momentary thought that he could bring his tools over and set about revitalizing the place, plant seeds, till soil, but for what? Soon Freida would be gone, he and Dawn and Jessie would split the sale of the house, and Dawn would probably move to wherever her daughter Julie wound up in for graduate school.

Dawn emerged from Freida's room. "Why are you taking this all so personally?" she asked. "Have a little Christian love, Franklin."

"Christian love my ass! Those words come from somewhere. It's like she's stockpiled them all these years."

"She's almost ninety years old," Dawn told him. "Try to understand."

"What is she, senile?"

Dawn shrugged. "Franklin, even your own mother doesn't hold it against her."

Franklin gritted his teeth, feeling his cheek muscles tense and untense. "When did you turn so good?" he asked.

"I've always been good. You just didn't notice. I've got to get going. See you in an hour or so."

It occurred to him that Dawn had not bothered to ask if he had anywhere to be this afternoon. She was just assuming he didn't. He could call Beverly later; plans hadn't been definite, and he was wearying of her anyway. Beverly was only for the moment; before her, there'd been Sabra, then Linda, Marquita, and Debra, a patchwork of women from beige to bronze, none of them ever managing to get it right. And he, Franklin, having to face himself the morning after, disappointed at the ease of trading one warm body for another, but pretending that was freedom.

For a moment he imagined that he and Dawn were still living together in Freida's house, that any moment she would emerge from the kitchen with the scent of red beans and rice trailing behind her, and she would be brushing against him with her long limbs, and her dark wild braids would slap across his cheek as she bent to pull him against her. She always smelled clean, her skin giving off a strong scent of something close to pine.

Franklin closed his eyes and listened for her breathing, the soft whispers against his neck that assured him of his rightful place in the world. "I believe in you, Franklin," she had said to him one night shortly after they were married. And he had thought that was all it took.

He turned and watched Dawn walk away, taking in the backs of her legs, or what he could see of them, still firm under her cotton dress. He longed for that familiarity, now out of reach and impossible.

II

Franklin sat on the screen porch with a glass of sun tea and thought of those early years when he and Dawn struggled on a shoestring in their falling-down gray shingle house, just three blocks from Freida's, where they slept on mats on the floor and gave more potlucks for causes than a hen has feathers. Their friends from those years, dashikied and afroed, their collective rage spiraling toward the Revolution, all culminating in one fateful summer, had over the years softened. They now followed careers around the country: attorneys, doctors, teachers, business people, one minister, and two jailbirds. Before the smoke had cleared, they'd all deserted the heart of the city, apologetic but firm in their resolve to give their children better lives. Yes, as soon as the opportunity presented itself, they opted for private schools and suburbs and what Franklin laughingly called "Maul Land." Holidays, Franklin was amazed by the arrival of their cozy family snapshots: kneeling children, dogs, sectional furniture, fireside hearths, nose rings and African trade beads replaced by modest button earrings and pearls, little newsy updates like "Teddy was made partner last year," or "Kwasi is president of his senior class."

The only one with any integrity left from the old days was Ollie, teaching poli-sci over at Wayne State, still riveting the next generation of students with his invocations of the times, the heat, the anger, the history that must never be forgotten. He scheduled walking tours every semester, and dragged his flock out there, black and white alike, poised over their notepads and pencils, moving awkwardly like elderly tourists on a nature walk through a bird sanctuary. Franklin had gone once and was struck that day by the irony that HONKY KILLS scribbled on the walls had simply been replaced by CRACK KILLS.

"Same dog, different collar," Ollie had mused to his students, most of whom didn't understand and might as well have been on an archeological dig after dinosaur bones.

Franklin skimmed through a magazine lying on the table in

front of him. He was restless, uncertain. He read an article about sailboating on Lake Erie. The article claimed that more people sailed in the Cleveland area than in sunny San Diego. A woman he'd once known, Angela, was from Cleveland, and now she worked in administration at the museum. At the last minute Franklin had changed his mind about her, counting on that deep feeling in his gut to keep him safe from entanglements.

"You're stuck in the past," Angela had told him, not unkindly. "Things change but you don't."

A year later she phoned and announced she was three months pregnant and marrying someone named Cedric. Most likely someone more progressive, Franklin thought bitterly, someone with a huge bank account and a Mercedes. This was pure speculation on his part, but it made him feel better. Cedric be damned! Franklin didn't go out all that weekend. Instead he sat in his living room watching old reruns: *I Spy, Bonanza,* the whole lot, with a vengeance.

III

It had been years since Franklin had been alone in his grandmother's house. With Dawn there, the place was usually overrun with relatives, kids mostly, nieces and nephews, people dropping by, church friends and neighbors, and Dawn's daughter Julie home from college with some of her friends. Franklin got up and went to look in on Freida. She was snoring.

He walked back down the hall to the living room where Dawn's piano took up one whole wall. On the mantel above the fireplace were framed photos of Freida and Henry at their wedding: young and expectant. Freida wore white lace and a veil; Henry, a dark suit. His hair was parted on one side and pressed and greased into submission. His ears were too big, her nose too pointed. There was the photo of their first house outside of Toledo, Henry's first car, Franklin's mother as a little girl with her brothers and sisters, the house before the screen porch was added, then Franklin and Bonnie and the boys as children posed stiffly on the front steps, dressed for Sunday. Jessie had them all confirmed Catholic, why, Franklin never really knew. Off in the corner was a snapshot of Franklin and Dawn that brought a smile to Franklin's lips: what Jessie had called their "African phase," when Dawn and Franklin had briefly joined the Black Muslims. Dawn wore a print head wrap, and Franklin's head was shorn.

The past always made him uneasy. He had a sudden urge to look around upstairs. He wanted to see what all had changed. Quietly he mounted the steps. Dawn still slept in the first room to the right. He walked past, and down to the end of the narrow hallway where the door to Dawn's daughter Julie's room stood partially open. Franklin peeked inside. It was pretty much as he'd remembered. An empty suitcase lay open on the floor. It had been several months, he knew, since Julie had been home from college, and the room had a slightly musty, unaired feeling to it. He closed the door. To his left were the narrow, steep stairs that led to the attic. In the summer, it was like a steambath up there. Franklin recalled the way the squirrels ran through, their scrambling claws as noisy as hail overhead. He pulled the attic door open and stared up the steps.

Dust motes danced before his eyes on a shaft of afternoon sunlight from the window at the top of the stairs. He imagined the vague figures of a small boy and a girl standing above, and he pictured himself and Dawn playing up there together as children in the sweltering heat, although that never could have happened. It was some other girl, a neighbor girl named

Chloe who moved away shortly after he'd kissed her, and the two events had always stayed linked in his mind.

He closed the attic door and roamed back down the hallway. A fist of apprehension tightened in his stomach. With the tense purpose of a trespasser, he moved into Dawn's bedroom and stood squarely in the center of the floor. The room was neat as a pin, but that came as no surprise. The quilt on the bed was smoothed tight, the surfaces of the furniture carefully dusted. He recognized her old dressing table, from their days together, where she would sit and painstakingly outline her eyes in kohl and pick out her giant afro with a cheesecutter. When he first met her she was in her mid-twenties—he was nineteen—and she wore her hair in a tall shellacked missile on top of her head. A year later she took the straightener out of her hair, grew an unruly natural, and donned army fatigues and black body suits.

Franklin parted the lace curtains at the window and stared down into the street. Below him was the slowly deteriorating neighborhood that had never been able to recover, growing more and more run-down as the city deserted its own soul. Sidewalks were broken, yards were overgrown with weeds, porches sagged, and houses were badly in need of paint. An old Chevy sat on blocks in the middle of what used to be the lawn of the brown house on the corner. There is a particular odor to despair; Franklin breathed that in, wondering just how far it extended. These streets had once burned and smoked, but the phoenix never rose from the ashes. Instead, he thought ruefully, it lay on its back, wings broken, claws stretched hopelessly upwards.

Across the street a family of poor whites, looking as if they'd just arrived from the mountains of West Virginia, crowded on the front stoop. Three fat teenage girls each held a round-faced infant. In front of the boarded-up storefront on the corner a group of young black men stood drinking something from a brown paper bag they passed around. There were no more neighborhood stores, just one Arab-run place two blocks over where you paid twice as much for a carton of milk as you would at a grocery. Dawn refused to go there, said she couldn't afford it. A brown-skinned woman strolled by in skin-tight pants and a short tank top. She was barefoot, and was hauling a toddler by his hand. As she passed, the men stopped drinking long enough to whistle. One stretched out his arm as if he were going to touch her. Franklin realized the woman couldn't have been more than fifteen. She yanked the child against her and snapped sharply at the men. They hooted loudly and stared after her.

Several children roared down the street on bicycles and skateboards. There was a toughness to them that Franklin couldn't remember himself having had as a child. He wondered how they had managed to make it this far in their short lives, and how much farther they would make it. His throat thickened. He turned away from the window, knowing what he was about to do.

He went straight to Dawn's closet and pulled open the door. Her clothes hung neatly on hangers. Most of them were new things he didn't recognize. She still kept her shoes packed in their original boxes, stacked one on top of another. On the top shelf were several more boxes, one which contained a wide-brimmed hat she had loved years ago but no longer had reason to wear. Franklin inhaled slowly and breathed in Dawn's familiar scent. Though he knew he had no business doing what he did, he ran his hand across the top shelf, feeling for the shoebox he knew she must still keep. She had promised, hadn't she? She had said she would safeguard it, he hadn't wanted to. What he hadn't told her was that he didn't trust himself with it.

The box wasn't on the shelf as he'd expected. He bent down then, his knees cracking, and explored the floor of the closet, taking care not to let his hands brush against Dawn's dresses. In a moment he found what he was looking for: a blue canvas duffel bag slouched in the corner. He pulled it out into the light. Inside was the small shoebox, bound loosely with old string and taped lightly along the sides. Over the years the tape had yellowed and cracked around the edges. He lifted the box out and set it cautiously on Dawn's bed. An ordinary child's shoebox, with the words "P.F. Flyers" in red written on the side. The box had once contained brand new sneakers that belonged to their son Phillip. Franklin could remember even now how he and Dawn had fussed at each other over buying those sneakers. Dawn thought they cost too much. He had insisted. He pulled off the string and carefully pried back the tabs of yellowed tape. The sound of his own breathing filled the room. Sweat stood out on his forehead. He peeled back the top of the box, too easily, he thought.

With a mixture of relief and anguish he stared down at the jumble of snapshots inside. Some lay face down, others only partially exposed. He caught a glimpse of a half-hidden face, a fragment of a Christmas tree, a child on a sled. He poked one index finger inside the box and flipped over a snapshot. He was startled by what he saw. It was himself, a young, hopeful man, leaning without a care in the world in a doorway he didn't recognize. He was shirtless and held a beer in his hand. Franklin pushed the snapshot aside and went further into the box. He came across an old pacifier with a red handle and a small ring of colorful plastic teething disks that made a clicking sound as he touched them. At the bottom of the box, in a brown wooden frame, was a black and white studio portrait of a small boy with Franklin's eyes, hair slicked back, obediently posed in white shirt and dark jacket on the edge of a large chair. There was a fierceness to his expression, a determination that struck Franklin like a blow to the gut. "Little Man," he murmured, but whether the words were actually spoken or simply stirred in his head he wasn't sure. He quickly covered the photo with the rest of the contents of the box as if he had just done something terribly wrong. He shoved the top of the box back on abruptly. He had meant no harm, he only wanted to be sure that Dawn had kept her promise. That she hadn't forgotten the pictures or lost them or, worse, thrown them away. He hoped that within her act of safekeeping there was forgiveness.

Funny how over the years his memory of that day had only sharpened, and now came into focus through the tropical heat of this day, not unlike the stifling heat in the streets over twenty years before when the National Guard, young white boys armed for war, poured through the same streets Franklin had played in as a child. How little anything really changes, Franklin thought. How long those summers could be. How long they still were.

He pressed his hands along the side of the shoebox, ironing the brittle tabs of tape down with his fingertips. He readjusted the string. He had a momentary urge to leave the box on Dawn's bed for her to find when she returned, but he was afraid she would misinterpret his gesture and finally accuse him of all the things she had never spoken about. He thrust the box back into the duffel bag, closed the closet door, and left the room quickly, breathing fast as if he were running uphill behind his house. Running as if he were trying to outrun something. Breathless.

His mind was knitting together the fragments of that day: the streets awash with heat and frantic people, clubs coming down on black heads, and the sound of breaking glass and screams, and he, Franklin, running among his neighbors and friends, carrying Phillip on his shoulders.

What exactly did Freida remember from where she had huddled inside her house while angry neighbors tore through her garden out back, and down the alley, to escape the clubs and tear gas and gunfire? For when it finally came down to it, she was a white woman—not Jessie's mother, nor Franklin's grandmother, but a stranger here in Detroit, suddenly afraid for her life and property. Without Henry, Freida seemed to forget she belonged. She had turned fearful and angry, a foreigner who could never comprehend the fearsome truths forcing the heat to the surface.

When she looked out of her window through the smoke, she saw Franklin running toward her, Phillip limp in his arms, a rag doll. Except then he hadn't realized Phillip was dead. He only knew that Freida was moving toward him on her porch, a small shape in yellow, crying out, "What have you done? How could you take him out there?"

No one in his family but Freida had outright accused him; how could they when they were able to comprehend his confusion and fear that day, as he zigzagged through the streets? Franklin's face and hands were streaked with blood, but he hadn't noticed when it happened. He remembered thinking only how his life and the lives of those around him no longer mattered. Smoke mixed with the muggy air. Glass seemed to shatter everywhere. He knew he was witnessing the death of a city, but he hadn't realized right away that he was also witnessing the death of his son. Phillip, the "Little Man," had loosened himself from Franklin's grip and charged off the curb. He ran headlong into the street, something he knew better than to do. For what reason, Franklin would never know. The car that hit Phillip never stopped. Franklin pulled the child up off the street as if he'd merely stumbled. Around him people yelled and pushed. Police were using bullhorns to order everyone off the streets. Franklin did the only thing his instinct told him to: he began to run, the boy's body tucked up tight against his chest.

Only Freida continued to denounce him. "How could you take him out there? How come you take a baby into those streets?" Because that was her fear. All he could do was stare at her in disbelief as he held Phillip's lifeless weight in his arms. He had cried out to Freida, "Because those are my people out there!" But her question haunted him long after.

In prison, where he subsequently spent three years for assaulting a police officer who refused to call an ambulance for a dead boy, Franklin grew impatient when the other inmates talked about the riots. He could silence them with a look and the cold reminder that none of them had sacrificed their own sons to that week of tempest.

Dawn visited him faithfully in the prison. At first she was hopeful, assuring him the lawyer would have him out any day now, that the appeals looked good. All those hours she put into his release, which seemed to grow more and more elusive by the day. Ollie and the others came too at first, full of talk and condolences. Then hope began to wear thin. Slowly Dawn wearied of his absence. She got busy, started missing visits. After all, it was a long way to come and Franklin had become impossible to talk to. Once he even slammed his fist against the glass window separating them. She stared at him long and hard, then murmured that the window between them had existed long before prison. That was the closest she ever came to admitting what she surely must have felt in her heart. Cautious not to ever blame him, there came a point when she could no longer see him.

When Franklin finally did come home, and it was to Freida's that he first came, the world had changed. Vietnam was in full swing, King was dead, and Dawn was living with some black South African guy named Winston, a Ph.D. engineering student who claimed to be a direct descendant of Zulu warriors.

After that day, Franklin's life never really took hold again. He moved in a surrealistic blur from one blunder to the next. After prison, he went briefly to his mother's, then to jobs that never lasted, prison again for violating parole, a degree that took him seven turbulent years to complete, and finally his current life of solitude, the only way he saw himself fit to live: in an ascetic apartment, dirty clothes in a heap on the living room floor, bed unmade, garbage stacked in bags by the back door, books scattered everywhere. It was as if by surrounding himself with decay he was safeguarding himself against the falling away of his own flesh. No woman to interfere for long. No limits. Without limits, he would die soon, he could feel it, just the way Freida would.

To her credit, Dawn had tried sticking with him out of pity or duty, he was never sure which, but finally she'd had enough. He read it in her face and eyes, and when she finally left him, it was the way a visitor steals quietly and hopelessly from the bed of a dying relative. That same look was reflected in Dawn's daughter Julie's face when she was growing up. She added her own little sour twist to it, refusing to look him in the eye and calling him "FRANK-lin," without the slightest care, as if he were merely an annoying classmate who had pulled her braids.

IV

"Dawn!" Freida's voice was surprisingly strong. It resonated through the house.

Franklin found her sitting up in bed, her bed jacket open across her thin chest. He bent over and kissed her cheek.

"Where's Dawn?" she demanded.

"She went to the center. She'll be back soon."

"I finished my nap."

"You want to come out and sit on the porch? Get some air?"

Freida nodded. Franklin folded back the sheet and helped arrange her nightgown over her legs. She could sit up on the edge of the bed, but couldn't trust her own legs to stand. He placed her arms around his neck and lifted her. "Don't drop me," she cautioned. He carried her out to the screened porch and set her down on the chaise with thick foam pillows. She peered up at him, childlike and expectant.

"I'll get you a drink."

"No ice," said Freida.

Franklin went to the fridge and poured juice into a glass. He diluted the juice with water. He found tea biscuits in a metal canister, and set three on a plate. When he returned to the porch, she was staring out at the yard. He placed the drink and biscuits next to her as an offering. Outside, the sky was clouding over. The air was thickening.

Franklin sat down in Henry's old wicker rocker. Freida continued to stare at the wide back yard, as if searching for something. From her expression, he gathered she was disappointed. He wondered if perhaps she had forgotten there was no garden anymore. And the arbor, once full of the sweetest grapes and blooms of sweet pea, now stood like an old weathered skeleton missing knuckles and joints.

"You never come see me anymore," she remarked without self-pity.

"I get busy," he said. "I'm sorry, Freida."

"Shoot, busy don't mean a thing." Her mind was momentarily sharp again. He saw the color rise in her face. She took a cautious sip of juice, holding the glass in trembling hands.

"Remember how the garden used to look?" Franklin said. "Remember the first time I helped you plant flowers?"

"I don't remember," said Freida. When she inhaled, her breath crackled like paper. She had always suffered with asthma. As a child, Franklin used to listen to her wheeze and snort at night. It was almost comforting when he woke in the night to be able to locate her in some distant part of the house, to hear her moving around, a nocturnal creature keeping everything safe.

"Sure," said Franklin, "I took your shovel one morning and got out there and tried to dig you a hole for your tomato plants and instead I ended up tearing up a bunch of your flowers. Boy, you whupped me good that day!"

"I don't remember any such thing," murmured Freida. "It sure is a mess out there. Look what they did to it."

"Nobody did anything to it. Time has done that," said Franklin.

"No," said Freida. "*They* did that, runnin through here like a bunch of crazy folks. Nothin was ever the same after that." A breeze stirred at one end of the porch, then moved gently across them both.

"The rose bush still blooms," said Franklin. "I could get out there and trim it for you." It had long ago outgrown the trellis and was now pushing pink and yellow blooms over the top of the garage where Henry's '63 Buick LeSabre was still parked. Franklin had asked Freida about that car more than once, even asked her outright to let him have it. "You must be outa your mind," she'd responded. "That car was Henry's pride. It doesn't have a scratch on it and it's staying right where it is."

She peered suspiciously into her juice glass.

"There's no ice in there," he said.

"Okay then," said Freida almost contritely, and she took another cautious sip. Her hand trembled over one of the tea biscuits, but she got it up to her mouth and chewed off a tiny corner. Thunder rumbled faintly in the distance.

Franklin sighed. "Remember how you showed me when to plant and how far apart to put things, and how to tell when vegetables were ready to be picked?"

"That was Henry showed you," said Freida, her voice warming. "Henry knew everything that was worth knowin. He had farmin in his blood, you know. Never belonged in the city, not Henry."

Thunder rolled boldly along the horizon. Phillip's face lit up with firecracker quickness in Franklin's mind. A pain, a headache. Funny, he'd go for months without getting a clear image like that. Sometimes he'd forget about it altogether. Phillip was the only person he'd ever really missed. Not Dawn. Not her daughter Julie. Not his mother Jessie. Not even his father when he died. Not his sister Bonnie or his brothers. When he'd served time, he stopped caring about those who were alive, and longed only for the dead child crumpled from the blow of a stranger's car.

"Henry," murmured Freida uncertainly. Her eyes searched the blackening sky. "Henry sure knew how to make things grow."

"Tell me all about how you two first met," Franklin urged feverishly, as if he hadn't heard the story many times before.

"Oh, I don't remember." Her eyes went filmy.

So Franklin seized upon the story himself and told it the way she had told it so many times when he was growing up.

Freida didn't interrupt, but listened quietly. When Franklin had finished, he saw that her eyes were closed and her chest was still.

He mistook her for dead. And then, he realized, he didn't want to try to wake her. But because he knew it was the right thing to do, he leaned over and gently touched her arm. That was when he saw the imperceptible heave of her thin chest, and in the corner of her eye was a glimmer of blue between her lowered lid and cheek, marking the narrow distance between sleep and death.

Franklin whispered, "Freida!"

Slowly she opened her opaque eyes and stared out with a face vacant of expression. It was the look of someone who has stumbled into foreign territory and now is uncertain whether she stares at friend or foe.

"I'm Franklin, Freida."

A very small, almost saucy, smile played in the corners of her mouth. Her eyes closed again, but her mouth was turned upwards.

"I know who you are," she murmured coyly. She reached one long white finger out and tentatively touched his dark brown arm. Franklin felt no more pressure than if it had been a raindrop. "You remember how my sweet peas used to climb way up over the fence?" she asked. "All over there, red and blue and white and pink."

"Yeah, and those hollyhocks you had. I loved those hollyhocks." Her grip tightened on his arm.

Round and round on the brick walkway they would go when he was a child, hand in hand, discovering the secrets she never shared with any of the others. "Just for you, don't tell nobody," she'd say as she popped open a pea shell and fed him straight from her palm.

Now he took her hand and drew it tightly into his, as if they could protect each other from whatever it was that would eventually claim them both. It suddenly mattered to him that she would soon be gone. He found reassurance in the warmth of her flesh. In the collecting darkness of the afternoon, a faint memory of happiness pulsed softly against his face like butterfly wings.

DEAD WOMEN

Just when I'm convinced night will never end, it's dawn. The air outside glows with a frosty fierceness that belies the flat, gold Castilian plains glistening on either side of the speeding train. To my right, in the autumn sky, an icy sun begins a long, cold climb away from the horizon.

The other three women in my couchette are French. Very French, I might add. We've all had a rough night of it, only they don't show it. Looking remarkably rested, they sit primly on their seats in their unwrinkled clothes. One wears a scarf with tiny red flowers. It is a peculiar trait of French women to appear eternally composed and well coiffed. Two of them are now elegantly sharing a small box of *petite beurre* biscuits, without dropping so much as a crumb, and staring placidly out the window as if we hadn't all spent a horrid night on Procrustean beds. Over and over our sleep was disrupted by the nightmarish shriek of brakes, followed finally by the slow jolts and grinds as we changed tracks at Hendaye.

I glimpse myself in the small mirror hanging above and quickly begin to work at my hair. I use my fingers to smooth out the skin on my face. Nothing to be done about the wrinkled blue jeans and T-shirt I slept in; nothing to be done about my stained socks. I work on tucking and zipping myself together, accepting a sympathetic smile from the thin brunette in the eggshell skirt-and-sweater set. When, I wonder, did she manage her makeup and hair, unnoticed? Now she sits nonchalantly peeling an orange, as we rattle and tumble along.

She told me last night she has a fiancé in Madrid, a Frenchman studying at the university. She herself works in a Paris bank in administration. "*Et vous?*" she asked so sweetly I didn't have the heart to explain I no longer have a life, that my old one is an empty skin hanging up in someone's attic catching cobwebs.

I never mention my pending divorce. Not to people I meet in my travels and not to Paloma at the Barcelona agency where, when I passed through a month ago, I was hired as a live-in governess for the Amado family in Madrid. María and Andreas Amado, Paloma had told me, would be back from vacation September 1. How quaint, I thought at the time, a governess. Like Jane Eyre. They still have such things here. "You'd be perfect," Paloma explained. "A real teacher. Let's see, you taught for three years . . . . Now, they had hoped for an English girl, but I told them you had a lovely American accent. Where are you from?"

I had been wearing my one dress that now lies rolled in tissue paper at the bottom of my duffel. My hair was neatly yanked back in a severe barrette, and I had squeezed my feet into the one pair of pumps I carry with me.

"Michigan," I'd said. "My accent is Midwestern American."

Paloma made more notes. "And you want to live in Madrid?" she asked.

"Very much," I said, without having a clue as to why. I was only passing through, I thought, and it was really Barcelona that caught my eye, but then . . .

She quoted the salary, which was hardly enough to feed a mouse, but I would be out of money soon and, besides, I was travel-weary. I added as an afterthought, "I'd like to learn Spanish."

This seemed to please her. "I think you will get on with this family very nicely." She smiled. "They are very literary. See you in September."

Spain has arrived this time around much too quickly, and I am expected to adjust in a matter of moments. I have had no time to get out of Paris.

In the Madrid station people are already swarming. Madrileños even look different from the French, who have over the last month actually become familiar. The severe faces strike me as frigid as the wind now polishing the air like glass. Countenances merge: a sea of long, angular El Grecos and round, stubby Goyas. I am in Spain, I keep telling myself, dragging myself past other travelers. I am in Spain. I say it over and over, in disbelief, like a child on the first day of school. It is my habit these days to remind myself where I am, or I will make a mistake and speak the wrong language or seek out the wrong places.

María Amado assured me she would be at home to meet me and pay the cab driver. I throw the driver a confident smile and wonder, if I suddenly ran off, how far he would go to chase me down. And what would María think, her new governess simply vanishing without a trace?

Ever since arriving in Europe, I walk everywhere, skip meals, sleep on lumpy mattresses in cheap *pensiones,* and wash out underwear by hand. I am a saver, not a splurger at all, and the length of this cab ride begins to work on my nerves. It's not my money being spent, I keep telling myself, watching the buildings flash by. But I'm as uneasy as if it were.

Autumn leaves swirl through the streets. Aproned shop owners are out already washing down the pavements in front of their *tiendas* with blasts of water from garden hoses. Madrid is repressive: rows of wrought-iron balconies and shuttered windows; at eye level, broad boulevards and plazas full of monuments. The city is big and unwieldy, not old at all.

The driver points out Retiro Park with its thick explosion of fall colors to my right. Two more turns and we lurch to a halt in front of a skinny plaster building the color of an old peach. The driver has, surprisingly, brought me the most direct route, and yet I think, if María has not kept her promise . . .

But she is waiting for me, or at least I assume it is she, standing three stories above on a wrought-iron balcony. She is not at all what I expected: much younger than her forty years, thin, tall, with one of those distinctly European faces that speak of centuries of tradition. Beautiful, not exactly, but sensual and natural, yes. Hers is a face that haunts. Besides, she is dark, with big eyes, long lashes, a hint of pout, a glimpse of Moorishness, and I have always envied dark women.

"Well," she says, after she's paid the driver.

She turns to me. "Welcome, Diana. I am so pleased you have come to my house." She states this as if my arrival were by accident and not design. Or as if I am a guest, which I am not, and we both know it.

I follow her up the scuffed and peeling linoleum steps. She makes small talk, cautiously testing out her English, which is less good than I expected. She speaks haltingly, with long pauses between words.

"So, you are a professor?"

"A teacher," I quickly correct her and explain the distinction in English.

"You look too young." She keeps turning around and studying me, Orpheus to my Eurydice. I now wish I'd changed clothes in the train station.

"I'm twenty-five," I tell her. "I taught high school in Detroit."

Already she is doubting me, I can see that. I know I will never tell this woman that I am still married, that I left my husband only four months ago, someone I now hardly remember who still calls me "wife."

At the top of the stairs she ushers me through an open door into the most chaotic jumble of a room I've ever seen. I set my bags down and follow her into the kitchen.

"Come, come, you must be hungry."

Before I can say I'm not, María pours powdered cocoa from a packet and turns on the flame under the teakettle. With a knife she assaults half a pallid Spanish omelette partially draped in Saran Wrap, and squeezes out a slice for me onto a plate. I collapse in an uncomfortable metal chair at the uneven table and take in my new surroundings.

I try to imagine myself in the disappointing light in which María must see me. I am an American, and not the fancy British governess she'd asked for: a far less evolved human being with a flat Midwestern accent and slovenly clothes.

María sits down across from me as I take perfunctory pokes at the omelette; she exudes a tremulous sort of humility, staring from dark, expectant eyes. Her long black hair is thick and loose. She has a habit of lifting it with her hands over one shoulder and then letting it fall down her back. She does this over and over until her arms grow tired or she gets distracted.

"So you're a writer," I say. It is my first stab at deference. I, too, am a writer: an avid writer of letters, postcards, and aerograms. I take notes, stash ideas in tiny notebooks. I write things no one will ever read.

A cautious smile spreads across María's face. Or is it self-complacence? Paloma at the agency told me how María had recently been catapulted to fame with an important collection of short stories called *Cantos de amor por las mujeres muertas*, for which she won the Spanish equivalent of the Pulitzer Prize.

I say boldly, "I'd like to read your book."

She waves her hand at me. "Boof! It is a small book. You cannot understand it. It is much, how do you say, surreal."

I persist. "I like surreal writing. I've read a lot of Latin American writers." But she is not listening, because she really does not care if I read her book or not.

I finish the cocoa and omelette, both of which conspire to turn my stomach. I am not completely present, but perhaps my air of preoccupation will appeal to María, who strikes me as only vaguely present herself.

"Come!" she says wearily. "I show you around." I have the sense that she has already tired of me, and wonder if I've done something to offend.

María and her husband Andreas rent a pair of second-story adjoining flats on the third floor of this building. María keeps everything padlocked—doors, cupboards, even the three boxy powder-blue telephones scattered about the main flat. She wears a number of keys on a bracelet around her wrist. "Because of the servants," she explains, referring to the two teenage girls, Cello and Isabel, who share a room just off the kitchen. "They are ignorant, silly girls from the provinces."

Cello and Isabel sleep on two mattresses shoved together. They are cousins, poor girls from the country, one skinny, the other as round and doughy as a biscuit. They are napping together when we poke our heads in, curled up like babies together under a dirty sheet. They have adorned their plaster walls with posters of American rock stars, all the way up to the high ceiling. A tiny black and white television teeters on top of an old dresser with mismatched drawers.

"They always sleep for an hour in the morning," explains María, as we withdraw ourselves. "They awaken at five-thirty to make breakfast, they clean, then sleep."

She begins unlocking and locking doors, carrying out her duty with the authority of a convent abbess.

She talks to me about my charges, her two sons, Tomás and Horacio, now off at school. I am to eat breakfast and speak English with them Mondays through Fridays. Evenings, they receive formal English instruction, an hour apiece. Saturdays I take them on a half-day, English-speaking outing. Sundays I have off, to do with as I please or, as María says, "To see friends," oblivious to the fact that I know no one here. In theory it sounds reasonable, certainly no less worthy than other things I could be doing. I'm certain she sees this as a favor to me, my living here with her and Andreas and the two boys.

We pause in the doorway of the boys' darkened room where the shades are still drawn. I make out the silhouettes of a set of bunk beds rising above a heap of dirty clothes thrown on the floor. A sour odor assails my nostrils: unwashed bedding and damp pajamas. María claims they are *lovely* children, and repeats this assurance at least half a dozen more times.

Andreas's study is the best room in the whole place, the only one unmarred by careless renovation. Andreas's absence is most conspicuous, perhaps because of the reverence María seems to hold for the empty room. Her voice pours like liquid over his name. "Andreas." Two of his walls are solid books, mostly in Spanish. I try to imagine Lady Macbeth crying out: "*Mira,* Macbeth!" How would one say "Screw your courage to the sticking place" in Spanish? When I stand on tiptoes to read titles, María gives me a look and informs me gently the *estudio* is *privado.*

"Andreas writes here," she explains deferentially. "Even the children do not come here." When we leave, she checks the lock twice.

What I know of Andreas from the agency is that he is a

poet of some repute, currently finishing up a week of lectures in Barcelona. He will be home in a few days. Like María, he teaches at the university on the outskirts of Madrid.

In both flats, the ceilings are twice as high as a person, and the rooms are spliced together haphazardly, creating odd sizes and shapes. There are all the awkward mismatchings of a place that has been the victim of careless occupants: a useless faucet jutting from an alcove wall; half a room painted royal blue, the other half a sickly pea green; a runner of dull brown carpet ending abruptly mid-room, like an unfinished sentence, and so on. María's mismatched furniture only adds to the lack of coherence. It is illogical: odds and ends stacked together, upholstery ripped at the seams, a broken table leg propped at an angle, bookshelves stacked with unsorted papers and manuscripts in battered folders.

"I'd really like to read your book," I try again.

"You may find it—how do you say—*aburrido*—uh—bored."

"Boring," I correct her companionably.

"Ah, yes, boring!"

"No, no, I'd find it very interesting." Why I persist, I'm not sure.

We move across the hall to the second flat, where my room is. The first door leads to the small filthy bathroom I will share with Cello and Isabel. Undaunted by the grime, María points out tub, shower, and toilet. We do not linger, and I make a mental note that my first task will be to scrub down the bathroom. Down the hall, she summons me into what appears to be a laundry room. The floor is littered with islands of sour-smelling clothing. About this, María muses, with a puzzled expression, "I must remember to tell Cello and Isabel they must wash the clothes soon."

A door through the laundry leads to a small unused kitchenette. It smells of stale coffee grounds left sitting in the electric pot on the counter. The room is a haphazard space that doubles as María's office. The floor is covered by cracked linoleum with one scatter rug shoved into the corner. Stacks of papers lie strewn across a tabletop. In the center is a Royal manual typewriter. Two beat-up bookshelves run from the floor to the ceiling, stacked with books and loose papers and cleaning materials. There on her desk are four more copies of *Cantos de amor por las mujeres muertas*.

"May I?"

With a shrug, she hands me a copy. The cover is stained with circular coffee-cup rings. I flip the book over to the black and white head-and-shoulders shot of María on the back. She wears that dreamy gaze often urged on subjects by well-meaning photographers hoping to capture the essence of artistry.

"Come, I'll show you your room." I clutch the book in one hand and we traverse the entire length of the hall to a room which, in comparison to the others, is surprisingly pleasant. A large window looks down into a small cement courtyard. There is a firm mattress with a stack of clean linens piled invitingly on top. María points out the antique armoire for my clothes. Just opposite is a writing desk. Someone has laid a dark blue throw rug on the floor to take the autumn chill off the linoleum.

"I think you will like it here," she says with certainty. "Our last governess was very happy."

"Thank you," I tell her, and am so startled by the relief of her warm smile that I don't bother to ask why the governess left. I'm not sure it would matter.

That afternoon I unpack slowly, spurning the drawers, keeping everything right where I can see it. My head is thick with disorientation. I keep feeling the most recent hands on my flesh, Marcos's warm breath on my cheek, his slender arms draped around me. He is a vague presence now, no longer real, but a postcard image from Paris, reduced to one dimension, a series of snapshots caught at various angles. I can smell his warmth and taste his mouth, but cannot remember what he looks like. It happens so fast, these things, and I wonder how long it will take for him to blur with the next one. Kevin is light-years away, a thing of the past. My marriage is over, even if not legally. There was a Greek fisherman and then an Israeli art student; before that, a Belgian biker, and preceding him, an architect from Argentina I met in a hostel. They all begin to collapse into one fragmented body which I have possessed over and over.

Outside in the hallway Cello and Isabel are giggling. But I don't open the door and soon they go away, murmuring about "*la señorita.*" I sit down at the desk and look around me. This is it, I think. This is what I've rushed off to. I take a peek out the window and down into the courtyard. There is the vague, incessant murmur of voices from neighboring open windows, but I can see no one.

I flip through María's book. The print job is awful, even faded in places. I scan the table of contents and then, with the help of my *diccionario,* begin to read. The first story focuses on an ill-fated love affair between an arrogant young man and a much older woman. Stumbling on idioms, I still manage to get the gist: the young man falls for another older woman, the first woman ends up committing suicide and haunts the young man for years after, tormenting his conscience and causing him to be impotent until his new lover abandons him.

The voice is passionate, the language feverishly erotic. Marcos's face suddenly reappears; he is the young man in the story, passionate, fearless, and cruel. I am drawn into the blur of romantic parables that make up this new fiction called my life. María's words, in a language I don't know well, invoke our parting: my train pulled out of the Paris station and Marcos ran alongside, striking the window with his fist and turning his stricken face, wet with tears, toward me. Just that morning he had dutifully confessed to me how he loved me, and I obediently reciprocated, knowing it wasn't true. But the words came easily, predictably. Arm in arm we strolled through Père Lachaise Cimetière and finally sat gloomily on Modigliani's tomb. The hour of my departure loomed over us. We both pretended to be sad, or maybe we were. One of us was crying. His vacation from law school was almost over, he was probably more despondent about returning to his books than my leaving.

"You must come back," he told me, but even then I was picturing the handsome Spaniard I was sure to meet in Madrid. I simply shrugged, the old restlessness rising in me, Marcos a thing of the past.

I finish María's story with only the slightest of pangs, wondering how long it will be again before I can't breathe, can't sleep. It was how I awakened that one night next to Kevin, sitting upright in bed, panting like a long-distance runner. I heard myself say, "There's no air in here," and then I knew. He knew too. "I could open a window," he told me, "but I don't think that's what you need." I put a coat on over my nightgown and went down into the street, just like that, and sat on the curb until Kevin came out and told me he was worried I'd catch cold.

María's boys, Tomás and Horacio, are twelve and eight. We are introduced just before they go to bed. The older, Tomás, carries a small marionette that he controls with strings attached to a wooden cross. He manipulates the doll to make it dance wildly. Tomás is tall and blond, almost Nordic. He looks unlike either of his parents. He wears an icy expression of privilege and superiority. When he shakes my hand, he treats it as a joke.

"It is a pleasure to meet you," he says with exaggerated courtesy.

Horacio is small and brown-haired, a nervous, giggly, bird-like boy. He wears soft wrinkled cotton pajamas with bunny rabbits on them. His two front teeth have grown in crooked and overlap each other.

María hovers, expectant and pleased.

"So, you are from America?" asks Tomás. He allows the marionette to hang limply from the cross. It is a clown with mismatched shoes and a pointed red cap.

"From Michigan."

"Michigan?" says Tomás sharply. "And where is that?"

"It's the mitten-shaped state."

"The what?" he asks curtly, as if I am the one who doesn't understand.

I draw a mitten in the air with my hand and repeat, "Mitten-shaped." María looks on approvingly.

"I don't know what you mean," he says petulantly. He jerks the marionette around.

"I'll show you on a map." I pretend to be conciliatory. I want María to see how you handle such a boy. But he has turned away, fiercely thrusting the marionette into the air.

I look at María, expecting her to address the boy's rudeness, but she seems oblivious.

"They are lovely boys, aren't they?" she says, and smiles with enough appreciation for both of us.

Over the next few days, María asks me about myself. Frequently, when I eat, she sits at the end of the long table and studies me, toying with the fringe at the end of her red scarf.

"You have a nice American accent," she says encouragingly.

"I asked for a British girl, but the agency recommended you. And I see how you are with the boys. You make them laugh."

I can tell she is trying to reassure herself that she has made a good choice.

"You are well educated," she continues. "You are like me."

"Not exactly," I explain. "I taught high school, you teach college."

"No matter, you are still young. Oh, by the way . . ." She moves cautiously over that expression, which she has picked up from talking to me, "I mean to tell you that Tomás uses a how-do-you-say, uh, a potty in his room, and every morning you must now empty into the toilet." Her eyes remain unblinking on me.

"Tomás? But he's twelve."

María's face tightens. "Yes, that is correct." An awkward silence comes between us, and then she reinforces, "But you have not been empty his potty." I don't answer, and she stands up with a sigh. "I must prepare for the university."

She is barely out of the room when the front door opens. I can hear the scrape of footsteps and the sound of a throat being cleared.

Andreas, back from Barcelona, pokes his face into the kitchen. "*Hola,*" he says and then enters.

He is not tall and he is frail in a too-sensuous, Byronic kind of way. He drops his satchel to the floor with a thump and removes his jacket.

He looks exactly the way a poet should: his pale olive complexion almost consumptive; dark curly hair and a mouth that is too carnal. He wears oversized corduroy pants, a battered sweater, worn Italian shoes, and a wool scarf around his neck. His eyes are wet and mournful, his expression one of eternal exhaustion with the world.

"Ah, and you must be . . ."

"Diana." I stand up, still chewing a mouthful of omelette.

"Andreas." He extends his hand. I grip his in mine and feel it go limp. "Welcome," he says, withdrawing his hand slowly. "You are all arranged here?"

His smile is angled sideways like a fish's.

María appears suddenly in the doorway behind him. A dark flush rises in her face. "Andreas . . ." She looks as if she has seen a ghost. "I heard the door."

He is breezy and unconcerned, unwrapping his scarf from his neck. "Busy trip," he says, and she stops short of embracing him. I realize they are speaking English for my benefit.

"You have met Diana, of course," she says, her eyes firm on his face.

Andreas smiles. He gives María a quick kiss on the cheek. There is something distinctly cold in his expression, and I suspect he is capable of great indifference.

"Diana is a very pretty girl, don't you think?" says María. Her tone has a stony control, but underlying it is a trace of anguish. Their eyes lock and I feel myself vanishing. Andreas's face goes blank, the way I have seen men do with women they no longer want.

"I'm very tired," he says. "Barcelona exhausts me." He crosses the room and disappears toward their bedroom. María gives me a wan smile, then picks up his satchel. She follows her husband like a hopeful child, her long legs and arms moving rapidly.

I throw the rest of my omelette in the garbage. I've lost my appetite.

I've just returned from walking the boys the four blocks to school to find a letter addressed to me on the hall table. It is too early for today's mail; I wonder when it came. At first I think

Kevin has found me. But the postmark is Paris, and the writing is unfamiliar, a tiny cramped hand. I carry the letter into the boys' room, turning the envelope around in my hand. Tomás's chamber pot awaits me like a wild creature about to spring. It is full of urine, a rich, dark orange color with a stench at once so sweet and pungent that it catches in my throat in that stuffy room, and if I don't hold my breath, I find myself tasting it over and over in my imagination.

I leave the chamber pot unemptied and wander out to the balcony. A heavy gray overcast hangs on the skyline. The letter, I realize, is from Marcos. Someone has lined through the agency address and forwarded it to Madrid.

The first paragraph is perfunctory; he's back in school, he's *très occupé*. But then he begins to describe walking in the Luxembourg Gardens where we had walked together, and how he was startled by a ray of sunlight through the clouds, which reminded him of my smile. He misses me. He misses the long afternoons in his stifling room, shades drawn against the outside world. The details are buried in the French words he has scrawled on the blue paper. It is only with great concentration that I move beyond the dreamlike foreignness of his words to the smells, tastes, sounds of our bodies together. Slowly the words disappear altogether. I close my eyes. Marcos and I first met beneath the gargoyles of Notre Dame. It was raining lightly, and neither of us had an umbrella. Within that first hour he had pressed his mouth against my damp neck, then onto my hair. His hands were inside my jacket, then under my shirt. Suddenly we were falling, fast, and he was no longer a stranger murmuring over and over, "*Viens, j'ai envie de toi.*" The voice seemed to come from inside me. By now my hair was soaked by the rain. We got under an awning and he told me I must come home to his place, that he would dry me and feed me.

The whole time he kept one hand wedged under my shirt, his fingers roaming warm over my bare skin. He was impatient, Marcos was, and I read it as passion. It was urgency I wanted, what dragged me out of my lethargy.

I finish the letter and turn the envelope over and over in my hands, repeating aloud his address from the ninth arrondissement as if it were my own.

"*Ma cherie . . .*" I start again. There is even more I have missed in the first reading. By the end of the second page I feel the heat in my face and the emptiness of longing. Marcos writes incautiously and beautifully in a language that belongs to neither of us. Marcos is from the Dominican Republic, and his native tongue is the language I hear all around me now in Spain. Marcos speaks no English.

I am back in his sparse room, with its single bed shoved against the white walls, the unburned candle by the bedside, and the view of the street from his window when the shutters were open. "*La semaine perdue.*"

He told me after we'd finished making love the first night, "No one knows we are here." This seemed to give him immense satisfaction.

He would be returning to law school after a two-week break; but where would I be returning to? I purposely told him all about Kevin, to make him jealous, and it worked. Marcos dubbed Kevin "*la pierre,*" the stone. And Kevin, poor gentle Kevin, came to represent all that was boorish and all that we detested, and Marcos spent the week proving to me he was everything Kevin was not. "I, too, had a stone," Marcos told me the second day we were together. Her name was Anne; she was French. He told me that at first she had offered him entreé into Parisian life. Bit by bit she had strung him with so many bourgeois expectations he began to feel like a puppet. "I can never be French," he told me wryly. "She wants a Frenchman in public . . ." He paused. ". . . and a black man in private." Only, in French what he said was "*un homme noir,*" and for some reason we both laughed.

So I became the antithesis of Anne, just as Marcos was the antithesis of Kevin. We often joked about introducing the two of them. As we lay sweating against each other at night, Marcos's hand moving between my legs, he would whisper, "*Je suis pas Kevin,*" and I would murmur, "*Je suis pas Anne.*"

María walks out onto the balcony. She wears a blue silk blouse, black corduroy jeans, the red scarf, and a wistful expression.

"Good morning, Diana. Did you sleep well?" She peers down at the street below. In one hand she has a small piece of dry biscuit, something they call toast, and in the other, a cup of cocoa. "I'm late for the university. I overslept again. I stayed up with Andreas, just the way we always do, talk, talk, talk, talk, talk. He is finishing an important book of poetry."

I am not sure why she tells me these things, for I am not her friend. Perhaps she wants me to envy their complex creative life. Perhaps it is a warning of sorts. She peers down at the envelope on my lap and then at the letter in my hand. She looks at me, as if I owe her an explanation, and settles into the metal chair next to mine.

"From France? Who writes from France?" she asks so sweetly that I break down and confess.

"A friend."

"Oh?" Her interest is pathetically girlish. "A man?"

I don't know how to explain Marcos, or any other men I've known, for that matter, but I suspect María is not so easily satisfied. "*Mi amigo,*" I say, because it sounds less dangerous in Spanish. But I have instantly formalized whatever passed between Marcos and me.

"Oh, you have a French lover!" María cries, delighted as a

child. She picks up the envelope and turns it over in her long fingers. She stares at his return address. "Oh, that is so wonderful he writes you! And in French too!"

Marcos is not at all what María is imagining, but I say nothing. His mother is actually Haitian and his father is Dominican. His parents never married, and he grew up poor, alone with his mother, in a small ugly house near fields of sugarcane. Starting when he was ten, he made monthly visits to his father, in Santo Domingo, a rich man with servants and many other children. It was on his father's money that he'd come to France to study.

"You know," María says earnestly, "passion is so precious. And young passion is the very best. You must miss him terribly."

Again, I recall Marcos at that last moment, how he ran along the platform next to the train. He kept up with me until the train groaned out of the station. In the frosty air his breath smoked. I could make out his parting words, "*Je t'aime, Diana,*" his face constricted in the cold. He wore a blue hat on his head that struck me as oddly comical, but now I cannot recall his face. It was only appropriate that he should say he loved me, I thought, as I leaned my head against the leather upholstery. They all have, and I've loved them, because it is actually very easy to fall in love. People talk about how hard love is, but they mean something else. Marcos grew smaller and smaller on the edge of the platform until he was just a speck. A moment later he was invisible, and I was on my way to Spain.

"You are so lucky," says María wistfully, as she stands up. "Your poet—Emily Dickinson—she said, 'Love is all there is, is all we know of Love.' Isn't that lovely?"

I nod. I want to say, "Love's stricken 'why' / is all that love can speak," but I don't.

"I am very glad for you," she persists from the doorway, "about your French lover."

"Thank you," I say and realize María has just assigned Marcos a place in my life. I get up and go to the kitchen for a cup of cocoa.

Andreas shuffles by me in his gray-and-red flannel bathrobe and pours cocoa mix into a mug. His sleep-stiff hair stands erect on his head. "Good morning," he murmurs grumpily in my direction, then casts an annoyed glance toward Cello and Isabel's room. The television blares. A woman's voice wails, "*Mentiras! Solamente mentiras!*" Violin music soars. Having been invited to their room a couple of times, I know fat Isabel and skinny Cello are slumped together on the mattress, their eyes riveted on the seductress La Rubia.

Isabel has a real boyfriend, scrawny, with hair like shoe polish, who meets her in the bushes downstairs and takes her for walks so they can smooch. Cello, on the other hand, is lonesome and probably a virgin.

"*Déjame sola!*" screams the tormented female voice. Andreas yells at the open door and the woman's cries dissolve into silence. I hear giggling, then Cello emerges earnestly with a mop in her hand and heads for the other flat.

Andreas settles down in a chair to drink his cocoa. "Stupid girls," he mutters to no one in particular. His bathrobe has risen up over one white leg, exposing coils of hair springing along his calf and thigh. I think of Marcos's milk-chocolate skin, the very smoothness of his hairless limbs, and wonder why Andreas doesn't cover himself up, he is revolting. I remain standing, leaning against the kitchen counter.

"María has left already?" he asks.

I nod.

"She likes you very much."

I don't answer.

"You know María is a famous woman." There is a hint of mockery.

"I know that."

"Very clever, very beautiful," he tells me. "An irresistible combination, don't you think?" I don't know what he is getting at, but his air of superiority hangs over him like mist.

"I finished one of her short stories last night. It was wonderful."

"Oh, good," he says. "Very good that you like her work. You must tell her. María is most insecure about people who must like her work. You know María was a student of mine. She was not yet a writer then, and certainly not a poet. She was young and very serious, and very—how do you say—uh, talented. I told her she must be a writer." He pauses. "You are very intelligent, Diana. I can tell, by your eyes. You understand much. You are good for María."

"Well . . . I don't know . . ." Uncomfortable, I turn and set my empty cup in the sink. There is an awkward silence and I can feel Andreas's stare.

Isabel appears from nowhere and begins stacking dirty breakfast dishes, giving me little conspiratorial winks. I've managed to piece together some of the less-than-flattering descriptions she and Cello use in reference to "*el senor.*" They have declared him "*muy feo,*" and "*flaco,*" stuck-up, and so on, but much of this is class warfare. The servants are expected to hate the master, and the master despises them for their subservience. Andreas plunges back into the newspaper, reading rapidly aloud and swinging his naked leg carelessly. There is a smirk on his face.

I take Marcos's letter and go back out on the balcony. It is turning into a smoky, smoggy day, the air choked with the smell of diesel. I read the letter through three more times, discovering more I've missed. With each reading, Marcos comes more clearly into focus, but it is not the Marcos I knew in Paris. I sit for a while staring down into the street. I have nothing else to look forward to except the return of the boys from school in the afternoon and the resumption of our ridiculous English lessons in which Tomás insists I am wrong and he is right.

Later, I take an aimless walk, the letter folded inside my sweater pocket. I've picked up a habit of studying people's faces, as if I could decipher a strange country by the countenances of its inhabitants.

I find the cafe several blocks away where I've come twice this week to sit and write postcards to friends in the States, detailing with crisp vanity my latest romance with Marcos and my new life in Madrid. My notes are breezy, written at the quick, careless pace I wish my life were actually traveling. The coffee is dark, served in a small white cup, Turkish style. I sit by the window and watch people pass. The women are haughty, stylish, and enviably dark. They walk quickly, with purpose. María has told me most Spanish women my age are married and have children. I am conspicuously American in my jeans and sweatshirt and sneakers, undignified to say the least. But I have no money for clothes, and I grow despondent, imagining how foolish I look. When I left the U.S., I just left. Kevin kept the apartment and all the furniture, not that it was much to speak of, and I took two suitcases and my duffel. We were both pretending, I suppose, that I might actually come back. I had my books and clothes stored at my parents' house. My mother made no comment, seemed to almost take the split for granted. "Of course you want to see Europe," she said, and that was the closest she came to discussing my divorce.

Today I read the title story from *Cantos de amor por las mujeres muertas*. It is told from the point of view of a woman who has died of breast cancer and now reflects sadly over her faithless husband's escapades during her illness. Now that she is dead he is unable to love anyone else. When he makes love to others, it is always her face that appears. When he finally finds someone he thinks he loves, he discovers it is his wife's decaying body he holds in his hands.

The following week passes slowly and I'm afraid I've made a terrible mistake. Each day in Madrid feels like Sunday, as if my life has closed down, windows shut, curtains drawn. I struggle against loneliness. I carry on conversations with myself in my head. I steer clear of Andreas, whom I have caught staring at me. I keep hoping that María will invite me to one of the social events she and Andreas always seem to be rushing off to. Hearing her in the hall one evening, I boldly plant myself in my door frame and smile brightly.

"Going out?" I ask.

"Yes, and you?" she responds cheerfully.

I shake my head.

"Oh, poor thing, you're thinking about *him*." She heaves a sympathetic sigh. "You must go out more," she says, as if I had somewhere to go, and disappears on down the stairs.

I am desperate to go out, but where, in a city in which women do not seem to go about by themselves much? I cannot afford to eat a leisurely dinner in one of the plazas downtown, hoping someone will take an interest.

On Wednesday two more letters arrive from Marcos. Each one accelerates in passion. I cave in and allow myself to believe.

You must write me. You must return to Paris. The fragile script has acquired a fever. *Diana, I must have you again. Why don't you answer my letters?*

Our letters have crossed in the mail. By now he should have received two from me, written with great pains and a lot of help from my *Petit Larousse* for *le mot juste.* Like María's dead women, I have invented hindsight, brought about by distance, ignorance, and my own absence. And all the time in the world, which Andrew Marvel lacked, to leisurely compose my romance in a borrowed language. I admit to him I am unhappy in Madrid. But I make no mention of returning to Paris. Instead, I speculate about heading down to Segovia, where it is warmer. I have heard it is a beautiful city, I tell him.

I write my third letter to Marcos in Spanish, as a surprise. *Mi amor.* I say things in Spanish I would never say in English. I borrow a line from María's book and forget to put it in quotes. So be it, I think.

I head down the street for a mailbox, returning with a heightened sense of my own importance in the world. I am loved. And I am sick of emptying Tomás's piss pot and cleaning up after Cello and Isabel. I have found blood on the toilet seat and dirty tissue wadded in a corner on the floor. Cello combs her stringy blonde hair into the sink and leaves bits of it there to clog up the drain. Isabel forgets to pick up her dirty underwear after a shower.

I plan to register these complaints with María as soon as possible. We are developing a friendly rapport born of mutual respect. After all, she often asks me about English literature, and we compare notes on things we've read. We occasionally sit and discuss books we've both liked. She seems pleased I am struggling with *Cien anos de soledad,* even though I'm cheating, because I already read it once in English. She tells me she's read Shakespeare only in Spanish, and I have offered to read her some of *Macbeth* in English. I want her to hear the rhythms, the sounds of the words themselves. She seems to like the idea, but never mentions it again.

Still, she often seeks me out, either in my room or on the balcony. No matter how the conversation starts, it inevitably turns to Marcos.

"Your French lover . . ." she remarks to me today, her voice thick with interest. "He has been writing you often?"

"Four letters. Four letters in *two weeks*."

"Ah," she sighs. "He is very much in love."

"Yes." I manufacture in my mind the moment Marcos and María actually meet. I am stuffing the widening gap in my daily life with the presence of Marcos.

"That is so wonderful." She runs her long slender fingers along the wrought-iron railing. "Love is everything. Will you go to visit him for Christmas holiday?"

"I suppose," I say. "I suppose I have to." I have not even thought that far ahead. But Christmas in Paris! Of course, that's it! The Amados will be off to the country for two weeks, and I have no desire to be left alone in Madrid.

María sits down next to me. There is sweet smelling oil in her dark hair. I resist the urge to reach out and stroke it. María is a child, someone who requires care.

"I was very much in love with a boy once—at university. Before I meet Andreas of course." She pauses, then adds, "He was the only other man I was *with*."

I try not to register surprise.

She continues in her plaintive voice. "It is very sad. His family wanted him to marry another girl, someone they choose. He was fighting, fighting with them all the time about me. And then I matriculated—into a class in Latin American poetry. Andreas was my teacher, and he seemed so . . ." Her face takes on a dark despair; her voice fills with hopeless yearning, as if she were speaking of someone who has recently died. Andreas is a brilliant poet, she informs me intently. Eight years older and, oh, so wise about life. Many women have loved Andreas, but his work always came first. But with her, things were different. He sought her out after class. They were married when she was not much older than I am now.

"We are the same, Andreas and I," she muses softly. "It is not always so good to be the same. We understand too much about each other." She pauses. "Sometimes," she adds, as if testing me, "I still remember the boy, but he is dead now."

"I'm sorry," I say, feeling a vague sense of my own losses, whatever they are. María has located hers, given them a name and a focus. I have never grieved over anyone, not Kevin, my husband of five years, not the boy I once loved who drowned in a lake just outside of Ann Arbor. But I feel for María.

Her eyes light up. "Oh, no!" she protests, as if I've misunderstood. "I am very happy to be with a man such as Andreas. He is a very important thinker, you know. I had never knew a man like him before."

Her eagerness makes me uneasy.

"I am happy you are here." She reaches out impulsively and touches my arm. "I hope you are happy too."

Sensing the time is ripe, I move our talk to the household sources of my irritation. I choose my words carefully. "María, I wonder if Cello or Isabel could empty Tomás's chamber pot in the mornings. It's a difficult thing for me to do." I pause. "Also, the girls leave a terrible mess in the bathroom and I am tired of cleaning up after them . . ."

María's smile fades. Her mouth stiffens and thins. "I don't know what you want me to do," she says coolly.

"I just thought . . ." I catch myself. Of course we're not friends. I am María's employee. I exist somewhere between the two boys and the two maids, someone she can confess herself to precisely because we are not peers.

I excuse myself and go to my room, where I lie down on

my bed, hands folded under my head, and consider how, after three months of travel, I have reached a dead-end. My thoughts cannibalize themselves.

I hear Marcos's words, "You must come back, Diana." I feel the strength of his desires, a balm for my present unhappiness. How stupid of me to come to Spain when I could have done so many other things.

I am awake most of the night, and the next morning when I rise to get the boys up in the still-darkened flat I find myself completely disconnected from my surroundings and wishing I were in Marcos's tiny room, his naked body against mine. I want to be touched again. It suddenly occurs to me just how lonely I have allowed myself to become.

I take up walking. I invent destinations for myself. I spend hours in the Prado, seeking companionship as much as the art. I did not leave Kevin merely to dead-end in dreary Madrid. I wonder if he has been taking good care of the cat I gave him right before I left.

One afternoon in a coffee shop near the Prado I spot a red-haired woman sitting across from me reading a bodice-ripper in English. The cover of the book shows a wild black-haired woman with a ruffled blouse open down to her navel. She is being seized from behind in lustful embrace by a shirtless blond man with an earring in one ear. The title of the book is *Savage Desire*.

The woman reading the book is a heavy person in a dress, probably younger than I, but very matronly, so that she appears older. Her dress is ankle-length, and she wears black clogs. She has caught me staring at the book.

"Are you English?" she asks.

"No, American. And you?"

"Australian. From Sydney."

She sets down her book and invites me to come sit with her. "Would you like another cup of coffee?" she asks. When I hesitate, she orders it, then insists on paying.

She is an au pair for a Spanish family who live on the outskirts of Madrid, and this is her day off. Once a week she takes the bus into the center of town and drinks coffee and reads trashy novels in English.

We introduce ourselves; her name is Jennie.

"Have you made friends here?" I ask.

"Oh, not at all," she says cheerfully. "I'm not really interested in making friends. Spanish men are so dreadful and Spanish women are too standoffish. I was friends with an English girl who worked for some neighbors, but she left. She had a boyfriend back home."

The second cup of coffee goes to my head. I find myself telling her about María and Andreas and the two boys, Cello and Isabel, and even Marcos. Funny I don't mention having been married. Somehow it just doesn't seem like anyone's business.

Jennie is so good-natured I take to her immediately, and it is sweet relief to speak English with someone so easily. She's lived in Madrid almost a year, but hasn't bothered to learn Spanish.

"I have no knack for languages," she says, "so I don't bother." She says the family she works for speak varying degrees of English.

The afternoon begins to merge into twilight, and I am suddenly horror-struck that I will be late for tutoring the boys. Jennie and I quickly agree to team up and take a day trip to La Escorial or Toledo. She insists on paying for my two cups of coffee and a biscuit I ordered, and leaves a generous tip. I envy her ease with money, and wonder if she has generous parents.

As I board the bus I catch sight of Jennie flagging down a cab. She doesn't see me, but I wave frantically anyway, the caffeine swarming in my head like gnats.

The following day María knocks on my door and invites me to come hear her lecture at the university on women writers of Latin America. We drive out together in her car and I mention how much I am enjoying her book. She seems pleased. I want to talk to her about the women in her book, to know why she uses dead women as both images and characters in her stories. But to my disappointment I see she is not listening at all.

"Anyway," I say to the passing scenery on my right, "I look forward to the rest."

At the university she deposits me in a seat in the back of the room and assures me I must not feel obligated to stay to the end. She even goes so far as to tell me which bus I might catch, and where to transfer. But I do stay, I remain the whole hour, taking pleasure in what I am able to understand, even jotting some notes in my notebook about Gabriela Mistral, Marta Traba, and María-Luisa Bombal, whose work I have read only in translation. Afterwards, María is so busy with students she doesn't seem to notice I am finally preparing to head off. Two girls about eighteen years old smile and I eagerly smile back. But then they put their heads together and begin a private conversation in Spanish too rapid for me to follow. Their intimacy, their youth, their shared experience, all serve to exclude me. I am an outsider.

I wander the campus outside, but it is unremarkable and gray. It has been almost a month since I've made love to a man, and I realize I could be as easily captured as the woman on the cover of Jennie's *Savage Desire*. I'm actually hoping to catch someone's eye. But the men here are all so young, and Jennie is right, Spanish men are not attractive.

I wander over to the bus stop to return to the center of town. María hadn't even acknowledged me when class ended. I think about this, wondering why she would go to the trouble of inviting me. She has extended herself in unexplainable ways and encouraged my connection to Marcos. I am not a maid, yet I am not an equal. She has allowed me to go only so far. This is her signal to me: this is why I still dutifully empty Tomás's chamber pot in the mornings and wrestle with his verb tenses in the afternoons, even though María will bring me tea and biscuits on the balcony and talk to me about love.

From the bus window I watch the bleak university campus passing. The bus makes a stop just on the edge, where half a dozen or so students wait. The girls are all dark-haired. They look like young Marías in their dark jeans and sweaters, scarves casually tossed around their necks. Their skin has a high color, their eyes flash. They begin to board, talking and laughing.

That is when I see him. He is coming up alongside the bus on the sidewalk, his curly hair tossed and windblown. It is Andreas, strolling intently down the sidewalk, but he is not alone. His arm is wrapped tightly about the shoulders of a tall, thin girl with long black hair. I recognize the carnal expression on the girl's face: it is passion at its most furious. I have never seen such a look on my own face, but I must have felt it, sometime, somewhere, in order to know it. Every few steps Andreas presses his lips against her neck. Her face is flushed and whipped by the wind; I catch a glimpse of her shining eyes, the curve of her full mouth. She is beautiful because she is so young, her hair spiraling downwards to her waist.

I am mildly unnerved by the coincidence, but not at all surprised by what I have seen. Of all the stupid luck, I think, being assigned the role of Andreas's secret sharer.

The bus starts up again and rounds a corner, leaving Andreas and the girl lost in a cloud of exhaust. My annoyance with María turns briefly to compassion. My first instinct is to protect her. María, with her nervous pacing and erratic gestures and plaintive eyes. María, whose heart bleeds like an open wound on the badly printed pages of her book. She writes so beautifully, I think, yet her life is such a mess. Two reckless and rude sons, slovenly maids, a messy flat, and now, a faithless husband. And I suspect Andreas is no stranger to faithlessness.

Now I know something for sure. I've suspected it, but now I know. María, I think, must be the better writer. But it pains her, because she loves Andreas, still views him as her mentor. How jealous he must be of her. The bus thunders through the center of Madrid and screeches to a halt. I get off and cross the street. I think of the young girl, pressed against Andreas, still radiating the afterglow of sexual enthusiasm. She is probably like María was years ago when Andreas first saw her in class, before María grew so sad.

I go to a cafe. I begin another passionate letter to Marcos. María would approve, I think. I write furiously, reaching for images: sun-drenched trees in the park, the smoky rose of dawn, the steamy gray of evening. I wonder with a pang if he has gone back to seeing his old French girlfriend Anne, and then I am sure of it. I think of the two of them now, sprawled across his bed, his hands working over her body as they worked on mine. I am consumed by utter jealousy, or desire, or maybe they are the same.

I know, as I finish the letter, my heart fattening on its own desires, that I can never tell María about Andreas's girl. He is the reason, I think, that she writes about dead women. He may even be the reason she writes. Anything I would have to say would be superfluous, a disruption of the balance they've managed in their lives. For María probably already knows, and it is that which drives her.

That evening, lessons go poorly with both Tomás and Horacio. I am irritable, in no mood for foolishness. Horacio plays distractedly with his pencil, poking holes in the paper. He is impatient with my corrections, and switches to a rapid Spanish I cannot keep up with. When I patiently work with him on idioms, he argues in a loud voice, then stabs his paper with the pencil. Finally, María drops in and sends him off to watch television.

"He is tired from school," she offers as an excuse. "Horacio has worked hard enough." There is maybe the implication that I am too hard on the boys, but I ignore it.

I don't mention to her that he hasn't worked at all. She sends Tomás in. He is in an equally foul mood. It is as if the boys' instincts are so finely tuned that they anticipate the uneasiness lying just beneath the surface of it all.

"Why do you say 'super' that way? It's pronounced 'supah,'" Tomás sulks.

"That's British, I'm American."

"You're stupid," he informs me. "Everything American is stupid." He produces a pen from his pocket and uncaps it. A mischievous smile plays on his lips. I watch him rolling the pen back and forth in his dirty little fingers. He has chewed his nails to the quick and the skin around the edges looks gnawed on.

I try to distract him. "Look, would you like to learn some American slang?" I suggest.

"I don't want to. I hate all this."

I keep my voice patient, half suspecting that María is poised just on the other side of the door. I am hoping she will overhear

Tomás's rudeness, and will come to my rescue. But when the door opens, it is Andreas who enters. He wears the same impatient but self-satisfied smile he always does. As he unwraps his scarf, I can almost imagine the smell of the girl wafting off him like a breeze. I look away, not wanting to meet his wet gaze.

"Good evening," he says, including both Tomás and me in his glance. "Is work going well?"

I take a chance. "No it's not, Tomás doesn't seem interested in anything."

Andreas grins at his son. "Are you giving Diana trouble?" He shrugs at me and says, "Boys will be boys, you know."

I can't help myself. "Sometimes men will too."

He doesn't hear, or else he doesn't understand. Instead he asks where María is.

"I don't know," I say, just to be stubborn. To myself I think, I can't keep all your doors straight, all the locking and unlocking that goes on in this household. I want to ask Andreas why he doesn't keep track of his wife himself.

Tomás pipes up, indignant. "She's in her bedroom."

He doesn't say "your bedroom," he says "her." I wonder if Andreas has noticed, but he only grunts and leafs indifferently through the stack of mail. He holds up an envelope to the light, peering at it closely. "Here's something for María," he says and opens it. He pulls out a letter and scans it. "Hmmmm," he says, as if pleased with something. "María has been invited to lecture in Sevilla." He folds the letter up, then saunters in his Italian shoes toward the bedroom. A moment later the door closes behind him, and Tomás looks at me triumphantly.

"I knew she was there," he says. Then, without warning, he points his pen at me and shoots ink all over my sweater, like an octopus.

I am too stunned to react immediately, but instead watch the dark ink stream like blood down the front of my sweater and onto my jeans. All I can think of is how I have no money for new ones. Tomás begins a demonic cackling, clutching his sides and rocking back and forth with laughter. The sight of the ink stains both outrages and depresses me.

"You little bastard," I say, sitting very still.

I imagine him running to María and repeating what I have just said, but I don't care. I want an excuse to leave Madrid, to be driven by some compulsion. I happily imagine boarding the train that night and heading back to Paris. I'd go to Marcos's, simple enough, and his bed would be empty, waiting for me. And from there?

Tomás doesn't budge. He looks at me as if I've pulled the plug on him, with an expression that borders on pity. "It's not real ink," he says softly. "It's the kind that disappears. It hasn't hurt you one bit. Watch, it will go away."

I look down at my stained sweater and, sure enough, as if by magic the ink begins to evaporate and the stains it has formed begin to shrink.

"End of lesson," I tell him. "Go do what you want. I really don't care."

I stand up, shaken.

"How can the lesson be over?" he challenges. "It's not even six yet. And the ink went away."

"The lesson is over," I repeat firmly and pick up my books and leave him sitting there. I go directly to my room and sit down hard in the chair by the writing desk.

I spend the next hour penning a letter to Marcos. I press down hard on the paper. I can no longer separate frustration from ardor. Marcos has become a goal, a place to return to each evening after I've faced my dreary tasks. When my wrist grows tired, I turn to María's book and finish another story of hers about a young village girl who has a passionate affair with a rich married man in town and is later found drowned in a well. The man's wife finds out and leaves him and the man is left alone to recall the youthful girl's beautiful body, which he may no longer have.

There is a knock on my door. I half expect to be punished for having called Tomás a bastard.

"Come in."

"I hope I am not molesting you, Diana," María says cautiously from the doorway. She holds her head the way a wounded animal will, slightly to the side.

I wait for her to mention my spat with Tomás, but she says nothing.

"I spoke to Cello and Isabel about the bathroom," she tells me earnestly. "I insist they clean more—for your sake." She labors over the words.

"Thank you." She makes no mention of Tomás's chamber pot.

"And about your trip to Escorial tomorrow. I hope you have a very nice time with your new friend Jennie."

I nod. María lingers in the doorway, peering at the letter I have written to Marcos. I do not ask her to come in and sit down, as I have done in the past.

"You are writing to *him* again."

"Yes."

Her features soften. "Ah, you are so in love. How many letters he has sent you now?"

"Seven, eight." I point to the stack, neatly rubber-banded on the corner of the desk.

"He is a poet?"

"No, just a law student, but he writes beautifully."

"Very good," María says approvingly. "And you write to him in French?"

"Yes. Sometimes I try a little Spanish."

She doesn't ask why. "Perhaps I should speak to you in Spanish, so you may practice."

"I couldn't ask you to do that. I speak like a child."

She looks at me gently. "You are . . ." She pauses. "You are a breath of fresh air." She says this with the speed of someone reciting a poem. I can tell she has rehearsed this line, something she has read somewhere. "I hope," she adds, "that you and your French lover are as happy as Andreas and I are."

The words fall like a curse on my head. She excuses herself to go in search of Andreas, who is late for a dinner engagement. I sit inside my tiny room and listen to the sounds from the courtyard, the voices rising up from below, the sound of dinner plates and chatter, of other people's lives. I realize now María has never asked me what Marcos's name is. And I realize how foolish it all is, my being here, that is.

All night I toss and turn in my bed, longing feverishly for Marcos and feeling terrified that this growing anxiety is the way real love feels. What if I never see him again? In my dreams I confuse him with Andreas, wrapped in the arms of another girl, and the next morning I awaken disoriented, in a frenzy of nerves. I confess to María at breakfast that I haven't slept well. She brings me a sleeping tablet for the next night and lays it on my writing desk.

"This will help you," she promises knowledgeably. "It will destroy the *diablos*." And she pulls her long hair back up into her hands behind her head and looks down at me with sympathy. I put the tablet away in the desk drawer.

The next morning I awaken late and take the bus down to Plaza del Sol, dropping my letter to Marcos into the mailbox on the way. The day is so warm I discard my sweater. I am relieved to be away from the dismal flat where Cello and Isabel listen to the endless parade of soap operas and María wanders about nervously locking and unlocking, searching for Andreas, and he for her, in that odd dispassionate ritual of theirs.

Jennie is prompt, and as cheerful as she was the other day. Today she carries a book called *Tawny Embrace*. We drink enough coffee to rattle my nerves, and I find myself feeling careless about everything, even Marcos who, now in the light of day with the promise of adventure, strikes me as remotely silly.

On the train to Escorial my earlier mood unravels into something close to ecstasy, and I realize it is the sound of the wheels on the tracks and the forward motion of the train that has shrunk my anxiety. Urged on by Jennie, I talk about Marcos. He is a good story, and our meeting and subsequent week together have all the requisite qualities of a good romance. She lays *Tawny Embrace* face down on the seat and listens. Seated across from me, she is taking most of the breeze on her pale, freckled face. Her red hair blows full and thick. She wears a long skirt and a neatly ironed long-sleeved blouse. I feel as if I am on an outing with my mother.

The train ride is nothing short of spectacular. The warm fall air blows in perfumed gusts through the open window. I stare at the countryside rolling by. Jennie has brought cheese and bread for us to eat, all neatly sliced up and wrapped in cloth napkins.

"I'm here for two years," she tells me, stretching out her thick white legs on the seat opposite. "I'm so glad to have gotten out of Sydney for a while. It was making me sick and I needed a big change."

She tells me about the wonderful people she is staying with and working for. She calls them her family. The mother is Swedish ("I'd never work for a Spanish woman," says Jennie) and the father is Spanish. There are the three children Jennie is quite attached to. The Swedish woman's English is excellent, Jennie explains, and the two of them have become very close. "I tell her everything. We're very open with each other." According to Jennie, her life here is perfect.

We wander through the church at Escorial. I want to see the art collection, Jennie has no interest. The palace is closed for repairs, but we sit outside nearby and eat an overpriced lunch for which Jennie insists on paying. I am overwhelmed by her generosity and offer to buy her coffee, but she won't hear of it.

"Save your money," she says magnanimously. And then she begins to tell me about Bill, the man she left behind in Australia. Bill is rich. He owns a yacht, he has flown her in a plane to Bali, he has even offered to leave his wife for her.

"His wife's name is Cynthia," Jennie tells me. "She's a model. I tell him not to leave her. She needs him and I don't. I mean, the sex is incredible, but you don't need to be in love to have good sex." For a moment I think she is making fun of me.

She lingers over her coffee and dessert, slowly licking the icing from her fork.

"Bill writes me just about every week," she says. "He's thinking of coming to visit at Christmas. Will you be around?"

I'm at a loss for what to say.

"I'll show you a picture of him." Jennie digs deep inside her purse. She produces a wallet bulging with stuff. She pokes around in it. "Ah," she says, "here's Bill," and she pulls out a small photo from behind plastic and hands it to me. It looks to me like a passport photo of a clean-cut, handsome man with dark hair. He is wearing a jacket and tie. I stare at it perfunctorily and return it to her. "He's quite good-looking." I look at the people walking by.

"Yes, isn't he?" she says with triumph. She smooths down her skirt over her wide lap. "He's an incredible lover. He likes to lick me all over." I don't look at her when she says this. I keep my eyes averted, but I am certain her expression is smug. She is lying, and lying badly. I desperately want to leave Escorial. I don't want to sit here with Jennie any more. I suggest we catch the earlier train back. I feel as agitated and nervous as María. I want to get away from Jennie. Suddenly Marcos is the bright light in my head and the burning in my body. I close my eyes. When I open them, Jennie has paid for my meal, against my protestations. We walk back to the train station.

"You know," says Jennie, interrupting my thoughts as the train glides along, "there's something I haven't told you about my family."

"What?" I brace myself for something awful about the Swedish woman and her Spanish husband.

"I take stuff from them," Jennie says quite calmly, as if testing me. She is cleaning her perfect fingernails with a small orange stick.

"What do you mean, you take stuff?"

"I take stuff." She smiles. "You know, a watch here, a ring there. I have a whole bag of stuff." She opens up her expansive purse again and produces a large plastic pouch. I say nothing and she begins to spread things out on the seat between us like prizes. There are rings and watches and necklaces, even a beautiful pair of gold earrings.

"What if they catch you?"

"They won't," she tells me confidently. "They have so much. They won't even notice."

"What are you going to do with it?"

"Sell it. Pawnshops or wherever. My family hardly pays me enough to make ends meet, so I figure I deserve it."

"I thought you liked the family. You're stealing from them."

She looks at me almost sympathetically and shakes her head. "They expect me to. That's why they barely pay us anything.

You mean to tell me you live off your measly 3000 pesetas a week?"

I regret having told her what I made.

"Well," she shrugs, folding up the bag of stolen paraphernalia and tucking it back inside her purse, "it's your loss."

I think of María with all her keys. I'd always assumed it was Cello and Isabel she suspected. Jennie and I fall into silence.

The train crawls back to the Madrid station where the winds have come up again. At the bus stop in town I lie and tell Jennie I'll call her the following week to see about walking in Retiro Park. She smiles patiently at me, her round face doughy around the edges. She knows I'm lying and she's enjoying it in a way I can't understand.

"Say hello to Marcos," she tells me in parting. "I'll tell Bill you said hello too."

María is waiting for me, pacing like a cat. At first I think I've gotten my days mixed up and there is some appointment I've missed with the boys.

"You've had a phone call," she tells me. I've never seen her smoke before, but she smokes now. "Your Frenchman telephoned. He speaks excellent Spanish."

I don't tell her why.

"He is at a friend's. He awaits your call. I have the number here." She hands me a slip of paper. "Andreas is very late again," she tells me, inhaling the cigarette smoke. But smoking seems to irritate her and so she stubs the long white butt out in a flowerpot on the table. "It is terrible of him to keep me waiting. I am getting an award tonight."

"An award?"

She doesn't answer. "He wants you to call him," she says, "right away," and for a moment I think she means Andreas. "Come with me."

She takes me to Andreas's study and unlocks the door. She flips through the keys from her wrist and finds the one to unlock the blue telephone.

"He will be here at this number until eight o'clock," she says urgently, "waiting for you."

"But this is Andreas's phone."

María nods vehemently. "You must not be disturbed." Then she proceeds to stand there as I pick up the phone to dial.

It has now been six weeks since I've been with Marcos in my arms, but the memory of his shape has been worn into them and reinforced by what I believe to remember. I cannot, though, remember clearly his face, or even how tall he is.

I dial the unfamiliar number with clumsy fingers, trying to piece together in my mind a reasonable likeness of the Marcos who emerges from those rainy nights in the words on blue paper.

María's arms are folded tightly across her chest, as if she is trying to keep them under control.

It is going to be difficult enough for me to speak to Marcos, let alone in French, or should I try Spanish, no not Spanish with María standing so close by. What I really want to speak is English and put an end to all this pretense. Yet speaking English all afternoon with Jennie has not yet cured me.

The phone line erupts into short spasmodic beeps. The line crackles with distance.

A man's voice answers, deep and rich.

"Marcos?" I say eagerly.

"*Un moment.*"

There is a clatter, a shout, a patter of feet. I hear male voices and then the phone is picked up again.

A voice, so high-pitched and unfamiliar I am taken aback, addresses me with excitement. "Diana?"

"*Oui, c'est moi,*" I say softly, hunched over the blue telephone. I feel relief at those words; a connection is made.

Marcos tells me I must come immediately to Paris. He can't stand how unhappy I must be in Spain and he is so unhappy in Paris without me. And how awful that I must try to teach such horrible boys.

"*Tu me manque,*" he says over and over. "*Je t'aime, Diana. J'ai envie de toi.*"

When I hang up, I am uncertain what I've just committed myself to. My chest constricts. María paces on the periphery of my awareness. She turns to me, stricken.

"He is coming here?"

"No," I say. "I am going there."

"You are going there?" María pauses, her face pensive. She turns to the window and parts Andreas's heavy dark drapes with her long fingers. She stares out into the harsh light. For the first time I notice how tired she looks. "He loves you so, Diana. Yes, you must go to him."

I say something that makes almost no sense. I ask her, "But what about you?"

We both hear the key in the lock at the same time. The sound echoes down the hallway. María bolts for the door and flings it open. "Andreas! At last you are here! We are late!"

He looks puzzled as we emerge from his office. His expression demands an explanation.

"Diana had an important phone call," she says in English for my benefit. Then in Spanish she begins to chide him for his tardiness.

"Yes, well," he says sheepishly, continuing in English. "I was—uh—detained, you know, at the university. I'm sorry. I know it is late."

"Hurry," María says, "you must get ready. Hurry, please."

She turns and locks the telephone behind us, then slides her wrist back inside the key ring as if into a manacle. We walk out together into the living room where María turns and says to me, eyes swimming with tears, "I wish you luck."

That night I take María's sleeping pill and fall into a black drop. I don't awaken until noon, and then it's to a clatter of plates and silverware from one of the open windows across the courtyard. It means I've missed getting the boys up, but no one bothered to remind me. I dress quickly, my mind blackened and singed by a hot, dreamless night. No one is about; María and the maids are out, and the boys are off at school. María has let me sleep.

I stand on the balcony watching the traffic below. I hear Marcos's voice, tinny and anxious. Higher-pitched than I recall. Back in my room, María's collection lies open on the desk. I'd begun something I hadn't finished. I sit down and read the last pages of the story before tucking the worn book into my duffel. Most finished books I simply discard to keep my travels light. But there is no place to toss this book that María wouldn't find it.

I have no regret saying good-bye to Tomás and Horacio. They barely notice, they are occupied with a board game. The night I leave, Andreas is out. María insists on helping me carry one of my bags down to the taxi. She seems almost relieved to see me go and presses cab fare into my hand.

"Go quickly to him," she says dramatically. "*Buena suerte.*" And she stands back wistfully on the curb and waves good-bye with one spidery hand.

Night trains are surrealistic, illuminated by garish compartment lights. The aisles are astir with travelers boarding and searching for their seats. I am overcome with a sense of panic, realizing I have no idea what I am going to. The couchettes are cramped. I step to one side while a steward stands in his sock feet to make up the linen on the top bunks. I share the sleeping compartment with five Spanish women who agree to watch my bags while I wander up to the dining car. Two of the women are already in nightgowns and stretched out on the upper bunks.

In the dining car a short, stocky Spanish man smiles at me from across the aisle. I have a sudden impulse to change my destination. The weeks of yearning for Marcos focus themselves in a new direction. Just like that! With the man grinning at me, my anguish is relieved. I splurge and order *merluza* and *arroz*, and flan for dessert. I drink two glasses of wine. The meal costs me half the money in my pocket, but I don't care. I am relieved to feel the motion of the train and I think how I never want to stop. The Spanish man invites himself over and takes the seat across from me. He speaks little English, and is willing to talk slowly in Spanish to accommodate me. He is amused by my awkward constructions, my foreigner's use of metaphor when vocabulary fails me.

Two shots of whiskey and my Spanish seems to have improved, or at least my impression of it has. The man's name is Diego. He's thirty-five and he's traveling to Paris to see his fiancée who works at a clothing shop. The dining car closes and Diego invites me back to his car to play cards with two of his friends. More whiskey is produced and I sing them all the old song "Passengers will please refrain / from flushing toilets on the train / while passing through the station / I love you. Every night just after dark / we goose the statues in the park / If Sherman's horse can take it, why can't you?" They have no idea what it means, but they laugh and slap me on the back. I try to teach them "Found a Peanut," but they tire of the repetition.

The groaning and clanking sound of the changing of the tracks at Hendaye signals the border crossing. I press the palm of my hand against the window and feel the chilled glass. Diego's friends leave the car one by one, and suddenly everything is very dark except for someone breathing low and soft against my ear. I keep hearing María's words, "If you love him you must go to him," and I think how they easily could have emanated from one of the soap operas in Cello and Isabel's room.

I consider getting off the train in some small town along the way, but it is dark now. I weigh the facts: with the little bit of money I put aside in the weeks at María's I could last only a week or so in hostels. Marcos would come down to the station and find I wasn't on the train, but he would get over it. I would go on to Barcelona and then Rome, maybe even Greece and Turkey.

But I have made a promise of sorts, one that should be seen through to the end. I am not going to get off the train, even though I know how things will be. At dawn I will meet Marcos as planned and go to live with him for as long as it will take us to tire of each other and for me to discover that the French girl named Anne has not gone away at all. She will arrive dramatically at the door one night when Marcos is studying at the law library and she will tell me in perfect English, with a defiant tilt to her beautiful head, that she intends to marry Marcos and I should get lost. But I don't and we sit and wait together. When Marcos gets home, we confront him. He is surprisingly unaffected. He escorts Anne out. He's back almost instantly, explaining that she is crazy, that she is suffering for no reason, and that he will end it once and for all tomorrow. But I leave, within minutes after, despite the fact that he hands me a straight razor and begs me to kill him. I throw the razor to the ground, disgusted with the whole business, and for the first time I have an unexplained pang about my ex-husband. I leave, teary-eyed more from weariness and anger than any real disappointment. Anne can have him, and good riddance.

I will wander hopelessly down through the Marais until I meet a Vietnamese hotel clerk who speaks good English and offers to let me sleep in his room while he works. He will show me how to double lock the door, and then leaves me the only key to the room to assure me I will sleep on clean, white sheets, undisturbed. In the morning he brings me fresh croissants and a paper, and then busies himself at the hot plate making me coffee. He pulls "Sergeant Pepper's Lonely Hearts Club Band" from a collection of Beatle albums in mint condition and puts one on the phonograph. I am thrilled by his kindness, but am already thinking how the world is full of generosity, if you know just where to look.

Now, as the train lurches along the tracks to Paris, I find myself, at two in the morning, urged on by the alcohol and my open-ended desires. I strain against Diego's presses as the train screams around curves and shudders through dark tunnels. After, I sleep briefly against the cold leather seats and awaken alone to a flat, gray dawn. I return unobtrusively to my couchette, where I fall into a deep sleep for another hour. I am worn out, and sorry to be heading for Paris. I check, but there are no more stops.

Diego buys me breakfast in the dining car, and I smoke a cigarette. "*No te preocupes,*" he teases, reaching over to flip my hair. "*Sola una broma?*"

I readily agree. "*Una broma.*"

Diego leans over and kisses me on the mouth. "I like you. *Qúe lástima!*" We grin at each other.

As we pull into Paris, the mist is so thick I mistake it for snow. I wait nervously until everyone gets off the train, wanting to avoid Diego. He has slipped me his address, invited me to come visit.

I find myself half hoping Marcos won't be here to meet me, and thinking how much easier it would be to hoist my bags over my shoulder and wander off penniless through the streets. But the conductor has come along and poked his head into the car. "Finished!" he announces, making a cutting gesture with his hand across his throat.

I pick up my duffel and knapsack, heave a sigh, and head for the exit. I spot Marcos before he spots me. He is not the same.

This is how I remember it all. He was the last one on the platform, small and agitated. I hadn't realized how frail he was, a brown mouse in his blue cap drawn over his ears, his shoulders dwarfed by the bulk of a red parka. His nose was red and swollen from the cold. He was anxiously searching the train windows for some sign of me, his beloved.

Of course he must have also been preoccupied by how he would eventually explain me to Anne, but at that moment I decided to believe, and so did he, as I stepped off the train, that I had returned to Paris for love, that what we had written each other was true. Even then I knew it would never work, but I came at him full force anyway, wrapping my arms and legs fiercely around him, burying my mouth in his thick, wiry hair. He spun me in the air just as Diego walked through the station hand in hand with a pretty young Spanish woman. I could have sworn he turned and winked at me. What did it matter? When Marcos whispered, "*Je t'aime,*" against my ear, I knew he was lying. But I'd come all this way, hadn't I, backtracking no less, to find him. I searched for his eyes, but caught instead the back of Diego's retreating head and the platform where the train track ended. I put my cheek against Marcos's and murmured back, "*Te amo,*" but it was not for him at all. It was for María, who believed in such things.

THE FLANNERY O'CONNOR AWARD

FOR SHORT FICTION

David Walton, *Evening Out*
Leigh Allison Wilson, *From the Bottom Up*
Sandra Thompson, *Close-Ups*
Susan Neville, *The Invention of Flight*
Mary Hood, *How Far She Went*
François Camoin, *Why Men Are Afraid of Women*
Molly Giles, *Rough Translations*
Daniel Curley, *Living with Snakes*
Peter Meinke, *The Piano Tuner*
Tony Ardizzone, *The Evening News*
Salvatore La Puma, *The Boys of Bensonhurst*
Melissa Pritchard, *Spirit Seizures*
Philip F. Deaver, *Silent Retreats*
Gail Galloway Adams, *The Purchase of Order*
Carole L. Glickfeld, *Useful Gifts*
Antonya Nelson, *The Expendables*
Nancy Zafris, *The People I Know*
Debra Monroe, *The Source of Trouble*
Robert H. Abel, *Ghost Traps*
T. M. McNally, *Low Flying Aircraft*
Alfred DePew, *The Melancholy of Departure*
Dennis Hathaway, *The Consequences of Desire*
Rita Ciresi, *Mother Rocket*
Dianne Nelson, *A Brief History of Male Nudes in America*
Christopher McIlroy, *All My Relations*
Alyce Miller, *The Nature of Longing*

ALYCE MILLER is a visiting assistant professor in creative writing at Ohio University.